Flyfisher's Guide to

Montana

Greg Thomas

Wilderness
Adventures
Press™

Belgrade, Montana

For my father, Fred, mother, Rita, and sister, Kim
for all their support

and

For Shadow and Moose
for enduring those cold nights in the back
of the pickup with hungry bellies

Table of Contents

Acknowledgements

There is no possible way to list individually all of the people who contributed to this book. But, without their help, this guide would not exist. Montana is far too large, with too many choice waters to pretend that I know them all intimately. I've spent 11 years, a good portion of those without the restrictions of a job, sampling this state's tasty attributes — ripping from one corner to the next, from the Kootenai to the Big Hole to the Bighorn to the Missouri, in search of trophy trout. Some years, I've spent better than 300 days astream. But, there are some waters that begged for insight from local experts. And, it is the people who live near and work on the Big Sky state's streams and lakes who understand them best. I'm talking about guides, outfitters, fly shop owners and biologists. In some cases it was not easy to drag information out of these people, but in the end we agreed — Montana's trout waters will not survive if the masses understand nothing about them. Instead, by offering information, it is the hope of the author and the guidebook's contributors that people will visit these waters, catch and release a few trout, see merit in protecting them, join forces and figure out a way to beat down the major conglomerations and political assassins. To all of you who offered information, insight, encouragement, those cold beers and free flies, thank you again.

Foreword

When I was young, trying to endure the monumental pelting rainstorms of southeast Alaska and western Washington, I dreamed of that place called Montana, where the climate was arid, you could see into the forest and, best of all, wild trout were abundant and eager to inhale artificial flies.

I moved to Montana in the mid-eighties under this guise: student at the University of Montana in Missoula. Trout fishing, of course, took the forefront; I graduated with a barely adequate GPA, although I suddenly harbored a PhD in the nuances of Rock Creek and its rainbow trout. Had I not divulged hatch knowledge and shared delicate mayfly patterns with university professors, I never would have made it out. Those errant papers, those failed tests and those unexcused absences would have destroyed me.

Fresh out of college and testing the writing market, I ventured around the Rocky Mountains, allowed to live in wonderful trout fishing locals, like Jackson Hole, Wyoming and Sun Valley, Idaho. But a voice, sounding most boisterous in my heart, kept calling from Big Sky Country.

I now live in Montana's Gallatin Valley, chasing trout whenever possible, which in recent years has amounted to 250-plus days a season. This is wonderful country, maybe the best place in the world for a flyfisher to reside, but it's frustrating in a way; how can a person possibly fish all of the wonderful waters and still maintain a few hours to tie flies and write? Unfortunately, it's not possible. You just have to fish the rivers, lakes and tributary streams highest on your hit list when the opportunity arrives.

Because time is short and life is finite, I hope this guide allows you to visit Montana's wonderful waters and make the most of your time, which, of course, includes putting a few hefty trout in your net. Don't think for a second that whirling disease, that ugly scrounge of a parasite that vaulted the Atlantic Ocean and planted its spore in the heart of Montana (the Madison River), has ruined fishing in this state. There are plenty of healthy fisheries around and even the Madison continues to offer big browns and rainbows.

During the past two years my friends and myself have taken rainbows over 10 pounds on the Blackfeet Indian Reservation; brook trout to six pounds at Georgetown Lake; grayling to 16 inches on the Madison and Big Hole Rivers; cutthroat trout to 23 inches on the West Fork of the Bitterroot; and brown trout to nine pounds, 28-inches on the unheralded Musselshell River. I am happy to report that prime flyfishing is alive in Montana and I don't expect that attribute to change anytime soon. See you on the river.

— Greg Thomas, Gallatin Gateway, MT
March 20, 1997

MAJOR ROADS AND RIVERS OF MONTANA

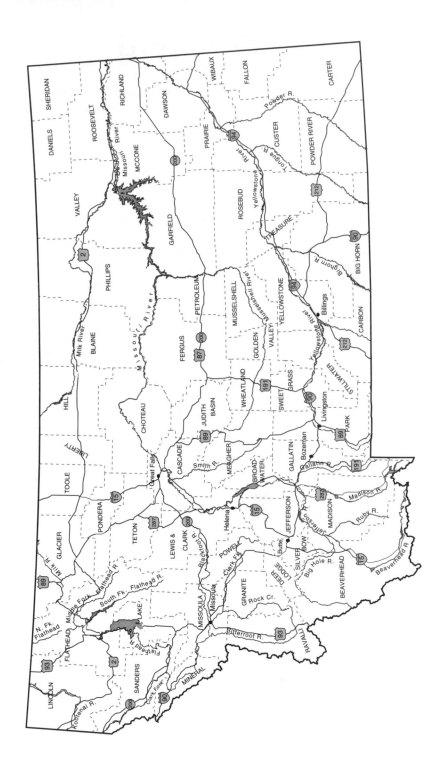

Montana Facts

Fourth largest state in the union
147,138 square miles
93,157,953 acres
550 miles across
275 miles north to south

Elevations: 1,820 feet to 12,798 feet
Counties: 56
Towns and Cities: 126
Population (1990 census): 790,000
    7 Indian Reservations
    2 National Parks
    11 National Forests
    68 State Recreation Areas
    12 Wilderness Areas
    11 State Parks

Nicknames: Treasure State, Big Sky Country, Land of the Shining Mountains
Primary Industries: Agriculture, timber, mining, tourism
Capital: Helena
Bird: Western meadowlark
Animal: Grizzly Bear
Flower: Bitterroot
Tree: Ponderosa pine
Gemstone: Montana agate
Grass: Bluebunch wheatgrass

Tips on Using This Book

Montana is a huge state with uncountable trout waters and many excellent bass and pike fisheries. I have compiled detailed information on all of the well known, destination rivers, along with some popular small streams and even some out-of-the-way, unknown waters like the Hog Hole, Dearborn River and Rattlesnake Creek.

Do not think that I have included all of the prime waters. There are hundreds of smaller lakes and streams that might provide "fishing of a lifetime" on any given day. However, most of those streams and lakes are too fragile, too vulnerable to cover here. By sending the masses, I would effectively, rightfully, garner blame for their demise.

However, the main rivers and lakes that I've covered, which can easily hold a fly-fisher's attention for a week or more at a time, offer a base of operations; those who desire to fish smaller waters that offer less predictable conditions can venture about if weather and water variables allow. If not, you still have the main river to fish. To learn about the smaller fisheries, obtain information from fly shop clerks, cafe waitresses, bartenders, the police—anyone who seems approachable and wants to offer information. Flyfishing is big in Montana and almost everybody has an idea of where to go and what fly to use—use this to your advantage.

Montana, despite its size, is listed under one area code—406. When no area code precedes a phone number, assume it is a Montana number. You must dial 1-406 for all in-state long distance calls. The information number is 1-406-555-1212.

This guide book is divided into five sections, covering each part of the state: northwest, far west, southwest, central and east. Each section contains detailed maps of rivers and lakes, hatch charts for each fishery and a list of amenities like hotels, airports, restaurants and auto repair joints for hub cities.

Although we have tried our very best to be accurate, it is always wise to call ahead before your arrival. Hotel owners may change, fly shops may close, restaurants may go under.

Motel cost key: $ — less than $30.00 per night
$$ — between $30.00 and $50.00 per night
$$$ — $50.00 a night and up

Also, before your visit, check with Montana Department of Fish, Wildlife and Parks for any emergency closures on the rivers or lakes (low water and faulty dams have, in fact, closed streams like the Big Hole and Rock Creek in the past five years).

Do not forget to ask permission and fully respect private property. Extend your respect to public areas also—pack out what you pack in!

Hatch charts list the main hatches of aquatic and terrestrial insects on Montana's rivers and lakes. However, the time frame of those hatches may change each year, depending on weather and water conditions. It's always advantageous to call a local fly shop before your arrival to check hatch progression. You can then tie the proper flies ahead of time, and you will not be caught by surprise when you arrive.

I hope that I've helped every one of you plan a successful trip. Catch and release lots of fish, enjoy Montana's scenery to the fullest and get to know some of this state's residents—you'll be hard-pressed to find better fishing, more impressive scenery, or better people anywhere.

—Greg Thomas, Gallatin Gateway, MT, January 1997

Whirling Disease Update

It seeped through Europe during the early 1900s, vaulted the Atlantic Ocean as an evil stowaway, then planted its ugly spore directly into the heartland of American flyfishing. Whirling disease found Montana, and it's here to stay.

Various accounts of the disease, sprinkled through every major outdoor magazine of late, decree its implications for Montana: the future of trout in Big Sky Country looks tattered at best.

But the presence of whirling disease does not mean you should cancel your flyfishing dates in Montana. There remain vast numbers of brown, brook, cutthroat, bull, golden, and yes, rainbow trout for the taking. Amid numerous reports on whirling disease, I'm happy to report that a fine coat of fish slime awaits your hands. And yes, that promise includes the upper Madison, where whirling disease has hit hardest; it ate 90 percent of that river's rainbows, dropping its population from historic levels of 1,600 a mile to 300 a mile. However, in addition to those remaining rainbows, Montana Fish, Wildlife and Parks estimates about 900 brown trout a mile. With 1,200 trout a mile in the "big riffle," a popular adage holds true today: If you can't catch fish in the Madison, you can't catch them anywhere.

Documentation of whirling disease in Montana shows that it has occurred in the Madison River, Ruby River, Beaverhead River, Poindexter Slough, Red Rock River, Clark Canyon Reservoir, Georgetown Lake, Swan River, Flint Creek, Willow Creek, Clark Fork River, Rock Creek, Little Prickly Pear Creek and the Missouri River, among others.

Fortunately, some of Montana's eastern rivers, such as the Bighorn and Big Spring Creek, tested negative. Time will tell if they, too, entertain an unwelcome guest.

Time will also tell if whirling disease will affect other streams as it did the Madison. These questions have not been answered: Was the Madison set up by a series of factors, not the least being years of drought? Has whirling disease always been present? Will some strains of rainbow trout tolerate the parasite?

While many flyfishers ponder those questions and choose to schedule trips in other Western states, I'll continue to grab my fly rod and take advantage of what we have in Montana. Even today, with whirling disease, Montana is the king of Western trout states.

Northwest Montana

Northwest Montana is the bastion of native trout species. Maybe nowhere else in the state are so many of the original occupants still finning in the depths. That does not mean environmental degradation overlooks this region; it is being torn down, beat up—obliterated—by mining, logging and hydroelectric interests within its own borders and neighboring states.

Fortunately, flyfishers can still access prime waters that harbor huge rainbows (fish between 15 and 30 pounds occupy the Kootenai), lots of meaty cutthroats (a 16-incher is nothing to raise your eyebrows at), monster bull trout (five- to 15-pounders are still quite common in the Flathead and Swan drainages) and some little wild rainbows that hold to the Yaak River tributaries. And the region's prairie lake fishing is unequaled anywhere in the West (four- to eight-pound rainbows are common, and 15-pound browns exist).

Northwest Montana receives the heaviest amount of precipitation in the state. Therefore, it's classified as a wet, cold, teeth-chattering, densely timbered region with lots of water and varied wildlife. You'll see mountain goats, mule deer and grizzly bears in the high country, and moose, white-tailed deer and elk in the lowlands. Huckleberry and blueberry patches are immense; late summer visitors can gorge on these seasonal delights (just watch out for Mr. Griz!).

Overall, northwest Montana, with its endless expanse of mountains, tight canyons and trees, is simply beautiful.

It's also very accessible. The Kootenai and Lolo National Forests control much of its land, and that means free access on most of the tributary streams. On the larger rivers like the Kootenai, Flathead, Yaak, Thompson and Swan, private lands eat up just small portions of the banks.

The main service hubs in the region are Kalispell and Libby on the west side of the Continental Divide, and Cutbank on the east side where the plains and excellent prairie pothole fishing begin.

Kootenai River

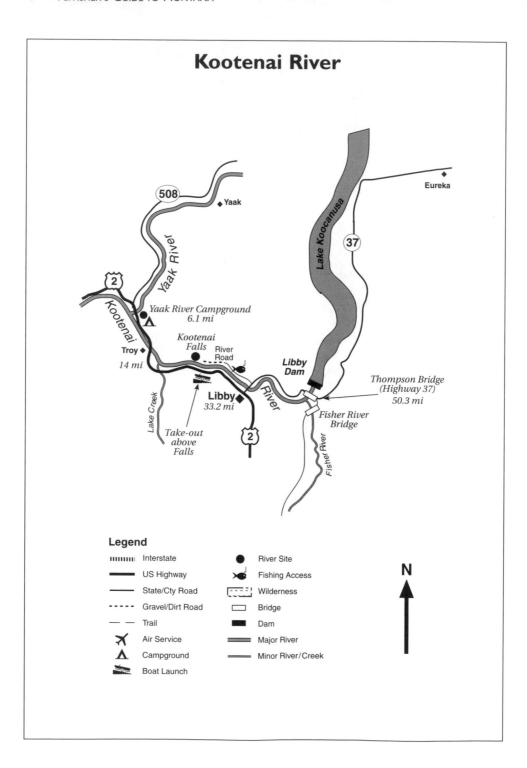

Legend

- ⊪⊪⊪⊪⊪ Interstate
- ▬▬▬ US Highway
- ▬▬ State/Cty Road
- ----- Gravel/Dirt Road
- — — Trail
- ✈ Air Service
- ⛺ Campground
- 🚤 Boat Launch

- ● River Site
- 🐟 Fishing Access
- ⫙ Wilderness
- ▢ Bridge
- ■ Dam
- ▬▬▬ Major River
- ▬▬▬ Minor River/Creek

N

KOOTENAI RIVER

Somewhere in the depths of northwest Montana's Kootenai River lies a 20-pound rainbow trout that is going to smack the hackle right off some unfortunate angler's dry fly.

Actually, that already happened. In 1995 a client of Dave Blackburn, who runs Kootenai Angler in Libby, hooked his size-4 Royal Wulff into an object that resembled a log. That log turned out to be a huge rainbow.

When the fish rolled, Blackburn yelled, "Did you see how wide it was across the back? That fish must be over 15 pounds! This is the biggest fish I have ever seen rise to a fly!"

The angler, who was using wispy 5X tippet exhaled, rightfully, "What do I do with this fish?"

Unfortunately, there was nothing to do except hold on. Ten minutes later, that rainbow felt a sting in its jaw, tore upstream and parted a 5X tippet like it was sewing thread.

"I will probably row the Kootenai another 13 years before I see another fish that size rise to a fly," Blackburn mused. "It took me several days to recover from the experience."

The Kootenai begins in the high mountains on the west slope of the Canadian Rockies, then races through northwest Montana and northern Idaho before turning farther north into the Kootenai Lakes region of British Columbia. During that course, the river slows for 90 miles, about half in Canada and half in Montana, at Lake Koocanusa.

The Kootenai's best flyfishing occurs in the tailwater section below Koocanusa and Libby Dam in Montana. From that point, extending 28.6 miles downstream to Kootenai Falls, flyfishers will encounter a variety of water types and some gorgeous, heavily-timbered mountain scenery. Rainbow trout numbers rate 2,400 a mile through that section, which should explain part of the Kootenai's appeal.

The Kootenai's "upper section", which runs from the dam downstream to Libby, is characterized by long runs, wide, extensive curves, gravel bars, islands, small side-channels, riffles and some very deep pools. Particularly productive are the mid-depth runs and the side-channels. The mouths of feeder creeks should not be overlooked either. Especially during spring, big rainbows will stage (hold in a con-fined area) at the mouth of those streams before pushing up the fast-flowing feeders to the origin of their birthplace.

Downstream from Libby the river is broken by a scattering of large boulders. Flyfishers can work the water below each boulder or the bankside habitat and draw fish from the depths. After the boulders, the river enters a section called China Rapids, which can be a challenge, if not downright deadly, for boaters.

The rapids earned their name in the 1860s when a party of Chinese miners from Canada tried to raft down the river with a load of gold. They avoided an overland route fearing white settlers would steal their fortune. Unfortunately, the gold shifted

Drift boats and rafts offer the best access to the Kootenai, especially when flows run high and fast, as they often do through summer. (Dave Blackburn Photo)

as they were negotiating the rapids and their raft upended. One miner made it to shore; the Kootenai ended up with the gold.

Today, only experienced boaters should try the rapids and it's advisable to scout them first if you don't want to end up like that infamous load of gold.

Just below China Rapids lies Kootenai Falls, and even the most experienced boater will not make it over the falls alive. Fortunately, a power line that crosses the river before the falls warns boaters of danger. There is a take-out site just above the falls.

Below the falls, the river remains turbulent for two miles. Only expert rafters and boaters should try that water. It harbors five major rapids that fluctuate in level of difficulty depending on how much water is being released at Libby Dam. During high flows, the river is quite intimidating—a place I would not tread.

After those rapids, below the town of Troy, beginners can float the river, although there are some large waves to avoid or negotiate, especially at the Yaak River confluence.

Fishing is less productive below Kootenai Falls, extending 20 miles downstream to the Idaho border. But there are good fish in that section, including some very large bull trout—they are just tougher to find.

Regulations through that stretch are less restrictive, which limits opportunity for the rainbows to grow as large as they do in the upper section. Fortunately, Montana Fish, Wildlife and Parks may soon change the regulations to accompany the upper river's limit of three trout under 13 inches and one over 18 inches. Currently, the lower river regulation allows a daily harvest of five trout with only one measuring over 14 inches. Whether considering the upper or lower river, those regulations allow the taking of too many fish. However, all bull trout, throughout the river, must be released. Other notable regulations cite: Floating is prohibited in the 500 yard section downstream from Libby Dam to the David Thompson Bridge; Kootenai River closed to fishing March 15 to the third Saturday in May from the dam to the Highway 37 bridge.

The most successful flyfishers ply the Kootenai from a raft or drift boat. But, all anglers can access the river adequately, especially along the upper river, via State Route 37 and U.S. Route 2, which parallel the river. State-run access sites do not exist, but boats and rafts can be dumped into the river at a few pullouts along the highway.

On the lower river, below the falls, access is more difficult with private land bordering much of the river.

Wade fishing can be productive at times, especially during late summer and fall when the water level drops and the swift currents of summer subside. During high flows, which can extend from April through August, wading can be downright dangerous. In 1995 an unfortunate flyfisher waded too deep and lost his life while skimming over Kootenai Falls. I can only hope that he was lined up on a huge 'bow, a 20-pounder, and figured he'd give it his best shot no matter what the consequences. Large trout drive men to do very crazy things, which I mostly support.

While the Kootenai offers excellent fishing, it does not make sense to push your luck to reach that one trout rising just beyond your casting range. Your trip could be severely spoiled. That could also be the case if you hit the Kootenai expecting to do battle with huge rainbows. While big rainbows exist, the state-record 29-pounder came from the upper river, most of the river's rainbows range from one to three pounds. Few flyfishers touch any of the truly monster rainbows. The huge fish hold in deep water where flyfishers rarely place a fly.

That's OK, the medium size 'bows are scrappy fish that seem particularly fond of dry flies. And there may be more of them swimming in the river soon.

According to Mike Hensler, a biologist for Montana Fish, Wildlife and Parks, those rainbows may be reacting to a three-year old slot limit that allows no harvest of trout between 13 and 18 inches on the upper river, above Kootenai Falls.

"We shocked sections of the river between the dam and the falls and what we saw was an increase in the number of large fish," Hensler said. "I do not consider it a trend yet, but it is very encouraging."

Encouraging? Check out these numbers: In 1991 the Kootenai held an average of just 93 trout age two or older every 1,000 feet. Now, the river holds about 307 of those larger fish every 1,000 feet. Numbers of three-year old and older fish jumped from 13 per 1,000 feet in 1991 to 45 every 1,000 feet in 1995. The total number of trout in the Kootenai runs about 2,400 a mile. Of those, about 1,500 a mile are seven inches or longer.

An increase in the population of larger trout could be the result of the slot limit, but two other factors may be contributing to the abundance of larger fish. First, flows on the Kootenai have been extremely high due to a salmon and sturgeon enhancement plan. During summer the Kootenai may flow more than 25,000 cubic feet a second. That high flow is intended to flush salmon smolts downstream to the ocean while benefitting sturgeon. Secondly, due to that high water, fewer anglers are plying the river.

For instance, in 1993 the Kootenai endured 31,000 angler days. That is not much compared to the Madison or Big Hole Rivers, but nearly all of the Kootenai's pressure was absorbed by the upper river. By considering pressure on the upper section only, Hensler calculates the number of angler days jumping to 700 a mile. That number would rank the river as fifth most pressured in the state. However, Hensler said, "If we did that survey again, the Kootenai would not be rated as one of the 10 most pressured rivers in Montana. Nobody wants to fish when the river is high."

The Kootenai is nearly impossible to wade fish during high flows, which are considered anything over 8,000 cfs. Prime floating occurs between 7,000 cfs and 11,000 cfs. Boat anglers can fish effectively at flows up to 20,000 cfs. Higher flows force those anglers into backwaters and side-channels where rainbows seek a calm place to rest.

"Often, larger rainbows will move into those spots to get out of the heavy current," Blackburn said. "There, they become very aggressive feeders. With the higher flows the bigger fish sometimes seem less wary. At those times float fishing is extremely productive."

The Kootenai's major hatches begin in spring before high water when some large western March brown mayflies emerge. A few Baetis may be seen at that time, too. Generally, flyfishers may encounter the March brown anytime from the second week in May to the first week of July.

"The western March browns are the first major hatch of the season," Blackburn said. "Sometimes there are just a few on the water and other times it can be a heavy emergence, but either way the fish get on them. I like to use a size-12 March brown tied in the parachute style, but a sparkle dun will work, too. I've found that the most effective patterns have a trailing shuck."

By mid June pale morning duns emerge and that is the hatch that most flyfishers target. The insects come off in abundance and the trout will focus their attention on them each day throughout summer. Be prepared for a slightly later hatch each day on the Kootenai than is typical of PMDs on other streams.

"The PMD is our bread and butter hatch," Blackburn said. "They come off every day as a spinnerfall in the morning and as duns in the afternoon around four. They live in riffles and shallow runs, but when they come off they will blanket the entire river.

"A lot of people will fish dun patterns throughout the hatch and that is a mistake," Blackburn added. "An emergence can go on for a few hours when the fish will only take small emergers in the surface film. Anyone fishing a dun is missing out at that time. After the emergence they will key in on the duns and dries will work. Then, the following morning we get a good spinnerfall and there can be millions of flies on the water at one time."

Flyfishers pop lots of big rainbows on the Kootenai, but there is always a chance that a big bull trout, like this monster, will pound your fly. (Dave Blackburn Photo)

Carrying plenty of PMD patterns is key on the Kootenai. According to Blackburn, those flies change in color and size throughout the season. Anglers who can't match the insects specifically are not going to catch as many fish as those anglers who can readily change patterns. Because of that fact, it pays to pack a fly-tying kit with other gear.

"You can never have enough PMDs," Blackburn said. "They can range from wine to an olive color. And they will change from large, size 14 and 16 bodies during early summer to size 18 or 20 bodies by the end of summer."

While PMDs dominate the summer hatch action, hopper fishing can be quite good on the Kootenai, too. But, only expect good hopper fishing during hot, dry summers.

"The hopper fishing is really variable with the climate," Blackburn said. "If we have a hot summer it can be terrific, but if it's a rainy summer it's poor. If we have some hoppers, I think fishing is best when the water is high. I'll float right down through the partially submerged grasses and slap that vegetation with my oar. It's like chumming.

When Kootenai River flows stabilize in late summer and fall, flyfishers can raise 20 to 60 rainbows a day. The typical 'bow runs 14 to 17 inches. (Dave Blackburn Photo)

"I'll anchor up and watch the fish feed on the hoppers I've knocked loose from the grass. Then I'll pick out the largest fish and go after him specifically."

Whether hopper fishing materializes or not, flyfishers can count on some excellent fall caddis action. Especially on the big October caddis, which may measure two inches long and really grab the attention of the Kootenai's rainbows. According to Blackburn, those rainbows can be taken on dry or wet imitations of the October caddis.

"Up top I like to fish a size-12 cinnamon stimulator tied on a long shank hook," he said. "You won't see a lot of bugs on the water, but you do see the fish key in on them. I also like to use a big caddis pupa fished under an indicator. Those pupa have a yellow body so any large pupa with a yellow coloration will work. A lot of people tie orange pupa because the adults have an orange coloration, but those guys don't do as well because the pupa are actually yellow."

Watch for October caddis action between mid-September and late October. However, it may be difficult to fish a caddis pattern at that time because the Kootenai offers intense blue quill and Baetis hatches throughout fall.

"It's tough not to tie on a Baetis during fall," Blackburn said. "During late August, September and October, you can stop in any riffle and fish for two hours without moving. There may be 50 or 60 fish rising in one riffle. It's not unusual to see 100 yards of rising fish ahead of the boat during a fall hatch. At times like that we can raise 100 fish a day on dry flies."

However, fishing small mayfly patterns is not easy. Flyfishers need to consider size, color and, maybe most importantly, presentation when culling fish from the river during a major Baetis and blue quill hatch.

"The Baetis actually look big compared to the blue quills," Blackburn said. "And it can be important to note the difference. Sometimes the fish will key on a certain size of fly when both bugs are emerging. The blue quills may go down to a size 24, but the Baetis will be size 18. You have to choose the right size or you're out of luck."

Size and length of tippet also play a key role in a flyfisher's success during fall when the water is low and clear. Standard on the Kootenai is a 12- to 15-foot leader tapered down to 5X or 6X for the Baetis and blue quill hatches. Stealth also contributes to an angler's luck, and that includes selection of a fly rod.

"There are times when the fish are so leader-shy you have to use a real delicate approach," Blackburn said. "I think a light rod that lays a fly over a fish nice and easy is the best. Nine-foot, four-weights are good, but even a three-weight works well."

Flyfishers who hit the river on an odd day, when little is happening hatch-wise, can still have opportunities for success. Nymphs and streamers are very effective on the Kootenai, and they often take the largest trout.

"Beadhead nymph patterns really work up here," Blackburn said. "A hare's ear beadhead is just the most effective pattern on this river. You can fish it any day of the year and do well. Prince nymphs work well, but they suck up a lot of whitefish, too. Often we use large nymphs just to discourage the whitefish from taking it."

Few whitefish will eat a woolly bugger, and they certainly won't eat a five-inch kokanee salmon imitation, such as those that Blackburn uses to probe the depths near the dam for the river's largest fish.

"Black and olive woolly buggers work really well here," he said, "but we like to use those big kokanee patterns with shooting heads and sinktip lines to reach the big fish. It's tough fishing and it's not pleasant, but that is about the only way you can catch the largest fish."

Whether you fish dry flies or big streamers on the Kootenai, visit the river with an open mind—don't expect to do battle with the next state-record rainbow. Instead, cherish an opportunity to work big water with delicate mayfly patterns for some very strong rainbow trout. With that approach, the Kootenai should not disappoint.

Stream Facts: Kootenai River

Seasons
- Open all year except from Libby Dam to Highway 37 bridge, which is closed to fishing from March 15 to May 18. Closed to intentional fishing or taking of bull trout. Fishing from boats or other floating craft is prohibited from Libby Dam approximately 500 yards downstream to David Thompson Bridge as posted.

Trout
- The Kootenai holds mostly rainbows with a few cutthroat and some large bull trout. Most rainbows run between 12 and 17 inches. However, there are some true hogs residing in the Kootenai's big current—20-pounders exist.

River Miles
- Libby Dam—0
- Fisher River—3.2
- Libby Bridge—17
- China Rapid—26.3
- Kootenai Falls—29.5
- Yaak River—44.2
- Idaho border—50.3

River Flows
- The Kootenai may run high anytime between April and August due to sudden releases from Kootenai Dam. Prime floating occurs at levels between 7,000 and 11,000 cubic feet a second. Prime wade conditions arrive when the river flows below 7,000 cfs.

Dangers
- China Rapids
- Kootenai Falls
- Yaak River confluence

Fishing Access
- Decent access points off of Highways and bridge crossings.

Area Fly Shops
- Kootenai Angler, 13546, Highway 37, Libby, MT 59923, 406-293-7578
- Lakestream Fly Shop, 15 Central, Whitefish, MT 59937, 406-892-4149
- Yaak River Lodge, 27744 Yaak River Road, Troy, MT 59936, 800-676-5670

KOOTENAI RIVER MAJOR HATCHES

Insect	J	F	M	A	M	J	J	A	S	O	N	D	Flies
Midge	■	■	■	■	■	■	■	■	■	■	■	■	Griffith's Gnat #18-24; Standard Adams #16-24; Palomino Midge #16-24; Serendipity #16-24; Brassie #18-24; Disco Midge #16-24; Reverse Suspender Midge #18-24;
Pale Morning Dun						■	■	■					PMD Cripple #16-22; Sparkle Dun #16-22; Parachute PMD #16-22; Rusty Spinner #16-22; CDC Transitional Dun #18-22; Woven PMD Nymph #16-20; Hare's Ear Nymph #16-20; Pheasant Tail Nymph #16-20
Caddis							■	■	■				Black Caddis Pupa #16-18; X-Caddis #16-18; Emergent Sparkle Pupa #16-18; Hemingway Caddis #16-18; Tan Caddis #16-18; Elk Hair Caddis #16-18; Soft Hackle #14-18
Blue-winged Olive				■	■	■			■	■			Olive Cripple #16-24; Parachute Adams #16-24; Sparkle Dun #16-24; Olive Thorax #18-24; Hare's Ear Nymph #16-22; Pheasant Tail Nymph #16-22; Poxyback Baetis #16-22; RS-2 Emerger
Grasshoppers							■	■					Dave's Hopper #6-8; Meadow Hopper #6-8
Iron Blue Dun						■	■	■	■	■			Baetis Parachute #18-24; Olive Sparkle Dun #18-24; Blue Quill #18-24
October Caddis										■	■		Elk Hair Caddis #8-12; X-Caddis #8-12; Yellow Caddis Pupa #8-10
Flying Ant								■	■				Chernobyl Ant #10-16; Flying Black Ant #12-16

BLACKFEET RESERVATION LAKES

You've probably heard those boisterous anglers in local fly shops—people who claim they caught some monstrous fish and then boldly display a photo of some pipsqueak trout.

I worked in Alaska's fishing industry for years, where large fish are the norm, and I know the dimensions of a five-pound fish. Let me tell you, a snaky 20-incher doesn't weigh over a few pounds. It's certainly no monster. And I am not particularly impressed with photos of large fish that scraped their fins off on the bottom of some concrete hatchery raceway a few days before their release into the local pond. In my mind, tame trout are unimpressive.

Instead of embarrassing themselves again by calling an average fish a monster or a finless trout a trophy, take pity and tell those braggarts to visit the Blackfeet Indian Reservation in northwest Montana. Never again will they need to expound the merit of some minuscule trout. They can catch enough hogs in one week on the reservation to quell their lies for a lifetime. Well, that might not be quite accurate. Once a flyfisher launches a line on the reservation, he will always want to return.

There is no place in Montana, maybe no place in the entire West, possibly no other place in the world that harbors so many appealing lakes with so many big rainbow trout. And the truth is, those reservation lakes do not see a whole lot of pressure compared to Big Sky rivers, like the Bighorn and Yellowstone. If there was ever a place to assure yourself a shot at a five-pound plus trout, maybe even a fish approaching 10 pounds, the Blackfeet Reservation is the destination.

Those lakes are loaded with five-pound fish and on some of them, the opportunity to catch a true monster, a trout approaching 30 inches, exists with each cast.

Many of the reservation's largest fish live in Mission and Duck Lakes, its two most popular fisheries. Mission offers a thriving population of large rainbows and Duck offers those huge rainbows, browns and, possibly, some very large bull trout.

In 1996, 11,000 two-year-old bull trout were planted in Duck to help control a burgeoning population of suckers. Bull trout are tremendously aggressive, and it's thought that they will grow fast and begin feeding on suckers by 1998.

While flyfishers may have to wait a couple years to tie into huge bull trout, some of those Duck Lake browns are already five-years old and reaching trophy size. And, with an expected life span of seven or eight years, they are only going to get larger.

"Duck may be the most productive lake in the Lower Forty Eight," said Ira Newbreast, director of the tribal wildlife department. "We stock fish each year when they are seven inches and in two years they'll measure between 17 and 19 inches. By the time they reach five or six years old, they average 20 to 25 inches with a few reaching 29 inches, say 10 pounds."

While Duck offers a shot at big browns, some rainbows, and possibly bull trout in the future, Mission harbors huge rainbows in staggering numbers. Each season, the lake receives a plant of about 81,000 juvenile trout. When those fish mature, they race into shallow water, searching for gravel beds to spawn in. Their sex efforts are

*The Blackfoot Reservation lakes: no better place in the west to take large
rainbow trout. Here, Paul Druyvestein points a six-pounder toward release.
(Dan Summerfield Photo)*

futile, but flyfishers find great joy landing one pig after the other. At times during
spring, 20-fish days can be had. The combined weight of those trout might exceed
100 pounds!

During late spring, summer and fall, those big trout will cruise the surface, looking for emerging insects. Hitting one of the reservation lakes during a full-blown
hatch borders on chaos. According to Joe Kipp at Morningstar Outfitters in Browning, those hatches begin with the Callibaetis mayflies in mid-May.

"The lakes vary in elevation, so the hatches begin on the lower lakes and they are
followed by the upper lakes a couple weeks later," he said. "We see those Callibaetis
and some large caddis come off in May, and then we get the big damselfly hatch
beginning around June 15. PMDs come off in early July and they extend into August.

"The most overlooked hatches are the terrestrial insects: hoppers, flying ants and
even lady bugs," Kipp added. "I really don't fish dry flies during any of the hatches.
The only times I use dry flies are during the grasshopper blow or when caddis are
skating across the surface and during true spinnerfalls. Otherwise, nymphs and
streamers are the ticket."

Kipp fishes the reservation an average of 150 days a year. If he could pick just
three days to fish the lakes, here's when you would find him bouncing in a floattube,
fighting the reservation's constant wind.

Blackfeet Reservation Lakes

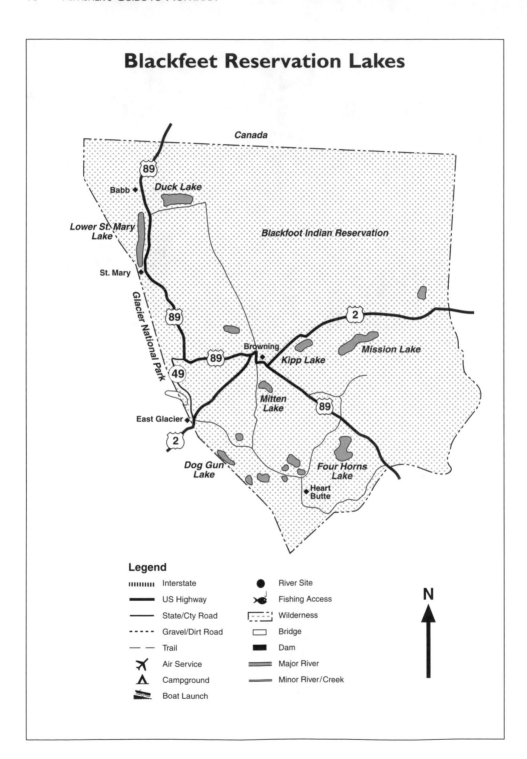

Canada

89

Babb ◆ Duck Lake

Lower St. Mary Lake

Blackfoot Indian Reservation

St. Mary ◆

Glacier National Park

89

89

Browning ◆

49

2

Kipp Lake

Mission Lake

Mitten Lake

89

East Glacier ◆

2

Dog Gun Lake

Four Horns Lake

Heart Butte ◆

Legend

ⅢⅢⅢ Interstate		● River Site	
—— US Highway		✕ Fishing Access	
— State/Cty Road		Wilderness	
---- Gravel/Dirt Road		▭ Bridge	
— — Trail		▬ Dam	
✈ Air Service		Major River	
▲ Campground		Minor River/Creek	
Boat Launch			

N

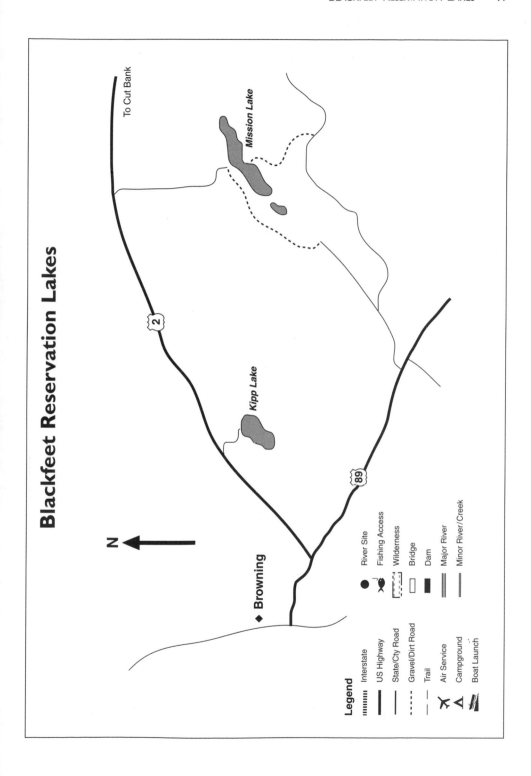

Blackfeet Reservation Lakes

N

To Cut Bank

Mission Lake

Kipp Lake

Browning

Legend

Interstate
US Highway
State/Cty Road
Gravel/Dirt Road
Trail
Air Service
Campground
Boat Launch

River Site
Fishing Access
Wilderness
Bridge
Dam
Major River
Minor River/Creek

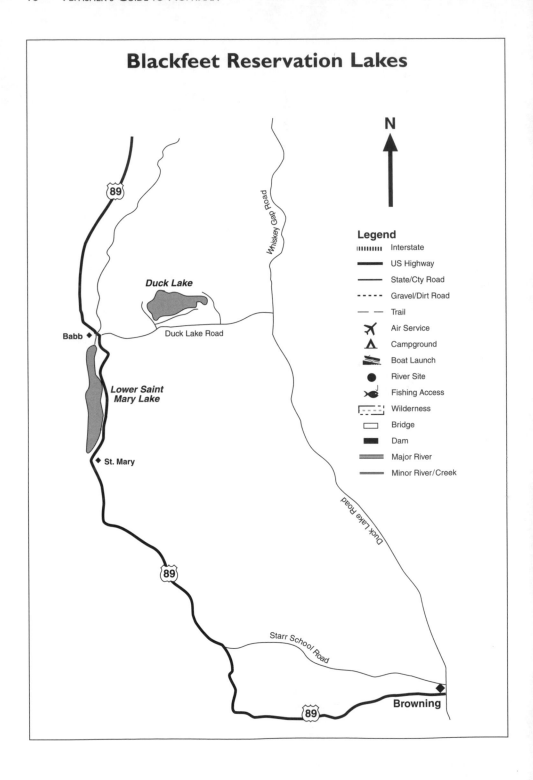

Blackfeet Reservation Lakes

Legend

┉┉┉┉	Interstate
▬▬▬	US Highway
——	State/Cty Road
- - - -	Gravel/Dirt Road
— —	Trail
✈	Air Service
⛺	Campground
🛥	Boat Launch
●	River Site
🐟	Fishing Access
⬚	Wilderness
▭	Bridge
▬	Dam
▬▬	Major River
══	Minor River/Creek

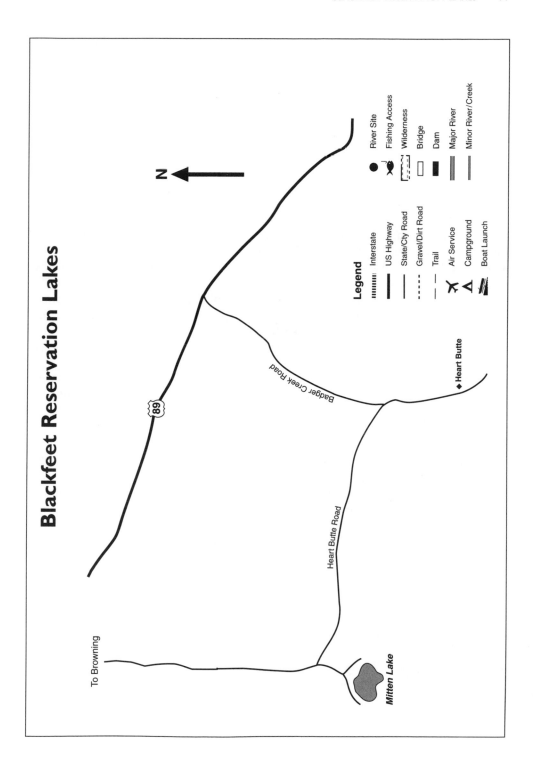

"I'd fish Mission or Kipp Lake in April for spawning rainbows," he said. "I'd fish again during the damsel hatch in June at Mission or Kipp—take your pick. I'd fish again in the fall at any of the lakes. Any time in late September or early October, the crowds are gone and the fish are all feeding. Browns and brook trout are trying to spawn, and they are very aggressive. It's the best time to catch large fish. They are really healthy and fat after feeding all summer and fall."

No matter when you visit the reservation and challenge its lakes, wind can be an evil. Here's what Kipp says about dealing with the wind: "Don't be a god-damned baby about it."

Point taken, but most floattube flyfishers prefer not to be swamped by five-foot breaking waves. They'd rather do their surfing on a boogie board in Hawaii. However, wind should not deter a flyfisher's efforts. According to Kipp, the reservation's weather is localized. When the wind is frothing on Mission or Duck Lakes, it may not be blowing on other waters. By jumping around to different lakes, a flyfisher may be able to avoid major gusts. But, in some cases, the wind can actually enhance a flyfisher's chances.

"What I hate are the dead-calm days," Kipp explained. "On a calm day the water is flat and really clear and the fish can be tough to approach. On a windy day, the food is stirred up. Often you can find a rip tide where the waves have stirred up mud around shore. I like to fish just outside of that mudline because that is where the fish will congregate."

While Mission and Duck draw most reservation anglers, there are other intriguing options. Here is a run-down on some other reservation fisheries, commonly utilized by nontribal members:

Dog Gun

A brook trout angler's delight. However, brookies can be difficult quarry. Fortunately, the lake is not huge—just 120 acres—and it is shallow, about nine feet deep on average. Some of the brook trout go four or five pounds, but the average fish will measure about 14 inches. Like brook trout everywhere, they'll feed mostly under the surface. Damselfly nymphs draw strikes, but streamer patterns work best.

Hidden Lake

Take note: Hidden Lake is located on private property, and landowner/angler relations are apparently strained. That is unfortunate for the flyfisher—Hidden holds some very large rainbow and brook trout.

"We've decided to stop stocking the lake," Newbreast admitted. "There was contention regarding access for tribal and nontribal members. A lot of that grazing land was inundated with mudholes from vehicles. Instead of being the whipping post, we decided to just stop stocking it and see what happens."

If you can get at Hidden, a 44-acre lake that lies just six miles northwest of Browning, expect brook trout and rainbows that go three to five pounds.

Dan Summerfield cradles a monster Mission Lake rainbow—one of a half dozen monsters he caught in two hours, without waders, from shore!

Four Horn

At 750 acres, Four Horn is a lot of water to cover. But, it holds browns and rainbows so it's worth listing on any trophy trout hunter's hit list. The browns are particularly fond of brown woolly buggers, although sculpin patterns draw strikes, too. Unfortunately, night fishing is not allowed on the reservation, but a mouse pattern fished early in the morning or just before dark could draw strikes as the big browns head away from the shallows for their daily dip into deep water.

Kipp

A heavily-fished lake just north of Browning, it manages to kick out some sizable rainbows.

"Kipp is looking really good right now," Newbreast said. "We stock it with about 30,000 to 40,000 juveniles each year. There are plenty of fish in the lake but they can be challenging."

There are many other waters to fish on the reservation and the best tactic is to stop at Northern High Plains Outfitters in Browning to pick up the latest report. If something sounds red-hot, you may want to venture to that water. However, if you want a safe bet, try the waters listed above. They should not disappoint.

Wherever and whenever you fish the reservation, there are some things to keep in mind. First, realize that you are on private land. The Blackfeet own the reservation, and they are not sold on visiting anglers. But as long as flyfishers respect property, both private and public, they should be all right. Oh yeah, you probably want to avoid any night life in reservation towns, especially Browning—it is a tough town and problems can arise.

Flyfishers can instead pitch a tent near one of the lakes or follow Highway 2 from Browning to Cut Bank where motels are available. There are also motels in Browning, East Glacier and St. Mary.

Do not necessarily count on sleeping in a tent or under the canopy of your truck, even if that was your initial game plan. The reservation's weather can be hideous at times. Snow can fall any day of the year. At other times the temperature may rocket into the nineties. During winter, the lakes freeze and ice does not generally come off before the first week of April. To assure fishing opportunities, you may want to plan a trip after the third week in April. Rainbows will still be spawning at Duck and Mission Lakes.

Another note: stock up on supplies before you hit the reservation. And if you visit around the high-school prom, there will be no alcohol available for sale, which is a story unto itself.

Four-wheel drive vehicles are best for the reservation, due to the variety of conditions you may encounter. Even a hard summer rain can turn the dirt roads into bottomless mud/gumbo. During spring and early summer and fall, snow may cause hazardous conditions even on the highways. If you visit in a two-wheel drive, park in a place where you can get back out to the highway whatever the conditions.

You do not have to buy a Montana fishing license to fish on the reservation, but you do have to purchase a reservation permit. Here are the options: $7.50 for one day; $20 for three days; $35 for the season. Lakes are open all year, and nontribal members under age 13 can fish without a license as long as they are accompanied by a licensed angler. The limit is five trout a day—it is hoped that flyfishers will choose to return their catch to the water. A photo, one that you can proudly display at the local fly shop or in your sportroom (hang it in your living room if you have an understanding spouse), should be enough.

BLACKFEET RESERVATION LAKES MAJOR HATCHES

Insect	J	F	M	A	M	J	J	A	S	O	N	D	Flies
Callibaetis		▓	▓	▓	▓	▓	▓						Callibaetis Cripple #14-16; Sparkle Spinner #14-16; Sparkle Dun #14-16; Parachute Adams #14-16; Hare's Ear #14-16
Sculpin	▓	▓	▓	▓	▓	▓	▓	▓	▓	▓	▓	▓	Matuka Sculpin #2-6; Woolhead Sculpin #2-6; Troth Bullhead #2-6
Midge	▓	▓	▓	▓	▓	▓	▓	▓	▓	▓	▓	▓	Parachute Adams #16-20; Glass Bead Midge #16-20; Midge Emerger #16-20; Hatching Midge #16-20; Midge Larvae #16-20
Damselfly					▓	▓	▓	▓					Marabou Damsel #10-12; Six Pack #10-12; Swimming Damsel # 8-12
Caddis					▓	▓	▓	▓	▓				Tom Thumb #6-10; Stimulator #6-10; Elk Hair Caddis #6-10; Clipped Hair Caddis #6-10
Leech	▓	▓	▓	▓	▓	▓	▓	▓	▓	▓	▓	▓	Rabbit Strip Leech (olive, black, brown) #2-6; Mohair Leech #2-8; Marabou Leech #4-8; Woolly Bugger #2-8
Dragonfly													Olive Dragon #6-10; Crystal Dragon #6-10
Scud	▓	▓	▓	▓	▓	▓	▓	▓	▓	▓	▓	▓	Gray Scud #14-16; Orange Scud #14-16

FLATHEAD RIVER

It's the presence of grizzly bears and the undeniable sensation that you just dropped a rung on the food chain that attracts me to the Flathead River, especially its South Fork.

Once, while walking along a trail that parallels the South Fork deep in the Bob Marshall Wilderness, I heard a "woof" emanate from the timber. The hair on my neck seemed to stand on end. My posture changed to defensive. I felt like a stick figure struggling with each step. A few limbs cracked above me. A dark, sizable creature moved through the timber. Black bear or grizzly?

Then nothing. Not the slightest noise. So I struggled to regain my composure for another 100 yards, then made like an Olympic sprinter and made tracks. If you happened to be there that day watching, I hope you enjoyed the spectacle: a man running flat-out under a full, heavy pack, pots and pans clanking, sleeping bag bouncing and a fly rod held out in front like a defense wand.

That is the beauty of the South Fork and the Flathead River in general. It flows through mostly wild country, offers native trout species in decent numbers, not to mention that native fauna, and it provides the option for intense solitude. And if you bump into a grizzly, you will probably do some deep introspection.

The Flathead River system should seem fairly intimidating to the visiting angler, whether gazing at its flow from a safe spot on its bank or as an intriguing, winding blue line on the northwest Montana map.

The Flathead contains so much water to fish and so many species of fish, the main question is where to start.

There are many options, including the lower river below Flathead lake. But let's start with the main river above Flathead Lake, including its forks, which provide the most consistent flyfishing for trout.

The Flathead has three forks, and two of them, the Middle Fork and South Fork, begin in designated wilderness areas. The Middle Fork commences in the Great Bear Wilderness, and the South Fork's headwaters, as mentioned, are located deep in the Bob Marshall Wilderness. The North Fork, although it has equally killer scenery and plenty of solitude, begins in Canada and follows the west edge of Glacier National Park before meeting with the Middle Fork at Blankenship Bridge, just southwest of Lake McDonald.

At Blankenship, the mainstem Flathead is born, and it flows freely, dropping just an average of four feet a mile through its 55-mile course to Flathead Lake.

Through that course the river meanders endlessly, especially below Kalispell where it offers lots of backwaters and sloughs.

As a native cutthroat, bull and wild rainbow trout fishery, the river is marginal. It hosts trout, but the river nowhere resembles what it could be if fish management debacles had not fouled up the Flathead River system.

The main culprit are lake trout. They were introduced into Flathead Lake, a 28-mile long, six-mile wide body of water, and they prospered. They fed heavily on kokanee salmon until that population crashed, in part due to competition from the

North Fork Flathead

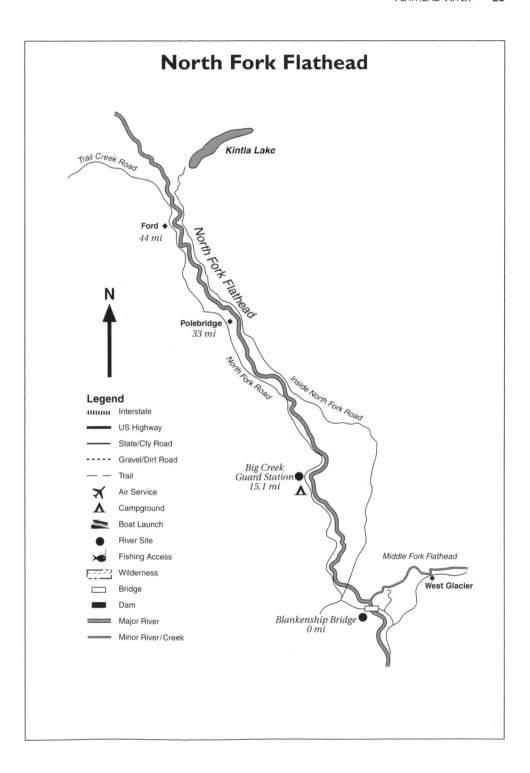

Kintla Lake

Trail Creek Road

North Fork Flathead

Ford ◆
44 mi

N

Polebridge ◆
33 mi

North Fork Road

Inside North Fork Road

Legend

ⅲⅲⅲⅲ	Interstate
▬▬▬	US Highway
▬▬▬	State/Cty Road
- - - - -	Gravel/Dirt Road
— —	Trail
✈	Air Service
⛺	Campground
🛶	Boat Launch
●	River Site
🐟	Fishing Access
⬚	Wilderness
▭	Bridge
▬	Dam
▬▬▬	Major River
▬▬▬	Minor River/Creek

*Big Creek
Guard Station* ●
15.1 mi ⛺

Middle Fork Flathead

West Glacier ◆

Blankenship Bridge ●
0 mi

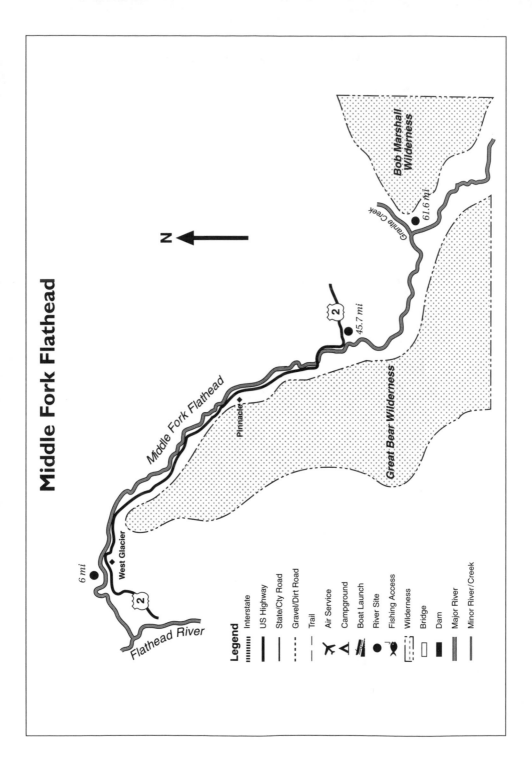

Middle Fork Flathead

Legend

- ▮▮▮▮ Interstate
- — US Highway
- — State/Cty Road
- — Gravel/Dirt Road
- — Trail
- ✈ Air Service
- ⛺ Campground
- ⛵ Boat Launch
- ● River Site
- 🎣 Fishing Access
- ▢ Wilderness
- ▮ Bridge
- ▮ Dam
- — Major River
- — Minor River/Creek

South Fork Flathead

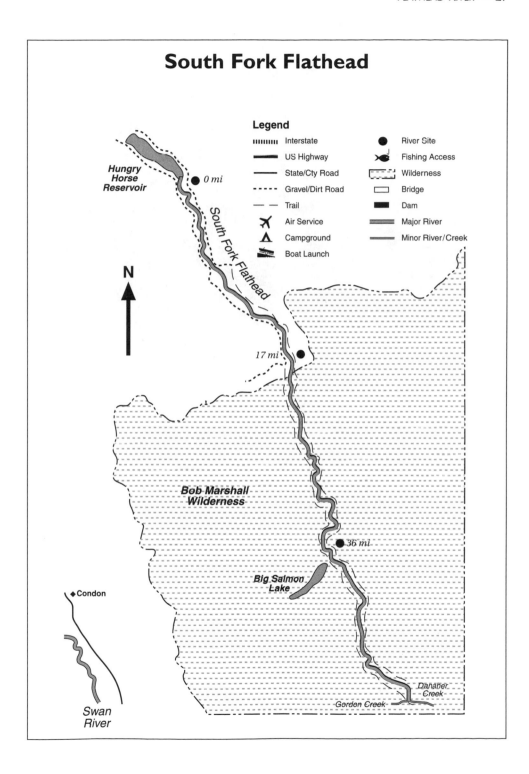

Legend

ⅲⅲⅲ Interstate		●	River Site
▬ US Highway		✖	Fishing Access
── State/Cty Road		⊏⊐	Wilderness
---- Gravel/Dirt Road		▭	Bridge
— — Trail		▬	Dam
✈ Air Service		▬	Major River
⛰ Campground		──	Minor River/Creek
🚣 Boat Launch			

Hungry Horse Reservoir

0 mi

South Fork Flathead

N

17 mi

Bob Marshall Wilderness

36 mi

Big Salmon Lake

Condon

Swan River

Danaher Creek

Gorden Creek

The Flathead's slow mainstream current and numerous sloughs are appealing to northern pike. Here, Scott Brown poses with an average pike before release. (Scott Brown Photo)

introduced *Mysis* shrimp and Lake Superior whitefish. Whitefish and lake trout combine for 80 percent of the lake's biomass.

As their food supply diminished, lake trout turned to cutthroat trout and bull trout for sustenance, and the smaller trout's populations have suffered.

The lake trout actually offer flyfishers a good opportunity when they cruise into the shallow shoreline areas during fall. Large streamers will draw their fair share of strikes but you will probably have to get them down near the bottom. Sinktip and high-density sinking lines are an advantage. Stout leaders are the rule—lakers will run between eight and 20 pounds on average.

The Flathead River between Blankenship Bridge and Flathead Lake receives seasonal runs of trout out of the lake. To catch the river during its prime, flyfishers must pick their times to visit.

During runoff or just when the big flows recede there are some large cutthroat trout in the main stem. Big nymphs and streamers offer the best chance to fetch trout at that time. In July and August, the main river attracts juvenile trout during their downstream migration from the headwaters to Flathead Lake. Interspersed between the small fish will be pods of adult risers. Flyfishers should target those pods.

"The main stem can provide excellent fishing during summer, but it is mostly for juveniles," said Jim Vashro, fisheries manager for the Montana Department Fish, Wildlife and Parks' office in Kalispell. "It's appealing because the fish rise so eagerly for dry flies. Really, you don't even have to fish nymphs."

In September, larger cutts move out of Flathead Lake into the river. Anglers who know how to work large nymphs and streamers can catch some nice trout. Most fly-casters avoid reaches below the mouth of the Stillwater River. That section is influenced heavily by fluctuating lake levels.

"I'd concentrate on the Flathead from the mouth of the Stillwater upstream to Presentine Bar, which is just opposite Glacier International Airport," Vashro said. "That's about a 10-mile section with large fish and easy access. Of any place on the Flathead River, we've seen an increase in popularity there."

Maybe the best way to approach the river is by raft or drift boat. By floating, a fly-fisher can cover plenty of water with those big nymphs or bushy dry flies. And cut-throats are not afraid to pound basic patterns.

Runoff generally subsides between June 20 and the Fourth of July holiday. As the water drops, watch for a decent hatch of gray drakes. According to George Widener at Lakestream Flyfishing Company in Kalispell, trout key on those insects.

"Normally, I just fish big stonefly nymphs and buggers, and I work them low and slow," Widener said. "The bigger cutts have moved out of the tributaries at that time, so there are some nice fish in the river. You can really have some good fishing when the gray drakes hatch. It's never a blanket hatch, but when it comes off, fish will really key on it. You can also see some large stoneflies at that time. There will be a variety of caddis too, but all you need to match them is a size 14 elk hair caddis. That pattern will work every day between July and August.

The mainstem Flathead above the lake can be characterized as a fairly sterile environment due to cold water that emanates from the high country of northwest Montana. However, part of the river's problem can be attributed to Hungry Horse Dam, which contains the South Fork and creates Hungry Horse Reservoir. During past years, the dam released water from the bottom of the reservoir that ran about 39 degrees. That release dropped the mainstem's temperature by 15 degrees, wiping out most of the solid aquatic insect hatches that occurred before the dam was constructed.

Fortunately, in 1996 Hungry Horse Dam was retrofitted so it can draw water from any depth in the reservoir. Controllers will try to maintain water releases from Hungry Horse at the same temperature as the undammed Middle and North Forks.

With warmer water temperatures, the mainstem Flathead below the South Fork confluence could see increased insect diversity in the next few years. And that could translate into a better fishery.

"We should see significant improvement," Vashro said. "Since 1950, drawing cold water from Hungry Horse Reservoir has really affected aquatic insect populations on the river. With warmer, more constant temperatures, some of those midsummer hatches should improve.

"We may see more of the big stoneflies and mayflies. I also suspect we will see a very significant change in growth rates and overall survival of trout. Really, we have no resident population of trout in the North, Middle or lower South Forks. They move from Flathead Lake to the rivers and back again. With stable water temperature, we expect a resident population of fish to hold in the South Fork."

While flycasters can look forward to a better cutthroat fishery in a few years, the mainstem Flathead already hosts excellent northern pike fishing. And those water wolves can be a riot on a light fly rod.

Focus your efforts during the spring and fall when pike move into the shallows. Church, Egan and Fennon Sloughs hold good numbers of northerns, although you may find them in many other backwaters and sloughs along the river.

The Flathead's trout fishery really comes into its own in the forks of the river, especially the South Fork, which flows for about 50 miles through the Bob Marshall Wilderness.

In fact, the South Fork above Hungry Horse Reservoir may rate as Montana's best native cutthroat fishery. And it offers excellent scenery to mesh with its eager rising fish.

"I think it's probably the best cutthroat fishery in the state," Vashro says. "We've had a wilderness trout limit there for 10 years, so you can catch some really nice fish. We haven't seen an inordinate increase in pressure on the river. The only complaint we hear is that people can't catch a fish small enough to keep."

If you want to fish the South Fork, you will have to don hiking boots and strike out on foot. If you want to keep a fish for dinner, try your luck below Meadow Creek where just 10 percent of the cutthroats exceed 12 inches. Above Meadow Creek Gorge, flyfishers should find healthy populations of resident cutts. They will stretch from 12 to 18 inches; a few may top the 20-inch mark. Farther upstream, 30 percent of the fish exceed 12 inches.

No matter where you fish on the upper South Fork or, for that matter, the Middle Fork or North Fork, be aware of bears. Flathead River country is big-time grizzly habitat, and backpacking flyfishers should follow all precautions when cooking and storing food.

"Of the forks, the South Fork is the hardest to get at," Widener said. "But it probably has the most pristine scenery and the best fishing. The fish move out of the reservoir in the spring to spawn in the small tributaries. By July the bigger fish back out of the tribs into the main river. Some of them remain in the river all year; others will move back to the reservoir. They are all native cutthroats, but you will encounter some big bull trout, too. If you are fishing a woolly bugger or another type of streamer you will pick up the bulls. They are a wonderful fish, but you have to be careful with them. Don't even lift them out of the water."

A fly box for the South Fork certainly should not resemble, say, a box full of tiny flies for some tricky spring creek venture. Instead, the South Fork lineup or, for that matter, any Flathead River fly box, should feature an array of bushy dry flies and terrestrial patterns.

Royal Wulffs, humpies, ants, beetles, grasshoppers and elk hair caddis are staples. Basic mayfly patterns like hare's ear and pheasant tail nymphs also draw strikes. Make sure to pack some parachute Adams in various sizes, too.

While the South Fork requires a long, planned-out hike to reach its best fishing, the North Fork allows anglers to hop off the gravel North Fork Road right into some excellent holes.

You can catch big, healthy native westslope cutthroat trout in the mainstem Flathead and its excellent tributaries. The author took this classic cutthroat on a parachute Adams.

The North Fork, which offers a beautiful view into Glacier National Park and the east side of the Continental Divide, is not rated as a top trout fishery, even though it holds fair numbers of native westslope cutthroat and bull trout.

"The North Fork is absolutely awesome for scenery," Widener said. "And it's a very pristine river to float. I just wouldn't do it when flows are high."

That is the truth. The North Fork is usually gushing between mid-May and July 4 each year. Then, as the river drops, some excellent options arise.

"The North Fork's fishery is primarily for out-migrating juvenile cutthroats," Vashro said. "In July and August it is full of eight- to ten-inch fish, and the action is fast and furious. Plus, it's an easy float in most reaches."

An easy four-mile float is from Big Creek Access to Glacier Rim. Another option is the Ford Creek Ranger Station to Polebridge, which could take all day.

The North Fork's trout will feed aggressively on various caddis and mayflies. And they will smack a streamer with abandon, too. While fishing streamers, you may strike into a monster bull trout. They run up to 20 pounds in the North Fork, and they are present throughout summer and fall.

"During summer, the section above West Glacier is overtaken by whitewater rafters, but there are some good fish in there," Widener said. "Some of the pools have rainbows, cutts, bull trout and even an occasional lake trout. None of those fish are picky eaters."

To avoid whitewater enthusiasts, flyfishers may want to lace up their boots and hike into the river's headwaters, which lie in the Great Bear/Bob Marshall Wilderness. Most of the Middle Fork's cutthroats run 12 to 14 inches, but the wilderness section holds plenty above 15 inches with a few true monsters stretching 20 inches.

All three forks offer classic cutthroat water in densely-timbered mountain habitat. Most of the river's food grows in the riffled sections. Due to that abundance in the riffles, flyfishers should focus just below those riffles most of the time.

"The fish like to feed, in particular, right below the riffles," Widener said. "The rainbows tend to hold out in slightly faster water than the cutthroats. Sometimes you will catch them right out in the middle of a riffle gorging on insects.

"Cutthroats prefer the soft, slower water right on the edge of the riffles. Any edge or current seam will hold them. You can almost always catch some fish on dry flies near the riffles, but some of the larger fish will hold near the bottom in deeper holes behind rocks and logs. That's usually where I catch the largest cutthroats. And I've seen them in the Flathead up to 23 inches. They are a beautiful fish."

While the upper Flathead offers the best trout fishing, the lower river is not without its temptations. And the greatest temptation between Kerr Dam and the river's confluence with the Clark Fork, about 72 miles, is the big northern pike. But you better get a tribal fishing permit before you cast those streamers because the river flows through the Flathead Indian Reservation. Flyfishers can gain access to the river in a few spots where Highway 200 parallels water.

Aside from those pike, the lower river offers some large rainbows, decent numbers of cutthroats and some big browns. But river flows are never stable and the water can run quite warm during the summer.

The lower Flathead should be a serious consideration for any flyfisher looking for a trophy pike. Twenty-pound specimens fin in the river. Larger fish probably exist. The common pike will run between five and 10 pounds and on light tackle, like a six-weight rod, they provide top sport.

Look for those pike, especially in late April, May and early June in the backwaters and sloughs where good weed growth occurs. Try a variety of large streamers patterns and strip-retrieve those offerings.

While there are ample fishing opportunities in the Flathead drainage, many frustrated fishers focus on the true potential of the river.

"The entire fishery is dependent on the health of Flathead Lake, and the lake is in disarray," Widener said. "It's all beautiful, pristine water, but until something is done about the lake, particularly the lake trout, the river will never regain itself as a top-notch cutthroat and bull trout fishery.

"I think the ideal situation would be commercial fishing for lake trout and putting no-bait, selective regulations on cutthroats," Widener added. "Then the river might live up to its potential."

Whether that scenario ever occurs is anyone's guess. Fortunately, while that question is being answered, flyfishers can continue to pursue a variety of species on a lot of gorgeous, wilderness water. For native westslope cutthroats and bull trout, the Flathead River and its wonderful, scenic forks can't be beat.

Stream Facts: Flathead River

Seasons

Mainstem Flathead

- From confluence of North and Middle Forks to mouth: extended season for white-fish and lake trout open December 1 through third Saturday in May. All other species of trout must be released.
- Above Kerr Dam closed entire year to taking of salmon.
- Flathead Reservation boundary to mouth open entire year.

South Fork Flathead

- Closed entire year to taking of salmon.
- Upstream from Hungry Horse Dam wilderness limits apply.
- Catch and release for cutthroats.
- Downstream from Hungry Horse Reservoir (dam to Devils Elbow) closed entire year.

North Fork Flathead

- Extended whitefish season and catch and release for trout open December 1 to the third Saturday in May.

Middle Fork Flathead

- Extended whitefish season and catch and release for trout open December 1 to the third Saturday in May.

River Miles

- Flathead Lake inlet—0
- Kalispell—27
- Presentine Bar—34
- South Fork mouth—44
- Blankenship Bridge (mouth of middle and north forks)—54

River Characteristics

- High flows may occur from April through September with a peak in June or July; early spring and fall offer the most predictable fishing conditions.

Fishing Access

- Good access throughout the main stem, South Fork, Middle Fork and North Fork.

Camping

- Lots of unimproved and maintained access sites throughout the entire river system.

Area Fly Shops

- Lakestream Fly Shop, 15 Central Avenue, Whitefish, MT 59937, 406-892-4641
- Snappy Sport Center, 1400 Hwy 2 East, 406-257-7525, Open 7 days
- Sportsman and Ski Haus, Junction of Hwy 2 and 93, 406-755-6484
- Open Season, 119 East Idaho, Kalispell, MT 59901, 406-755-1298
- Glacier Country, 945 4th Avenue East, Kalispell, MT, 406-756-7128
- Glacier Wilderness Guides, West Glacier, MT 59936, 800-521-7238

FLATHEAD RIVER MAJOR HATCHES

Insect	J	F	M	A	M	J	J	A	S	O	N	D	Flies
Caddis					■								Elk Hair Caddis #14-16; Stimulator #14-16; Emergent Sparkle Pupa #14-16; Drifting Cased Caddis #14-18; X-Caddis #14-18; Electric Caddis #14-16
Salmonfly *Pteronarcys californica*					■								Seducer #4-8; Stimulator #4-8; Bitch Creek Nymph #4-8; Kaufmann's Stone #2-6; Brook's Stone #2-6
Baetis				■						■			Parachute Adams #16-20; CDC Baetis #18-20; Sparkle Dun #18-20; Poxyback Baetis #16-20; CDC Biot Comparadun #18-20
Grasshoppers								■					Joe's Hopper #6-10; Dave's Hopper #6-10; Madame X #4-10; Meadow Hopper #4-8
Midges	■											■	Griffith's Gnat #16-20; Parachute Adams #18-22; Pheasant Tail Nymph #16-22
Gray Drake						■							Parachute Adams #14-16; Sparkle Dun #14-16; Comparadun #14-16; Hare's Ear Nymph #14-16; Pheasant Tail Nymph #14-16
Pale Morning Dun								■					Sparkle Dun #14-20; Parachute Adams #14-20; PMD Cripple #16-20; Lawson's Thorax Dun #16-20; Hare's Ear Nymph #16-18; Pheasant Tail Nymph #16-18; CDC Floating Nymph #16-18; Half Back Emerger #16-18
Flying Ant								■					Cinnamon Ant #12-16; EZ Sight Foam Ant #12-16

FORKS OF THE FLATHEAD RIVER MAJOR HATCHES

Insect	J	F	M	A	M	J	J	A	S	O	N	D	Flies
Caddis					■	■	■	■	■				Elk Hair Caddis #14-16; Stimulator #14-16; Emergent Sparkle Pupa #14-16; Drifting Cased Caddis #14-18; X-Caddis #14-18; Electric Caddis #14-16
Salmonfly *Pteronarcys californica*						■							Seducer #4-8; Stimulator #4-8; Bitch Creek Nymph; #4-8; Kaufmann's Stone #2-6; Brook's Stone #2-6
Flying Ant								■					Chernobyl Ant #10-16; Flying Black Ant #12-16
Baetis				■	■				■	■			Parachute Adams #16-20; CDC Baetis #18-20; Sparkle Dun #18-20; Poxyback Baetis #16-20; CDC Biot Comparadun #18-20
Hoppers							■	■	■				Joe's Hopper #6-10; Dave's Hopper #6-10; Madame X #4-10; Meadow Hopper #4-8
Midge	■	■	■	■	■	■	■	■	■	■	■	■	Griffith's Gnat #16-20; Parachute Adams #18-22; Pheasant Tail Nymph #16-22

Thompson River

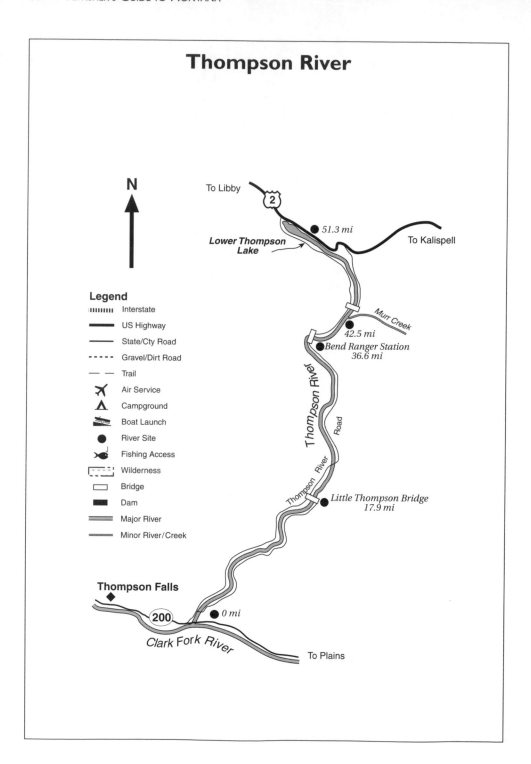

N

To Libby

2

51.3 mi

To Kalispell

Lower Thompson
Lake

Murr Creek

42.5 mi

Bend Ranger Station
36.6 mi

Thompson River

Thompson River Road

Legend

‖‖‖‖‖‖	Interstate
——	US Highway
—	State/Cty Road
- - - -	Gravel/Dirt Road
— —	Trail
✈	Air Service
⛺	Campground
🚣	Boat Launch
●	River Site
✦	Fishing Access
⌐⌐⌐	Wilderness
▭	Bridge
▬	Dam
══	Major River
—	Minor River/Creek

Little Thompson Bridge
17.9 mi

Thompson Falls
◆

200

0 mi

Clark Fork River

To Plains

THOMPSON RIVER

Simply stated, the Thompson River is not the trout fishery it could be. And it may not reach its potential anytime soon.

Still, the Thompson remains the best trout-fishing tributary on the lower Clark Fork River—a distinction avid flycasters gobble with a grain of salt. However, any fly-fisher in his right mind should not pass up an opportunity to fish that beautiful stream, especially as a day-long side trip away from its larger cousin.

The Thompson is a fun river to fish, due to its intimate size and its eager trout. In most places, it is less than a double-haul wide, which makes it a perfect river for fly-fishers of all skill levels. And of course, it beckons for that sexy three-weight rod you have been waiting to throw.

The Thompson flows out of Lower Thompson Lake west of Kalispell and south-east of Libby. From there it cuts almost directly south 50 miles until it meets the Clark Fork just west of Thompson Falls. It offers easy access with two dirt roads paralleling the river for most of its length.

In its upper reaches, the Thompson twists through a series of pretty meadows before bolting down through a forested canyon, spreading out a little before it reaches the Clark Fork. Through those sections, flyfishers find a variety of water types and trout habitat. There are deep pools, slick glides, shallow riffles and boulder-laden pocket water. Four types of trout and one species of char stalk the river.

Brook, rainbow, brown and cutthroat trout make up the majority of the catch, but a few bull trout strike up from the Clark Fork, providing an element of surprise that only the unexpected big fish brings.

Most of the river's trout run eight to 12 inches, but there are some legitimate rainbows for the taking. Many of the larger fish are located on the lower end, likely spending part of the year basking in the big flows of the Clark Fork. Those big fish represent the potential of the Thompson. With proper management and a helping hand from the river's anglers, large fish could be the norm. More on that later. In the upper 10 miles, which run from the Murr Bridge upstream to Lower Thompson Lake, an angler will find mostly small cutts and brookies.

What those fish lack in size they make up for in eagerness to strike a dry fly. And because the Thompson runs particularly clear almost all year, even during spring runoff, it is a good bet when other rivers are blown out.

The river's prime hatches begin in May, with a solid emergence of Grannom caddis and the early salmonfly hatch, which can draw bigger fish to the top for massive dry-fly patterns. Because of the presence of salmonflies, a black or brown Kaufmann's stonefly and woolly buggers work on the river any day of the year.

Throughout summer a variety of caddis emerge. An angler should inspect those insects closely and choose the best match from his fly selection. Thompson River caddis may run the gamut in color, ranging from tan to olive to dark brown.

In August, grasshoppers, gray drakes, and Trico and Baetis mayflies make their appearance. Gray drakes and Baetis should hatch best on overcast days extending through September, and Baetis all the way into November.

Gray drakes are particularly interesting because the dun stage of the hatch does not hold much merit. Gray drake nymphs are excellent swimmers, so they usually reach the shore before emerging. Therefore, duns generally fly away from the shoreline without ever having to present themselves as a surface target to trout. On the other hand, gray drake spinnerfalls can be monumental. Generally, spinnerfalls occur between 9 AM and noon. It pays to get out of bed and hit the river early.

Normally, flyfishers don't need to worry about matching the hatch exactly. Oh, there are times when patterns and tippet make a difference, but normally, fish will rise steadily to attractor patterns. The Thompson hardly resembles technical rivers like the Bighorn or Bitterroot when its comes to picky fish.

"Those fish are young and they act like it," offered Jim Vashro, regional fisheries manager for Montana Department of Fish, Wildlife and Parks. "Any of the attractor patterns will work. I like to use an elk hair caddis or grasshoppers during late summer. Royal Wulffs and renegades are good choices, too, and they will work most of the year. Any of the nymph patterns like a hare's ear or Prince nymph will work, and the streamers are good choices, too."

While the fish rise eagerly, you may not find trout in every hole. During the summer season, the Thompson can see its fair share of pressure from visiting anglers. Trout quickly disappear from the accessible holes. They move to areas that are relatively unfished.

"It's really a fun stream to fish," said Vashro. "It's not big enough to float, so most of the traffic is on foot. I try to pick areas where the river bends away from the road. You'd be surprised how few people are willing to walk out through the trees to the river. Spots like that will provide the best fishing."

While fishing on the Thompson can be rated good, logging, sediment overload and trout poachers weigh heavily on the river's potential. Its trout and char numbers are far less than what could be produced with prime conditions and considerate anglers. And it could use some special regulations placed on it.

It had a seven-mile section reserved for catch-and-release angling, but that provision was dropped by FWP in 1990. Most of the Thompson's anglers called that section "Closed," which should give a clear indication of their mentality. Meat-sackers is the correct term, I believe.

FWP's decision to drop the catch-and-release section left the Thompson with little hope of becoming a significant trophy-trout fishery. Surprisingly, the Thompson's demise could ultimately save the river.

Vashro said that improving roads that parallel the river and gaining support for restrictive regulations from the river's hungry angling community might turn the tide in the Thompson's favor.

"Plum Creek (the timber company that has plundered the Thompson's banks and cut the heck out of the forests surrounding the river—they do it everywhere in western Montana) is going to do some work on their road, and that will be a tremendous help to the fishery," Vashro said. "There are dirt roads on either side of the river, and sediment runs heavy off both of them. Plum Creek's work on the road will reduce sediment input directly, which should allow the river to use its own sediment flushing system."

Sediment affects production of trout because the river's rainbows and cutthroats use shallow riffles and runs during spawning season.

FWP biologist Joe Huston says, "If an air quality guy went up there and measured dust levels, they would be very high. And it all ends up in the river. Sediment increases egg mortality for fish, and it decreases aquatic insect production, too. That has a major effect on a fishery. If you don't have any insects, you don't have any fish. If you don't have good egg survival, you don't have any fish, either."

Of course, if anglers keep every fish they catch, you never gain a population of large trout.

"There was a lot of noncompliance when we had the catch-and-release section," Vashro admitted. "Plus that section was too short. We had fish moving 20 miles, right out of the catch-and-release area and into places where it is legal to catch them. In order to make the regulations work, we need to put them on a large section of the river, like 20 miles or even the whole thing, but we don't have public support for that type of management yet."

That does not mean the Thompson won't hold a population of big fish in the future. A curious phenomenon occurs when fisheries are stripped of their large trout. Often, fish-bonking phenoms turn pro-active. They blame everyone except themselves for the trout's demise, then quickly support restrictive regulations.

"I think this fishery will continue to slide downhill," Vashro said. "There are about 400 to 500 fishing days a year per mile on it. The number of large fish in the river is way down compared to the past. At some point, the quality will drop to a level that is unacceptable. Then, people may support our efforts. Until that time, you won't see many large fish in the Thompson."

Whether there are any large fish or not, Skip Cenis, a long-time Montana fly-fisher, will always return to the river. He's been fishing the river for 15 years, and trout size does not mean as much to him as the opportunity to fish beautiful water with a dry fly.

"I'm not really after trophy trout when I fish the Thompson," Cenis said. "But it is one of my favorite places to fish. It is almost always clear, and 75 percent of the time those trout will hit anything you throw to them. Only occasionally are there times when you don't get fish on top. When that happens you should go with a small nymph and fish the deeper, darker waters."

If Cenis had to pick one day of the year to fish the Thompson and he could only throw one fly, he'd pick a day in August and would work a parachute Adams to those risers.

"August is the best time because the water has dropped and the fish are hungry," Cenis said. "In August the river is beautiful and we see a lot of wildlife; moose standing in the river, deer and elk on the sidehills, ospreys, eagles and blue herons flying overhead.

"I would probably throw a parachute Adams at that time, because I can see it on the water and the fish seem to eat it. Really, they'll hit just about anything, especially in the evenings, rather late. All the basic patterns will work fine. Royal Wulffs and small caddis are real productive."

Stream Facts: Thompson River

Seasons
- Open third Saturday in May through November 30. Whitefish season and catch and release for trout runs November 30 through third Saturday in May.

Trout
- Rainbow, cutthroat, brook and bull trout. Most fish taken are rainbows that run between six and 12 inches with a few Clark Fork migrants to 20 inches.

River Miles
- Clark Fork confluence—0
- Little Thompson River Bridge—17.9
- Bear Creek Bridge—23
- Bend Access—36.6
- Murr Creek Bridge—42.5
- Lower Thompson Lake—50

River Flows
- Flows rise in April, peak in May and drop to desirable levels by July.

River Characteristics
- The Thompson is a fun stream to fish, relatively small and easy to wade. It is slowest at its upper end, picks up speed in the middle and carries that turbulent water to its confluence with the Clark Fork.

Fishing Access
- Flyfishers can jump off roads that parallel the river almost anywhere. Bridge crossings offer the easiest access and there are plenty of bridges.

Camping
- Plenty of public, nonmaintained campsites up and down the river on adjacent National Forest land.

Area Fly Shops
- Lakestream Fly Shop,116 9th Street, Kalispell, MT 59923, 406-293-4641

THOMPSON RIVER MAJOR HATCHES

Insect	J	F	M	A	M	J	J	A	S	O	N	D	Flies
Caddis													Elk Hair Caddis #14-16; Stimulator #14-16; Emergent Sparkle Pupa #14-16; Drifting Cased Caddis #14-18; X-Caddis #14-18; Electric Caddis #14-16
Salmonfly *Pteronarcys californica*													Seducer #4-8; Stimulator #4-8; Bitch Creek Nymph #4-8; Kaufmann's Stone #2-6; Brook's Stone #2-6
Flying Ant													Chernobyl Ant #10-16; Flying Black Ant #12-16
Baetis													Parachute Adams #16-20; CDC Baetis #18-20; Sparkle Dun #18-20; Poxyback Baetis #16-20; CDC Biot Comparadun #18-20
Grasshoppers													Joe's Hopper #6-10; Dave's Hopper #6-10; Madame X #4-10; Meadow Hopper #4-8
Midge													Griffith's Gnat #16-20; Parachute Adams #18-22; Pheasant Tail Nymph #16-22

Yaak River

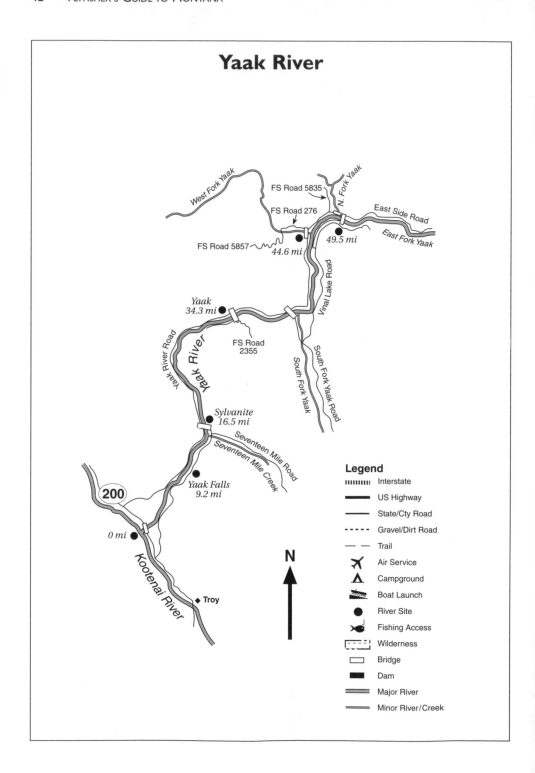

West Fork Yaak

FS Road 5835

N. Fork Yaak

FS Road 276

East Side Road

East Fork Yaak

FS Road 5857

49.5 mi

44.6 mi

Vinal Lake Road

Yaak
34.3 mi

FS Road 2355

South Fork Yaak

South Fork Yaak Road

Yaak River Road

Yaak River

Sylvanite
16.5 mi

Seventeen Mile Road

Seventeen Mile Creek

200

Yaak Falls
9.2 mi

0 mi

Kootenai River

◆ Troy

N

Legend

ⅢⅢⅢ	Interstate
—	US Highway
—	State/Cty Road
- - - -	Gravel/Dirt Road
— —	Trail
✈	Air Service
⛺	Campground
🚤	Boat Launch
●	River Site
🐟	Fishing Access
[ⁱⁱⁱⁱⁱ]	Wilderness
▭	Bridge
▬	Dam
▬▬	Major River
—	Minor River/Creek

YAAK RIVER

You will not catch many, if any, large trout from the Yaak River, but you may walk away from the water with a new appreciation for dry flies and the merit of brook trout.

Despite that lack of large trout, the Yaak is worth fishing, especially as a day or two-day side trip during your northwest Montana visit. There are plenty of fish to catch, and they are mostly eight- to 15-inch rainbows, brookies and cutthroats. On a good day the Yaak may put a couple dozen or more trout in your net. That is often more fish than the nearby and better-known Kootenai River provides, but they are smaller trout.

The length of the Yaak's trout may not be of concern to the flyfisher because nobody should complain about catching fish while floating on a beautiful, intimately-sized stream that winds its way through sections of pristine, deep, dense rain forest. Unfortunately, in other sections, a flyfisher will have a perfect view of the river's neme-sis—clearcut logging above the river and throughout the valley that has hampered the fishery for years and continues to do so today.

In fact, the Yaak River Valley stakes claim to an unwelcome distinction: it gives up more timber than any valley in the Lower Forty-Eight. Just 30 years ago there was only one road through the valley. Now there are thousands of miles of logging roads that facilitate the direct flow of sediment into the river and its precious, tiny tribu-taries. Didn't anybody read Ed Abbey's *The Monkey Wrench Gang*? Where are you guys hiding? Sound the alarm. Sledgehammers unite!

The Yaak begins in the mountains of southern British Columbia, Canada, east of Kootenai Lake, with the North Fork Yaak. The North Fork then drains into Montana and runs about three miles before its confluence with the East Fork Yaak.

The North Fork, a meandering meadow-type stream, offers decent fishing for native inland redband rainbow trout—a species that has been proposed for the Endangered Species List. But because of a silty bottom, fish populations are low. Access is limited due to private land along the river's banks.

The West Fork Yaak begins in Montana, just south of Marmot Mountain, before swinging briefly into British Columbia. Then the river turns south into Montana for about 10 miles before its confluence with the East Fork Yaak. Where those forks meet, the mainstem Yaak begins.

The West Fork is surrounded by Forest Service land, which provides easy access. Above the falls, which occur just a few miles upstream from its mouth, the West Fork provides some steady action on smallish native westslope cutthroat trout.

The East Fork Yaak flows for about 18 miles in Montana before meeting with the waters of the West Fork. Brook trout are the predominant species on the East Fork, and there is good access along its banks, which are surrounded mostly by Forest Service land. Most of its brook trout run eight to 10 inches. Flyfishers may also encounter some native redbands, and they should run similar in size.

Because those redbands are genetically pure and because they are threatened due to consumptive resource use, Joe Huston, who for years watched over those waters as a biologist for Montana Fish, Wildlife and Parks, urges total catch and

The Yaak offers rainbows, brook, cutthroat and bull trout—plus scenery galore.
Keep an eye on the bankside brush for rogue grizzlies and love-stricken moose!

release. Do not think that taking a few small fish for dinner is not a crime. If you eat native redbands, you are no different than that meat sacker you may have chastised on the lower river.

The South Fork Yaak also offers good flyfishing, but you will have to deal with nasty backcast conditions to catch its brook trout, which average about 10 inches. The South Fork is small and it is surrounded by swampy, brushy terrain. Watch out for moose, especially cows with calves. Also, the entire Yaak River Valley is considered grizzly bear country, although much of the bear's precious habitat is leaving with the logs strapped to the back of those obnoxious diesel-billowing trucks. Flyfishers, no matter where they fish on the Yaak, should just keep an eye out for grizzlies when they are working through the brush. There are lots of black bears around, too, although they tend to be less aggressive.

Back to the fishing. On the lower end, at its violent confluence with the Kootenai River (there can be some huge waves where the rivers meet), the Yaak is a midsize stream that offers some large rainbow trout and a few huge bull trout during spring and early summer.

However, the rainbows run out of the Kootenai to spawn during high water, which makes them difficult quarry for the flycaster. The lower river runs about four miles from the falls to its confluence with the Kootenai and is characterized by riffles and runs with a steep gradient and boulder-laden banks through its deep canyon. Large nymphs and streamers that reach the bottom have been known to catch fish, but chucking big patterns is not an easy proposition.

"If you want to get some good rainbow fishing in the canyon, you should go around July 1, just as the water is dropping," offers Cliff Dare, a guide who has fished the river for 40 years. "If you are stout-hearted and you can climb into the canyon, you can really get some big rainbows that pile up at the bottom of the falls. You'll also pick up some bull trout down in there, too. They are tough to catch though—they just head downstream and they do not stop. There's nothing a guy can really do—the banks are rocky, slick and steep."

Dare suggests large streamers for the canyon section, like woolly buggers, spruce flies and muddler minnows.

Access to the canyon is available by walking upstream from Highway 2 at the confluence with the Kootenai or by scaling the canyon walls down to the river.

Above Yaak Falls, extending to the Pete Creek Campground and the mouth of Pete Creek, the river offers ample access, and trout fishing can be quite good.

According to Huston, flyfishers will encounter classic pool-riffle habitat and a river that averages about 80 feet wide from Pete Creek downstream to Sylvanite. Below Sylvanite the river winds through a boulder field, which is nearly impossible for boaters to float. Boaters should find no problems from Pete Creek downstream to Sylvanite, which encompasses about 12 miles of the river—a perfect full-day float.

"It's pretty fair flyfishing through that section," Huston said. "There are a mix of inland and native rainbows that run up to 18 or 20 inches, and there are a few brook trout that will go 16 inches or slightly more. The fish are really pretty good size."

According to Dare, the best time to float that section is during the early season when the water is up. Later on, you're likely to rip the bottom of your boat off on some sizable boulders.

"Floating is fine when the water is high, but you don't want to go any farther downstream than the Burnt Dutch Road at the mouth of Dutch Creek," he said. "There is actually a pretty hairy set of rapids at the mouth of Spread Creek, and the section between Hellroaring Creek and Burnt Dutch is pretty fast and hard, too. There are some fish to be had, but it's tough from a boat. I think the best time to fish those sections is in August after the water drops and there are tons of small rainbows around. You can catch and release fish all day on dry flies."

From Pete Creek upstream to the Yaak's confluence with the West and East Forks, flyfishers will encounter lots of private land along the river's banks. While wade fishers could have trouble gaining access, floaters can dump a boat in off the Yaak River Road, which parallels the water from its mouth upstream to the headwaters of the East Fork. Floating is only advised below the forks.

"Above Pete Creek the Yaak is a slow meadow-type stream that holds some real nice brook trout," Houston said. "There are a few rainbows in that section also, but the brook trout—with an occasional fish to four or five pounds, measuring maybe 18 or 20 inches—are the real draw."

Big brook trout are an anomaly in the West. They are difficult to find, harder to catch. The Yaak provides one of the best opportunities to fish over truly huge brookies. But, they are not easy to catch due to their choice of habitat.

"The only way you are going to catch the big brook trout is with streamers," Dare said. "I've caught a lot of brookies on gray ghosts, muddlers, spruce flies and even Mickey fins. You have to get those to the bottom of the pools, but there are lots of logs and I've lost a lot of riggings over the years. The largest brook trout I've caught in the Yaak weighed five and a half pounds, but I've seen larger fish."

Trout in the Yaak River do not hold PhDs in entomology. Instead, most rise willingly to bushy dry flies and a variety of nymphs. Dare does not get technical with his selection of flies for the river.

"We get a variety of mayflies and a few types of caddis, but it's not overly challenging to draw fish to the surface," he said. "For the mayflies I use a gray paradun in various sizes. Sometimes a royal Wulff works well. During the early season we see a dark caddis on the water and I use a dark bodied elk hair. Later in the summer a light bodied elk hair works fine. We also get some action on hoppers in late August and September and the standard patterns work. They usually draw the larger trout up top. Around October 1 we get the big Western sedge, which a lot of people call the October caddis. I have a particular pattern to mimic them that looks a lot like a Joe's hopper. Essentially if you just darken the wings on a Joe's you have what I use. The big fish really get after those caddis and the hatch is spread out through the entire river."

While the Yaak may not offer numbers of large trout like its neighbor, the Kootenai, Dare rates it as one of the state's top wade fishing, dry fly waters.

"If you are zeroing in on the Yaak, the main thing is it's an excellent wading stream," he said. "All of the sidestreams even have little brookies in them that offer a great time for kids. Myself, when you get right down to it, I like to go with dry flies and you can do that here. It's one of the best places I've seen to catch lots of trout on a dry fly."

To reach the Yaak, follow Highway 2 northwest out of Libby. Turn right on Yaak River Road. From Eureka, follow Highway 37 west for a few miles and turn right on Yaak River Road. There are few amenities in Yaak, so stock up before you leave Libby or Eureka.

Stream Facts: Yaak River

Seasons
- Open third Saturday in May through November 30.

Trout
- Rainbow, cutthroat, bull and brook trout. The upper reaches harbor most of the brook and cutthroat trout. Rainbows and bull trout dominate on the lower end.

River Miles
- Kootenai River confluence—0
- Yaak Falls—9.2
- Sylvanite—16.5
- Pete Creek—31
- Yaak Bridge—34.3
- West Fork Yaak—44.6
- East Fork Yaak—49.5

River Flows
- Peak flows occur during April, May and June. Flows taper off in July and are prime from August through March.

River Characteristics
- The Yaak is a medium size stream that winds through densely timbered mountains, where they are not ruthlessly clearcut. Floater fishers will find the river pleasant except on the lower end below Yaak Falls where the river provides some big rapids and heavy waves.

Fishing Access
- Most access is via Yaak River Road, which parallels the river for most of its length. Maintained access sites exist just below Yaak River Falls, at Red Top, Whitehall and Pete Creek.

Area Fly Shops
- Kootenai Angler, 13546, Highway 37, Libby, MT, 406-293-7578
- Lakestream Fly Shop, 15 Central, Whitefish, MT 59937, 406-892-4149
- Yaak River Lodge, 27744 Yaak River Road, Troy, MT 59936, 800-676-5670

YAAK RIVER MAJOR HATCHES

Insect	J	F	M	A	M	J	J	A	S	O	N	D	Flies
March Brown Drake					▓								Sparkle Dun #14-16; Sparkle Spinner #14-16; Pheasant Tail Nymph #12-16;
Pale Morning Dun							▓						Sparkle Dun #14-20; Parachute Adams #14-20; PMD Cripple #16-20; Poxy Biot Nymph #16-20; Lawson's Thorax Dun #16-20; Lempke's Extended Body PMD #16-18; Hare's Ear Nymph #16-18; Pheasant Tail Nymph #16-18; CDC Floating Nymph #16-18; Half Back Emerger #16-18
Midges	▓												Griffith's Gnat #16-20; Parachute Adams #18-22; Pheasant Tail Nymph #16-22
Caddis						▓							Elk Hair Caddis #14-18; Diving Caddis #14-16; X-Caddis #14-16; Drifting Cased Caddis #14-18; Emergent Sparkle Pupa #12-18; Deep Sparkle Pupa #12-18; Electric Caddis #14-16; Caddis Variant #14-16
Baetis				▓									Parachute Adams #16-22; CDC Baetis #16-22; Sparkle Dun #18-20; Thorax Baetis #18-22; Poxyback Baetis #16-20; Hare's Ear #16-20; Pheasant Tail Nymph #16-20
Grasshopper								▓					Joe's Hopper #6-10; Dave's Hopper #6-10
Callibaetis									▓				Callibaetis Cripple #14-16; Sparkle Spinner #14-16; Sparkle Dun #14-16; Parachute Adams #14-16; Hare's Ear #14-16

SWAN RIVER

For those true romantics who dream of the good ol' days, when Lewis and Clark, some Indians and few other people roamed the western countryside, the Swan River is a good place to set up a camp.

The Swan is not tremendously isolated; you'll find a few campgrounds nearby, massive log cuts on the slopes above the river and diesel-belching log trucks ripping past its banks. But you'll also find two Western originals in pretty good numbers— the westslope cutthroat trout and large bull trout.

The Swan begins in mountain benchland between the Bob Marshall Wilderness to the east and the Mission Mountain Wilderness to the west. From its beginning, where it flows out of Lindbergh Lake to its entry with Swan Lake nearly 30 miles later, the river exhibits one extremely distinctive trait—brushy, log-riddled banks.

"The Swan is a classic native trout stream," says Jim Toth, who runs Grizzly Hackle in Missoula and frequently heads north to probe the river. "It lies in a heavily-timbered mountain setting with extremely brushy banks, and it has the native species that like that habitat. It's more fertile than the forks of the Flathead River, but it has trouble with siltation. However, the fishing is surprisingly good above Swan Lake."

While cutthroats and bull trout love that brush and downed logs, rainbows and a smattering of brook trout are present, too. However, that snarling tangle of willows, berry bushes, downed timber, stumps and vines play hell with anglers, especially during high water periods. Fortunately, few anglers test the river during that time, due to its lack of good wading spots when the water is up.

"The Swan is a mountain river, and it stays cold up there pretty late into the season," Toth said. "It's always a challenge to wade, but especially so when the water is high, which usually begins around May 1; people really can't get at it until July. Sometimes the river will be fishable by late June, but you can count on it after July 4, when we see a real good stonefly hatch. The hatch lasts through the summer. It isn't the giant stone that comes off, it's the yellow sally or Isoperla. Small stonefly imitations work during that time. After that, through summer, attractors are the ticket; a size 10 H&L variant, royal Wulff, or a peacock-body elk hair caddis will work fine."

Don't expect any trophy rainbows, cutthroats or brook trout from the Swan; its trout average eight to 12 inches with only a few stretching 16 inches or more. And don't dare think about taking one from the stream between Piper Creek and Swan Lake—that section, thankfully, stands as catch and release.

"The fish aren't really big, but their numbers seem to be coming back (timber cutting has hammered the trout populations), and they are really eager for dry flies and small nymphs," Toth said. "You'll see some caddis and PMDs on the river during summer, but you rarely have to match them closely. The river is brushy and fast so it does not facilitate long casts or delicate presentations. You don't hunt fish here. Instead, you just cover the water—it has a lot of good habitat. You just have to hit a fish that's looking to feed."

Bull trout are technically off-limits to flyfishers, just like they are in all waters of the western fishing district. The regulations read: "all waters...are closed to taking

Swan River

N

Bigfork

Bigfork Dam

83

Swan Lake

Flathead Lake

◆ Swan Lake

● 0 mi

35

Porcupine Creek

Point Pleasant
9 mi ●

Fatty Creek
● 15 mi

Piper Creek
● 23 mi

Salmon Prairie
27 mi ●

□ *Cold Creek Bridge*
29 mi ●

◆ Condon
● 34 mi

Mission Mountains Tribal Wilderness

Swan River

Holland Lake

83

◆

Lindbergh Lake

Legend

׀׀׀׀׀׀׀	Interstate
▬▬▬	US Highway
———	State/Cty Road
- - - -	Gravel/Dirt Road
– – –	Trail
✈	Air Service
▲	Campground
🚤	Boat Launch
●	River Site
🐟	Fishing Access
▭	Wilderness
▭	Bridge
▬	Dam
▬▬▬	Major River
▬▬	Minor River/Creek

Brushy banks and downed logs are synonymous with the Swan River. So are huge bull trout and some decent cutthroats and rainbows.

and/or the intentional fishing for bull trout." However, anyone who fishes a woolly bugger or muddler minnow in the river—viable patterns for rainbows and cutthroats —is also inviting a strike from the bulls.

Swan River bull trout, which run upstream out of Swan Lake during the summer, average about four or five pounds with a few stretching to double digit weight.

"You stumble upon a few now and then," Toth says. "Most will go 18 to 25 inches, but I've seen a few reach 29 inches. They really go for the muddlers."

Public access isn't a huge problem on the Swan, but because of the brush and dense forest, getting to the river can be difficult. Easy access is available at the bridges, but Toth is convinced that flyfishers will find the fishing is better the farther they can get from easy access spots.

You can reach the upper Swan, above Swan Lake, by taking Highway 83 south from Bigfork. Productive trout fishing begins just beyond the town of Swan Lake and extends to Lindbergh Lake. The lake, which rates a little more than 700 acres, is decent for cutthroats.

There are plenty of primitive places to camp just off the highway. Take any of the logging roads and pitch a tent or park a trailer. A nice little camping area that isn't maintained rests right on the bank of the Swan on the west side of the Fatty Creek Bridge. Bring enough mosquito repellent to fight off the hordes. Mosquitoes can ruin your trip if you let them. Bears, blacks and a few grizzlies frequent the river corridor, too. Store your food appropriately.

Stream Facts: Swan River

Seasons
- Piper Creek Bridge downstream to Swan Lake is catch and release only for rainbow and cutthroat trout, artificial flies and lures only. Fishing for bull trout is closed year-round.

Trout
- Rainbow, brook, cutthroat and bull trout. Bull trout must be released.

River Miles
- Lindbergh Lake outlet—0
- Condon Bridge—11.5
- Piper Creek Bridge—25
- Fatty Creek Bridge—32
- Swan Lake inlet—52.5

River Flows
- Runoff begins in mid May, peaks in late June and subsides in early July.

River Characteristics
- The Swan is a medium size river in its upper portion, above Swan Lake. It harbors brushy, densely timbered banks and lots of downed logs. Deep pools will hold bull trout.

Fishing Access
- Lindbergh Lake
- Condon Bridge
- Piper Creek Bridge
- Fatty Creek Bridge
- Point Pleasant
- Swan Lake

Area Fly Shops
- Grizzly Hackle, 215 W. Front Street, Missoula, MT, 406-721-8996
- Streamside Anglers, 301 S. Orange St. Missoula, MT, 406-543-6528
- Missoulian Angler, 420 N. Higgins Ave., Missoula, MT, 406-728-7766
- The Kingfisher, 926 East Broadway, Missoula, MT, 888-542-4911

SWAN RIVER MAJOR HATCHES

Insect	J	F	M	A	M	J	J	A	S	O	N	D	Flies
Little Yellow Stone *Isoperla*							▉						Stimulator #12-16; Elk Hair Caddis #14-16
Caddis								▉					Elk Hair Caddis #14-16; Caddis Variant #14-16; Goddard Caddis #14-16; Emergent Sparkle Pupa #14-16; Deep Sparkle Pupa #14-16; X-Caddis #14-16; Drifting Cased Caddis #14-16
Pale Morning Dun								▉					Parachute Adams #16-18; Sparkle Dun #16-20; PMD Cripple #16-18; Hare's Ear Nymph #16-20; Pheasant Tail Nymph #16-20; Poxyback PMD #16-20
Attractors							▉						Royal Wulff #14-16; Stimulator #14-16; Renegade #14-16

FLATHEAD BASS LAKES

Montana is justly famous for its excellent trout fishing, but it is often overlooked for its warmwater options, not the least of which is a healthy population of five-pound largemouth and some sizable smallmouth bass on the highly accessible, yet underfished, Flathead Indian Reservation.

The Flathead Reservation rests in northwest Montana, just 50 miles north of Missoula at the base of the Mission Mountains and their 9,000 foot peaks. When wading into Nine Pipe, Kicking Horse or Crow reservoirs for the first time, you might automatically consider pilfering your fly box for dainty trout flies instead of the four-to-eight inch streamers required to catch bass. Resting under the Missions and the pine-tree covered slopes that race down to their shores, those reservoirs just scream of trout. Fortunately, they are a bastion of warmwater opportunity in a land where trout is king.

The typical largemouth bass from Kicking Horse and Nine Pipe reservoirs runs about 12 to 15 inches, maybe two or three pounds. However, there are much larger fish to be had; the state record, a 7¼ pound monster, was taken at Nine Pipe and numerous four and five pounders show up each season. Many local flyfishers, including bass enthusiast Rob Shrieder of Ronan, believe that the new state-record largemouth is finning in Kicking Horse or Nine Pipe right now.

The smallmouth bass in Crow Reservoir run slightly smaller. A two-pounder is a decent fish, a four-pounder really turns heads and a five-pounder would probably end up on someone's wall. But, even the smaller versions hold that standard smallmouth attribute—they fight like determined dogs!

Overall, the Flathead draws little attention from anglers when compared to public land opportunities in Big Sky Country. It's as if the requirement of a tribal license is too much to handle when, essentially, the $30 fee is nothing more than you might blast through at the reservation's Bucksnort Saloon in a few hours on a weekend night.

If you pass up on one of those nights out on the town and you fork out the very worthwhile money for a license, you're in for a surprise—the Flathead offers excellent, uncrowded fishing.

In fact, one night, when I could have saddled up to the Bucksnort's bar, I joined a friend for a late-night excursion to Kicking Horse. We harbored in our fly boxes a dozen meaty, black woolly buggers, a couple ugly deer hair mouse patterns (it was my first attempt at spinning deer hair) and a sincere determination to avoid any inadvertent pow-wow's with rogue skunks in the tall grass.

Risking that sour encounter paid off—with a sweet introduction to Kicking Horse's pre-spawn potential in early May.

Despite my fear of skunks, I ditched my friend and wandered around Kicking Horse's west shore, stumbling into holes and spooking wayward herons while casting those woolly buggers to likely looking points in a shallow bay. On my fifth cast, I caught a three-pounder, a largemouth that drilled my offering before it sank an inch under the surface. The fish leaped maybe a half dozen times, each aerobatic maneu-

It looks like a trophy trout lake, but under the watchful eye of the Mission Mountains, Kicking Horse Reservoir pumps out some large bass. Four-pounders are not uncommon and fish to seven pounds have been landed.

ver highlighted by the moon glow. I let out a holler, half hoping my buddy would get jealous, also trying to verify that our crazy notion was paying dividends.

I had not made two more casts when a shout echoed across the water, followed a few moments later by another. I cast more frantically, feeling that instinctive urge to catch at least one more fish than my partner, not really hoping that he would have a less enjoyable time than myself, but definitely desiring that extra fish.

When another shout raced over the surface a few moments later, followed by "Four pounds!", I relented to the fact that a long, loud drive home was likely in store.

Our luck that night on Kicking Horse—the score wound up nine to five in my loud-mouthed friend's favor—was not unusual. All three Flathead Reservation reservoirs pump out big bass consistently from April through September, although Nine Pipe's south half remains closed until July 15, due to waterfowl nesting activities. It closes again during waterfowl season in early October.

According to Shrieder, who works at Ronan Sports and Western when he isn't flailing the water, possibly the best time to fish the reservation for bass is during late spring and early summer.

As it does almost everywhere in the nation, the largemouth bass spawn arrives just as the water warms up after a long, cold winter and late spring, but before it becomes too hot from incessant summer sun. Generally, prime temperatures arrive in May and June in Montana and it doesn't hurt that those conditions coincide with the bass spawn. However, don't overlook the prespawn.

"Usually, the reservation's bass get active sometime in April, and the warmth of the water determines how fast things will happen," Shrieder said. "You'll want to work a fly slower during the early season. That retrieve will speed up as the water warms. In April and early May, you'll want to carry some black leeches, girdle bugs and dark zonkers—and you'll want to work them real slow. I'll fish those off of a floating line that time of the year because you'll find the bass in shallow water. They are not really looking for spawning beds at that time, but they like to congregate in front of any inlets where the water is heavily oxygenated."

While you can catch bass at any hour during spring, Shrieder says an interesting phenomenon takes place during the first two hours of light and again during midafternoon, when most flycasters give up on the day and point their trucks toward home.

"During spring the fishing can be very, very good in the morning," he said. "Just as the sun comes over the Mission Mountains and spreads its light over the water, the bass really get active. Then it slacks off for three or four hours. But right when you think it's over, around noon or 1 PM, it picks back up and you get another hour or two of prime fishing. Why, I'm not sure, but it happens and it's worth being there for it."

Especially during spring, but again later in summer and fall, the reservation's bass are tied to structure. At Kicking Horse, that means unpronounced bunches of submerged grass, grass banks, rocks and earthen depressions. You can wade, floattube or fish from a boat at Kicking Horse, and with any tactic, you should keep an eye on the bottom, note where the structure exists and log it in your brain. Although the reservoir does not hold a lot of structure, that can be advantageous when a large fish is on the line; play him gently and you will land him—there is very little to break off on.

At Nine Pipe, which harbors much more structure, including incredibly thick cattails and moss beds, the fish lie in along shore, moving in and out of cover. Casting to them can be quite difficult at times; Nine Pipe is off-limits for boats and floattubes and that vegetation can extend out into the water many yards when the reservoir is high. That mass of moss and cattails also makes it difficult to land a hog. Heavy tippet, with enough strength to drag a fish out of the moss or keep him from tearing into the cattails, is a good idea.

Crow Reservoir is a little different than Nine Pipe or Kicking Horse. Its banks are steep and rocky rather than gentle and grassy. And its smallmouth bass prefer rocky shorelines and gravel depressions in three to 10 feet of water. Stalking the banks is treacherous, so most flyfishers hit the reservoir in a boat or floattube.

By the second week of May, Montana's cool spring weather finally relents, and a series of 75- to 80-degree days cast a warmth over the land. Green grass sprouts from the ground, barren cottonwood and pine trees sprout new growth, and probably most important, the reservation's bass start searching for spawning beds in earnest.

When that happens, some fabulous bass fishing occurs. But you want to make sure the water temperature is at or near 60 degrees. Until it reaches that point, the

*Scott Brown hoists a nice largemouth from the Flathead Reservation bass lakes.
As the water warms in late April and May, those bass will hit streamers and poppers with abandon. (Scott Brown Photo)*

bass will remain scattered. When it reaches a suitable warmth, they head for the
shallows in mass.

"If you have calm water with no wind during the spawn, a lot of times a popper
will work better than anything," Shrieder said. "Those poppers really make bass mad
when they come over the top of a bed. They don't like the noise a popper makes.

"If you fish a subsurface pattern, like a leech, and you get a strike and miss it they
may not take it again. But if you put on a popper and work it over a nest, they'll hit it
almost every time."

While it's true that you'll find bass in shallow water during the spawn, you won't find many situations where classic sight and cast options exist. From my experience, if you can see a bass, it can see you, and it is very unlikely to snap at a fly, whether it's defending its nest or not.

By mid-June, the spawn tapers off and the bass become fussy. However, there is a period of three or four days, just after the spawn, when the bass are extremely aggressive.

"It seems like they go on a feeding binge for a few days," Shrieder said. "You just have to be on the reservoirs at the right time to hit it."

After that binge, the fish spread out and rest. It does not help matters that the water warms up considerably and dissolved oxygen levels deteriorate. The bass, essentially, become nocturnal, choosing to feed occasionally in the morning, but mostly during evening and the dead of night. During that time, alternative tactics, like fishing at night, are required for success.

"I like to go with a longer fly during the dog days of July and August," Shrieder said. "You want something about eight inches long that imitates a perch, mouse or snake. You have to go back to working those flies very slow, just crawling them along.

"If you fish at night, you'll find it's a little different, not to mention more difficult," he added. "There are Canadian thistles and those cattails that will eat your lunch on backcasts. But there is great fishing at night. Usually, I'll throw a popper because I can keep in contact with how far the fly is away from me from its noise and the disturbance it puts on the surface. Also, when I hear that splash, it makes the hair stand up on the back of my neck. It's the most exciting fishing there is. Sometimes the bass will wait until a popper is right up to your feet before they take. It lights up your life!"

When September arrives in Montana, the water cools quickly with the first few frosts. At that time, the largemouth and smallmouths feel an urgency to eat as much as they can before winter arrives and ice coats the water's surface. Because hunting seasons open at that time, fewer anglers will be found on the water—you can have a reservoir to yourself during weekdays.

"I like to use the flashier patterns in September, and the fishing can be really good at that time," Shrieder said. "That crystal flash and flashabou really excites them. And you can work a fly faster again. They'll move quite a ways to take something; they are more active because there's more wind during fall that churns up the surface and creates more oxygen in the water."

Crow Reservoir can be especially good during fall, and Shrieder says those bass act a lot like trout in September and October.

"The smallmouths are a lot more like trout than a largemouth," he said. "I've seen them hit humpies and small nymphs and at times of the year, especially August and September, they pound terrestrials."

While the Flathead Reservation is certainly no Texas when it comes to bass fishing, it does offer excellent options for largemouths up to seven or eight pounds and smallmouths to five pounds on fly tackle. And you will not find a more beautiful spot to fish for bass. The Mission Mountains and the Flathead Reservation offer some of

Montana's most impressive vistas. All you need to fish the Flathead's bass waters is a nontribal license—the new state record could be waiting.

Getting There

Nine Pipe and Kicking Horse Reservoirs: Nine Pipe rests just west of Highway 93, six miles south of Ronan. Kicking Horse lies east of Highway 93 about three miles south of Ronan. Both reservoirs are noted by highway signs.

Crow Reservoir: Turn west onto Roundbutte Road at the Highway 93 stoplight in Ronan. Follow Roundbutte for six miles and turn south on Crow Dam Road. Go one mile to a T in the road. Turn left at the T and follow the road one mile to the dam.

Suggested Flies for Flathead Lakes

Woolly Buggers: Size 2 and 4 olive, black, brown, red and yellow
Zonkers: Size 2 and 4 olive, black, brown, red and yellow
Muddler Minnow: Size 2, 4 and 6 olive and brown
Mohair Leech: Size 2, 4, 6 and 8 brown and red
Clouser Deep Minnows: Size 2 and 6 in black and white or green and white
Poppers: Dahlberg Divers and Cork and Deer Hair poppers in sizes 2 and 4, various
    colors

METCALF LAKE

Located just a mile off the Swan River and Highway 83 south of Swan Lake, Metcalf Lake, a little, 13-acre gem that sits in a beautiful timbered bowl, is well known for its large rainbow trout.

Fish over 22 inches are taken there each season; larger trout were taken in past years and there could be some holdovers stretching to 26 inches or more (once I saw a fish as long as my arm swimming calmly past my floattube fins!). The average Metcalf rainbow tapes an honest 15 inches.

The lake is managed for trophy trout, and a 22-inch minimum size limit exists. Only artificial flies and lures can be used. Most flyfishers, thankfully, return their catch no matter what it measures. It should be noted that overharvest and poaching have hampered the fishery in the past.

The best times to fish Metcalf are during spring and fall when its trout head for the shallow silt/sand flats. During May and June, after ice-out, big rainbows will cruise over the white bottom and are highly visible. A float-tuber needs only to hold in one spot and wait for pods of fish to cruise by. Calm mornings are ideal for spotting fish.

Especially important during late spring is the midge emergence. These small cream-colored bugs, which rate about a size 16 or 18, will draw the trout up top. Flyfishers can pound fish with a variety of patterns, but an RS-2 emerger seems to work best. A small parachute Adams trailed by a midge pupa or emerger is also a good bet. Scuds will also draw strikes.

Another prime emergence is the damselfly hatch in mid-June. That hatch extends into late July. Patterns like a marabou damsel, six pack, or a larvae lace damsel work well. Especially effective is a slow strip retrieve that draws the damsel out of deep water and over the shallow flats.

Terrestrials also take fish at Metcalf—black ants, beetles and even grasshoppers draw curious strikes.

Ideal rods for Metcalf range from a 3- to a 6-weight. A longer rod, such as a 9.5- or 10-footer, is best while fishing from a floattube. Floating lines offer all you need in spring, early summer and fall. A 10-foot sinking line or a full sink are ideal for mid-summer when the fish drop to the bottom.

By midsummer, water temperatures have warmed up and trout have had time to learn a few tricks, which can make fishing a little more difficult. Early mornings and late evenings are the best times to fish the lake during the midsummer doldrums. Anglers may want to probe the depths during midday. Big rainbows will hold on the deep dropoffs, just off shore, where large downed logs dip into the water and offer plenty of cover.

Whatever the time of day, flyfishers will want to fish from a floattube, boat or raft. However, access to the water is not ideal. Boats and floattubes must be hauled down a steep bank on the north side of the lake. And yes, they must be hauled up that same treacherous bank. A boat larger than 10 feet would prove impossible without a few buddies along.

Floattubes offer excellent access to Metcalf Lake, which is managed for trophy rainbow trout. Here, Kent Sullivan lands a hard-earned, 18-inch Metcalf rainbow that ate an RS-2 emerger.

When fishing the lake, expect company. Metcalf appeals to a variety of interests, from dedicated flyfishers to romantic teens to beer guzzling parents with unruly kids. Plus, there's a monster rope swing on the north end of the lake that can fling you 25 feet above the water, and it's a serious temptation when the fishing slows. The first time I launched, an embarrassing scream raced across the water, just before my stomach slapped flat on the surface. Friends later told me that a muffled "ooh" emanated from the spectators. Really, from early July through August, the lake's water temperature is ideal for swimming.

If you want to camp at the lake, there are some nice grassy slopes among the big pine trees that offer excellent unimproved sites to pitch a tent. To reach Metcalf, take the Fatty Creek Road south off Highway 83, about 13 miles southeast of Swan Lake. A note: the Fatty Creek Road sign is only visible while driving south on Highway 83. If you are driving north, you will need to really search hard to see the sign. To reach the lake in early spring or late fall, a 4WD vehicle may be needed; the dirt road is rough and, at times, snowcovered or muddy. Mosquitoes attack in unbelievable hordes.

More Seeley/Swan Valley Lakes

There are many more lakes in the valley than I have covered here; they offer excellent fishing for a variety of species, ranging from brown, cutthroat, brook and bull trout, to largemouth bass and pike. A national forest map and some local inquiry can lead you to seldom fished, yet productive, waters.

Van Lake

Van is larger than Metcalf but nearly as pretty. Timber drops down to the edge of the lake and the fish, all rainbows running from eight to 18 inches, congregate on shallow shoals during spring and fall. During summer they hide under downed logs that reach into the water from shore.

A floating line is good for morning and evening rises, and a sinking line will get down to those fish that need to be dragged out from the logs.

Midges are an important food item at Van and the same patterns, such as RS-2 emergers, that work at Metcalf will work here. Damsels come off sometime in June and last into late July.

To reach Van, turn east off of Highway 83 just a mile or two south of Fatty Creek Road. A sign to Van Lake is marked on the highway. Follow the logging roads two miles to the water.

Unlike Metcalf, Van offers easy access for a larger boat, up to 14 feet, or raft. Floattubes are ideal, also. During spring and fall, the road into the lake can be muddy, and a 4-wheel drive vehicle may be needed.

Harpers Lake

This little prairie pothole is located west of Highway 83, just north of Clearwater Junction. It is plainly marked by a public fishing access sign.

Harpers is not about to gain recognition as Montana's next great trophy trout water, but it did once kick out a 20-pound rainbow. Unfortunately, that fish was of the Arlee strain, and its fins were rubbed raw by years of hatchery life. The fish was caught the day it was planted.

In fact, all of Harpers trout are hatchery rainbows. If you want to take a trout or two home for dinner, this is the place to do it. Catch and release is taboo for most of Harpers' anglers. "Take to bake" is the motto here.

However, the lake can provide excellent action on some large, four to eight-pound rainbows during spring. And they are a blast to hook and fight. They strip what seems like miles of line off your reel when they feel the bite of a hook for the first time ("What the hell was in that fish pellet, anyway?" you might ask).

Harpers' rainbows are planted randomly, beginning in late April or May. Contact Missoula's fly shops for word of a plant. The getting is very good until anglers fish the lake out, which doesn't take long.

Floattubes or small boats are great for Harpers, but the fish can be taken from shore, too. There is very little bankside brush to fowl a cast. Floating lines will work at Harpers, but fullsink or medium sinklines are best.

The best pattern I've found for the lake is the Six Pack. It works prior to, during and after the damsel hatch. Midge emergers and even scuds work, as well.

Salmon Lake

The lake is loaded with kokanee salmon and has some brown trout, but they are meaningless to a flyfisher. The draw at Salmon Lake is the recent discovery of northern pike.

Hey, they're not wild, but they drill damsel patterns and can take you to your backing. Author releases a Harper's Lake rainbow.

Pike haunt the shoreline shallows and weedy ends of the lake. They can be taken on large bunny-strip flies. Kent Sullivan of Missoula, Montana, who fishes the lake when he isn't chasing black bears or bugling in huge bull elk, indicates that yellow is the best color.

Large motor boats or small skiffs will work on Salmon Lake. A floattube will work, too, but often the best pike fishing is opposite the highway on the far shore. It's quite a kick to the other side in a floattube, and a sudden wind could make dangerous conditions.

If you are going to fish Salmon Lake for pike, hit it in April and May when the fish are spawning and aggressive. Work the shallow flats or the edges of islands.

Salmon Lake is easy to find: it is located about 10 miles north of Clearwater Crossing, and Highway 93 curls around its east edge the entire distance. Maintained boat launches are available. Camping can be found on National Forest lands that surround much of the lake.

One note: there is a run of brown trout that exits the north end of the lake, stacking up in the Clearwater River during fall. The brush around the stream is dense, which makes hiking difficult and dangerous. A decent backcast in that tangle is a fabrication. Floating the stream is not easy, either. Logjams cross the entire creek. I floated a 12-foot Achilles down that section of the Clearwater one spring and almost died. Fishing fall browns is only for hard-cores.

METCALF LAKE MAJOR HATCHES

Insect	J	F	M	A	M	J	J	A	S	O	N	D	Flies
Midges													Palomino Midge #18-20; RS-2 Emerger #16-18; Serendipity #16-20; Parachute Adams #16-22; Griffith's Gnat #16-20
Damselfly													Marabou Damsel #10-12; Six Pack #10-12; Swimming Damsel #8-12
Caddis													Elk Hair Caddis #14-16; Caddis Variant #12-16
Scud													Scud (gray, olive) #16-18

NORTHWEST HUB CITIES
Libby
Elevation – 2,066 • Population – 2,800

Libby is located in a beautiful valley surrounded by the awesome 2.5 million-acre Cabinet Mountain Wilderness. Bordering the north edge of town is the blue-green Kootenai River. Kootenai National Forest (over 2 million acres) provides extensive public land in some of the most beautiful and rugged country in northwest Montana.

Lincoln County leads the state in commercial lumber and wood products, which, of course, leads to the demise of many area tributary streams. Libby has a host of fine restaurants, motels, and services, and its people are known for their friendliness.

ACCOMMODATIONS: LIBBY
The Caboose Motel, West Hwy 2 / 406-293-6201 / 28 rooms / Hunters and dogs welcome, $5 pet fee / $

Sandman Motel, Hwy 2 West / 406-293-8831 / 16 units / Hot tub, cable, microwaves and refrigerators in each room / Dogs welcome, $5 pet fee / Your hosts are John and Christine Heinlein / $

Super 8 Motel, 448 West Hwy 2 / 406-293-2771 / 42 units / Cable, indoor pool / Dogs welcome, $5 fee / $$

Venture Motor Inn, 443 Hwy 2 West / 72 rooms / Cable, indoor pool, exercise room, adjoining restaurant / Dogs allowed / $$

ACCOMMODATIONS: TROY
Yaak River Lodge, 2774 Rt 508 / 406-295-5463 / 5 rooms and a dorm room that sleeps 9 / Located in the beautiful Yaak river valley / Dogs welcome / Laundry service, gourmet dining, hot tub and sauna / Hosts are Don and Gloria Belcher

Overdale Lodge, 1076 Overdale Lodge Road / 406-295-4057 / Two-story, 5 bedrooms / Fully equipped kitchen / Overlooks a pond and a lake—a beautiful, secluded setting / Dogs welcome / Hosts are Jim and Mary Jackson

Tamarack Lodge, 32855 South Fork Road / 406-295-4880 / Quaint private cabins and main lodge —excellent setting and easy access to Yaak and Kootenai rivers. Guided river fishing and alpine lakes trips

CAMPGROUNDS AND RV PARKS
Big Bend RV Park, 13 miles from Libby on Rt 37 / 406-792-7277 / 25 tent, 25 RV sites / Water, electric, sewer, dump / 10 acres on lake, restaurant, and bar

Russell's Conoco, 2 miles west of Libby on Hwy 2 / 406-293-4942 / 5 tent, 20 RV sites / Water, electric, sewer, dump, shower, laundry, store

OUTFITTERS
Linehan Outfitting Co., 22408 Yaak River Road, Troy, MT 59935 / 406-295-4872 / Kootenai and Yaak River guide service

Kootenai Angler, 13546 Highway 37, Libby, MT 59923 / 406-2937578

RESTAURANTS

Beck's Montana Cafe, 2425 Hwy 2 West / 406-293-6686 / Open 8AM–10PM daily / Specializing in broasted chicken / Thursday night prime rib special

4B's Restaurant, 442 Hwy 2 / 406-293-8751 / Open 24 hours

Henry's Restaurant, 407 West 9th / 406-293-7911 / Family restaurant

MK Steakhouse, 9948 Hwy 2 South / 406- 293-5686 / Open for dinner 6 days, closed Mondays / Beautiful log building / Cocktails, specializing in steaks and prime rib

Venture Inn Restaurant, 443 Hwy 2 West / Open 6AM–11PM / Family restaurant

VETERINARIANS

Treasure Valley Veterinary Clinic, 845 Hwy 2 West / 406-293-7410 / Doug Griffiths, DVM

FLY SHOPS AND SPORTING GOODS

Libby Sport Center, 116 East 9th / 406-293-4641 / Complete supplies and licenses

Kootenai Angler, 13546 Highway 37, Libby, MT 59923 / 406-293-7578

Pamida, 1600 West Hwy 2 / 406-293-4151

AUTO REPAIR

Auto Haus, 808 Hwy 2 West / 406-293-4351

Carr's Towing, 4063 Hwy 2 South / 406-293-3988

AIR SERVICE

Libby Airport, Keith Kinden / 406- 293-9776

MEDICAL

St. John's Lutheran Hospital, 350 Louisiana Avenue / 406-293-7761

FOR MORE INFORMATION:

Libby Area Chamber of Commerce
905 West 9th Street / P.O. Box 704
Libby, MT 59923-0704
406-293-4167

Kalispell

Elevation – 2,959 • Population – 26,000

Kalispell is one of the fastest growing areas in Montana and has become a summer and winter playground. Glacier National Park is 32 miles north of Kalispell, and Flathead Lake is seven miles south of town. Located in the broad Flathead Valley and surrounded by the Flathead National Forest, Kalispell is a regional trade center with shopping malls and numerous stores. The Salish Mountains lie to the west, and the Whitefish and Swan Mountains are to the east.

ACCOMMODATIONS

Blue and White Motel, 640 East Idaho Street / 406-755-4311 / 107 rooms, sauna, hot tub, pool, and restaurant / Dogs allowed in rooms / $$

Kalispell Super 8, 1341 1st Avenue East / 406-755-1888 / 74 rooms / Dogs allowed in smoking rooms only / $$

CAMPGROUNDS AND RV PARKS

Rocky Mountain "Hi" Campground, 5 miles east of Kalispell on Rt 2 / 406-755-9573 / Open year-round / 20 tent and 70 RV spaces / Full facilities including laundry and store

Spruce Park RV Park, 3 miles east, Junction US 2 and 93 on Hwy 35 at Flathead River / 406-752-6321 / Open year-round / 60 tent and 100 RV spaces / Full facilities including laundry and store

RESTAURANTS

Bulldog Steak House, 208 1st Ave East / 406-752-7522 / Spirits, beer, fine steaks, and salads / Steamed shrimp is their specialty

Que Pasa Restaurant, 75 Woodland Park Drive / 406-756-8776 / Open 7AM–10PM daily / Serving breakfast, lunch, and dinner / Fine Mexican food, beer, wine, and margaritas

Fred's Family Restaurant, 1600 Hwy 93 / 406-257-8666 / Open 5:45AM–11PM daily / Serving breakfast, lunch, and dinner

VETERINARIANS

Animal Clinic, 1408 City Airport Rd / 406-755-6886 / 24-hour service

Ashley Creek Animal Clinic, 3251 Hwy 93 South / 406-752-1330 / 24-hour service

FLY SHOPS AND SPORTING GOODS

Lakestream Fly Shop, 15 Central Avenue, Whitefish, MT 59937 / 406-892-4641

Snappy Sport Center, 1400 Hwy 2 East / 406-257-7525 / Open 7 days

Sportsman and Ski Haus, Junction of Hwy 2 and 93 / 406-755-6484

Open Season, 119 East Idaho, Kalispell, MT 59901 / 406-755-1298

Glacier Country, 945 4th Avenue East, Kalispell, MT / 406-756-7128

Glacier Wilderness Guides, West Glacier, MT 59936 / 800-521-7238

AUTO REPAIR AND RENTAL

Conoco Car Care Center, 229 3rd Avenue / 406-755-3797

Avis, Glacier Park International Airport / 406-257-2727

National Car Rental, Glacier Park International Airport / 406-257-7144

AIR SERVICE

Glacier Park International Airport, 4170 Hwy 2 East / 406-257-5994

MEDICAL

Kalispell Regional Hospital, 310 Sunnyview Lane / 406-752-5111.

FOR MORE INFORMATION
Montana Department of Fish, Wildlife, and Parks
490 North Meridian
Kalispell, MT 59901
752-5501

Kalispell Chamber of Commerce
15 Depot Loop
Kalispell, MT 59901
752-6166

Thompson Falls

Elevation – 2,463 • Population – 1,300

Thompson Falls is a small, friendly, northwest Montana town resting on the banks of the Clark Fork River. Timber and agriculture are its dominant industries. The beautiful Cabinet Mountains and the Cabinet Mountain Wilderness Area lie east of town. The Bitterroot Mountains frame its western border. Thompson Falls is a good overnight location for those fishing the lower Clark Fork and the Thompson rivers. It's also a good resting spot if heading for the Kootenai or Yaak.

ACCOMMODATIONS
Falls Motel, 112 South Gallatin / 406-827-3559 / 22 rooms / Dogs allowed, $10 per dog, per night / $
Rimrock Lodge, Hwy 200, 1 mile west of town overlooking the Clark Fork River / 406-827-3536 / Cable, restaurant / Dogs allowed / $$

CAMPGROUNDS AND RV PARKS
Riverfront RV Park, 1 mile west on Hwy 200 / 406-827-3460 / 3 tent and 10 RV sites / Full facilities

RESTAURANTS
Granny's Homecooking, 915 Main Street / Open for breakfast, lunch, and dinner
Rimrock Lodge, Hwy 200, 1 mile west / 406-827-3536 / Beautiful dining room overlooking the Clark Fork River / Open for breakfast, lunch, and dinner / Fine food and western hospitality

VETERINARIANS
Thompson Falls Lynch Creek Veterinary Clinic, 1 mile east on Hwy 200 / 406-827-4305

FLY SHOPS AND SPORTING GOODS
Krazy Ernie's, 602 Main Street / 406-827-4898

AUTO REPAIR
Bob's Auto Repair, 33 Prospect Creek Road / 406-827-4811
Ken's Auto Repair, Hwy 200 East / 406-827-3940

AIR SERVICE
County Airstrip, Frank Barbeau / 406-827-3536

MEDICAL
Fork Valley Hospital, in Plains, 22 miles east / Emergency: call 911

FOR MORE INFORMATION
Thompson Falls Chamber of Commerce
P.O. Box 493
Thompson Falls, MT 59873
406-827-4930

Cut Bank

Elevation – 3,838 • Population – 3,300

Cut Bank is an oil and gas town that sits on the Montana Hi-Line at the eastern edge of the Blackfeet Indian Reservation. Most of Glacier County is comprised of Glacier National Park and the Indian reservation.

ACCOMMODATIONS
Glacier Gateway Inn, 1121 East Railroad Street / 800-851-5541 or 406-873-5544 / 19 rooms at the Inn, 9 more (budget) at another motel owned by the same people / Dogs allowed, $2.50 per dog / Some theme rooms, hot tub, free breakfast / Your hosts are Irene and Keith Gustafson / $$

CAMPGROUNDS AND RV PARKS
Riverview Campground, end of 4th Avenue SW / 406-873-5546 / Open year-round / 9 tent and 36 RV spaces / Full service except for sewer / Laundry and store

RESTAURANTS
Maxie's, 1159 East Railroad Street / 406-873-4220 / American fare / $$-$$$
Golden Harvest, Main Street / 406-873-4010 / 6AM–10PM / Breakfast, lunch, and dinner

VETERINARIANS
Northern Veterinary Clinic, 55 Santa Rita Hwy / 406-873-5604 / Gary Cassel, DVM

FLY SHOPS AND SPORTING GOODS
Many Feathers Trading Post, 519 Main Street / 406-873-4484

AUTO REPAIR
Auto Tune Diagnostic Center, 1122 East Main / 406-873-2126
Northern Ford-Mercury, 120 West Main / 406-873-5541

AIR SERVICE
County Airstrip, Arnie Lindbergh / 406-873-4722

MEDICAL
Glacier County Medical Center, 802 2nd St SE / 406-873-2251

FOR MORE INFORMATION
The Cut Bank Chamber of Commerce
P.O. Box 1243
Cut Bank, MT 59427
406-837-4041

Far West

There are more prime trout waters in far west Montana than a flyfisher blessed with 10 lives could ever fish.

Unlike much of Montana, this region, stretching from the Canadian border south to central Idaho and east from the Idaho Panhandle to Butte, Montana, is comparatively wet.

In this area, flyfishers will find big-name rivers like the Blackfoot, Bitterroot, Clark Fork and Rock Creek. Or they can while away in solitude on lesser-known prime streams like Lolo Creek, Flint Creek, and the West and East Forks of the Bitterroot. Throw in some excellent lakes, where trophy rainbow, brook, brown and native cutthroat trout thrive, and you have a flyfisher's nirvana.

Many flyfishers consider far west Montana the most varied trout country in the state. Its terrain runs the gamut from near vertical, densely-timbered mountains, where mountain goats, grizzly bears and mule deer toil, to broad, flat stream valleys where domesticated cows, white-tailed deer and elk gather.

In the mountains, public land dominates; you can step into a stream just about anywhere you choose. Water, spawned in the ice and snowfields of the mountains races down narrow canyons and gullies, forming small, timber-sheltered tributary streams that can be loaded with small cutthroats and rainbows. Larger, migratory brown, rainbow and bull trout can be found in those streams seasonally. Wade fishers will find the small streams ideally suited to their pursuit.

In the agricultural areas that harbor the larger rivers, you may have to pound on a door or two to test a river. However, public access sites allow wade fishing below the high water mark, and floaters in boats, rafts, water otters and floattubes can drift large sections at their leisure.

Compared to other portions of the state, far west Montana receives lots of rain, but it does not compare with northwest Montana, which endures spells of drizzle that last for weeks. Instead, far west Montana complements its partially cloudy winter, spring and fall weather with unending days of sun extending from May through early October. Winter extremes are generally less pronounced than in other portions of the state—far west Montana is a banana belt of sorts, and flyfishers can find opportunity almost any day of the year.

The main service hubs in far west Montana are Missoula in the Missoula Valley, where the Clark Fork, Bitterroot and Blackfoot Rivers join, and Hamilton in the Bitterroot Valley.

Clark Fork River
Anaconda Ponds to Gold Creek

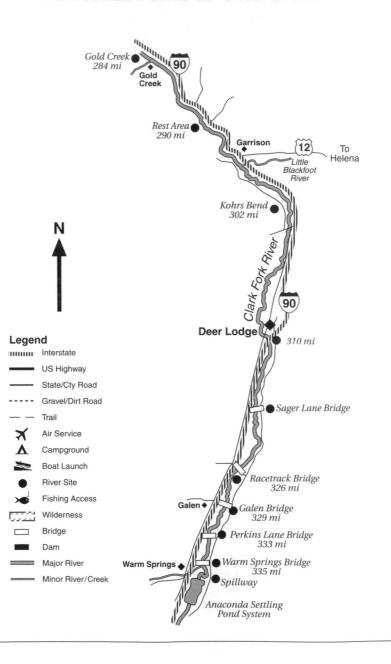

Gold Creek
284 mi

Gold
Creek

Rest Area
290 mi

Garrison

To
Helena

Little
Blackfoot
River

Kohrs Bend
302 mi

Clark Fork River

N

Deer Lodge

310 mi

Sager Lane Bridge

Legend

- ⅢⅢⅢ Interstate
- ▬ US Highway
- — State/Cty Road
- ----- Gravel/Dirt Road
- — — Trail
- ✈ Air Service
- △ Campground
- 🛥 Boat Launch
- ● River Site
- 🐟 Fishing Access
- ⬚ Wilderness
- ▭ Bridge
- ▬ Dam
- ▬ Major River
- ▬ Minor River/Creek

Racetrack Bridge
326 mi

Galen

Galen Bridge
329 mi

Perkins Lane Bridge
333 mi

Warm Springs

Warm Springs Bridge
335 mi

Spillway

Anaconda Settling
Pond System

CLARK FORK RIVER

If you asked flyfishers to point at the single most beleaguered river in Montana, most digits would be directed at the Clark Fork. The river has been raped by consumptive interests for a century.

Fortunately, if not entirely amazing, the Clark Fork remains an excellent option for rainbow and brown trout on a fly. And it also offers decent action on cutthroat, brook and bull trout in spite of destructive forces, both past and present, that haunt its banks.

Whether it has been timber cut from its banks, minerals dug from neighboring mountains, heavy metals dumped into its streambed, or irrigation drawing its levels down, the Clark Fork has weathered it all.

Near the mining mecca of Butte, the river's headwaters are heavily channeled and slag heaps (piles of dark, ugly, toxic mine tailings) line its banks. Often, heavy rains cause flooding, which flushes the heavy metals into the river and causes major fish kills.

Mine tailings are felt farther downstream, too. Seven miles east of Missoula, tailings accumulate behind Milltown Dam, providing a loaded gun effect for Missoula residents and the lower river's excellent rainbow fishery.

In February 1996, massive releases at Milltown Dam sucked up some of that sediment and deposited it downstream in the Clark Fork's town section, which weaves directly through Missoula and offers a post-work fishery—a place to throw a line for a few hours before heading home to the dinner table.

Unfortunately, tests showed high levels of toxic heavy metals in February, including copper, zinc and arsenic, flowing through town. Levels of copper ran at 693 parts per billion below Milltown Dam. At the same time, copper levels ran 18 parts per billion in the headwaters of the Clark Fork at Silver Bow Creek, which has been called an industrial ditch and harbors no aquatic life. The state limit for copper is 18 parts per billion. Unfortunately, until that sediment is removed from the entire upper river, if it can be removed, the lower Clark Fork and Missoula's wonderful town section should expect similar debacles in the future.

A report by Montana's Natural Resource Damage Program—cited in the state's $634.4 million damage claim against Atlantic Richfield Company (ARCO)—chronicles and documents "multiple and pervasive injuries to fish and aquatic life in the Clark Fork River and Silver Bow Creek from more than a century of mining and milling in Butte and the surrounding area." The report says numbers, sizes and kinds of trout have been reduced because of decades of heavy metals pollution.

The report describes damage to aquatic resources, surface and groundwater, air, soil, vegetation and wildlife habitat from hazardous wastes by Anaconda mining operations. The state contends that ARCO, which bought Anaconda in 1977, is responsible for the damage and cleaning it up.

The report concludes that natural reclamation of the Clark Fork's fishery would take "hundreds if not thousands of years."

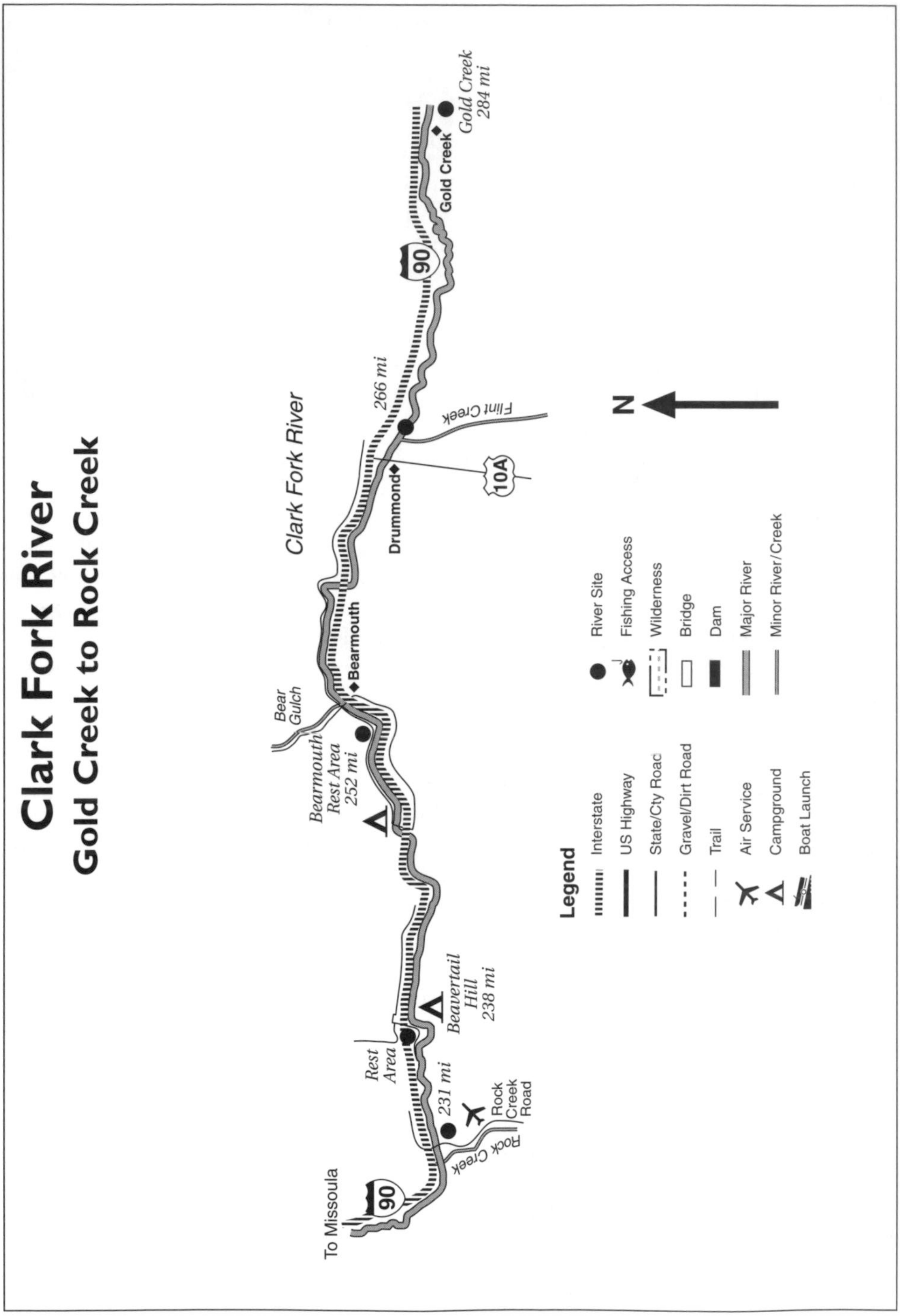

Clark Fork River
Gold Creek to Rock Creek

Clark Fork River

Gold Creek 284 mi

Gold Creek

266 mi

Flint Creek

Drummond

10A

Bear Gulch

Bearmouth

Bearmouth Rest Area 252 mi

Beavertail Hill 238 mi

Rest Area

231 mi

Rock Creek Road

Rock Creek

To Missoula

90

N

Legend

▪▪▪▪▪ Interstate	● River Site	
── US Highway	🎣 Fishing Access	
│ State/Cty Roac	⌐¬ Wilderness	
┆ Gravel/Dirt Road	▢ Bridge	
⌐ ¬ Trail	▮ Dam	
✈ Air Service	── Major River	
⛺ Campground	── Minor River/Creek	
⛵ Boat Launch		

Clark Fork River
Rock Creek to Alberton

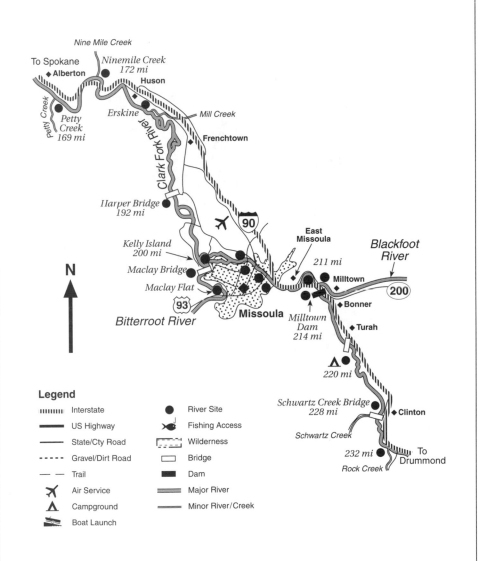

Nine Mile Creek

To Spokane

Ninemile Creek
172 mi

◆ **Alberton**

Huson

Petty
Creek
169 mi

Petty Creek

Erskine

Mill Creek

◆ **Frenchtown**

Clark Fork River

Harper Bridge
192 mi

✈ 🛣 **90**

East Missoula

Blackfoot River

Kelly Island
200 mi

211 mi

Maclay Bridge

Milltown

N

Maclay Flat

93

Missoula

Milltown Dam
214 mi

◆ **Bonner**

200

◆ **Turah**

Bitterroot River

▲
220 mi

Schwartz Creek Bridge
228 mi

◆ **Clinton**

Schwartz Creek

232 mi

To Drummond

Rock Creek

Legend

⑊ Interstate	● River Site		
▬ US Highway	🎣 Fishing Access		
— State/Cty Road	〰 Wilderness		
- - - Gravel/Dirt Road	▭ Bridge		
– – Trail	▬ Dam		
✈ Air Service	▬ Major River		
▲ Campground	▬ Minor River/Creek		
🚢 Boat Launch			

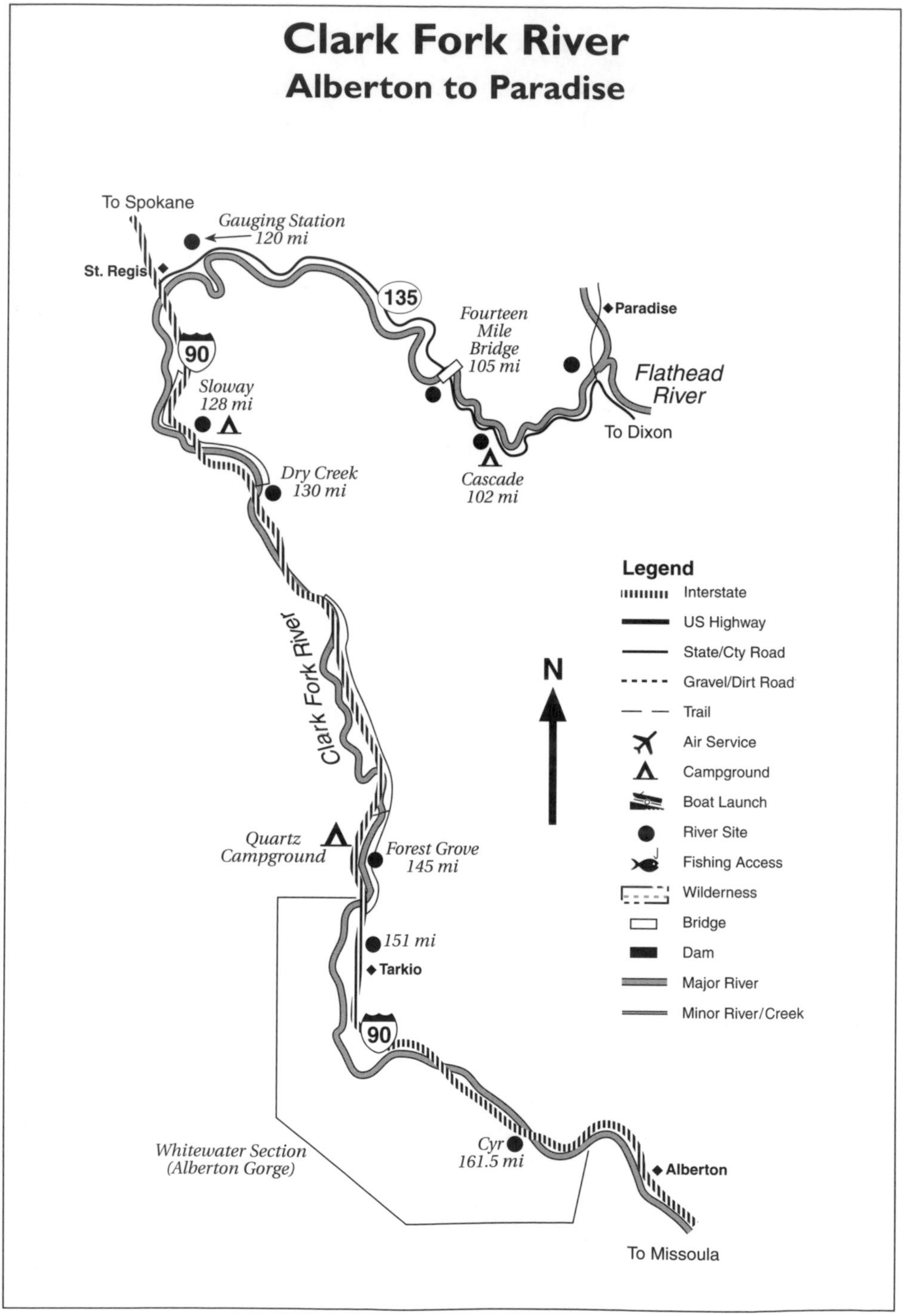

Clark Fork River
Alberton to Paradise

To Spokane

Gauging Station
120 mi

St. Regis

(135)

Fourteen
Mile
Bridge
105 mi

◆**Paradise**

(90)

Flathead
River

Sloway
128 mi

To Dixon

Dry Creek
130 mi

Cascade
102 mi

Legend

‖‖‖‖‖	Interstate
—	US Highway
—	State/Cty Road
- - - -	Gravel/Dirt Road
— —	Trail
✈	Air Service
△	Campground
🪵	Boat Launch
●	River Site
🐟	Fishing Access
⌁	Wilderness
▭	Bridge
▬	Dam
━	Major River
━	Minor River/Creek

Clark Fork River

N

Quartz
Campground

Forest Grove
145 mi

151 mi

◆**Tarkio**

(90)

Whitewater Section
(Alberton Gorge)

Cyr
161.5 mi

◆**Alberton**

To Missoula

The lower Clark Fork at Petty Creek: big water, small flies and healthy rainbows are its trademark.

Heavy metals are not the Clark Fork's only concern. Downstream from Deer Lodge, most acute between Drummond and the mouth of Rock Creek, the river may be nearly devoid of water during summer due to irrigation demand. Water temperatures have been measured in the high 70s in that section, and flyfishers must battle mounds of moss and algae floating down the river. During those hot months, trout move to distant sections of the river, where water quality is better, or they swelter and die.

With a tainted history and ongoing problems, including four major mine proposals on three of her tributaries, many anglers reject the Clark Fork on their way to big-name destinations, like the Beaverhead, Big Hole and Missouri Rivers.

And there is a lot of water to snub your nose at. The Clark Fork is western Montana's longest river running from its conception at the joining of Warm Springs and Silver Bow Creek near Butte, to its terminus 200 miles downstream at Lake Pend Oreille. However, at Paradise, where the mouth of the Flathead River doubles her flows, the Clark Fork ceases as a quality trout stream. Warmwater species, like pike and smallmouth bass, offer decent action from Paradise to Lake Pend Oreille.

With her size and length, the Clark Fork claims dominance over all waterways of western Montana. In fact, in all of the Big Sky Country, only the Yellowstone River drains so many fine tributary streams. A list of Clark Fork feeder streams reads like a guidebook to flyfisher's heaven: the Little Blackfoot, Big Blackfoot, Bitterroot, Rock Creek, Thompson, Rattlesnake and Flathead Rivers, along with some excellent, lesser-known waters, all gather in the Clark Fork on their journey to the Columbia River and their freshwater exodus into the Pacific Ocean.

Near Galen, the upper Clark Fork's brushy banks provide cover for brown trout that occasionally push 30 inches.

Throughout the Clark Fork, which is easily accessed from Interstate 90 for most of its length, the river offers two distinct faces—narrow, brushy brown trout stream vs. massively wide rainbow water.

Those two sections hold a variety of water types, trout species and aquatic insects—something to suit every flyfisher's needs. As fishermen race by on a blind bolt for the big-name rivers, Clark Fork's local flyfishers tip their caps in appreciation while trying to tame wide smiles.

They're smiling because the Clark Fork can fish as well as any stream in the state during major hatches, such as the salmonfly emergence in June, the caddis hatch in July or the Baetis (blue-winged olive) blanket in September and October. And we're talking about some healthy browns, cutthroats and rainbows roaming this river.

Brown trout and caddisflies are the trademark of the upper river, which extends from the confluence of Warm Springs and Silver Bow Creeks near Butte downstream to Milltown Dam near Missoula.

According to Wayne Hadley at Montana Department of Fish, Wildlife and Parks, brown trout on the upper Clark Fork average between 12 and 14 inches. And their population, although it too fights the effects of heavy metals and frequent fish kills, is strong—a testament to the determination of these fish.

Currently, the Clark Fork's brown trout population is highest at Warm Springs, where Hadley estimates about 1,500 trout a mile, which is very high considering that the river is only 10 or 15 yards wide in most places. While brown trout dominate that population, a few large rainbows can be taken, too.

"A nice fish in that section goes about 16 inches," Hadley said, "and a real exceptional trout would go 20 inches or more. There are very few fish over 20 inches, just

The author took this 26-inch, snakey brown at Warm Springs. Winter fishing can be productive when air temperatures rise above 30°F.

a few rainbows and browns that slip down from the ponds (Anaconda Settling Ponds)."

Downstream at Deer Lodge, the brown trout population drops to about 500 a mile. From Drummond to the mouth of Rock Creek, the population drops to about 30 fish a mile. From the mouth of Rock Creek, extending to Milltown Dam, rainbows and brown trout numbers jump back up to about 300 a mile.

The entire upper Clark Fork is classic caddisfly water, and the first five miles are managed under special regulations. The section near Deer Lodge is where angling author and publisher Gary LaFontaine, a.k.a Mr. Caddis, studied those insects for his extraordinary book, *Caddisflies*. According to LaFontaine, the early caddis hatch on the upper Clark Fork is well worth hitting.

"It's the thickest hatch you can imagine," he said. "I think everyone should see it once in their life. If you were standing 60 feet upstream from me, you'd have a hard time seeing me through the flies. They are an absolute blizzard in the evening and the fish just go wild."

The upper Clark hosts two caddis species, and they are both netmakers. The spotted sedge (*Hydropsyche*) is about a size 12 mottled wing insect with a brown or dull yellow body, almost a rust color.

The other type is the little sister sedge (*Cheumatopsyche*), which is closely related to the spotted sedge but slightly smaller. It runs about a size 16 with a tan wing and body. Fortunately, these caddis are the dominant species across Montana, so if you learn to fish them on the Clark Fork, you pretty much have the entire state nailed for caddis fishing.

"They emerge as soon as runoff is over, which usually occurs on the upper Clark Fork in late June or early July," LaFontaine said. "People see fish rolling and taking insects in the surface film, so they tie on a dry fly and that is a mistake. The fish are taking pupa in the surface film that are half-in, half-out of the water. When the pupa emerges, it's the fully-formed insect with a sheath around it. The sheath is clear and transparent, and it holds tiny air bubbles.

"The fly that they will take is the emergent sparkle pupa," LaFontaine added. "The reason it's special is it's tied with antron yarn, and antron mimics air bubbles."

LaFontaine suggests fishing that pattern with floatant on the wing so that it rides half-in, half-out of the water like the natural. It should be dead-drifted with little movement.

If flyfishers can't take trout on the emergent pupa, a diving caddis might work.

"It's a wet fly that I like to fish unweighted," LaFontaine said. "I cast upstream and let it dead-drift just under the surface. I use an elk hair caddis or an X-caddis as the dry fly indicator, and I'll drop the diving caddis about nine inches below the dry fly."

Upper Clark Fork flyfishers may also encounter egglaying female caddis. Generally, they can be seen in the air before fish start rising to them. Then, during the last hour of light, the females return to the river where they crawl under the surface and deposit their eggs. That is when the fish key on them.

In that situation, LaFontaine fishes a diving caddis in various colors. Choose the pattern that matches the color of the naturals.

Look for most of the caddis action to occur in the evenings, just before dark. However, flyfishers can nail trout all day long if they fish a free-living caddis larvae.

"I like to fish those in size 12, 14 and 16, and I like bright green patterns best," LaFontaine said. "It's a really good searching pattern that can work all day."

While caddisflies provide the best action on the upper river, there are other important emergences.

Beginning in March and April, a few Baetis mayflies come off, and the trout will turn to the top for them. They appear again in September, October and early November as the water cools down after the hot summer months.

The tiny Trico mayfly also comes off in the fall, lasting from late August through September. Brown trout will form pods and feed on Tricos as they accumulate in the backeddies and slackwater pools.

Craneflies are an important insect during the first high flows of the season, which usually occur in April. The upper Clark Fork winds and cuts through the Deer Lodge Valley, creating lots of mudbanks that are laced with willows. When the first high flows arrive, cranefly larvae are washed right out of banks, and the trout gorge on them.

The upper Clark Fork between Rock Creek and Clinton provides excellent rainbow and brown trout habitat. The author, Shadow and Moose, check out this pool.

Drakes, both green and brown, make an appearance in June and early July, especially below Rock Creek in the braided water extending to Milltown Reservoir.

Grasshoppers are the most important terrestrial on the upper Clark Fork, and they fly out of the hayfields en masse, beginning in late July, extending through September.

Another hatch to note, occurring below the mouth of Rock Creek, is the giant salmonfly (*Pteronarcys californica*). Generally, the Clark Fork's salmonfly emergence occurs in mid- to late May about a week before Rock Creek gets its big hatch. Big stonefly nymph patterns draw the most consistent action, but large dries like sofa pillows and stimulators work well, too.

Below Milltown Dam, the Clark Fork changes character, becoming a large river with major mayfly hatches and fewer brown trout. Rainbow trout, a few cutthroats and some large bull trout round out the menu.

In the best water of the lower river, extending from Milltown Dam to the Clark Fork's confluence with the Flathead River at Paradise, trout populations are less dense, approaching only 600 fish per mile. But large trout, especially big rainbows, are her trademark. Two big-water rainbows over 30 inches were pulled from the river in 1995.

Lower Clark Fork flyfishers concentrate on the wide riffles, long, smooth glides and the deep holes. And they pass up a lot of flatwater, dead stretches.

At first the water can seem overwhelming, simply by its size, but the rainbows rise eagerly, and it will not take an observant flycaster long to locate pods of hungry, slurping trout. Rainbow trout on the Clark Fork are social creatures—they prefer to pod up and feed.

While most of the action can be had on mayfly dun and emerger imitations or small mayfly nymphs like hare's ears and pheasant tails, there are good options for those who prefer the big nasty stuff like size 4 woolly buggers, sculpins and zonkers.

In particular, the area between Harper Bridge and Huson, just west of Missoula, holds decent numbers of brown trout, and some of those fish are quite large. Twenty-inch-plus specimens are not uncommon, but flyfishers won't find big trout slurping minuscule mayflies up top. Instead, they will have to throw big stuff into the deep holes and slow-water pockets behind obstructions like diversion dams, bridge pilings and downed logs.

The lower Clark Fork's important hatches begin with the emergence of Baetis mayflies in March, April and May, before runoff.

The best way to fish the lower Clark Fork is by floating it. But there are good options for the bankfisher, and the Baetis hatch provides an excellent chance to catch fish from shore, especially below the Petty Creek Bridge where fish accumulate on both sides of the river and gorge.

But flyfishers must demonstrate stealth to score. I like to walk downstream from the bridge, presenting a size 16 or 18 CDC Baetis or an olive parachute with a downstream dead-drift. Tippets need to be light, say 5X or even 6X, or the trout will get fussy and refuse offerings. Many big rainbows will sit tight to the bank in three feet of water where they can, unfortunately, spot any movement along the banks. Flyfishers may need to approach on a knee or use the bankside brush (it loves to gobble backcasts) as a screen.

In mid-March extending into April, skwala stoneflies are present on the lower river, and big rainbows respond to stonefly nymphs in size 6 and 8. These stoneflies are not present in massive numbers, and they are rarely, if ever, seen flying. Flyfishers may catch a few floating downstream on the surface, but they could also go an entire day without seeing one. However, that doesn't mean the fish aren't eating nymphs underneath.

Flyfishers should tip over rocks near the banks and check for the skwala nymphs. If they are present in good numbers, slap a stonefly nymph along the banks. Some large fish may be produced.

The Clark Fork's summer mayfly hatches begin with the pale morning dun and gray drakes just as runoff subsides. On the lower Clark Fork that might not happen until late June or mid-July.

The PMD and gray drake hatches last through August, enhanced by the presence of green drakes sometime in July. The number of mayflies on the water at one time can be staggering, and the fish may key in on one particular insect during one stage of the hatch, which makes the flyfisher's job particularly difficult. To compound matters, those rainbows' preference for food items may change every few hundred yards of the river.

One way to avoid the confusion is to fish a grasshopper pattern in August and early September. Huge hayfields parallel the lower Clark Fork in many places. If you can time a float when a rancher is cutting a hayfield, the action can be epic. Really, a grasshopper slapped along the banks will take fish at any time of the day in late summer, even when those trout are keying on mayflies.

Spillways between the Anaconda settling ponds offer some big rainbow and brown trout. Here, the author hoists a four-pound "football" below the Pond 2 spillway.

In early August, extending into September, there are plenty of Trico mayflies on the water. And the early morning spinnerfall, which extends until noon, is the best stage of the hatch to fish.

There can be literally hundreds of thousands of bugs on the water during the spinnerfall and the trout will be slurping greedily. The flyfisher's task is to time the rise of one particular trout and present a size 18, 20 or even size 22 spent wing black Trico pattern, just when that fish is ready to rise. Frustrating fishing to be sure, but incredible to watch due to the sheer numbers of bugs on the water and the greediness of those rainbows at that time.

Baetis reappear in September and they are present through early November. A day spent on the river during fall, when ducks and geese scream by on their southerly migration with the cottonwoods lit up in crimson and gold coloration, is tough to beat. The trout gorge like they are eating their last good meal for five months, which they are, and the scenery is outstanding. I will take a fall float on the Clark Fork any chance I get.

During fall floats, extending from early September through October, those Baetis will be joined by the larger mahogany duns. Size 14 or 16 CDC mahogany duns or pheasant tail nymphs produce nicely.

After November 30, the lower Clark Fork falls under winter whitefish/catch and release trout regulations and the only real option is fishing midges or throwing big streamer patterns. Winter fishing on the lower Clark Fork does not rate high on my hit list, but a few big fish are produced by dedicated anglers during the winter season.

According to flyfishing guide Eric Ruberg at Grizzly Hackle in Missoula, if he could pick just one week of the year to fish the lower Clark Fork, he'd quit his job and fish two weeks—the first week of April and the first week of October.

"In April you will see gray drakes, *Nemoura, Capnia* and skwala stoneflies, plus Baetis and midges," Ruberg said. "The fishing can be phenomenal, with pods of feeding fish stacked along the current seams.

"The gray drake hatch is particularly good," Ruberg added. "I like to fish size 12 comparaduns, parachute Adams and paradrakes. I use the same patterns for the gray drake and green drake hatches, too. I think those patterns work because they all offer a low profile and that is key, especially in the glassy, smooth runs during low, clear water, which is what you will encounter during early spring and fall."

In the fall, Ruberg suggests using smaller flies like size 14 or 16 drake patterns. And he encourages flyfishers to skip through the dead sections, searching instead, for pods of rising fish.

"During fall, the fishing can be really good throughout the lower river," Ruberg said. "But the way they get podded up, it can take some exploratory work to find them. There are good fish in all sections, but it's just a matter of finding out where to spend your time."

Although the slow, glassy sections (some may extend for a half-mile or more) hold fewer fish, the fish they do offer can be quite large.

"They tend to be bigger in the slack water, but they are more selective, tending to eat smaller insects," Ruberg said. "I've fished to them when gray drakes are passing right over their heads. I've used 15-foot leaders tapered down to 6X, and they still seem skeptical of a big fly. It's like you have to go with a small midge pattern or something to take them."

One place on the lower Clark Fork where you don't have to worry about selective trout and small patterns is the 12-mile jaunt through Alberton Gorge, just west of Alberton.

However, only the most experienced rafters should attempt that water, which harbors rapids with names like Rest Stop Rapids, Cliffside Rapids, Tumbleweed Rapids and Boateater Rapids. One particularly intimidating wave is simply referred to as Fang.

The Gorge offers little wade access but lots of trout. FWP says trout populations are significantly higher in the Gorge than other portions of the lower river. And many of those big-shouldered rainbows run over 20 inches.

Woolly buggers and other streamer patterns are most effective through the Gorge and its deep, swirling water.

Wherever flyfishers choose to fish the Clark Fork, whether on the upper river for browns or the lower sections for big rainbows, realize the precarious position of the fish you pursue. Each is a treasure, a symbol of the fighting spirit inherent to all trout. For a fish to thrive in the waters of the Clark Fork, it must harbor a strong will to live. That gives me enough reason to release every one I catch. I hope you, too, will see the merit of those trout and follow suit.

Stream Facts: Clark Fork River

Seasons
- Third Saturday in May through November 30. Extended whitefish season/catch-and-release trout November 1 through third Saturday in May.
- The exceptions are from the mouth of the Thompson River to the Idaho border, which is open all year. Also open all year from the Pond 3 spillway to Warm Springs Bridge at the Anaconda Settling Pond System. Open all year from Warm Springs Bridge to Perkins Lane Bridge.

Special Regulations
- Warm Springs Bridge to Perkins Lane Bridge: Five trout under 12 inches or four trout under 12 inches and one over 20 inches. Artificial flies and lures only.
- Milltown Dam to mouth of the Thompson River: five trout only one over 16 inches.
- Mouth of Flathead River to mouth of Thompson River, open all year for northern pike.

Trout
- Upper river: Dominated by brown trout, with lesser numbers of cutthroat and rainbows. Whitefish abound.
- Lower River: Dominated by rainbow trout with lesser number of cutthroat and browns.

River Miles
- 200 miles from its origin at the confluence of Warm Springs and Silver Bow Creeks to the Idaho border. It is floatable throughout its entire length.

River Flows
- Flows peak in June and drop by mid- to late July.
- The upper river is heavily dewatered from June through early September by irrigation needs. The section affected runs from Deer Lodge downstream to the mouth of Rock Creek.

River Characteristics
- The Clark Fork is a small stream at its headwaters, but it quickly grows to a medium size stream in its first 15 miles. It remains that size until it reaches Milltown Dam east of Missoula where it picks up flows from the Blackfoot River. Four miles west of Missoula it picks up flows from the Bitterroot River and becomes a large western river. Most of the river provides easy floats, but the Clark Fork drops into a narrow canyon just west of Alberton. Only excellent boaters should attempt a series of rapids that extend through the canyon. Below Alberton Gorge to the Idaho border, it is big water that is easily floated.

Fishing Access

- Numerous side roads offer ample access to most of the river, especially in the upper river and between Missoula and St. Regis on the lower river.
- Developed access sites include (upper river to lower river): Warm Springs, Galen Bridge, Racetrack Bridge, Deer Lodge, Kohrs Bend, Little Blackfoot, Gold Creek, Flint Creek, Bearmouth, Beavertail, Rock Creek, Clinton, Turah, Milltown, Sha-Ron, Kelly Island, Harper Bridge, Erskine, Huson, Ninemile, Petty Creek, Cyr, Forest Grove, Dry Creek, Sloway, St. Regis, Fourteen Mile Bridge, Cascade.

Shops/Outfitters

- Fish-On Fly and Tackle (Butte), 3346 Harrison Ave., Butte, MT, 406-494-4218
- Rock Creek Fisherman's Mercantile (mile 1, Rock Creek Road), 15995 Rock Creek Road, Rock Creek, MT, 406-825-6440
- Grizzly Hackle, 215 W. Front Street, Missoula, MT, 406-721-8996
- Missoulian Angler, 420 N. Higgins Ave., Missoula, MT, 406-728-7766
- The Kingfisher, 926 East Broadway, Missoula, MT, 888-542-4911
- Crain Guide and Outfitting Services, Plains, MT (Excellent trout, smallmouth bass and pike options on lower Clark Fork), 406-826-5566

Camping

- There are numerous campgrounds along the Clark Fork, including options for trailer hookups. Motels and hotels are located in Butte, Anaconda, Missoula, Alberton and St. Regis.

CLARK FORK RIVER MAJOR HATCHES

Insect	J	F	M	A	M	J	J	A	S	O	N	D	Flies
Grasshopper								X	X				Dave's Hopper #2-8; Meadow Hopper #2-8; Dave's Hopper #4-8
Skwala Stonefly			X	X									Bullethead Skwala #6-8; Olive Stimulator #6-8; Rubberleg Brown Stone #6-8
Gray Drake					X								Parachute Adams #14-16; Sparkle Dun #14-16; Comparadun #14-16; Hare's Ear Nymph #14-16; Pheasant Tail Nymph #14-16
Midge	X	X	X	X	X	X	X	X	X	X	X	X	Griffith's Gnat #16-20; Parachute Adams #18-22; Pheasant Tail Nymph #16-22
Trico							X	X					Parachute Adams #18-22; Parachute Trico #18-22; CDC Trico Biot #18-22; Sparkle Dun #18-22; Trico Spinner #18-22
Salmonfly *Pteronarcys californica*						X							Seducer #4-8; Stimulator #4-8; Bitch Creek Nymph #4-8; Kaufmann's Stone #2-6; Brook's Stone #2-6; Black Rubberlegs #2-8
Baetis				X	X				X	X			Olive Cripple #16-20; Parachute Adams #16-20; Sparkle Dun #16-20; Hare's Ear Nymph #16-20; Pheasant Tail Nymph #16-20; Poxyback Baetis #16-20
Golden Stone *Hesperoperla pacifica*						X	X						Whitlock's Golden Stone Nymph #4-8; Montana Nymph #4-8; Betts' Brown Stone #4-8; Whitlock's Revised Golden Stone #4-8; Poxyback Biot Golden Stone #6-12

CLARK FORK RIVER MAJOR HATCHES (cont.)

Insect	J	F	M	A	M	J	J	A	S	O	N	D	Flies
Caddis				▮	▮								Elk Hair Caddis #14-18; Diving Caddis #14-16; X-Caddis #14-16; Drifting Cased Caddis #14-18; Emergent Sparkle Pupa #12-18; Deep Sparkle Pupa #12-18; Electric Caddis #14-16; Caddis Variant #14-16
Pale Morning Dun						▮	▮						Sparkle Dun #14-20; Parachute Adams #14-20; PMD Cripple #16-20; Poxy Biot Nymph #16-20; Lawson's Thorax Dun #16-20; Lempke's Extended Body PMD #16-18; Hare's Ear Nymph #16-18; Pheasant Tail Nymph #16-18; CDC Floating Nymph #16-18; Half Back Emerger #16-18
Mahogany Dun									▮				CDC Emergent Crippled Dun #14-16; Sparkle Dun Mahogany #14-16; CDC Spinner #14-16; Comparadun #14-16; Pheasant Tail Nymph #14-16; Floating Nymph #14-16
Green Drake/Little Western Green Drake							▮	▮					Olive Sparkle Dun #10-16; Cripple #10-16; Green Drake Emerger #10-16; Comparadun #10-16; Hare's Ear Nymph #10-16

LESSER CLARK FORK TRIBUTARIES

Little Blackfoot

The Little Blackfoot joins the upper Clark Fork River near Garrison, which serves as the cutoff for flyfishers heading from the upper Clark Fork, Rock Creek and Georgetown Lake to Helena and the Missouri River via U.S. 12.

Less noted than its big brother, the Blackfoot of *A River Runs Through It* fame, the Little Blackfoot can fish quite well during all seasons, and some of its brown trout run to impressive size—16- to 20-inchers are not rare.

The successful flyfisher seeks pockets of productive water on the Little Blackfoot —some sections are sabotaged by ranchers. Those sections hold skimpy trout populations and poor habitat. Other sections, however, will be noted as some of the finest looking small water habitat in the state.

Fortunately, flyfishers can gain access to the river via numerous side road bridge crossings. The highway also crosses the river at several points. Remember, you can fish below the high water mark on private land but not above it. You'll have limited success pounding on doors: some ranchers will readily grant access across their land; others, selfishly, will not.

Flyfishers should carry a variety of patterns when fishing the Little Blackfoot— its hatches can be diverse and heavy at times.

Beginning before runoff in the spring, anglers will find the typical fare—blue-winged olives and some midges. For the olives, try olive sparkle duns, parachute Adams, olive cripples and, of course, a hare's ear or pheasant tail nymph prior to and during the infancy of the hatch. Watch for bugs on the water between 11 AM and 4 PM, with peak activity between noon and 3 PM.

In late spring (late April and May) look for the first solid caddis hatches of the season. The standard patterns, such as elk hair caddis, X-caddis, and Goddard caddis, work fine. Emergers like the LaFontaine sparkle emerger are productive, too.

Sometime in May, the river will blow out, turn the color of chocolate milk and send flyfishers away like it carried the plague. But by mid-June or early July in excessively high water years, the river will drop into shape and provide some nice mayfly hatches. Watch for pale morning duns during late morning and midday hours. Try sparkle duns, parachute PMDs and cripples.

As the PMDs subside, watch for a late caddis flurry. Throw elk hair caddis and sparkle emergers late in the day and into dark.

Grasshoppers take plenty of fish during late summer and early fall, and the standard varieties, such as Joe's and Dave's hoppers, work fine.

As the hoppers subside after the first few solid frosts of the year, watch for brown trout, both resident fish and monsters that move out of the upper Clark Fork, to go on the spawn. They'll turn aggressive toward most streamer patterns; I've had the best luck with a size 4 brown woolly bugger, with long palmered brown hackle and a brown marabou tail. In the tail, I'll tie a few strands of olive sparkle.

If you're looking for something other than brown trout, try the upper reaches of the river above Elliston, where some brookies and cutthroats are known to roam.

In many areas the Little Blackfoot is springfed, and it holds open water most of the winter. Because of that, it remains open for whitefish and catch-and-release trout fishing between November 30 and the third Saturday in May. It's a worthwhile winter venture.

Private land borders much of the lower river, but those with tents, a truck with a canopy or a trailer can enter the Deer Lodge or Helena National Forests near Elliston. A note: bring your food and drink because eateries are nonexistent on the highway between Garrison and Helena. There is a small gas station at Garrison that offers a few groceries, a post office and a pretty mean cup of coffee. Avoid the cheese-and-onion-covered long dogs.

Rattlesnake Creek

There is a common misconception about Rattlesnake Creek—most flyfishers believe the river is closed to fishing from Beeskove Creek in the Rattlesnake Wilderness all the way downstream to the creek's confluence with the Clark Fork River in Missoula.

Actually, Rattlesnake Creek is open from its mouth, which pours into the Clark Fork just east of the Red Lion Inn, upstream to the Missoula water supply dam, which is about six or seven miles of water. However, the creek is closed all year between the dam and Beeskove Creek, which is about nine miles of very attractive water that runs through the Rattlesnake Wilderness Area.

Fishing can be quite good in the open sections above and below the dam. Look for seasonal runs of rainbows, cutthroats, bull trout and brown trout in the lower river, which opens the third Saturday in May and closes November 30.

Often, the river can be blown out on the opener, lessening a flyfisher's opportunity to hit some of the bigger rainbows that move out of the Clark Fork. But, even if you miss the spawning run, there are good options through summer. Rainbows and cutthroats will rise willingly to a variety of mayflies and caddis. Watch for March browns, blue winged olives and pale morning duns. Caddis are also present and they will be eaten by the Rattlesnake's trout between late May and September 1.

The lower Rattlesnake offers mostly pocketwater fishing with very few truly deep holes. It is highly wadable, spans just 15 yards in most places and offers vehicle-less students at the University of Montana first-rate flyfishing.

To reach the upper river, you need a good set of lungs or a mountain bike. In my mind, a mountain bike with full cargo stowed in a backpack is the way to go. Many times I've taken off on a whim and pedaled upstream to Beeskove Creek where the open section of the upper river begins. On a June or July day, with the sun beaming down and the anticipation of a full summer of fishing looming ahead, there are not many better or prettier places to be. You may find a few friendly bikers or hikers on the trail (watch out for overzealous bikers), but by bushwhacking to the river, you have your solitude.

Fish the river anywhere above Beeskove—you will find good water throughout. You will also find plenty of hungry cutthroat trout and maybe a few bull trout in the deep pools. It's all catch and release, so bring food with you if staying overnight. And remember, there are grizzly bears and a ton of black bears in the Rattlesnake Wilderness (my friend Hank whistled around a corner on his mountain bike—he's

The Little Blackfoot offers a great day trip away from the bigger Clark Fork River. Brown trout and brushy banks should be expected.

one of the "radical" crew—and nearly dusted an immature griz). Store and dispose of your food properly.

There are decent caddis and mayfly hatches on the upper river, and the standard patterns like elk hair caddis, pale morning duns, hare's ear and pheasant tail nymphs, and caddis pupa, will take fish.

Woolly buggers and large woolhead sculpins will draw takes from aggressive cutthroats, too. They may also draw strikes from bull trout, which run up to eight or ten pounds on occasion. A 2X or 3X leader will hold a large fish if played properly.

The Rattlesnake is a truly great day trip away from the region's more noted, larger rivers. On its lower end, the Rattlesnake offers prime flyfishing, literally in Missoula's backyard. On the upper end, you can find a wilderness experience and some of the most ideal-looking cutthroat water in the world. If you take a mountain bike with you, you can enjoy that wilderness solitude by day and be home by 8 PM to taste Missoula's night life. That is a tough, yet very appealing, combination to find anywhere.

Ninemile Creek

Ninemile Creek, an important spawning stream with decent populations of resident trout, flows into the lower Clark Fork River just east of Alberton.

On its lower end, the creek is bordered by much private property, while its upper end offers access via the Lolo National Forest.

For such a small creek (in most places it's a medium cast wide), good flyfishing and some meaty specimens of rainbows, cutthroats and a few bull trout can be found throughout. Its size does make it unapproachable to those who would prefer to float.

Access can be a problem on the lower creek's most productive stretches, and that keeps many potential anglers away. However, if you can get on, the getting is good. Ninemile Road crosses the highway at several spots, and the stream access law can be applied (stay below the high water mark).

Early in the year during high water (after the opener on the third Saturday in May), try large weighted nymphs like a Kaufmann's stone or George's brown stone, or streamers like a woolly bugger. When the water subsides, watch for decent PMD and caddis hatches extending from June through August. During fall, Baetis and general attractors will take fish. Woolly buggers and muddler minnows also draw strikes.

While Ninemile Creek can be tremendously frustrating to those who have trouble securing access, it is worth the effort. If all else fails, grab a bite to eat at the Nine Mile House, which serves excellent dinners and can have some entertaining night life on Friday and Saturday nights.

To reach Ninemile Creek, take Exit 82 from Interstate 90. Follow Ninemile Road upstream.

Fish Creek

Fish Creek, one of the lower Clark Fork's most important spawning tributaries, offers excellent flyfishing for some nice rainbows and cutthroats and scenery galore. Just don't try to sneak on this creek before the opener (third Saturday in May).

Montana Fish, Wildlife and Parks patrols the creek regularly, and they are eager to hand out citations. Fortunately, local judges don't look kindly on Fish Creek poachers—if they threw away the keys and closed the shades, it wouldn't bother me.

One option is to fish the Clark Fork just below the mouth of the creek—big rainbows, heading upstream to spawn, will suck in streamers and large nymphs.

The upper portion of Fish Creek is accessible via the Fish Creek logging road. That section provides good fishing for smallish rainbows and cutthroats in the six- to 12-inch range; however, some larger spawning rainbows can be encountered shortly after the season opens.

The lower river is accessible by hiking away from Fish Creek Road into a narrow canyon. Flyfishers will encounter bouncy pocketwater with some deeper pools. If you arrive early in the season, before high water or just after high water diminishes, you should find some large rainbows at the tailouts of those pools.

Throughout the creek, wading is the way to go. Floating is not an option.

Attractor dry flies work best on Fish Creek—anglers need a fly that floats high and is buoyant. Royal Wulffs, stimulators, elk hair caddis, humpies and renegades draw strikes. For the early season, don't be afraid to pitch larger nymphs and streamers like rubberleg brown stonefly nymphs, woolly buggers and woolhead sculpins.

To reach Fish Creek, take Exit 66 from Interstate 90 just west of Cyr. Head west on Fish Creek Road. Private ranches border the river in some stretches, but Lolo National Forest offers plenty of access and camping sites all along the road.

Rattlesnake Creek offers some of the best scenery in Montana. It also offers sizable cutthroat, rainbow and bull trout. Here, Jim Nave rigs up, 12 miles deep in the wilderness.

St. Regis

The St. Regis has endured its fair share of environmental nightmares, but it is still an important spawning tributary for the lower Clark Fork's big rainbow and brown trout.

Flowing into the Clark Fork just east of St. Regis, the river can be covered with a 30-foot cast in most places. It's an excellent wade stream that offers ample access throughout. It is not a good stream to float.

The lower end should be the target of flyfishers in the spring when the river opens (third Saturday in May), and when big rainbows can still be found in the deep pools. Look there in the fall, too, when some big browns move upstream to spawn.

Spring-run rainbows will eat a variety of streamers; I've taken some brutes on olive woolly buggers with palmered grizzly hackle and white rubberlegs. Fall-run browns, which stack up behind midstream boulders and other obstructions, will succumb to similar offerings. Egg patterns will also take rainbows that follow the browns upstream.

The St. Regis is not hard to find, and access is plentiful. Just follow Interstate 90 west from St. Regis—I-90 parallels and often crosses the river.

Flint Creek

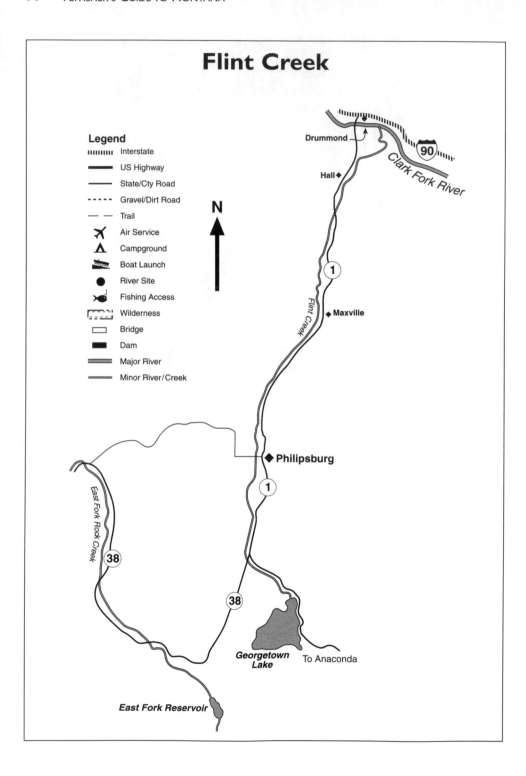

Legend

‖‖‖‖‖	Interstate
▬▬▬	US Highway
———	State/Cty Road
- - - -	Gravel/Dirt Road
— —	Trail
✈	Air Service
⛰	Campground
⛴	Boat Launch
●	River Site
🐟	Fishing Access
▨▨▨	Wilderness
▭	Bridge
▬	Dam
▦▦▦	Major River
▬▬▬	Minor River/Creek

N

Drummond

Hall ◆

Clark Fork River

90

① Flint Creek

◆ Maxville

◆ Philipsburg

①

East Fork Rock Creek

38

38

Georgetown Lake To Anaconda

East Fork Reservoir

FLINT CREEK

It sits out there in the Philipsburg Valley like a whipped puppy watching its litter-mates munch treats. In other words, Flint Creek gets no attention compared to nearby and highly praised Rock Creek.

In some ways that is a shame, because Flint Creek offers respectable brown trout and some purely choice water as it cuts, twists, and generally meanders through a beautiful mountain valley. For any age angler with a strong imagination, Flint Creek is perfect.

Flint Creek begins as the North Fork Flint Creek on the east side of Georgetown Lake. It receives a spawning run of the lake's big rainbows, but flyfishers can't get at the creek until July 1, which is after the spawn. Don't grumble—if they left the creek open it would be a bait-casting, treble-hooking, trout-snagging debacle. Flint Creek proper is born at the base of the dam that contains Georgetown Lake.

From there, the creek winds through a steep canyon before spilling out into the valley bottom. It parallels Highway 1 for most of its length, dodging away from the pavement into the middle of the valley near Philipsburg. At times it is barely visible, but you can still follow its path by watching the snaky course of willow bushes that line its banks throughout its course. North of Philipsburg, between the entrance of Sawmill Creek and Maxville, the river runs through a canyon, and by looking off the highway, a flyfisher can feast his eyes on some of the most ideal-looking, twisted trout and mosquito habitat in Montana. Just north of Hall, the river again cuts away from the highway, this time east through private land, before plunging into the Clark Fork River at Drummond.

Flint Creek's undercut banks, its medium-depth runs, its downright deep, dark holes, and its propensity to kick out the occasional Godzilla brown make it a viable day venture away from Montana's big-name and, at times, heavily-crowded rivers. You will not find much competition on Flint Creek, but you will find a healthy population of blaze orange fenceposts. Those posts are almost as populous as the bends in this stream, which is to say there are a ton of them.

Private property borders the creek for most of its length, and there is very little public access to the river. Floating through private sections is not an option—the creek is simply too small for a boat or raft. However, landowners in the Flint Creek Valley are quite cordial, and the respectful flyfisher who asks for permission should be rewarded with free reign to fish. Oh, it's true you will find the occasional sourpuss, but most ranchers give the go-ahead. Just do not go pounding on doors at 6:30 AM on a Sunday morning! One way to assure access to the creek is to jump into the river at one of the four highway bridges. Just remember to obey the stream access law.

"Brown Trout Water" is the easiest way to describe Flint Creek. And that is exactly what a flyfisher should expect to catch. There are lesser numbers of cutthroat, brook and rainbow trout, but they can range between 12 and 15 inches. They should be considered a bonus. The brown trout average about 12 inches, but fish to 20 inches become active late in the day, at night, when the grasshoppers arrive in late summer, and during the fall when some fish migrate out of the Clark Fork and into Flint Creek.

Most of the creek's larger browns are fish eaters, but the smaller specimens plus the cutthroats and rainbows will rise diligently for mayfly and caddisfly morsels. And there are a variety of both species on the creek.

During April and May, flyfishers should watch for Baetis and Western March brown mayflies. As the air temperature heats up in May and June (winter drags in the valley), watch for a few Callibaetis mayflies and two species of caddis—*hydropsyche* and *cheumatopsyche*.

For the Baetis, try a size 16 CDC Baetis or olive parachute on top. For a nymph, try an olive flashback hare's ear or a small pheasant tail nymph. March brown and Callibaetis can be represented with a size 14 or 16 parachute Adams up top and a similar size hare's ear or pheasant tail underneath. You can use those patterns throughout summer, because Callibaetis will carry on through August on random days.

For both caddis species, flyfishers can probe the depths during bright light hours with an olive free-living caddis. When the sun begins to drop and a hazy light spreads over the valley, a flyfisher can whip out dry fly and emergent pupa patterns to give the late caddis emergence a try.

Watch for trout making splashy rises as the surface action begins. Those fish will take pupa that are half-in, half-out of the water. Try an emergent caddis pupa and make sure to put a little fly floatant (dressing) on the hair wing. Shortly after, the fish may focus on egg-laying females. Try dead-drifting a diving caddis pattern. Don't get upset about going high-tech for Flint Creek's trout. If all you have in your fly boxes are a few elk hair caddis, you will probably catch plenty of fish. But by carrying extra patterns and fishing them during specific stages of the hatch, you stand a good chance to double your tally.

During the midday heat of summer, most Flint Creek flyfishers choose to fish a free-living caddis or a large streamer. If you choose to fish a streamer, bring a bunch of spares—you will need them.

Flint Creek eats flies like the Hamburgler swallows Big Macs. There are enough rocks, submerged willows, downed logs and hidden sections of barbed wire in the creek to last an angler a lifetime. And if my loss of streamers is any suggestion, that mess seems to be magnetic. Oh yeah, tall willows nab those streamers on errant backcasts, too.

However, even the best anglers will lose flies to this creek if they fish it properly. Larger browns will not be found out in the open during the day. Instead, they hold deep under the banks or in structure like logs and rocks. When they hold like that, it is nearly impossible to place a streamer in front of their snouts. Essentially, the prospecting flyfisher must simply admit that this cast is either going to catch a fish or the streamer will be lost to the river. Most of the time, a streamer ends up busted off, but on occasion that bug will swing in front of a big fish, and when it does, they'll take. Then it's just a matter of extricating the fish from the rocks, sticks and that darned barbed wire.

Author's father, Fred Thomas, works an appealing bend on Flint Creek. Not noted as a top fishery, Flint does offer some big brown trout from the deeper holes.

One way to draw some larger fish out of their lies, without having to drop an offering down to them, is to fish grasshopper imitations. Because a flyfisher can follow the hopper's drift by sight, they will lose far fewer flies than anglers throwing streamers. On Flint Creek, hoppers are present in good numbers from late July through mid-September.

Big browns love hoppers. Those big terrestrials are really the only substantial food item they see floating by on the surface. But a flyfisher won't draw many strikes fishing that pattern daintily. Hoppers should be slapped down on the water with the intention to make a commotion. That's what the naturals do. They fly out of the hayfields, like wounded helicopters and when they hit the surface they send up a plume of spray. The trout key on that disturbance, slip out of their comfortable lies and detonate on those writhing, longlegged creatures.

While hoppers draw some big fish to the top, quite possibly the best way to nail a big Flint Creek brown is to wait until fall when those big spawners move out of the Clark Fork.

There are some deep pools and riffles near the mouth of the creek, and the browns stack up there. They also accumulate below the mouth of the creek in the Clark Fork. Especially effective at that time are size 4 bunny leeches, black and brown woolly buggers, zonkers, muddler minnows and matuka sculpins.

Flint Creek is readily accessible from many directions. Flyfishers suffering through a slow day on the Bitterroot, upper or lower Clark Fork, Blackfoot, or even Rock Creek could be on Flint Creek for a change of pace and the evening caddis action in an hour.

Whenever you visit the creek, make sure you have some extra clothing. The Flint Creek Valley is not very warm. Even in May, there can be some serious snowstorms racing through the mountains. By fall, when those browns are spawning, temperatures may hover in the low 30s at night. They might only bounce up into the 50s during midday.

From the Bitterroot Valley, take Skalkaho Road (Highway 38), which cuts east from Highway 93 just south of Hamilton. This mostly dirt road holds many potholes, but even small cars can make the grade. There is an absolutely spectacular falls to stop and marvel at on the west side of the Sapphire Mountain Range. Spray shoots across the road to cool scorched skin on a hot summer day. Skalkaho Pass generally opens in late June and closes again in November or December.

From Missoula, lower Clark Fork and Blackfoot River flyfishers can take Interstate 90 to the Drummond exit and follow Highway 1 southwest. Flint Creek parallels the highway.

From Rock Creek, simply follow Rock Creek Road to its intersection with Highway 38 and turn east.

Although Flint Creek will never be mentioned in the same breath as other notable small streams like Rock Creek, the Little Blackfoot or even the Thompson River, it provides interesting options for the flyfisher. And it will always capture the imagination of those who love small streams. If fished often enough, sooner or later reality will catch up with fantasy. Big brown trout are there.

FLINT CREEK MAJOR HATCHES

Insect	J	F	M	A	M	J	J	A	S	O	N	D	Flies
Grasshoppers							▮	▮	▮				Dave's Hopper #2-8; Meadow Hopper #4-8
Callibaetis						▮	▮						Callibaetis Cripple #14-16; Sparkle Spinner #14-16; Sparkle Dun #14-16; Parachute Adams #14-16; Hare's Ear #14-16
Midge	▮	▮	▮	▮	▮	▮	▮	▮	▮	▮	▮	▮	Griffith's Gnat #16-20; Parachute Adams #18-22; Pheasant Tail Nymph #16-22
March Brown Drake					▮	▮							Sparkle Dun #14-16; Sparkle Spinner #14-16; Pheasant Tail Nymph #12-16;
Caddis *Hydropsyche* *Cheumatopsyche*					▮	▮	▮	▮					Elk Hair Caddis #14-18; Diving Caddis #14-16; X-Caddis #14-16; Drifting Cased Caddis #14-18; Emergent Sparkle Pupa #12-18; Deep Sparkle Pupa #12-18; Electric Caddis #14-16; Caddis Variant #14-16
Baetis				▮	▮					▮			Olive Cripple #16-20; Parachute Adams #16-20; Sparkle Dun #16-20; Hare's Ear Nymph #16-20; Pheasant Tail Nymph #16-20; Poxyback Baetis #16-20

Rock Creek

Rock Creek Fisherman's Mercantile

Valley of the Moon
2 mi

Clark Fork River

I-90

Soloman
6 mi

Sawmill
8.5 mi

Norton Campground
11 mi

Grizzly Campground

Dalles Campground

Harry's Flat Campground
23 mi

Bitterroot Flat Campground
28 mi

32.7 mi

Squaw Rock
37 mi

To Phillipsburg

Gilles Bridge
42 mi

Rock Creek

To Hamilton

West Fork

◆ East Fork

East Fork

N

Legend

‖‖‖‖	Interstate
▬▬	US Highway
▬	State/Cty Road
-----	Gravel/Dirt Road
— —	Trail
✈	Air Service
⛺	Campground
🛥	Boat Launch
●	River Site
🐟	Fishing Access
⬚	Wilderness
▭	Bridge
▬	Dam
▬▬	Major River
▬▬	Minor River/Creek

ROCK CREEK

Flowing between the densely timbered Sapphire and Garnet mountain ranges, western Montana's Rock Creek offers flyfishers just what they need: classic mountain trout water, major insect hatches and eager-rising inhabitants.

More than one flyfisher has labeled Rock Creek "a trout stream made in heaven." I buy that line, although the river suffers the effects of drought and disease. In fact, Montana Fish, Wildlife and Parks indicates that numbers of juvenile fish are down 40 percent over all-time highs. And whirling disease is present in the system in as many as 80 percent of the juvenile trout. I am sure Rock Creek will go through its cycles of heaven and hell in the coming years; however, on a good day, Rock Creek may put 30 or more beautiful trout in your net, which is a testament to the river's true potential.

Rock Creek begins as the west fork high in the Sapphires. It picks up pace at the entrance of the east fork. Throughout its 50-mile length, Rock Creek offers fast-flowing water in the form of gorgeous riffles, deep alluring runs and a few tantalizingly dark pools. Plus, it harbors five species of trout: brook, bull, cutthroat, rainbow and brown. When Missoula flyfishers say they nailed the grand slam, you know they spent the day on Rock Creek and caught a representative of each species.

To take the grand slam, Rock Creek flyfishers must tactfully probe microhabitat where trout hold. Anything less than a precise cast should draw refusals. However, few anglers would call Rock Creek a demanding stream or mention it in the same vein as, say, the Beaverhead River.

While young flyfishers must read the varying currents and master their mending techniques, what the river demands in presentation it more than makes up for in an opportunity to read all types of water and catch eager fish that rise willingly to the river's excellent hatches. Rock Creek's major emergences include salmonflies, golden stoneflies, a variety of summer caddis, pale morning duns, midges, October caddis and Baetis. Unfortunately, the creek's prime hatches draw anglers from around the world, and crowding can be a problem.

Rock Creek leaped into prominence during the 1950s and 1960s when it was labeled blue-ribbon trout water. Throngs of anglers visited, and most of the creek's large trout were destined for the bottom of a dark creel and a well-used frying pan.

Understandably, Rock Creek's population of large fish plummeted. By the mid-1970s, the problem became so acute that it became difficult to catch a decent fish. In 1979, Montana Fish, Wildlife and Parks changed the creek's regulations. Anglers are now allowed to keep three trout, none under 12 inches, or two trout under 12 inches and one over 20 inches. Only artificial flies and lures are allowed except for kids under 14 years old.

Today, populations of large fish, most in the 14- to 17-inch range, have rebounded, and Rock Creek has regained its reputation as a premier flyfishing river. Crowding is again a problem, and it becomes most intense during the salmonfly hatch. That debacle reflects the general trend on Rock Creek: its popularity is its only downfall.

"In the six years I've lived here, I've seen the pressure go way up," said Doug Persico, who, with his wife Caroline, runs Rock Creek Fisherman's Mercantile, an excellent fly shop and motel at the base of the river. "The salmonfly hatch on this river is absolutely nuts. But you can avoid the pressure by fishing in March and April or October and November—with a blaze orange cap on. The only hope is that most of the yahoos like to float rivers during summer, and you can't float this creek after June 1 (Forest Service regulation). That fact will hopefully keep some people off of Rock Creek."

Fishing the river in March and April is a good idea. There are two important hatches that occur then: the skwala stonefly and the March brown drake. Like me, Persico rates the March brown drake as the river's premier hatch. The skwala is less pronounced. Fish do key in on skwala nymphs, but that is no different from their year-around routine. Persico says you can catch Rock Creek's trout on a stonefly nymph any day of the year. However, the March brown drake hatch is a short-lived occurrence that every flyfisher should try to catch at least once. If you plan to visit Rock Creek from far away, allow yourself at least a few days to catch this hatch. It can be hit and miss, due to weather conditions and the river's flow.

"I would much rather fish the March brown drake hatch in April than the salmonfly hatch in May or June," Persico said. "It's not an all-day thing, but boy, you can have fun for a half-hour to an hour a day on dry flies. The rest of the time you can do well on a big hare's ear nymph."

Persico's right. The March browns may only emerge for a short time each day. Therefore, if you are driving along the road and you see a fish rise, immediately pull off and tie on a parachute Adams. Action can be intense until the hatch suddenly shuts off.

"When it's on, you can't beat it," Persico says. "I've caught as many as 20 trout over 16 inches in the space of an hour or two. And those fish were not picky at all. They'll hammer a size-10 anything."

When the hatch subsides, hare's ears and pheasant tail nymphs will draw strikes. But you have to get a nymph to the bottom.

"I use a seven and a half foot leader that tapers to 3X," Persico said. "I'll dead-drift nymphs under an indicator with some lead. I like to adjust the indicator for the depth of each particular hole. You want that nymph right down to the bottom. The trout probably take a big hare's ear as a March brown nymph or a skwala."

You don't have to fish small nymphs or dry flies to catch fish on Rock Creek. Woolly buggers are super productive, especially during spring and early summer. If beginners have trouble matching any of the river's hatches, they can admit defeat and always tie on a bugger. They'll catch fish, their eyes will light up, and you can get your fly back on the creek's surface.

Buggers can be fished in a variety of ways to match a number of different food items. Dead-drifted through the deep runs and holes, buggers may be taken for stonefly nymphs. Stripped through the deep holes or slack water pools below obstructions like bridge pilings, logs and boulders, they resemble small fish. Allowed to swing at the tailout of riffles and runs, small buggers may be mistaken for emerging drakes or large caddis.

While buggers provide good action for anglers of all skill levels, it's the summer hatches that draw most people to Rock Creek. And summer hatches begin with the

Western Montana's Rock Creek is one of the prettiest, if not most productive, trout streams in Montana. Walk the banks and you might find a moose, mountain lion, black bear, elk, mule or white-tailed deer. Step into the stream anywhere, always, there will be prime trout water ahead.

big salmonflies, *Pteronarcys californica*, which emerge any time between mid-May or early June.

During that emergence, Rock Creek Road resembles a super highway as fly-fishers scramble for the best runs. If you prefer solitude, stay away from the river during the salmonfly emergence. However, hitting the salmonfly hatch on the right day can provide lifetime memories.

According to Persico, in 1994 the hatch started on May 18. In 1995 it started on May 19. During extreme high water years, the hatch may be pushed back a week to 10 days.

There are three trains of thought when approaching the salmonfly hatch, which extends throughout the river: fish adult insect patterns at the site of the emergence, fish nymphs ahead of the hatch, or fish nymphs and drowned salmonfly patterns behind the hatch. Each offers unique possibilities.

The salmonfly hatch begins on the lower river and progresses about five miles upstream a day. It is not difficult to tell where the hatch is happening. Through a cloud of dust, courtesy of anglers ripping by in their pickup trucks, large winged insects can be seen negotiating the wind currents above the river. They'll also cling to bankside brush in the mornings, before the sun warms their bodies and they take flight. Oh yes, they will also crawl on your hat, in your hair, down your shirt and under your vest—not a particularly pleasant sensation for the squeamish.

"About two weeks before the hatch starts, the big nymphs are crawling into the shallow shoreline areas, and that is when I like to fish best," Persico said. "I think fishing nymphs ahead of the hatch beats the hell out of the hatch itself. But you can do well fishing nymphs behind the hatch, too. Most people fish right at the hatch with dries and drowned dries and they do well, but that is where everybody else is at, too."

Floaters are the beneficiary of Rock Creek's high flows during the salmonfly hatch. Wade fishermen may have trouble reaching many of the creek's best runs and holes. And mending line in those swift currents can wear an arm out in no time. Wading can be dangerous, too, especially for flyfishers who have trouble maintaining their balance. Rock Creek was named aptly, and its boulders are slick as grease.

Novice boaters should steer clear of the creek. Each year rafts are eaten when inexperienced rafters round a corner and lodge against an unexpected diversion, like logjams, boulders, bridges and sweepers.

If you do choose to float, quality rafts like an Avon or Achilles, should be used. A 12-footer is about ideal, and 14-footers are fine, too. Plan on floating at least 10 miles of the creek each day—the bank will be ripping by, and you can cover a lot of miles quickly.

If you want to fish with a guide, which isn't a bad idea, book a trip six months ahead of your chosen date. Guides are available through fly shops in Missoula.

After the salmonfly spectacle, which lasts about three weeks, Rock Creek flyfishers focus on a lesser-chased golden stonefly hatch that can provide some excellent fishing. Then, around July 4, the creek settles into its summer pattern, as high water and boat fishermen make their annual exodus. That is the time to tie on an X-caddis.

"Every morning there will be caddis coming off," Persico offered. "I like to fish just as the sun hits the water and dew melts off the grass. You are not going to see a blizzard hatch, but there are enough caddis to get the trout feeding. You can cast blind or try for individual rising fish. Either way, (catching) 10 to 12 fish is a good morning."

Pale morning dun mayflies make their annual appearance in early July, also. According to Persico, chasing the spinnerfall is the best way to deal with that insect.

"You can find them hatching in the mornings, and the fish will be taking duns, but I treasure the PMD spinnerfall," he said. "Usually they start falling in the afternoon and early evenings. It's never really dense, but it extends throughout the river and the trout will key on them."

As summer winds down, watch for sporadic Baetis hatches. These small olive mayflies, about a size 18, should come off best on overcast days extending from mid-August through October. Rock Creek flyfishers should also encounter Baetis during spring. Fall and spring Baetis hatches can provide excellent fishing, especially when the trout are slurping duns, but the hatch rarely extends longer than a couple hours during the warmest part of the day. While Baetis provide sporadic action, most Rock Creek flyfishers key on two significant events during fall: the migration of big spawning brown trout and the emergence of October caddis.

"From mid-August through October, the trout will turn to these big caddis," Persico said. "But I don't fish the October caddis with dry flies; I have a secret weapon."

Persico's secret weapon is a orange serendipity. That is the nymph he uses to catch large fish, especially fall-run brown trout.

Jenny Howard picks her way across Rock Creek, below the Dalles, in April. Early spring fishing offers an awesome March brown drake emergence and a decent skwala stonefly hatch.

"You don't get very much activity on dry flies because October caddis hatch in the evening after dark," Persico said. "Most of the time, you get them when they are ovipositing or drinking. I like to dead-drift a serendipity and then let it swing."

While fall fishing may be best on the lower river due to an influx of brown trout, Rock Creek can be divided into three sections, each covering about 18 miles. Classic water exists throughout.

At its upper end, immediately below the confluence of the east and west forks, Rock Creek hosts gentle pocketwater, plenty of riffles, some deep pools, and a healthy population of rainbow and cutthroat trout. In this section, the river ranges between 50 and 70 feet wide. Access is somewhat limited because the creek is bordered mostly by private land.

The middle section begins near Big Hogback Creek, where the river becomes narrow and fast. Holding water becomes scarce—if you find a slow-moving pocket there should be a trout waiting.

In the Dalles section, a unique area strewn with huge boulders that slow the flow and create deep pools, look for a few large browns and some acrobatic rainbows.

You may also encounter bull trout and some of them run quite large. Bulls in the 20-inch class are common. Fish to five pounds are less frequently encountered, but they do exist. Look for bulls in the deep pools and the slow water behind obstructions, especially the huge boulders in the Dalles area. Weighted streamers stripped through the deep holes draw strikes. Remember, fight bull trout fast, do not remove them from the water, and take time to release them at full strength.

Below the Dalles, lower Rock Creek offers its greatest variety of trout habitat. In that section, you can find rainbows and browns hiding under logjams or in deep riffles, long runs and undercut banks. There are also a few channels and feeder creeks to probe.

Fall may be the prettiest season to fish the creek. During September and October, the river lights up with orange and yellow cottonwood leaves, and the surrounding hills offer yellow tamaracks to highlight massive sweeps of dark green forest. An occasional elk can be heard bugling from a distant ridge. Mule deer and whitetails frequent the surrounding hills. Rifle shots can be heard as hunters fill the freezer.

While fishing Rock Creek, flyfishers can stay at six public campgrounds located up and down Rock Creek. They are maintained by Lolo National Forest, and they are extremely popular. However, finding a place to pitch a tent in one of these campgrounds during summer can be futile. Fortunately, there is much public ground located away from the river, and a tent or trailer can be pitched or parked there. If you're looking for more amenities, Missoula bustles just 25 miles west of Rock Creek. Motel and hotel accommodations are available there. One note: if you are hungry after a day on the water and you don't want to fire up the Coleman stove, treat yourself to chicken and dumplings or a juicy steak at the Stage Station Restaurant, located next to Fisherman's Mercantile at the base of the creek.

Even with depressed trout numbers, Rock Creek provides some of western Montana's best flyfishing in an unmatched setting. However, two proposed mines near the creek's banks have environmentalists and flyfishers scrambling.

Cable Mountain Mining is proposing a cyanide heap-leach mine in Cornish Gulch, which flows into Rock Creek downstream from Gilles Bridge. American Gem Mountain wants a sapphire mine in the headwaters of Rock Creek on the west fork.

"One good thing about Rock Creek is that it is such a treasure, just a couple phone calls can get thousands of people out in the streets shouting about it," Persico said. "People are concerned about this area, and they do what is necessary to protect it.

"This is a world treasure," Persico added. "There's only one place like it, and when it's gone, there won't be any place to turn."

Stream Facts: Rock Creek

Seasons
- Third Saturday in May through November 30.
- Extended whitefish season/catch and release for trout December 1 through third Saturday in May.

Special Regulations
- Artificial lures and flies only.
- Limit is three trout daily under 12 inches or two trout under 12 inches and one over 20 inches.
- Closed to fishing from boats July 1 through November 30.

Trout
- Rainbow, native westslope cutthroat, brown, brook and bull trout. Whitefish are also present in large numbers.
- Rainbow populations heaviest in upper and middle river. Average about 14 inches.
- Cutthroat populations heaviest in upper river. Average 12 to 14 inches.
- Brook trout spread throughout the river, including side-channels and spring creeks. Average eight to 11 inches.
- Bull trout are spread throughout the river, but populations are heaviest in the middle and upper sections. Average about 18 inches. Fish between five and 10 pounds have been taken.
- Brown trout populations are heaviest in the middle and lower river. Average about 14 inches. A few fish above 22 inches are taken each year.

River Miles
- Exit 126, Rock Creek—0
- Valley of the Moon—2
- Spring Creek—6
- Sawmill—8.5
- Norton Campground—11
- Harry's Flat—23
- Bitterroot Flat—28
- Squaw Rock—37
- Gilles Bridge—42
- East Fork Rock Creek—52

River Flows
- High water begins in mid-May and extends through mid-June. Low flows make for challenging fishing conditions by mid-August.

Fishing Access
- Rock Creek provides some of the best stream access in Montana. The lower and middle sections are paralleled by Rock Creek Road. Access is slightly worse through the upper section, although an angler can still get to the river.

Area Fly Shops
- Rock Creek Fisherman's Mercantile, 15995 Rock Creek Road, 406-825-6440, is the only shop on the creek. It is located at mile 0.5 on the lower river.
- The Kingfisher, 926 East Broadway, Missoula, MT, 888-542-4911
- Grizzly Hackle, 215 W. Front Street, Missoula, MT, 406-721-8996
- Streamside Anglers, 301 S. Orange St. Missoula, MT, 406-543-6528
- Missoulian Angler, 420 N. Higgins Ave., Missoula, MT, 406-728-7766

Camping
- There is unlimited camping on National Forest lands that surround the river. There are also a number of Forest Service campgrounds along the river, including Norton, Sawmill, the Dalles, Harry's Flat and Bitterroot Flat. Private cabin rentals also available. Try Elkhorn Guest Ranch, 406-825-3220, or Rock Creek Fish Tale Resort, 406-721-1880 or 406-825-4054.

ROCK CREEK MAJOR HATCHES

Insect	J	F	M	A	M	J	J	A	S	O	N	D	Flies
Salmonfly *Pteronarcys californica*					█								Seducer #4-8; Stimulator #4-3; Bitch Creek Nymph #4-8; Kaufmann's Stone #2-6; Brook's Stone #2-6
Golden Stone *Hesperoperla pacifica*						█							Whitlock's Golden Stone Nymph #4-8; Montana Nymph #4-8; Betts' Brown Stone #4-8; Whitlock's Revised Golden Stone #4-8
Baetis				█						█			Olive Cripple #16-20; Parachute Adams #16-20; Sparkle Dun #16-20; Hare's Ear Nymph #16-20; Pheasant Tail Nymph #16-20; Poxyback Baetis #16-20
Caddis						█	█						Elk Hair Caddis #14-18; Diving Caddis #14-16; X-Caddis #14-16; Drifting Cased Caddis #14-18; Emergent Sparkle Pupa #12-18; Deep Sparkle Pupa #12-18; Electric Caddis #14-16; Caddis Variant #14-16; Orange Serendipity #6-12
March Brown Drake			█	█									Sparkle Dun #14-16; Sparkle Spinner #14-16; Pheasant Tail Nymph #12-16; March Brown Drake #14-16
Skwala Stonefly			█	█									Bullethead Skwala #6-8; Olive Stimulator #6-8; Rubberleg Brown Stone #6-8
Pale Morning Dun						█	█	█					Sparkle Dun #14-20; Parachute Adams #14-20; PMD Cripple #16-20; Poxy Biot Nymph #16-20; Lawson's Thorax Dun #16-20; Lempke's Extended Body PMD #16-18; Hare's Ear Nymph #16-18; Pheasant Tail Nymph #16-18; CDC Floating Nymph #16-18; Half Back Emerger #16-18
Midges	█	█	█	█	█	█	█	█	█	█	█	█	Griffith's Gnat #16-20; Parachute Adams #18-22; Pheasant Tail Nymph #16-22
Grasshopper								█	█				Joe's Hopper #6-10; Dave's Hopper #6-10

BITTERROOT RIVER

The river had me where I didn't want to be. My bow was three feet from oblivion, being sucked into a wicked logjam by the Bitterroot River's deceptively powerful late spring flows.

My two terrified guide clients were silent, their fingers coiled in death-grips around their Sage rods. I detected fear and offered, "Oh shit, hold on!"

I ripped my right oar through the current, a well-timed maneuver that allowed the perpetuation of our hatch-chasing affliction. We breathed a collective sigh of relief as the Achilles' stern swung downstream and skirted disaster.

My elderly client called it a near-death experience. I told him, "it would not have been a bad place to die; now hit that nice riser two feet off the left bank." No need to dwell on the obvious.

If you were to die on the banks of a river, western Montana's Bitterroot would be a good one to do it on.

Of the Western valleys I have known—and I've lived in many of them, including Jackson Hole, Wyoming; Sun Valley, Idaho; and Montana's Gallatin Valley—western Montana's Bitterroot Valley is quite possibly the prettiest.

Bordered by the impressive, sheer granite Bitterroot Mountains to the west and the pastel Sapphires to the east, this lush agricultural valley stakes claim to one of the most impressive vistas in Big Sky Country. Summer sunsets, which carve through the Bitterroot's long canyons illuminating the eastside green alfalfa fields and the Sapphires, are legendary—the type that find me on the front porch for a couple hours worth of gin and tonics at least a few evenings each year.

Still, the valley would not draw me in if it were not for its excellent trout fishing on the Bitterroot River, its east and west forks, and many small, private spring creeks.

Rated less productive as an ecosystem than Montana's more famous rivers, such as Rock Creek to the east and the Big Hole to the southeast, the Bitterroot maintains its fair share of faithful flyfishers who sample the river at its prime. On those occasions, every rainbow, cutthroat and brown trout seems to go out of its way to impale itself on your dry-fly hook. And we're talking about trout that commonly stretch 16 inches. Twenty-inch fish are not uncommon, although they are considerably more difficult to find.

The east fork of the Bitterroot begins east of Sula in the Anaconda-Pintler Wilderness, just a stone's throw from the Continental Divide. The west fork of the Bitterroot tumbles out of the mountains west of Conner near the Idaho/Montana border and the edge of the Frank Church River of No Return Wilderness. The west fork slows at Painted Rocks Reservoir but picks up pace again below the reservoir in its 14-mile dash to the confluence of the east fork.

Where the forks meet, just north of Conner, the Bitterroot River and 70 miles of prime, diverse, classic western trout water begin. One or another stretch should meet almost every flyfisher's criteria: pocketwater, braided channels, deep pools,

Bitterroot River
Missoula to Kootenai Creek

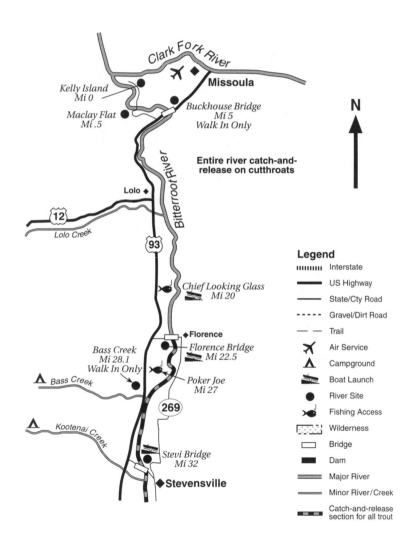

Kelly Island
Mi 0

Maclay Flat
Mi .5

Clark Fork River

Missoula

Buckhouse Bridge
Mi 5
Walk In Only

N

Entire river catch-and-
release on cutthroats

Bitterroot River

Lolo

12

Lolo Creek

93

Chief Looking Glass
Mi 20

Florence
Florence Bridge
Mi 22.5

Bass Creek
Mi 28.1
Walk In Only

Bass Creek

Poker Joe
Mi 27

269

Kootenai Creek

Stevi Bridge
Mi 32

Stevensville

Legend

ⅢⅢⅢ	Interstate
▬▬	US Highway
──	State/Cty Road
- - - -	Gravel/Dirt Road
— —	Trail
✈	Air Service
▲	Campground
🚤	Boat Launch
●	River Site
🐟	Fishing Access
▦	Wilderness
▭	Bridge
▬	Dam
═══	Major River
──	Minor River/Creek
▭▬▭	Catch-and-release section for all trout

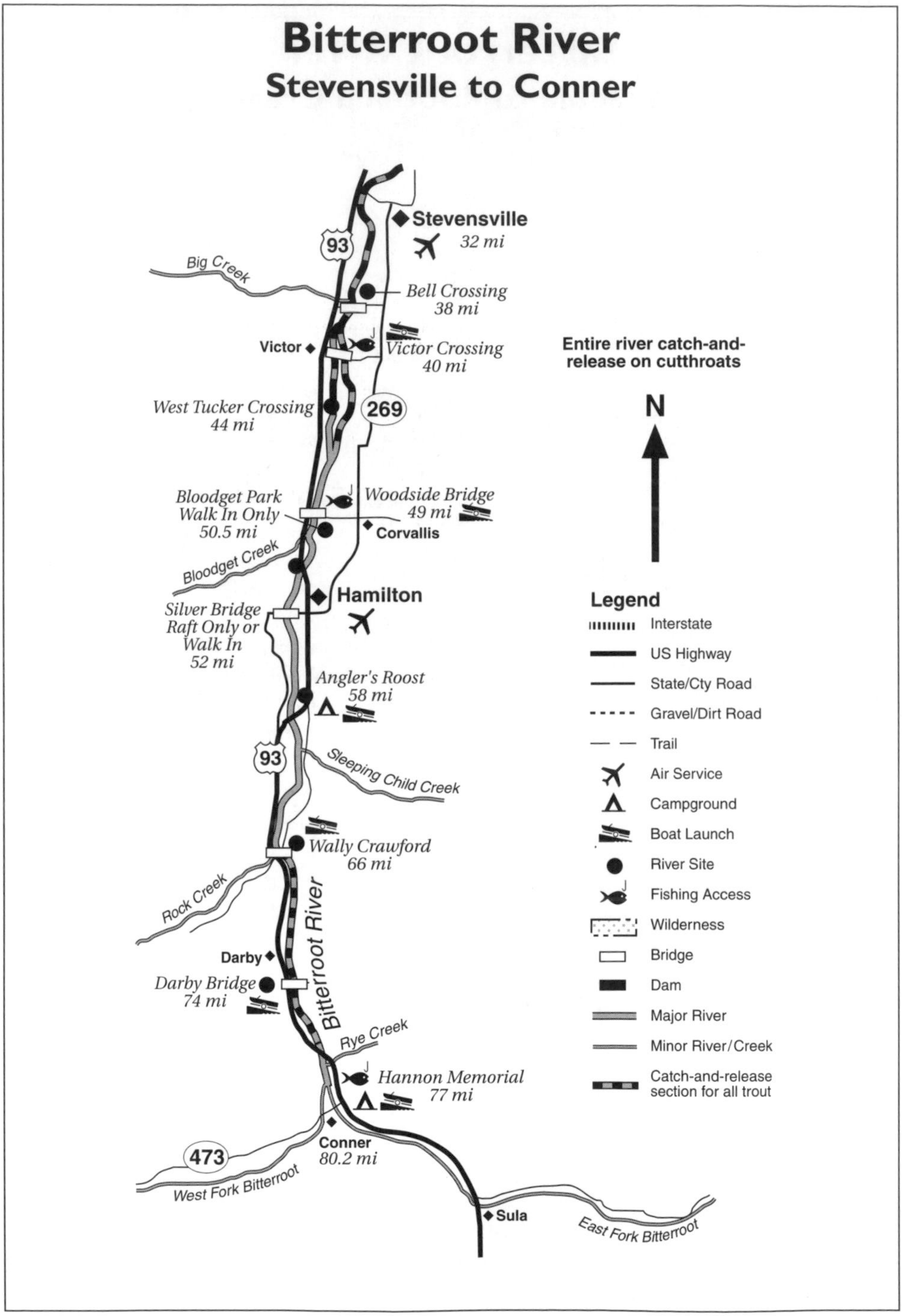

Bitterroot River
Stevensville to Conner

Big Creek

93

◆ **Stevensville**
✈ *32 mi*

Bell Crossing
38 mi

Victor ◆

Victor Crossing
40 mi

269

West Tucker Crossing
44 mi

Entire river catch-and-release on cutthroats

N

Bloodget Park
Walk In Only
50.5 mi

Woodside Bridge
49 mi

◆ **Corvallis**

Bloodget Creek

◆ **Hamilton**
✈

Silver Bridge
Raft Only or
Walk In
52 mi

Legend

⊪⊪⊪⊪	Interstate
▬▬▬	US Highway
───	State/Cty Road
- - - -	Gravel/Dirt Road
─ ─	Trail
✈	Air Service
⋀	Campground
⊨	Boat Launch
●	River Site
⊱	Fishing Access
▦	Wilderness
▭	Bridge
▬	Dam
	Major River
	Minor River/Creek
	Catch-and-release section for all trout

Angler's Roost
58 mi
⋀

93

Sleeping Child Creek

Wally Crawford
66 mi

Rock Creek

Bitterroot River

Darby ◆

Darby Bridge
74 mi

Rye Creek

⊱ *Hannon Memorial*
⋀ *77 mi*

◆ **Conner**
80.2 mi

473

West Fork Bitterroot

◆ **Sula**

East Fork Bitterroot

Skwala stoneflies emerge in March and April on the Bitterroot. They offer an excellent diversion for the winter blues. Here, the author displays an early-season 'bow taken on a rubber leg brown stonefly nymph.

long riffles and glassy glides. The Bitterroot ends where it meets the Clark Fork River, just west of Missoula at Kelly Island.

While the main river is where most flyfishers focus their attention, the east and west forks offer stimulating opportunities that should not be ignored, especially during the early summer salmonfly hatch, which can be feast or famine, depending on the nuances of Mother Nature and her choice to dump all of the Bitterroot Mountain's snowpack into the system at one time or prolong runoff over several weeks.

If the forks are in shape during the salmonfly hatch, which generally arrives in late May or early June, floaters pound the banks with large dries or size-4 stonefly nymphs. Wade fishers offer similar patterns, including Bitch Creek nymphs, while maintaining a grip on the bankside brush. Risking a cold dunking in the river is worth it for many flyfishers, especially those who call themselves "cutthroat connoisseurs." The reason: the west fork, in particular, has seen its population of native westslope cutthroat, some of them quite large, rise steadily since the implementation of special regulations. The west fork offers small cutts above Painted Rocks Reservoir; larger fish, including browns and rainbows, swim in the lower section. The reservoir itself offers little for the flyfisher.

"The Bitterroot's bright spot is definitely cutthroats," indicated Chris Clancy, a biologist for Montana Department of Fish, Wildlife and Parks. "We went to catch and release on cutthroats in 1990, and their numbers are increasing, especially on the upper river. A lot of those fish are in the West Fork above Darby and Conner."

While cutthroats are on the road to recovery, the Bitterroot's browns and rainbows just manage to hold their own.

According to Clancy, most browns are found in the upper river near Darby, where they average about 800 to 1,000 trout a mile. Rainbows account for nearly the same number in that stretch.

Below Hamilton, especially near Victor, trout numbers drop to 100 rainbows and just 75 browns a mile. Clancy suggests that low water and marginal habitat during summer irrigation season accounts for the drop.

At Stevensville, rainbow numbers rebound to about 300 a mile, due to groundwater recharges to the river. Brown trout numbers tail off at Stevensville; if you hook one on the lower river, feel very lucky.

At Chief Looking Glass, extending downstream to its confluence with the Clark Fork River, Clancy estimates about 350 rainbows a mile.

While those numbers do not hold up to more prolific rivers, such as the Big Hole and Bighorn, there are enough trout in the Bitterroot to keep an angler busy during its major hatches.

The most popular hatch on the Bitterroot, an emergence of skwala stoneflies, begins in March before the general season opens. Anglers who want to fish during the hatch can catch and release fish to their heart's content.

Because of the skwala hatch, the largest emergence of flyfishers occurs at the same time, generally between March 1 and April 30. Normally, the Bitterroot is uncrowded. Summertime can see its fair share of use, but angler hours tail off drastically by September. In October, a few dedicated flyfishers have the river to themselves. But don't plan on having the river to yourself during the skwala emergence. Flyfishers, drift boats and rafts congregate on the banks of the river like a plague when the hatch comes off. And you should not blame them. Winters are long in Montana. Too much time is spent indoors dreaming of bikini-clad bodies in Hawaii. When the skwala hatch arrives, spring fever begins in earnest.

Skwala stoneflies do not come off in droves like the more famous salmonflies. Instead, skwala may be encountered sporadically. As with almost all stoneflies, nymphs crawl out of the water. The dry-fly fishing begins when females return to the river to lay eggs. A few may be seen floating on the surface, and few, if any, in the air. But an inspection of the shoreline rocks should produce lots of big, olive nymphs. The Bitterroot's trout will key on those nymphs, but they can be taken on size 8 dries, as well.

For pre-runoff fishing, remember to wear long underwear, neoprene waders, fingerless gloves and plenty of warm shirts. A stocking hat will see some use, too.

The Bitterroot's side channels offer excellent fishing during late spring, early summer and again during fall. Here, the author hits a braid north of Corvallis.

Daytime temperatures may range from 25 to 60 degrees in western Montana, so be prepared for any weather.

Do not expect to be on the water all day, as you might during multiple hatches of the summer season. Early spring fishing on the Bitterroot means you will be casting flies only during the warmest hours. Generally, there is a productive three-to-five-hour period between 10:30 AM and 4 PM, and then you are off the river to thaw fingers and toes.

Despite the Bitterroot's popularity during the skwala hatch, you will not battle the 17-boat deep debacle you might find on, say, the Bighorn River during the summer season.

As with most large rivers, floating is the best way to fish the Bitterroot, and there are enough public access sites (see map) to allow easy access. Same holds true for wade anglers.

Here are a couple of my favorite floats: Angler's Roost (just south of Hamilton) to Silver Bridge (watch out for the diversion dam); Woodside Bridge (at Corvallis) to Bell Crossing; Conner (six miles south of Darby) to Como Bridge; and Fort Missoula to Kelly Island (mouth of the Clark Fork).

My recommendations for wade fishers are Hannon Memorial (three miles south of Darby), Woodside Bridge, Bell Crossing (two miles north of Victor), Poker Joe (four and a half miles south of Florence), and Fort Missoula (a few miles southwest of Missoula). All major access sites are clearly marked along Highway 93, which parallels the river from Missoula to the forks near Conner.

Sparse emergences of blue-winged olives and speckle-winged gray drakes follow the early stoneflies in mid-April. By mid-May, the Bitterroot and Sapphire Mountains' snowpack sails through the valley, which makes floating treacherous and fly-fishing the river an afterthought.

By mid-June, the river recedes and flyfishers find hungry trout rising to a variety of meals, including pale morning duns, golden stones, green and brown drakes and multiple caddis species—plenty of opportunity for the dry-fly aficionado.

"You can fish through June and July on the Bitterroot without having to tie on anything smaller than a size 10 dry fly," said Chuck Stranahan at Riverbend Flyfishing in Hamilton. "Attractor patterns will work fine, especially for beginners. Experienced guys who want to play games with large fish can get specific with patterns, but you don't have to."

During late May and June, flyfishers can focus their attention on pale morning duns and a variety of caddis species. PMDs emerge from 9 AM through late afternoon, and anglers should carry a variety of PMD patterns, varying in size and color. For the caddis, which bring fish up top early in the morning and again late in the afternoon, an elk hair works fine.

Some of the best fishing for large trout occurs during the green drake hatch, especially on overcast days. In 1994, the green drake emergence was particularly heavy, and anglers to this day recall the action with a sparkle in their eyes. Fish to 20-inches could be taken during every float. Fourteen- to 16-inchers impaled themselves on dry flies around every bend. However, in 1995 the hatch was sparse, although I managed to catch up with those bugs and some large trout a few times.

The dun stage of a green drake emergence is most important on the Bitterroot. Green drake duns have three tails, large gray wings and a body that may vary from olive to dark green to nearly brown.

Nymphs can take fish that are keying-in on green drakes, too. Those nymphs run about a size 8 or 10, with stocky bodies, three tails and pronounced legs.

Green drakes usually emerge between 10 AM and 4 PM, although you can catch hatches before or after those times, depending on the nuances of the weather. During heavy hatches, which generally occur on overcast days or during or after thundershowers, duns may be shunned for floating nymphs or stillborn, crippled drakes. Olive sparkle duns and Quigley cripples work well to mimic those stillborns or cripples.

"June is our wettest month in the valley," Stranahan said. "Light rain and occasional thundershowers are the norm. That's when the drake fishing is best. You can fish a variety of patterns, but a Quigley cripple seems to work as well as any pattern. You could fish one all day and never be required to change flies."

After the drake hatches subside, watch for a smaller mayfly that has a similar appearance to the Western green drake.

Drunella flavilinea, often called the little Western green drake, or simply a *flav*, makes its appearance on the Bitterroot anytime between mid-July and late August.

Timing of the hatch depends heavily on weather conditions. On sunny, warm days the hatch will come off late, around sunset or just after. On a rainy, cold day flavs

Jim Nave plays a Bitterroot rainbow below the Missoula suburbs. Is there a better in-town fishery than the Bitterroot through Missoula? Maybe not.

should emerge earlier, say 5 or 6 PM. The spinnerfall provides very consistent late evening action, too. The flav spinner is best matched with a size 14 clear wing spinner.

As is typical of all western Montana rivers, the Bitterroot provides excellent fishing with grasshopper patterns from mid-July through mid-September. And, of course, those anglers who pound the banks, plopping a hopper noisily on the surface, pick up the most and often the largest trout.

While hoppers should work fine on the main river, flyfishers may need to be a little more specific when fishing side channels and flatwater stretches, which occur more frequently the farther one travels downstream toward Missoula. Especially on the flatwater reaches of the lower river, long, light leaders, delicate presentations and stealthy wading affect success tremendously.

"I like to use parachute patterns on the flatwaters because they lie flush with the surface and mimic the actual insects best," Stranahan said. "This is a freestone stream with lots of riffles and runs, but there are long flat glides, and they need to be fished like a spring creek. The fish can be quite wary and very selective. They will not settle for anything less than a perfectly tied and subtly presented fly."

Long leaders and light tippets are required on the entire river during fall, just when the Bitterroot receives an explosive hatch of *Tricorythodes*, Baetis and mahogany dun mayflies. If there is any time to turn a Bitterroot River skeptic into a believer, this is it.

For an avid flycaster who can taper down to a 10-foot, 6X tippet and present a size 20 Trico or Baetis in front of a trout's snout—without ruffling the surface or lining the target—landing 15 or 20 fish in an afternoon is the norm.

Personally, I have always liked Trico mayfly hatches better than any other emergence, no matter what river I have plied. The Bitterroot's Trico hatch can be explosive and very productive, but it is the Baetis hatch that gets me drooling.

While living in Corvallis in 1995, I ventured down to the river with my two Labradors each fall afternoon, smug in the knowledge that I was about ready to slay!

Every day, on cue, the Baetis popped at noon. I could walk up and down the river, in any section, and pick out pods of rising fish. I worked size 18 and 20 CDC olives or parachute olives to them. Any drag-free drift over a trout's holding position brought a rise. September and October, more than any other time of the year, are the most predictable months on the Bitterroot.

In fact, I would suggest fall as the best time for visiting flyfishers. It's not the time for a family vacation, because the weather is cold in the morning and evenings, snow may fall from the sky, and holding a wet flyline in your hand is not too pleasant. But the fish are eager to rise, predictable and very healthy after gorging on the river's large insects all summer. Water conditions are ideal and they do not change rapidly as they might during spring and early summer.

While flyfishers catch mostly rainbows and cutthroats up top on Baetis patterns, mature brown trout get aggressive during fall, too. They can be taken near the bottom on big streamers and nymphs. But don't expect to catch a wall-hanger. There are large browns in the Bitterroot, but they are infrequently encountered.

"In our electrofishing during fall, we check about 2,000 fish," Chris Clancy said. "Normally, we see only a couple that would go five pounds or better. The largest one we saw last season (1995) was an eight-pound brown. We seldom see rainbows over 21 inches, although there are a few around. Especially for people who fish dry flies, the chance to land a large fish on the Bitterroot is limited. You have to get down to the bottom where they feed on large nymphs and minnows to get the big boys."

Advantages to fishing the Bitterroot, rather than some isolated stream, include accommodations located just a half-mile off the river's banks.

Excellent food, lodging, flies and nighttime entertainment can be found in Missoula, Stevensville, Victor, Corvallis, Hamilton and Darby.

Hamilton may be the ideal location to stay. From there you can hit the upper river, including the forks, or venture downstream to the flatwater sections without backtracking.

If you do lodge in Hamilton, try La Trattoria for excellent Italian food or The Banque for a variety of fine meals. Make sure to bring your own wine or beer to La Trattoria; they will pour it in a glass for you, but they do not sell wine, liquor or beer. At The Banque, venture upstairs after your meal to the bar. The scenery can be quite nice. For pitchers of beer and large-screen television, try Cedars Lounge at the south end of town. Bands play rock and country music each weekend and, again, the scenery is prime. For a family fill-er-up, try Bad Bubba's BBQ for burgers and ribs.

While the Bitterroot may not offer tremendous numbers of large fish, it holds deep pools and classic runs, which are beautiful enough to tempt anybody's imagination. With an increasing population of native cutthroats and scenery that rivals any Western river, the Bitterroot should be on any flyfisher's hit list.

Stream Facts: Bitterroot River

Seasons
- Third Saturday in May through November 30. Extended whitefish/catch and release trout December 1 through third Saturday in May.

Special Regulations
- Mainstem Bitterroot and East Fork to mouth of Martin Creek and West Fork upstream to Painted Rocks Reservoir: *Cutthroat trout*—catch and release only; *Limit:* Three rainbow or brown trout alone or in any combination with only one over 14 inches.
- From Tucker Crossing to Florence Bridge and one mile downstream from Darby to Como Bridge: Catch and release only, all year. Artificial flies and lures only.

Trout
- Westslope cutthroat from 10 to 20 inches
- Brown trout from 12 to 24 inches
- Rainbow trout from 12 to 24 inches
- Bull trout from 16 to 25 inches
- Numerous whitefish

River Miles
- The river runs 80 miles from the confluence of the East and West Forks to its confluence with the Clark Fork River at Missoula.
- Missoula—0
- Lolo—10
- Florence—16
- Victor—38
- Hamilton—49
- Darby—74

River Flows
- The Bitterroot runs low and clear during fall, spring and winter. High flows occur between May 15 and July 4.

River Characteristics
- The Bitterroot is a medium-size stream in its upper reach above Hamilton. It measures about 20 yards wide near Hamilton. Below Hamilton to its confluence with the Clark Fork it measures about 30 yards wide. For its entire length the river runs between the Sapphire Mountains to the east and the Bitterroot Mountains to the west. It is one of the most scenic rivers in the West.

Fishing Access
• Private land surrounds much of the river, but there are excellent public access sites throughout the Bitterroot Valley that allow wade and boat anglers ample opportunity to reach the river.
• Maclay Bridge (Missoula), Buckhouse Bridge (Missoula), Chief Looking Glass (between Lolo and Florence), Florence Bridge (Florence), Poker Joe (between Florence and Stevensville), Bass Creek (between Florence and Stevensville), Stevensville Bridge (Stevensville), Bell Crossing (between Stevensville and Victor), Victor Crossing (Victor), West Tucker and East Tucker (between Victor and Corvallis), Woodside Bridge (Corvallis), Bloodget Park (between Corvallis and Hamilton), Silver Bridge (Hamilton), Main Street Bridge (Hamilton), Angler's Roost (just north of Hamilton), Como Bridge (south of Darby), Hannon Memorial (north of Darby).

Area Fly Shops
• The Kingfisher, 926 East Broadway, Missoula, MT, 888-542-4911
• Riffles and Runs, Highway 9,3 Corvallis, MT 59875, 406-961-4950
• Grizzly Hackle, 1108 N. 1st, Hamilton, MT, 406-363-4290
• Riverbend Flyfishing, N. Highway 93, Hamilton, MT, 406-363-4197
• Fishaus Tackle, 702 1st N. Hamilton, MT, 406-363-6158
• Angler's Roost, 815 Highway 93 south, Hamilton, MT, 406-363-1268
• Blackbirds Lodge and Fly Shop, 1754 Highway 93, Victor, MT, 406-642-6375
• Missoulian Angler, 420 N. Higgins Ave., Missoula, MT, 406-728-7766
• Grizzly Hackle, 215 W. Front St., Missoula, MT, 800-297-8996

Campgrounds
• There are plenty of public campgrounds on national forest lands throughout the Bitterroot Valley. Try the West Fork Bitterroot, Lick Creek Campground, Lake Como, Anglers Roost (south of Hamilton, with trailer hookups), or Bass Creek.

BITTERROOT RIVER MAJOR HATCHES

Insect	J	F	M	A	M	J	J	A	S	O	N	D	Flies
Grasshopper								▮	▮				Dave's Hopper #2-8; Meadow Hopper #2-8;
Skwala Stonefly		▮	▮										Bullethead Skwala #6-8; Olive Stimulator #6-8; Rubberleg Brown Stone #6-8
Gray Drake					▮								Parachute Adams #14-16; Sparkle Dun #14-16; Comparadun #14-16; Hare's Ear Nymph #14-16; Pheasant Tail Nymph #14-16
Midge	▮	▮	▮	▮	▮	▮	▮	▮	▮	▮	▮	▮	Griffith's Gnat #16-20; Parachute Adams #18-22; Pheasant Tail Nymph #16-22
Trico								▮					Parachute Adams #18-22; Parachute Trico #18-22; CDC Trico Biot #18-22; Sparkle Dun #18-22; Trico Spinner #18-22
Salmonfly *Pteronarcys califorrnica*						▮							Seducer #4-8; Stimulator #4-8; Bitch Creek Nymph #4-8; Kaufmann's Stone #2-6; Brook's Stone #2-6; Black Rubberlegs #2-8
Baetis					▮					▮			Olive Cripple #16-20; Parachute Adams #16-20; Sparkle Dun #16-20; Hare's Ear Nymph #16-20; Pheasant Tail Nymph #16-20; Poxyback Baetis #16-20

BITTERROOT RIVER MAJOR HATCHES

Insect	J	F	M	A	M	J	J	A	S	O	N	D	Flies
Golden Stone *Hesperoperla pacifica*							▮						Whitlock's Golden Stone Nymph #4-8; Montana Nymph #4-8; Betts' Brown Stone #4-8; Whitlock's Revised Golden Stone #4-8; Poxyback Biot Golden Stone #6-12
Caddis						▮			▮				Elk Hair Caddis #14-18; Diving Caddis #14-16; X-Caddis #14-16; Drifting Cased Caddis #14-18; Emergent Sparkle Pupa #12-18; Deep Sparkle Pupa #12-18; Electric Caddis #14-16; Caddis Variant #14-16
Pale Morning Dun							▮						Sparkle Dun #14-20; Parachute Adams #14-20; PMD Cripple #16-20; Poxy Biot Nymph #16-20; Lawson's Thorax Dun #16-20; Lempke's Extended Body PMD #16-18; Hare's Ear Nymph #16-18; Pheasant Tail Nymph #16-18; CDC Floating Nymph #16-18; Half Back Emerger #16-18
Mahogany Dun								▮					CDC Emergent Crippled Dun #14-16; Sparkle Dun Mahogany #14-16; CDC Spinner #14-16; Comparadun #14-16; Pheasant Tail Nymph #14-16; Floating Nymph #14-16
Green Drake/Little Western Green Drake							▮						Olive Sparkle Dun #10-16; Cripple #10-16; Green Drake Emerger #10-16; Comparadun #10-16; Hare's Ear Nymph #10-16

LOLO CREEK

During spring and early summer, Montana's large rivers can wreak temperamental torture on visiting flycasters.

Even when high flows drop and insect emergences come off full-swing, the river's residents can remain lockjawed on the bottom. Often, big names, such as the Clark Fork, Yellowstone and Bitterroot, seduce the flyfishing hordes, only to tell those greenhorns upon arrival, "A long winter has made me too darn tired to play! Now get on, little doggy!" Fortunately, the Bitterroot River offers a nice little tributary that can bail an angler out when bigger rivers are playing hard to get.

Lolo Creek, a 10- to 15-yard wide, intimate stream that twists its way off the Montana/Idaho border, offers plenty of small rainbow, cutthroat, brook and brown trout, some excellent hatches, and plenty of timbered mountain scenery.

Destructive, cut-and-run logging kills Montana's fisheries. Due to this clearcut, combined with many others, Lolo Creek runs muddy during spring and cannot reach its true potential as a trout fishery.

It's a popular stream with Missoula residents—and for good reason. The lower end of Lolo Creek lies just 15 miles south of Missoula. Highway 12 runs west from there, and the river is easily accessible. Plus, a few large fish frequent the system during spring and fall, when rainbows and brown trout of Bitterroot and Clark Fork origin, respectably, run up the tributary to spawn.

Lolo Creek is fishable shortly after runoff, which can vary from late May to early July. Typically, you can throw a line on the river by mid-June. Just don't tempt the creek's currents when it is high—I nearly lost my Labrador, Moose, when he was young and challenged by a hen mallard during high flows. Then I nearly lost my own life saving him.

When the creek starts fishing, look for a variety of mayflies like pale morning duns, March brown drakes, green drakes and even a few Baetis. Caddis are abundant, too.

Those bugs draw trout to the surface, and juvenile fish are not too picky about their table fare. I've found that standard attractors like a parachute Adams or an elk hair caddis will work fine. Specific patterns like a sparkle dun or X-caddis will take the wary, larger fish during appropriate stages of a hatch. But this is not the stream to play technical warfare with trout; instead Lolo Creek offers fun fishing, right off the highway for anglers of all experience levels. Take beginning flyfishers to Lolo Creek, and they'll have the opportunity to catch the grand slam: a rainbow, brown, cutthroat and whitefish on their first day astream.

Expect to catch 15 or 20 fish a day when the fishing is good; more trout are possible but should not be expected. Almost all of those trout will run between five and 10 inches; a 14-incher is a trophy. Only on occasion will a larger fish show up.

To reach Lolo Creek from Missoula, follow Highway 93 south. At Lolo, turn west on Highway 12. The highway parallels the creek for nearly 30 miles. Some sections are posted as private, others run through National Forest lands and offer easy access.

LOLO CREEK MAJOR HATCHES

Insect	J	F	M	A	M	J	J	A	S	O	N	D	Flies
Baetis			▓	▓	▓						▓		Olive Cripple #16-20; Parachute Adams #16-20; Sparkle Dun #16-20; Hare's Ear Nymph #16-20; Pheasant Tail Nymph #16-20; Poxyback Baetis #16-20
March Brown Drake				▓	▓								Sparkle Dun #14-16; Sparkle Spinner #14-16; Pheasant Tail Nymph #12-16
Caddis					▓	▓	▓	▓					Elk Hair Caddis #14-18; Diving Caddis #14-16; X-Caddis #14-16; Drifting Cased Caddis #14-18; Emergent Sparkle Pupa #12-18; Deep Sparkle Pupa #12-18; Electric Caddis #14-16; Caddis Variant #14-16
Pale Morning Dun						▓	▓	▓					Sparkle Dun #14-20; Parachute Adams #14-20; PMD Cripple #16-20; Poxy Biot Nymph #16-20; Lawson's Thorax Dun #16-20; Lempke's Extended Body PMD #16-18; Hare's Ear Nymph #16-18; Pheasant Tail Nymph #16-18; CDC Floating Nymph #16-18; Half Back Emerger #16-18
Salmonfly *Pteronarcys californica*					▓								Seducer #4-8; Stimulator #4-8; Bitch Creek Nymph #4-8; Kaufmann's Stone #2-6; Brook's Stone #2-6

Anaconda Settling Ponds

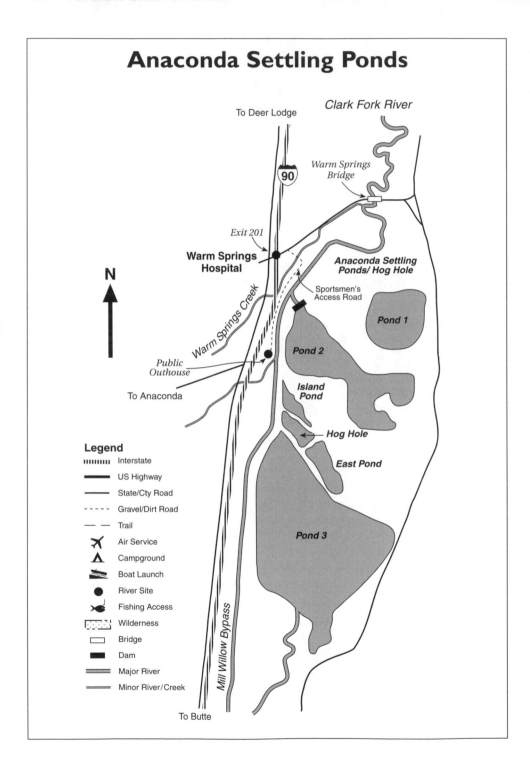

ANACONDA SETTLING PONDS: THE HOG HOLE

I followed the typical progression of a demented flyfishing junkie. At first, small and medium-size trout were just fine on bushy dry flies. Soon I yearned for a 20-incher or two on small nymphs and light tippet. What a rush, catching a trout I couldn't see. But even that was not quite enough.

Today, if I go very long without catching a true hog, I get the shakes. So I fish for them anywhere they can be found.

Call them what you want—major pounders, pigs, orcas, toads, meats—I am not afraid to throw all type of ugly creations at any hour of the day or night to score on a fish wearing one of those titles. So when I glanced at my Montana fishing regulations and saw that there actually exists a place called the Hog Hole, I realized immediately I would spend time, probably a lot of it, on that water.

The Hog Hole is just one small pond in a series of ponds and sloughs that are collectively called the Anaconda Settling Pond System. They rest smack-dab in the middle of the nation's largest Superfund Cleanup site, just west of Butte at Warm Springs.

Massive amounts of heavy metals from mining operations in Butte and Anaconda earlier this century were flushed straight into the upper Clark Fork River. They still do today but not in the amounts they used to (the river used to run red, all the way to Missoula on occasion). Much of the progress in water quality can be attributed to the Settling Ponds. Toxins, including zinc, arsenic and copper, flow into the ponds where much of that waste sinks to the bottom.

Surprisingly, aquatic vegetation grows readily in the ponds. And where there is dense aquatic vegetation there exist heavy populations of aquatic insects. And where there are lots of aquatic insects (you're catching on, aren't you?), there are generally a lot of big trout. That is the case at the ponds. And the Hog Hole may have the densest insect populations and the most fish.

Because many others share my large-trout affliction, the Hog Hole is the most popular among the ponds. However, fast-paced flyfishing it is not. And for scenic splendor, it leaves a lot to be desired. It more resembles a lunar landscape than a setting you might see pictured on a glossy Montana travel brochure. Still, I would take a shack near the banks of the Hog Hole before I would immerse myself in a big city, even if I was forced to buy bottled water at the grocery store for fear of swallowing tainted mine scum.

It was not until the early 1980s that a small hit-group of flyfishers spearheaded an assault on the Settling Pond's population of large trout. Most flyfishers just didn't believe trout could live in that mess. Browns up to 14 pounds and rainbows over 10 pounds were taken before other anglers caught on to the secret.

There are still some huge fish to be had, but they are not pushovers. Patience and persistence are virtues if a flyfisher wants to hook a fish in one of the ponds. That massive insect population is the double-edged sword that makes these trout such a challenge to catch. There is simply too much food available. Casting tiny midges here is similar to false-casting mosquito patterns for flying bats and swallows.

When it opens, the Hog Hole provides one of Montana's best bets for trophy trout. Big rainbows and browns slurp diminutive patterns like midge larva and scuds when they are not chowing four-inch leeches.

"There are some very large fish in those ponds," says Wayne Hadley at Montana Fish, Wildlife and Parks. "I'd say the average size is about 2.5 pounds, but there are some fish that reach double-digit weights. Casual fishermen won't catch those trout, and even good fishermen shouldn't be ashamed to get skunked. I'd say a couple of fish is a pretty good day."

A couple of fish a day would be monumental for me. My success at the Hog Hole has been limited. The place seems to hold a curse for me.

During an initial trip, my single air chamber floattube blew out in mid-Hog Hole. Kicking like a madman, taking gulps of water over the back of my waders, I barely managed shore.

I ventured back a year later with a friend. We planned to fish the Hog Hole at midnight of opening day. When we arrived, the main access road was closed. We tried hiking in to the Hog Hole, wearing neoprene waders with floattubes laced to our backs. Five miles later, drenched in sweat on a moonless night, we finally found the Hole.

Just after we geared up, the wind grew in ferocity, frothing the water into whitecaps. Inside my waders I believe frost was building. My friend was even less happy, especially when our olfactories went on high alert. Our chosen spot to wait out the blow was a sucker graveyard. Hundreds of rotting suckers were strewn around shore —probably the work of sadistic raccoons or just part of my curse. Snowflakes began falling from the sky.

I visited the Hog Hole again, after a three-year hiatus. The plan was to fish at midnight when those big browns probably attack every mouse or vole pattern stripped across the surface.

Unfortunately, the temperature registered 33 degrees and the action was not fast enough to keep me warm. In fact, there was no action to speak of.

A few anglers from Missoula toughed out the weather longer than me. I talked to them in the morning—they had not touched a fish. At least I am not alone in my plight.

"I suggest being patient and persistent when fishing those ponds, especially Pond 3," Hadley suggested (Wayne, you mean it could be slower than the Hog Hole?). "I know guys who fish that pond successfully, but they tell me the catch rate is lower than on the Hog Hole. There is a lot of food in all the ponds and that is why we see such good growth rates. But, throwing flies to those fish is just like being fed a slice of bologna after eating a prime rib dinner!"

One person who has experienced success at the ponds is John Oswald who works at Fish-On Fly and Tackle in Butte. He insists that those trout can be caught.

"I think it is a fun place to fish and you have the chance to take some really large trout," Oswald said. "We used to say an eight to 15-fish day was good on the ponds, but I think the average has dropped off some. Still, it holds huge fish; the largest rainbow I took was eight pounds and I caught a brown that was just under that. The largest fish I've seen taken was a 12-pound rainbow."

Major hatches in all of the ponds, which are strictly catch and release, include Callibaetis, damselflies, caddis and midges. There are also huge numbers of scuds, leeches and snails.

For the Callibaetis hatch, Oswald suggests a size 14 flashback nymph or a Callibaetis cripple.

"Those nymphs and emergers work far better than dries," Oswald added.

For the damselflies, which emerge between the May 25 opener and June 1 each year, Oswald suggests a size 10 marabou damsel.

"My personal preference is to fish that pattern very slow, just creeping along," he said. "I don't think you can fish a damsel nymph slow enough. You see guys stripping those patterns like mad, but I think a slow retrieve is best."

The big brown trout in Pond 3 get particularly active when the damsels come off. Browns up to 18 pounds have been taken from the pond and you might catch a fish with similar dimensions chasing damsel nymphs into shallow water.

"When the damsels are moving those fish move out of the deep water and slurp along the banks," Oswald said. "A lot of the time they work most actively in the evenings. I just cruise along in my floattube, watching for rises and working those banks."

Leech patterns also draw strikes and a size 2 or 4 brown mohair leech is always a good choice.

"You can't believe the number and size of the leeches in here," Oswald warned. "It's amazing; they look like water snakes."

Watch for strong caddis emergences late in the day, often just before dark. Oswald says most of the caddis are dark brown or even black. They rate about a size 14.

Scuds are also an important food item, and a variety of colors and sizes will work. The two patterns Oswald fishes most are the gray and olive scuds in sizes 14 and 16.

Pond 3, in particular, is best fished from a floattube or canoe. The banks drop off steeply, and it can be difficult to reach fish from shore. However, on the Hog Hole and other ponds, you may want to leave the floattube behind.

"One of the secrets to fishing those ponds is to stalk individual fish that you spot from shore," Oswald said. "A lot of guys get out in floattubes and fish blind. They just drag a woolly bugger around for half the day. I like to just look for fish, try to figure out what they are eating, and then throw something out in front of them."

Of course, sight-fishing can be ruined when the wind pops up late in the morning, extending through the afternoon. The best conditions bring no wind and an overcast sky. Bright days, in Oswald's opinion, are a "waste of time." The big trout will bury their snouts in the weeds, and you won't see any action until the sun goes down.

Floating lines will work best at the Settling Ponds, with the exception being Pond 3. For Pond 3, a sinktip or a high-density, fullsink line will allow a flyfisher to drop a streamer or damsel down in the depths.

If you choose to fish the Hog Hole or one of the other ponds, take the Warm Springs exit and turn left under the Interstate. Follow the road for 100 yards and turn right. Follow that dirt access road to its end. Then ford the Mill-Willow bypass to the ponds.

Special regulations apply to these waters. The Hog Hole opens May 25, and it will remain open through June 30. It reopens August 15 through September 30. Pond 3 also opens on May 25, and it remains open through September 30. All other ponds and canals are open August 15 through September 30. Best fishing occurs early and late in the season. Summer brings high water temperature and less feeding activity.

If you visit the ponds, arrive armed with a sturdy fly rod, plenty of patience and pray that a curse doesn't affect your success. And whatever you do, don't lie in a pile of rotting suckers. Three years after that rotting sucker debacle, my waders still smell!

You can camp near the ponds in primitive parking areas. Bring your own water to drink!

ANACONDA SETTLING PONDS MAJOR HATCHES

Insect	J	F	M	A	M	J	J	A	S	O	N	D	Flies
Leech													Rabbit Strip Leech (olive, black, brown) #2-6; Mohair Leech #2-8; Marabou Leech #4-8; Woolly Bugger #2-8
Callibaetis													Callibaetis Cripple #14-16; Sparkle Spinner #14-16; Sparkle Dun #14-16; Parachute Adams #14-16; Hare's Ear #14-16
Midge													Parachute Adams #16-20; Glass Bead Midge #16-20; Midge Emerger #16-20; Hatching Midge #16-20; Midge Larvae #16-20
Damselfly													Marabou Damsel #10-12; Six Pack #10-12; Swimming Damsel #8-12
Caddis													Elk Hair Caddis #14-16; Caddis Variant #14-16; Hemingway Caddis #12-16; Emergent Sparkle Pupa #14-16; Deep Sparkle Pupa #14-16; X-Caddis #14-16

Gold Creek Ponds

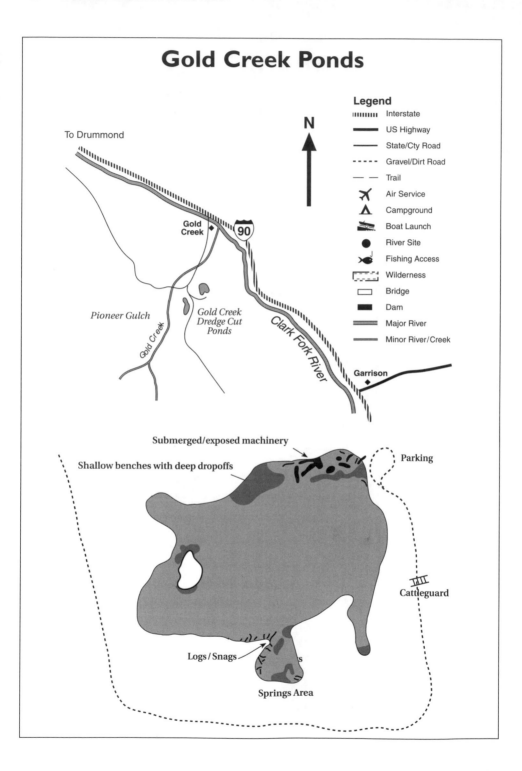

Legend

Interstate		
US Highway		
State/Cty Road		
Gravel/Dirt Road		
Trail		
Air Service		
Campground		
Boat Launch		
River Site		
Fishing Access		
Wilderness		
Bridge		
Dam		
Major River		
Minor River/Creek		

N

To Drummond

Gold Creek

90

Pioneer Gulch

Gold Creek

Gold Creek Dredge Cut Ponds

Clark Fork River

Garrison

Submerged/exposed machinery

Shallow benches with deep dropoffs

Parking

Cattleguard

Logs / Snags

Springs Area

GOLD CREEK PONDS

At first glance, these ponds resemble another industrial debacle—a far cry from what you might find in glossy travel brochures. A heap of rusting equipment lies restless and half-submerged in one of those flooded trenches cut into the flat, low-brush valley. Nearby, piles of sterile, oversized rocks climb toward the sky, in places suppressing the surrounding scenery, which includes a bona fide peek into Deer Lodge National Forest.

When approaching the ponds, through a sea of bottomless mud gumbo if you arrive after a recent spring rain, you might consider, "what the hell are those? where's the map?" After closer inspection, you might realize that the ponds and abandoned equipment offer lots of deep, quality trout habitat for growing large fish.

That impression is accurate. One year an ice-fisherman hauled out an 18-pound brown. Trout to several pounds are commonly sighted cruising the shoreline and, less frequently, landed. Remember, the larger fish are mostly brown trout that do not come to the net readily, especially when hooked near downed, woody debris or razor-edged metal equipment.

While browns hold to deep dropoffs, underneath logs, brush and old machinery, the ponds' cutthroat and rainbow trout cruise throughout the lake, often rising to the surface during hatches. If you hit the ponds on the right day, numerous fish will be greedily gobbling bugs off the surface. I found that situation one mild May afternoon. Callibaetis mayfly duns rode the wind-riffled surface, and the trout were on them.

I was accompanied by a friend, Sarah Hoskins, who was just cutting her flyfishing teeth. I wanted her to tie into a few fish, so she set out in my floattube with a Scientific Angler floating line and a size 16 Callibaetis nymph trailing behind. In short time she was fast into a small rainbow that had recently been stocked. Then she caught and released another. Then another and then another. Content, I mused.

At that point, I struck out along the shore toward the equipment and whipped my fast-sink line out among the ruins. Promptly, a big brown, maybe a four-pounder, raced out from its lie and smacked my olive woolhead sculpin. The fish went airborne, then dove deep and sliced my leader off on an edge of rusted metal. Sarah kicked by in the tube and offered, "Hey, you're supposed to land those." That's the true beauty of these ponds; Sarah was never outside of earshot, and I could offer instructions while she learned. And I was perfectly content on shore. In fact, a shore fisher can catch just as many fish as a floattuber.

However, to catch the big browns, a floattuber or a flyfisher limited to the shore should concentrate on the deep dropoffs (in some places the banks drop down 30 feet), the submerged equipment area, or the springs area (a small cove located on the southwest side). A shorebound angler should pay particular attention to the spring-fed cove. Big browns and some larger cutthroats frequent that area, and on a windless day, an angler can sight the fish, sneak close, and try to present a proper fly (generally small) without spooking the quarry.

However, the fish are extremely wary. I have seen them shy away from a fly, when it seemed they were prepared to grub, because of a heavy tippet. Tippets of 5X or even 6X may be needed. Then, once you hook a fish, the real challenge begins.

Big brown trout frequent the spring creek-like conditions on the south side of Gold Creek ponds. Tiny patterns like midge larvae, hare's ears and pheasant tail nymphs are required. The author fooled this pretty brown on a black pheasant tail.

Once, I hooked a big five-pound plus brown in the springs area. The fish inhaled a black hare's ear and dove for a log. I wrenched that brown back toward the surface. That's when it went skyward and landed in a snarl of downed branches. Of course, the fish broke me off, which demonstrates the difficulty of the ponds. It's downright hard to catch a large fish. However, the smaller fish are pushovers.

What the ponds lack in aesthetics, they more than make up for in ample bank access and opportunities for beginning flyfishers to learn while catching fish. For advanced flyfishers, its large brown trout are a huge draw.

While most of the large fish can be taken on streamers, there are some decent hatches to consider. Midges hatch all year long, and then a solid Callibaetis hatch begins in May. Rainbows and cutthroats can really come up top for Callibaetis duns. Most of the browns will stick to the nymphs underneath.

A few caddis will skip across the surface or hover around the bank brush during summer. Standard patterns like the deep sparkle pupa or the LaFontaine emergent caddis will take fish. Elk hair caddis can sometimes tempt a trout to the surface, too.

To reach the ponds, take the Gold Creek exit about 15 miles east of Drummond (fishing licenses are available at the Exxon in Drummond). Turn right off the exit , follow the dirt road seven miles, then follow the left fork. The ponds are first visible to the left. There are no maintained campsites, but there is ample room to park a trailer or set up a tent. Just don't be surprised if a few wayward cows cruise through in the night.

GOLD CREEK PONDS MAJOR HATCHES

Insect	J	F	M	A	M	J	J	A	S	O	N	D	Flies
Callibaetis					▮	▮							Callibaetis Cripple #14-16; Sparkle Spinner #14-16; Sparkle Dun #14-16; Parachute Adams #14-16; Hare's Ear #14-16
Midges		▮	▮	▮	▮	▮	▮	▮	▮	▮	▮		Parachute Adams #16-20; Glass Bead Midge #16-20; Midge Emerger #16-20; Hatching Midge #16-20; Midge Larvae #16-20
Damselfly						▮	▮	▮					Marabou Damsel #10-12; Six Pack #10-12; Swimming Damsel #8-12
Caddis					▮	▮	▮	▮	▮				Elk Hair Caddis #14-16; Caddis Variant #14-16; Hemingway Caddis #12-16; Emergent Sparkle Pupa #14-16; Deep Sparkle Pupa #14-16

Blackfoot River

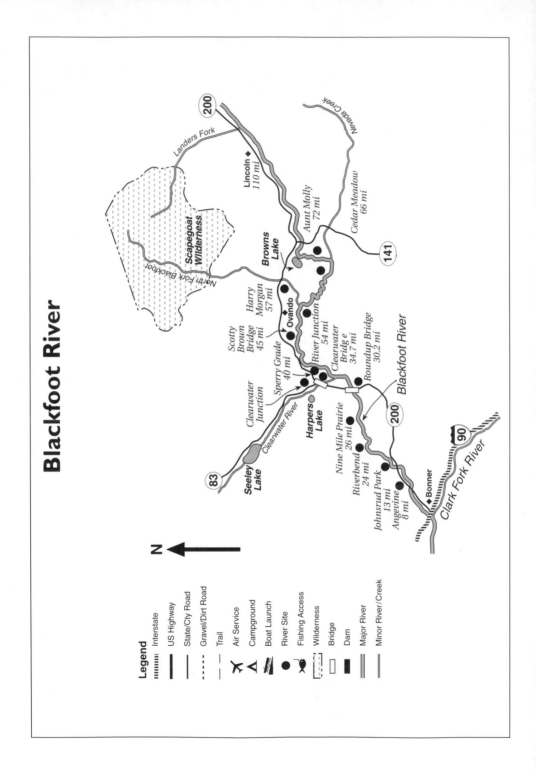

BLACKFOOT RIVER

You can get so damn frustrated covering environmental issues on Western rivers that, over time, it becomes a question of when, not whether, to get out the double-barrel shotgun and lay waste to the enemy.

I am feeling very much that way about the Blackfoot River, but who should I blame? Executives of the mining companies that stand to plunder the river, fill their pockets, and leave behind an environmental nightmare? Or should I blast the creators of the 1872 mining law? Can't do that, they're already dead. Maybe I should take out the Montana governor who was arrogant enough to oppose listing the bull trout on the Endangered Species List, which would have effectively curtailed much mining and logging in this great, yet severely raped, state.

Instead of protecting the Blackfoot River, the governor allowed legal steps for a massive mine at the headwaters of the river to keep plowing ahead full bore.

Maybe if I could show the governor the Blackfoot on a good day, when the salmon-flies hover over the river in dense clouds and the fish rise greedily to dry flies, maybe then he might say, "My pocket is full and this river is worth saving." Am I only dreaming?

The Blackfoot is a gorgeous, 130-mile long western Montana river that gained national fame when Norman McLean's book, *A River Runs Through It*, was released as a big-screen movie in 1992.

Immediately, the Blackfoot became a focus around the United States, even across the world. At that time, the environmental group, American Rivers, placed the Blackfoot on its 10 most endangered rivers list. Unfortunately, it deserves to be there.

Despite threats, the river maintains an excellent fishery for native cutthroat and bull trout and the introduced species, browns and rainbows.

Since 1990, when catch-and-release regulations for cutthroat and bull trout and a slot limit (none over 12 inches) for browns and rainbows was implemented, the river has produced larger fish with many trout measuring 18 to 20 inches. During the early spring season, fish exceeding 20 inches, mostly browns, are caught regularly.

During some of its better hatches, and it has a lot of good emergences, the Blackfoot fishes as well as any western Montana river, and you can't beat it for scenery.

"It's the most perfect, classic trout water in the state," says Mike Hillygus of High Plains Drifter in Missoula. "All the sections are beautiful, and the only difference between them is one runs next to the highway and the others do not. I never really recommend a certain time for people to visit. I just tell them to get here when they can; it's almost always good fishing."

The Blackfoot begins in the high, timbered mountains near Rogers Pass and the Continental Divide. From there it flows southwest toward Missoula. Highway 200 follows the river for most of its lower length, offering easy access.

From its headwaters to Lincoln, the river is unproductive due to a silt-ladened streambed and plenty of slack water. Below Lincoln, extending to Cedar Meadow, the river continues its winding, slow pace, and fishing remains marginal, although there are a few good browns hidden under the logs, brush and undercut banks. Fishing

The Blackfoot is one of Montana's prettiest rivers. However, a massive cyanide heap-leach mine at its headwaters may kill flyfishing opportunities soon.

through that heavily-timbered section may bring encounters with white-tailed deer, moose, black bears, mule deer and elk.

Where the North Fork Blackfoot dumps in near Ovando, the mainstem Blackfoot enters a broad plain, becoming a much faster river where trout habitat and populations increase.

In its middle section, the Blackfoot glides through endless boulder fields that create some serious rapids. Trout will hold behind any boulder or obstruction they can find, trying to stay out of the fast flows. Flyfishers must deftly cast flies to that microhabitat while screaming by in a raft or, tougher yet, while wade fishing. Above the river, habitat runs the gamut: sagebrush covered hills, stands of thick lodgepole pine and colorful rock cliffs.

In its lower section, the Blackfoot curls around the north end of the Garnet Mountain Range, cutting between rock walls and timbered slopes. In that section, flyfishers will find all types of water. There are deep runs, boulder pockets, major riffles and some flatwater slow stretches—all excellent trout water. The fact that the Black-foot offers first-rate flyfishing for 60 miles is no small feat. Montana Department of Fish, Wildlife and Parks biologists deserve much of the credit.

During the 1980s, the river suffered from overfishing and liberal limits. It also was subjected to habitat degradation and sedimentation problems caused by poor land-use practices, including accelerated logging, road construction and overgrazing by livestock. Also, the water was polluted and habitat fouled by mining in the head-waters. Naturally occurring low flows compounded the problems. Under these cumulative conditions, the Blackfoot's fishery was foundering.

However, in the early and mid-1990s, FWP was involved in 19 fisheries-related rehabilitation and enhancement projects of varying sizes. More than 100 miles of the Blackfoot's mainstem tributaries were reopened to spawning and fish passage. Now the Blackfoot again provides a viable fishery that is getting better each day with large trout making up a good portion of its specimens.

On a good day, the Blackfoot can put a dozen or more solid trout in the net. During a major hatch, when everything seems to go right and the fish are up top gorging, 60-fish days are not unheard of.

Those fish, mostly brown, brook, and cutthroat trout on the upper end and a mix of rainbows and browns on the middle and lower river, will rise eagerly from April through October for a variety of flies, including mayfly morsels, stonefly feasts and caddis cuisine.

Flyfishing begins for local casters in late March and April, before high flows take back the river. Unfortunately, during that time, a flyfisher must battle Montana's weather. Long underwear, wool gloves, stocking caps, a thermos of coffee or hot chocolate, and plenty of extra socks make a day on the river barely tolerable.

But for the flyfisher who can take the weather, there are plenty of big browns up against the banks or behind midstream obstructions and a woolly bugger or zonker will draw strikes. Some of those fish may run to four or five pounds.

Those fish may key on the movement of skwala stonefly nymphs, which make their annual pilgrimage to shore between March 15 and the end of April. Stimulator patterns draw fish to the surface on occasion, but those streamers or size 8 skwala nymphs produce most frequently.

"Especially toward the end of April, you will see some skwala activity, and we also get a good hatch of March browns (*Rythrogena morrisoni*)," Hillygus said. "You don't see many skwalas, but the fish are definitely eating them. You can throw skwala nymphs beneath the surface or stimulators up top and they'll nail them. Really, at that time of the year they will eat any olive streamer. For the March brown drakes, you can swing mayfly nymphs effectively."

Through April, extending into May, Blackfoot River flyfishers should also encounter Baetis hatches on the warm days. Any time the air temperature rises above 40 degrees, expect some action. Size 16 CDC Baetis or olive parachutes work well.

High water generally arrives in mid-May and puts a damper on a flyfisher's chances to catch trout. Essentially, the Blackfoot becomes unfishable, resembling chocolate milk with a mass of floating logs and ugly debris bouncing downstream. Unfortunately, the salmonfly hatch, which can be quite intense, often comes off during high water. However, if the river clears even slightly, offering at least a foot of visibility, float fishers can pound the banks with size 4 black stonefly nymphs and find success. Often, fishing the upper river near Scotty Brown Bridge during the last week of the hatch brings the best action. By June 10 the water usually drops a little and clears, especially on the middle and upper river, and fishing big salmonfly patterns can be quite good.

"It's always a crapshoot with the salmonflies," Hillygus said. "Really, you can see salmonflies anytime in June, and usually there will be some point where the water conditions are good enough to have a crack at the fish."

At times the Blackfoot can be a bust throughout its entire length due to high, muddy water. If that is the case, flyfishers may want to concentrate on the mouth of the Clearwater River, which true to its namesake, runs clear while the Blackfoot is unfishable. Some large bull trout and a good number of rainbows and browns stack up at the mouth of the Clearwater where they can breathe.

Caddis hatches, especially *Brachycentrus*, can be dense on the Clearwater during the early season. If conditions are decent on the Blackfoot, those flies will be present there, too. Flyfishers should throw elk hair caddis and caddis pupa when the hatch is on. During lulls, try buggers in the deep, dark slots behind boulders.

Caddis, especially *Hydropsyche*, are also present in dense numbers along the Blackfoot all summer. Because of the river's nature as a fast, riffled stream, buoyant patterns like elk hair caddis, stimulators and Goddard caddis—patterns that ride high—seem to draw the most strikes. Caddis pupa fished six or eight inches under a dry-fly indicator are also effective.

Attractor patterns work well on the Blackfoot during all seasons, too. Just bounce a royal Wulff, parachute Adams, humpy or trude through any of the splashy riffles and you are bound to draw strikes, even during midday.

One hatch that is not very well known, but is well worth looking for, is the green drake emergence (*Drunella grandis*). According to Hillygus, the trout go nuts when the hatch comes off. During low flow years, flyfishers may see it the first week of June. When the water is up, it won't be present until the end of June.

"It can be incredible," he said. "When it comes off, just quit what you're doing and tie on a big fatty mayfly pattern. I like to float a big dun pattern best. An extended body fly is the ticket. Lawson's extended body, parachute Adams or big Quigley cripples work well, too."

If the drakes aren't coming off, try a big stimulator against the banks. From June 1 through July, golden stoneflies are present in good numbers along the Blackfoot. But don't expect to see many of the bugs.

"They will be out, but you won't see them," Hillygus said. "All you have to do is believe they are there and cast stimulators."

Grasshoppers are important food items during late summer. Pounded up against the banks, or even fished through the midriver runs, a hopper will draw some large fish to the top. Joe's hoppers work as well as any pattern I've thrown.

Jenny Jo Snyder works a prime North Fork Blackfoot run in September. The North Fork offers big native cutthroat and bull trout from small waters. (Scott Brown Photo)

I remember one particularly large brown that rolled three times at my Joe's hopper and drifted along a riprap rock bank without imbedding the hook in its mouth. The fish probably stretched 23 inches and it may have weighed five pounds. Its snout, back and tail parted the water each time it rose, and each time I got too excited and yanked the morsel right out of its gaping mouth.

In August, the Blackfoot offers a marginal Trico mayfly hatch. Tiny size 20 and 22 black polywing spinner patterns, fished off light 5X and 6X tippet, draw strikes.

Tricos will accumulate in the mornings wherever there is slack water—big, slow pools behind large boulders, downed logs and in the foamlines. Pods of trout form and sip selectively on those tiny flies. Flyfishers must present a pattern with a dead-drift to score.

A very worthy side trip to the Blackfoot is a day on the North Fork Blackfoot. It is one of Montana's prettiest streams, and its water quality is excellent due to its emergence in the Scapegoat Wilderness north of Ovando.

The North Fork offers excellent but nonmaintained campsites along with plenty of native westslope cutthroats and a number of quite huge bull trout—five- to 10-pound fish are caught each year.

The North Fork is a good late summer bet. Its water drops by that time, and excellent caddis and mayfly emergences remain. Standard caddis patterns and general mayfly imitations like a parachute Adams in the proper size will fool the North Fork's fish. They are not tricky.

There are great camping areas and plenty of access to the mainstem Blackfoot, too. In fact, 30 miles of the river run through the Blackfoot recreation corridor, which provides flyfishers access to the river within the first 50 feet of land around it. The corridor runs from Scotty Brown Bridge downstream to Johnsrud Park.

Actually, the Blackfoot offers easy access and plenty of public land along most of its banks. However, floaters may want to avoid certain sections of the river.

Upstream from Lincoln, the Blackfoot is extremely narrow and provides little opportunity for floaters.

From Lincoln downstream 40 miles to Cedar Meadows, the river is characterized by slow water that meanders through some excellent scenery. There are some brown trout and cutthroats to be had, but there are logjams to negotiate and, during low water, lots of shallows to drag a boat, painstakingly, through.

From Cedar Meadows downstream to River Junction, about 11 miles, there is slightly better trout water and faster flows. It is a decent float as the water drops after runoff.

River Junction to Scotty Brown Bridge, about an 11-mile float, is excellent during the salmonfly hatch. Big bushy dries and black stonefly nymphs can produce nicely. The water is fast through that section, and inexperienced boaters may have trouble dodging boulders through the five-mile long Box Canyon. There is a dangerous set of rapids at the end of the canyon that may need to be portaged.

From Scotty Brown Bridge to Ninemile Prairie, about 18 miles, the river really picks up pace, and a flyfisher must make precise, quick casts to prime bankside habitat.

The first four miles of the float, to Russ Gates, is easy water, but from Russ Gates to Ninemile Prairie, only experienced rafters need apply.

From Ninemile to Johnsrud Park, about 12 miles, fishing can be excellent. The first six miles of the float are easy, but the last six require some quick navigating around boulders and a few formidable rapids.

From Johnsrud Park to the Bonner Weigh Station, the water is more like a lake. Anyone can maneuver a raft down that section. Fishing can be decent, especially when trout are rising.

Wherever you fish on the Blackfoot, Hillygus suggests keeping an open mind. River conditions and hatches can vary day by day, mile to mile.

"The best advice I can give someone is to be versatile and do not plan on fishing a dry fly the entire time," he said. "We all would like to fish dry flies all of the time, but that is not realistic here. Something I like to do is fish a big, slightly weighted muddler minnow just under the surface. I can see it out there, so it's almost like fishing a dry fly when you actually have a wet fly."

Hillygus also advises not to concentrate strictly on the banks of the river. Instead, cast to the center of the river if it looks good.

"Look for any variation in the water depth," he suggested. "Especially after high water, those trout will move back from the banks and relocate in any of the prime lies throughout the river."

No matter what section of the Blackfoot you want to fish, you can find a campsite near the river. But if you prefer a motel, there are a few options.

Missoula has plenty of hotels and motels that run the gamut in price and quality. You probably do not want to stay at one that offers a different color door for each room.

There is also a motel at Clearwater Junction, and there are motels at Lincoln.

Unfortunately, almost all of the information I've given you, especially facts about the insects and fish, may not hold true if a major mine proposal goes through on the Blackfoot.

That monstrosity would be located on private and state land about 11 miles east of Lincoln. Excavation of a mile-wide, 1,200-foot deep pit would occur. Gold would be extracted from the ore by a cyanide heap-leach process, which has a history of failure.

The mine poses an enormous threat to the Blackfoot River, its native and non-native trout species, and the perpetuation of one of the West's most scenic and productive trout waters. If the mining operation goes through, take all of my advice with a grain of salt. Your guess is as good as mine as to how the mine will affect fly-fishing. Judging by what the Berkeley Pit did to the nearby Clark Fork River, the impact of this mine will not be good—devastating would be more accurate. Until that time, enjoy the Blackfoot thoroughly.

Stream Facts: Blackfoot River

Seasons
- Mainstem and all tributaries open third Saturday in May through November 30. Extended whitefish and catch-and-release season for trout runs November 30 through third Saturday in May.
- NOTE: North Fork Blackfoot is catch and release only for cutthroat downstream from wilderness boundary.

Trout
- Brown, bull, rainbow and cutthroat trout. The mainstem is primarily a brown trout stream with some rainbows thrown in on the side. The North Fork shows good numbers of cutthroats and rainbows. Some monster bull trout can be found throughout the drainage.

River Miles
- Clark Fork/Blackfoot confluence at Bonner—0
- Marco Flat—4
- Angevine—8
- Johnsrud Park—13
- River Bend—24
- Ninemile Prairie—26
- Roundup—30.2
- Clearwater River—34.7
- Sperry Grade—40
- Russell Gates—42
- Scotty Brown Bridge—45
- River Junction—54
- North Fork—54
- Aunt Molly—72
- Landers Fork—120

River Flow
- Runoff begins in April, peaks in late May and drops in mid or late June.

River Characteristics
- Brushy at its upper end, the Blackfoot broadens out below the North Fork. It runs through some whitewater between Sperry Grade and Clearwater Bridge and again near Roundup Bridge. Floaters will find some heavy waves between Whitaker Bridge and Sheep Flats, too.

River Access
- The Blackfoot offers some of the best river access in the state. There are numerous launch and hike-in sites located along Highway 200, which parallels the river for its entire length.

Area Fly Shops
- Rock Creek Fisherman's Mercantile, 15995 Rock Creek Road, Rock Creek, MT, 406-825-6440.
- Grizzly Hackle, 215 W. Front Street, Missoula, MT, 406-721-8996
- Streamside Anglers, 301 S. Orange St., Missoula, MT, 406-543-6528
- Missoulian Angler, 420 N. Higgins Ave., Missoula, MT, 406-728-7766

BLACKFOOT RIVER MAJOR HATCHES

Insect	J	F	M	A	M	J	J	A	S	O	N	D	Flies
Grasshopper								▮					Dave's Hopper #2-8; Meadow Hopper #2-8; Joe's Hopper #4-8
Skwala Stonefly			▮										Bullethead Skwala #6-8; Olive Stimulator #6-8;; Rubberleg Brown Stone #6-8; Olive Stone #6-8
Gray Drake				▮									Parachute Adams #14-16; Sparkle Dun #14-16; Comparadun #14-16; Hare's Ear Nymph #14-16; Pheasant Tail Nymph #14-16
Midge	▮												Griffith's Gnat #16-20; Parachute Adams #18-20; Pheasant Tail Nymph #16-22; Palomino Midge #16-20
Trico									▮				Parachute Adams #18-22; Parachute Trico #18-22; CDC Trico Biot #18-22; Sparkle Dun #18-22; Trico Spinner #18-22
Salmonfly Pteronarcys californica						▮							Seducer #4-8; Stimulator #4-8; Bitch Creek Nymph #4-8; Kaufmann's Stone #2-6; Brook's Stone #2-6
Baetis						▮				▮			Olive Cripple #16-20; Parachute Adams #16-20; Sparkle Dun #16-20; Hare's Ear Nymph #16-20; Pheasant Tail Nymph #16-20; Poxyback Baetis #16-20
Golden Stone Hesperoperla pacifica							▮						Whitlock's Golden Stone Nymph #4-8; Montana Nymph #4-8; Betts' Brown Stone #4-8; Whitlock's Revised Golden Stone #4-8
Caddis							▮						Elk Hair Caddis #14-18; Diving Caddis #14-16; X-Caddis #14-16; Drifting Cased Caddis #14-18; Emergent Sparkle Pupa #12-18; Deep Sparkle Pupa #12-18; Electric Caddis #14-16; Caddis Variant #14-16
Pale Morning Dun									▮				Sparkle Dun #14-20; PMD Cripple #16-20; Poxy Biot Nymph #16-20; Hare's Ear Nymph #16-18; Pheasant Tail Nymph #16-18; CDC Floating Nymph #16-18

Georgetown Lake

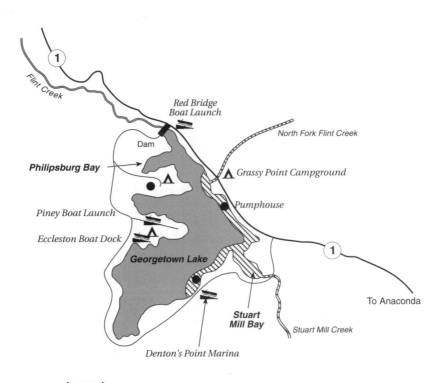

Flint Creek

1

Red Bridge
Boat Launch

North Fork Flint Creek

Dam

Philipsburg Bay

Grassy Point Campground

Pumphouse

Piney Boat Launch

Eccleston Boat Dock

Georgetown Lake

1

To Anaconda

**Stuart
Mill Bay**

Stuart Mill Creek

Denton's Point Marina

Legend

ⅢⅢⅢ Interstate	
▬▬ US Highway	⤜ Fishing Access
—— State/Cty Road	▭▭ Wilderness
- - - - Gravel/Dirt Road	▭ Bridge
— — Trail	■ Dam
✈ Air Service	▬ Major River
⋀ Campground	═ Minor River/Creek
🚤 Boat Launch	▨ Special Regulation Water

N

GEORGETOWN LAKE

When contemplating mountain lakes, most flyfishers picture small, intimate, trout-dimpled waters nestled at the base of glacial cirques. Georgetown Lake hardly paints that image.

Resting in the mountains at 6,000 feet, Georgetown has the proper altitude and high-country scenery to be called a mountain lake, but its fertility, including lush plant growth, hordes of aquatic insects and squadrons of large brook and rainbow trout, just do not fit the mold. That is why Georgetown ranks high on most Montana flyfishers' hit lists, including mine.

Georgetown lies just 20 miles west of Anaconda and 15 miles south of Philipsburg off of Highway 1. From Butte or Missoula, it takes about an hour drive to unleash a fly line on its surface. From Butte, take Interstate 90 west to the Anaconda turnoff. From Missoula, follow Interstate 90 east to Drummond, then turn south on Highway 1. From the Bitterroot Valley, turn east onto Skalkaho Road (Highway 38) from Highway 93 just south of Hamilton. That route requires about a 1.5-hour drive.

When Georgetown's trout are on the feed, a full-day drive would be regarded as a minor inconvenience. Big rainbows and brook trout may leave flyfishers dazed, their eyes wide, their casting arms sore and their smiles wide.

The lake's brook trout are particularly intriguing, if not for their cosmic fall coloration and impressive size, then certainly for the fact that they persist in a land where the brook trout is often called a bum.

In fact, the brook trout is universally unpopular in the West. Despite its colors, it is often regarded as an easier fish to take than rainbows, cutthroats or browns, and its fight is typically less pronounced when compared to the aerial antics of its cousins, particularly rainbows. Presented with the option to fish for any type of trout, brook trout would likely fall to the bottom of a Western angler's list.

However, a brook trout, with its olive, worm-tracked back, its white-tipped fins and its orange-slashed sides, is a beautiful fish, and many of them are not pushovers in Georgetown. In my mind, a colorful trout that weighs in from two to five pounds and offers a serious flyfishing challenge is a fish worth pursuing. And Georgetown is the best water in western Montana to do just that.

Georgetown's big brook trout get most active in the fall when my friend, Scott Brown of Missoula, says, "there's a pretty good egg-sucking leech hatch."

To tempt the lake's trout, flyfishers throw large streamers like egg-sucking leeches, woolly buggers, zonkers and mohair leeches. And the fish are easy to find, especially along the east shore where natural springs are located. Brook trout will be nestled along the shallow water gravel beds, guarding their nest and eggs.

While there are ethics to deal with when fishing trout on their spawning beds, the fishery remains open from the third Saturday in May through March 31. And during fall, brookies, some up to five pounds, are more than a little eager to smack a streamer.

According to John Oswald at Fish-On Fly and Tackle in Butte, brookies and even rainbows will concentrate on rocky points during fall and again in the spring.

"The brook trout look for the rocky points during fall when they spawn, and the rainbows seek them out in the spring to spawn," he said. "At that time they focus on minnows, and the best patterns I've used mimic the redsided shiner. I tie it as a size 8."

If you do fish brookies during fall, keep your fish in the water for photos and consider when you have disturbed a trout enough. Do not repeatedly move a fish off its bed by dragging a leech or bugger over its back. And please do not take any home for the wall — take a photo instead. In my mind, flyfishers with lots of photos of big fish on their wall are cool. People who have a house full of fakey looking stuffed trout are reaching for something they will never find.

From opening day, the third Saturday in May, extending into September, Georgetown offers a variety of hatches and plenty of big trout, including three strains of fast-growing rainbows. But it hasn't always been that way.

During the 1940s and 1950s, before national outdoor media discovered its tasty attributes, Georgetown Lake was one of the best trophy trout waters in the West. Large rainbows were numerous, five pounders not uncommon. Then the lake was rocked by two major predators: anglers and the kokanee salmon. Fortunately, both play a lesser role in the fishery today.

"After its peak in the Fifties, the lake declined because kokanee salmon came into the drainage," said Wayne Hadley, a biologist for Montana Fish, Wildlife and Parks. "They are incredibly efficient predators on plankton, and they deny rainbows access to that food base. Even today, a significant amount of biomass in the lake is tied up in 10- to 11-inch kokanee. And the lake is full of suckers and shiners, too."

Two major changes contributed to the rejuvenation of Georgetown's rainbow fishery. In 1985 the catch limit was changed from 20 brook trout and 10 other trout to a combined five trout a day. Also, FWP altered from stocking only Arlee strain rainbows to stocking Kamloops and Eagle River rainbows, as well. Kamloops and Eagle River rainbows are more predatory than Arlee, and biologists hoped that they would put a dent in the kokanee population.

"As soon as we changed the regulations and the type of trout we were planting, we saw the maximum size and average size go up," Hadley said. "We try to manage for a 14-inch average, because almost nobody will scoff at a 14-inch trout. Some years we've been close to that average size, but we've never exceeded it. But you have to remember, if that is the average size, there is a major portion of larger trout in the lake."

A big Georgetown rainbow will go five pounds. Hadley says the largest fish they've seen weighed over 10 pounds. Seven-pound rainbows, mostly Kamloops and Eagle River strains, are fairly common. Currently, the average rainbow goes 13 inches, while the average brook trout goes 14.8 inches, which is up from 12 inches in 1990.

Unfortunately, the Eagle Lake and Kamloops strain rainbows may not be eating as many kokanee as originally projected. Instead, their diet consists mostly of shiners and aquatic insects.

"Shiners act as a buffer for the kokanee," Hadley said. "We know those rainbows are taking some kokanee, but they aren't keeping the numbers down like we hoped they would."

You won't find a better looking brook trout anywhere. This huge, fall-caught Georgetown brookie, taken by Ryan Lutey, fell for an egg-sucking leech. (Scott Brown Photo)

Over the next five years, flyfishers should keep a close eye on Georgetown Lake, because whirling disease could take a bite out of the naturally spawned population of rainbows and brook trout.

Whirling disease was detected in Georgetown's two main spawning tributaries in fall 1995. According to Hadley, he first considered that there was a problem with the Georgetown Lake system in 1994.

"Our winter catch rates for ice fishermen declined in 1994," he said. "That's when I heard about whirling disease in the Madison (River). I said, 'There's our problem.'

"Right now (spring 1996), it looks like natural reproduction from rainbows is about zero in the spawning tributaries," he added. "It's been severely damaged. The question that remains is what will happen to the brook trout? They survive in the lake entirely by natural reproduction, and they are certainly infected with the disease."

Fortunately, Georgetown's rainbow trout populations should remain strong due to intense stocking efforts — to the tune of 180,000 rainbows a year. Fish consist of three subspecies, including Arlee, Kamloops and Eagle Lake strains. Because of the threat of whirling disease on young trout, Hadley will now plant fish when they reach eight or 10 inches instead of the standard three or four-inch fish. With that added size, rainbows should be able to fight off the effects of whirling disease, which attacks the cartilage of young fish.

"We will plant larger rainbows that are less vulnerable and keep our fingers crossed that the brook trout are going to be just fine," Hadley said. "Those are the steps that are available ... I'm thinking that stalking the larger trout will work, it's just more expensive. And I have a feeling that the brook trout may be less susceptible to the disease than rainbows."

Despite its problems, Georgetown Lake is a tremendous high mountain trout fishery, and it should maintain its reputation despite whirling disease. According to Hadley, most lake fisheries are limited by extremely successful reproduction. Lakes can actually harbor too many fish and competition for food limits growth rates. By losing natural production from the rainbows, Hadley and his cohorts may actually be able to boost the average size of the lake's trout.

"I think the rainbows will do fine with our stocking program," Hadley said. "My only concern is the brook trout. But before I get too nervous, I'll watch them over the next two or three years. If it looks like brook trout are being negatively affected, we'll try to help them out."

Prime hatches bring the best fishing opportunities at Georgetown, beginning with the Callibaetis mayfly emergence in May and June. If you visit Montana during those months, you may find rivers and streams blown out. But Georgetown should be prime, and the lake's recreational boaters, including waterskiers, generally wait until July to carve up the surface.

Expect excellent Callibaetis emergences during morning when the wind is calm and the fish are active. Big rainbows will cruise just under the surface sucking down emerging insects. Patterns with trailing shucks like a size 12 olive sparkle dun do wonders during the hatch. Anglers can anchor a boat or navigate a floattube in any of the mudbottom, weed-riddled bays. Try to pattern a trout by watching its rises. Then cast a fly in front of its snout. Leaders in the 4X or 5X range are subtle enough not to spook fish, yet strong enough to stop a big rainbow when it dives for Georgetown's prolific weedbeds.

"The Callibaetis hatch is interesting because it comes off in a series of sizes," said Oswald. "Early in the season bugs will run size 12. By midsummer they will measure about a size 14. Then, during late summer, you will have to tie on a size 18 to match them."

Because Callibaetis require dense weed growth, Oswald focuses on two particular bays during the hatch.

"I like to fish Stuart Mill Bay on the south end or Fin Bay on the west side of the lake," he said. "You have to find mud bottom and weed growth to find good numbers of Callibaetis."

Georgetown's biggest hatch takes place around the Fourth of July when damselfly nymphs leave aquatic vegetation and swim to shore in masses. Flyfishers can work any depth of water with many different patterns (a size six or eight six pack works well). When the fish are on, they'll drill those patterns. Using anything lighter than 5X tippet spawns frustration because a big fish may dive into the weedbeds and break you off.

"During the damsel hatch, I again focus on the mudbottom, weedy bays," Oswald said. "Stuart Mill Bay and Fin Bay are the best places, although you can find damsels throughout the lake. I like to fish those patterns as slow as possible at a variety of depths."

Damselfly nymphs should work well weeks before and after the hatch, too. Crawl those patterns along the bottom, between the weedbeds, and hold on tight.

In late July and well into August, Georgetown offers an amazing caddisfly, a size 6 or 8 insect, for flycasters to mimic. According to Hadley, this is not a hatch for the faint of heart.

"These are great big caddis," he explained. "They are bigger than a golden stonefly and almost as big as a salmonfly. And the fish are looking for it. It comes off late in the evenings…sometimes you can't see your fly, but you will know when you get a hit. It brings up the biggest fish, so use heavier tippets or they'll bury themselves in the weeds and break off."

Georgetown's caddis, which belong to the *Limnephilid* family, have a strange preference for travel. Strange, that is, until you understand why they do what they do. Those big bugs swim to the shore instead of flying because they are so large and they offer such a substantial target for birds; they figure they are less susceptible to trout than the birds. Trout key in on the wake that the insect leaves behind. Flyfishers should try to mimic that surface disturbance.

According to Gary LaFontaine, anglers should strip a high-floating fly across the surface as fast as they can. LaFontaine places the rod under an arm and strips with both hands, which allows him to keep a steady motion to the fly. A pause in your retrieve is less effective.

Oswald fishes a couple of high-floating patterns effectively.

"We tie a Tom Thumb, a large elk hair, stimulators and even a clipped-hair body caddis on size 8 long shank hooks," Oswald said. "I skate them right across the surface, just like a bass bug. I don't fish blind. I wait until I see a fish working and then cast. Some of the best caddis action is in Stuart Mill Bay and Fin Bay, especially along the southern willow-lined bank."

If you want to take fish home from Georgetown Lake, visit during winter and jig for kokanee salmon through the ice. By bonking kokanees, you will contribute to the success of Georgetown's rainbow and brook trout.

Lake Facts: Georgetown Lake

Seasons:
- Third Saturday in May through March 31.

Special Regulations
- The south and east shoreline is closed to fishing from shore or within 100 yards of shore from April 1 to July 1 to protect spawning rainbows. Closed area extends from a point 200 yards west of Denton's Point Marina, easterly and northerly along the shore including Stuart Mill Bay and its entirety, to a point 200 yards north of the mouth of North Fork Flint Creek.
- Tributaries to Georgetown Lake open July 1 through November 30.

Trout
- Kamloops rainbow trout: Long-lived rainbow that reach 10 pounds in Georgetown. Most fish run 14 to 18 inches.
- Arlee rainbow trout: Short-lived rainbow that reaches a few pounds in Georgetown. Most fish go 14 to 16 inches.
- Eagle Lake rainbow trout: Long-lived rainbow that reaches seven pounds in Georgetown. Most will go 14 to 18 inches.
- Brook Trout: Most fish average 15 to 17 inches. There are some fish to five pounds.

Lake Size
- 3,000 acres

Lake Character
- Rests at over 6,000 feet in a large mountain valley. Maximum depth is 38 feet. Most of the bays are shallow and rich in aquatic vegetation. The river can become unfishable in heavy winds. Mornings and evenings are generally calm.

Area Fly Shops/Outfitters:
- Fish On Fly and Tackle, 3346 Harrison Ave, Butte, MT, 406-494-4218
- Georgetown Landing, 14411 Hwy 1 West, Georgetown Lake, MT, 406-563-5900

GEORGETOWN LAKE MAJOR HATCHES

Insect	J	F	M	A	M	J	J	A	S	O	N	D	Flies
Callibaetis					▮	▮							Callibaetis Cripple #14-16; Sparkle Spinner #14-16; Sparkle Dun #14-16; Parachute Adams #14-16; Hare's Ear #14-16
Midge	▮	▮	▮	▮	▮	▮	▮	▮	▮	▮	▮	▮	Parachute Adams #16-20; Glass Bead Midge #16-20; Midge Emerger #16-20; Hatching Midge #16-20; Midge Larvae #16-20
Damselfly						▮	▮						Marabou Damsel #10-12; Six Pack #10-12; Swimming Damsel #8-12
Caddis							▮	▮					Tom Thumb #6-10; Stimulator #6-10; Elk Hair Caddis #6-10; Clipped Hair Caddis #6-10
Leech	▮	▮	▮	▮	▮	▮	▮	▮	▮	▮	▮	▮	Rabbit Strip Leech (olive, black, brown) #2-6; Mohair Leech #2-8; Marabou Leech #4-8; Woolly Bugger #2-8

FAR WEST HUB CITIES
Missoula
Elevation – 3,200 • Population – 43,000

Missoula is located in a broad valley in western Montana. It is at the center of five scenic valleys: the Flathead to the north, Frenchtown to the west, Bitterroot to the south, Blackfoot to the northeast, and Hellgate to the east. Flowing through the center of town is the Clark Fork River, which is joined by the famous Bitterroot River from the south. Home to the University of Montana, Missoula is a major retail and cultural center of western Montana with excellent access to a number of prime waters.

ACCOMMODATIONS
The House on Butler Creek, 215 West Front, Missoula, MT 59802 / Run by Jim and Cassie Toth who own Grizzly Hackle / Five bedroom cedar sided guest house in private, quiet setting / arrangements can be made for airport pickup / guide trips and gourmet dining available 406-721-8996

Bel Aire Motel, 300 East Broadway / 406-543-7183 / 52 rooms / Dogs allowed in smoking rooms, $5 fee / There is one nonsmoking room in which dogs are allowed / $$

Days Inn/Westgate, Rt 93 and I-90 / 406-721-9776 / 69 rooms / Dogs allowed, $5 fee / Restaurant on premises / $$

4B's Inn North, 4953 North Reserve / 406-542-7550 / 67 rooms / Dogs allowed / Restaurant on premises / $$

4B's South, 3803 Brooks / 406-251-2665 / 79 rooms / Dogs allowed / Restaurant on premises / $$

CAMPGROUNDS AND RV PARKS
Missoula El-Mar KOA, Reserve St exit, 1½ miles south / 406-549-0881 / 36 tent and 164 RV spaces / Open year-round / Full facilities including hot tub and store

Out Post Campground, I-90 exit 96, 2 miles north on Rt 93 / 406-549-2016 / 10 tent and 35 RV spaces / Open year-round / Full facilities

RESTAURANTS
4B's, located at 4B's motels north and south / Open for breakfast, lunch, and dinner

Finnegan's Family Restaurant, 700 East Broadway / 406-542-2752 / Open 24 hours, 7 days for breakfast, lunch, and dinner

McKay's on the River, 1111 East Broadway / 406-728-0098 / Restaurant/lounge open 7 days for breakfast, lunch, and dinner / Unique antique gun display / Steaks, prime rib, and seafood

New Pacific Grill, 100 East Railroad Avenue at the old Northern Pacific Railroad station / 406-542-3353 / Open 7 days for lunch and dinner / Casual dining / Fresh seafood and beef

Paradise Falls, 3621 Brooks / 406-728-3228 / Restaurant, lounge, casino / Open 6AM–2AM for breakfast, lunch, and dinner / Steaks and baby-back ribs

The Depot, 201 W Railroad Ave, 406-728-7007 / Restaurant, lounge, outside deck / excellent steaks, salads, seafood and microbrew

VETERINARIANS

Missoula Veterinary Clinic, 3701 Old 93 South / 406-251-2400 / 24-hour emergency service

Pruyn Veterinary Hospital, 2501 Russell / 406-251-4150 / 24-hour emergency service

FLY SHOPS AND SPORTING GOODS

Bob Ward and Sons, 2300 Brooks / 406-728 3220 / Open 7 days

Sportsman's Surplus, Tremper Shopping Center / 406-721-5500 / Open 7 days

Grizzly Hackle, 215 West Front Street, / 406-721-8996

Missoulian Angler, 420 North Higgins Ave / 406-728-7766

AUTO RENTAL AND REPAIR

Avis, Missoula International Airport / 406-549-4711

Hertz, Missoula International Airport / 406-549-9511

National, Missoula International Airport / 406-543-3131

Ram Towing and Repair, 3402 Grant Creek Road I-90 at Reserve Street / 406-542-3636 or 800-870-3634 / 24-hour auto and diesel repair

Skip's Orange Street Sinclair, 400 West Broadway / 406-549-5571 / Open 7 days.

AIR SERVICE

Missoula International Airport, Hwy 93 north of town / 406-728-4381 / Delta, Horizon, and Northwest airlines

MEDICAL

Community Medical Center, 28227 Fort Missoula Road / 406-728-4100

St. Patrick Hospital, 500 West Broadway / 406-543-7271 / 24-hour emergency services / Life flight

FOR MORE INFORMATION

The Missoula Chamber of Commerce
825 East Front Street
Missoula, MT 59802
406-543-6623

U.S. Forest Service
340 North Pattee
Missoula, MT 59802
406-329-3511

Montana Department of Fish, Wildlife, and Parks
3201 Spurgin Road
Missoula, MT 59801
406-542-5500

Hamilton

Elevation – 3,600 • Population – 2,800

Hamilton is a nice little community, located in the beautiful Bitterroot Valley. The Bitterroot Mountains form the western border of the valley, and the Sapphire Mountains are to the east. The famous Bitterroot River runs north through the valley. Logging and log home manufacturing are the main industries of Ravalli County.

ACCOMMODATIONS

Bitterroot Motel, 408 South 1st Street / 406-363-1142 / 10 rooms / Dogs welcome / $

Sportsman Motel, 410 North 1st Street / 406-363-2411 / 18 rooms, restaurant / Dogs allowed in smoking rooms only / $

TownHouse Inns of Hamilton, 115 North 1st Street / 406-363-6600 / 64 rooms / Restaurant / Dogs allowed, $5 charge / $$

CAMPGROUNDS AND RV PARKS

Angler's Roost, on Bitterroot River 3 miles south on Rt 93 / 406-363-1268 / 15 tent and 60 RV spaces / Open year-round / Full facilities, including cabins, store, gun and tackle shop, fishing licenses, boat launch facility and gas

RESTAURANTS

Rocky Knob, Highway 93 south of Conner / 406-821-3520

Trapper's Family Restaurant, 561 Main / 406-821-4465

Coffee Cup Cafe, 500 South 1st Street / 406-363-3822 / Home-style cooking and pastry / Breakfast served all day

4B's Restaurant, 1105 North 1st Street / 406-363-4620

Staver's Restaurant, 163 South 2nd Street / 406-363-4433 / The Bitterroot's finest bar and grill

Bad Bubba's BBQ, 105 North 2nd / 406-363-7427

Sportman Restaurant, adjacent to the Sportman Motel / 406-363-2411

The Banque, 225 West Main / 406-3631955

VETERINARIANS

Basin Veterinary Service, 58 Roaring Lion Road / 406-363-4579

Bitterroot Veterinary Clinic, 1116 North 1st Street / 406-363-1123

FLY SHOPS AND SPORTING GOODS

Bob Ward and Sons, 1120 North 1st Street / 406-363-6204

Riverbend Flyfishing, 302 North Hamilton / 406-363-4197

Riffles and Runs, Highway 93 North of Hamilton / 406-961-4950

Fishaus Tackle, 702 North First, Box 583 / 406-3636158

AUTO REPAIR

Al's Car Care Center, 324 South 1st Street / 406-363-3700

AIR SERVICE
Ravalli County Airport / 406-363-3833

MEDICAL
Marcus Daly Hospital, 1200 Westwood Drive / 406-363-2211

FOR MORE INFORMATION
Bitterroot Valley Chamber of Commerce
105 East Main
Hamilton, MT 59840
406-363-2400

Deer Lodge

Elevation – 4,688 • Population – 3,378

Deer Lodge rests in the Deer Lodge Valley on the banks of the Clark Fork River west of Butte. It's most noted for Montana's state prison, however flyfishers should recognize Deer Lodge for its real claim to fame—Gary LaFontaine calls the town home. Deer Lodge is centrally located: the upper Clark Fork runs through town, the Big Hole, Missouri, Little Blackfoot, Jefferson and Beaverhead rivers, plus Rock Creek, Clark Canyon Reservoir, the Hog Hole and Georgetown Lake, are located within a two-hour drive. Deerlodge National Forest borders the western part of the county and the Helena National Forest is east of town. Timber and agriculture are the main industries. Terrain consists of intermountain grassland and montane forest.

ACCOMMODATIONS
Deer Lodge Super 8, 1150 North Main Street / 406-846-2370 / 54 rooms / Dogs allowed in smoking rooms only, $5 per dog / $
Scharf Motor Inn, 819 Main Street / 406-846-2810 / 44 rooms / Dogs allowed / Restaurant on premise / $

CAMPGROUNDS AND RV PARKS
Riverfront RV Park, Garrison Mtn, off I-90, 10 miles north / 800-255-1318 / Open year-round / 12 tent and 16 RV spaces / Full facilities including store

RESTAURANTS
4B's Restaurant, I-90 interchange / 406-846-2620 / Breakfast, lunch, and dinner / 24 hours
Country Village, I-90 interchange / 406-846-1442 / Open 7:30AM–9PM, 7 days
RJ's Steakhouse and Casino, 317 Main / 406-846-3400 / Open for dinner 7 days a week
Scharf's Family Restaurant, 819 Main / 406-846-3300 / Serving breakfast, lunch, and dinner 7 days a week / Family style dining

VETERINARIANS
Clark Fork Veterinary Clinic, 390 North Frontage Road / 406-846-1925
Paul Bissonette, DVM / 9AM–5PM M–F, 9AM–1PM Sat

FLY SHOPS AND SPORTING GOODS
Hiatts Sporting Goods, 101 Milwaukee Avenue
Ace Hardware, 506 Second Street / 406-846-2461

AUTO REPAIR
Riverside Service Center, 228 Mitchell / 406-846-3113

AIR SERVICE
County Airstrip, Ralph Besk / 406-846-2238 or 846-1771

MEDICAL
Powell County Memorial Hospital, 1101 Texas Avenue / 406-846-1722
Deer Lodge Clinic, 1101 Texas / 406-846-2212

FOR MORE INFORMATION
Powell County Chamber of Commerce
P.O Box 776
Deer Lodge, MT 59722
406-846-2094

Butte

Elevation – 5,750 • Population – 34,800

For many years, Butte, located at the crossroads of Interstates 15 and 90, was a booming mining center. Today, it is a diversified commercial city that offers plenty of lodging for the travelling flyfisher and easy access to a number of excellent rivers. The terrain in Silver Bow and Jefferson counties is primarily montane forest, where it is not unearthed from mining activities. The Beaverhead National Forest forms the western part of the county and the Deerlodge National Forest is east and north of the county.

ACCOMMODATIONS
TownHouse Inns of Butte, 2777 Harrison Avenue / 406-494-8850 / 150 rooms / Dogs allowed, $5 fee / $$
War Bonnet Inn, 2100 Cornell Avenue / 406-494-7800 / 134 rooms / Dogs allowed, $10 fee / Restaurant on site / $$$

CAMPGROUNDS AND RV PARKS
Fairmont RV Park, 17 miles west of Butte off I-90 / 406-797-3535 / 84 RV spaces / Full facilities including showers, laundry, store, and cabins

RESTAURANTS
4B's Family Restaurant, 1905 Dewey and Rocker Interchange / 406-494-1199
Perkins Family Restaurant, 2900 Harrison Avenue / 406-494-2490 / Open 24 hours
The Uptown Cafe, 47 East Broadway / 406-723-4735 / One of Montana's finest

VETERINARIANS
Animal Hospital, 2330 Amherst Avenue / 406-494-4044
Butte Veterinary Service, 6000 Harrison Avenue / 406-494-3656

FLY SHOPS AND SPORTING GOODS
Bob Ward and Sons, 1925 Dewey / 406-494-3445
Fran Johnson's Sports Shop, 1957 Harrison Avenue / 406-782-3322
Fish-On Fly and Tackle, 3346 Harrison Avenue / 406-494-4218

AUTO REPAIR
Mark's Sinclair, 1200 South Montana, 3 blocks north of I-90 / 406-723-3351 /
Open 7 days

AIR SERVICE
Bert Mooney Field, Harrison Avenue South / Delta (Sky West), 406-494-4001 /
Horizon, 406-494-1402

MEDICAL
St. James Hospital, 400 South Clark Street / 406-782-8361

FOR MORE INFORMATION
Butte Chamber of Commerce
2950 Harrison Avenue
Butte, MT 59701
800-735-6814, Ext. 10

Anaconda
Elevation– 5,331 • Population – 10,700

Anaconda, a town built by copper magnate Marcus Daly, is home to one of the
largest copper smelters in the world. The "stack" as it's called, is out of service now,
but it continues to rise over the landscape like a trusty sentinel. Deer Lodge County
is comprised of montane forest and intermountain grasslands. Flint Creek, the east
fork of Rock Creek, Georgetown Lake and the Anaconda-Pintler Wilderness are
located in the western part of the county.

ACCOMMODATIONS
Georgetown Lake Lodge, Restaurant and Lounge, Denton's Point Road / 406-
563-7020 / 11 rooms / Dogs allowed / $$
Seven Gables Inn Restaurant and Lounge, Georgetown Lake / 406-563-5052 /
10 rooms and one cabin that sleeps 8 / Dogs allowed / $
Trade Winds Motel, 1600 East Commercial / 800-248-3428 / 24 rooms /
Kitchenettes available / Dogs allowed / $$

CAMPGROUNDS AND RV PARKS
Georgetown Lake KOA, 14 miles west on MT 1, 2 miles south at lake / 406-563-6030
/ Open year-round / 10 tent and 48 RV spaces / Full services except for sewer /
Store and laundry

RESTAURANTS

Barclay II Supper Club, 1300 East Commercial / 406-563-5541 / Open for dinner / Italian food

Georgetown Lake Lodge, Denton's Point / 406-563-7020

Granny's Kitchen, 1500 East Commercial / 406-563-2349

VETERINARIANS

Anaconda Veterinary Clinic, 1501 East Park / 406-563-2440

FLY SHOPS AND SPORTING GOODS

Don's Sport Center, 1310 East Commercial / 406-563-3231

Rainbow Sporting Goods, 605 East Park / 406-563-5080

AUTO REPAIR

Anaconda Automotive, 1400 East Commercial / 406-563-8126

AIR SERVICE

Bowman Field, Warm Springs, MT / Contact John McPhail / 406-563-8112 or 563-9984

MEDICAL

The Community Hospital of Anaconda, 401 West Penn / 406-563-5261

FOR MORE INFORMATION

Anaconda Chamber of Commerce
306 East Park Avenue
Anaconda, MT 59711
406-563-2400

Southwest

Flyfishers call it the Golden Triangle, a title referring to a section of the West that might be unparalleled anywhere in the world in trout fishing options.

Included in the Triangle, which encompasses parts of northwest Wyoming, Yellowstone Park and eastern Idaho, is Montana's southwest region, where rivers as notorious as the Madison, Gallatin, East Gallatin, Red Rock, Jefferson, Beaverhead and Bighole beckon to flyfishers.

What do you want? Big browns in fast pocket water? Hit the Madison near Slide. Prefer large rainbows on dry flies? Head to the Bighole River during its early summer salmonfly blitz. Desire scrappy cutthroats in a mountain stream? Cast a flyline on the upper Red Rock River. Looking for a truly trophy brown? Tie on a size 20 palomino midge and sink it to the bottom of the Beaverhead River. Then hold on and say your prayers—those fish will part a 5X tippet like sewing thread. How about grayling? Southwest Montana hosts the West's last viable populations of native fluvial grayling. Try them on the Red Rock, Gallatin, and especially on the upper Big Hole. If you are really lucky, you might tie into one on the Madison.

For those who prefer stillwaters, cast tiny Trico or midge patterns on Hebgen Lake, where two to four-pound rainbows and browns are standard fare. Or launch a floattube on Clark Canyon Reservoir—a rainbow or brown trout from that reservoir must exceed seven pounds to turn an old salt's head!

You name it for flyfishing opportunity, southwest Montana has it. The problem for those of us fortunate enough to live in the region is this: with so many good options, where do you start and how do you choose where to fish on any given day of the year?

Fortunately, it's a problem each of us accepts readily. Hey, we could be locked in an office in the city, punching keys at the computer, dreaming of the difficult choices those Montanans have to make!

A flyfisher could live in southwest Montana a full lifetime and never fish all the appealing waters the region holds. Nonresidents face a greater, more harsh reality. In effect, that is an invitation to get started.

Big Hole River

With whirling disease eating the Madison, angling crowds reaching nearly unbearable status on the Bighorn, and major floods turning the Yellowstone to mud during much of the summer season, the Big Hole River could be labeled "Montana's finest" overall flyfishery.

The Big Hole is almost always fishable, even during strong runoff months. It has varied, yet heavy, aquatic insect hatches, and its trout—large, scrappy specimens that rise avidly to a dry fly—are as beautiful as you might find anywhere in the world. And the Big Hole's scenery is equally awesome.

Lifelong flyfishers, fond memories, and major yearnings for the wild places of the West are born on the Big Hole.

George Grant of Butte so likes the river and the valley that he has admirably dedicated his life to preserving the Big Hole. His efforts speak loudly for the perpetuation of an undammed river and the continuation of a diverse fishery in the stronghold of ranching. We, as flyfishers, cannot thank the man enough. He helped spawn modern conservation on the river by creating the Big Hole River Foundation in 1989, following the worst dewatering year on the Big Hole in memory.

The Foundation, concerned anglers, Montana Fish, Wildlife and Park's biologists, plus a few good ranchers continue Grant's legacy. Currently, the river still offers native fluvial grayling—a species so dependent on quality cold water that its only viable population in the lower 48 states resides in the Big Hole.

All this admiration for the river seems strange because in 1994, just a scant few years ago, the river was closed to fishing due to a series of drought years that were compounded by irrigators whose demand for water outstripped the river's ability to fulfill their needs.

Huge numbers of the river's trout were thought to have perished during that low water period. A lot of fish probably did die, including significant numbers of juvenile trout and grayling. But the fish have rebounded, and as of spring 1996, biologists estimate more than 3,000 trout per mile in some sections of the river.

Even without trout, the Big Hole would be a recreational draw. Throughout its 150-mile length, visitors might sneak a glimpse of mule deer, elk, black bears, Shiras moose, mountain lions and coyotes. There are also plenty of forested mountains, sagebrush covered flats and lush riparian lowlands to gawk at.

The Big Hole begins at Skinner Lake, which rests at 7,340 feet and is surrounded by the 10,000-foot peaks of the Beaverhead Mountains just south of Jackson, Montana. To the north, the 10,000-foot spires of the Anaconda Range border the valley.

Its tributary streams, including the North Fork, offer small brook trout and a few remnant cutthroat and grayling. Below the entrance of the North Fork, the river braids extensively while flowing between cutbanks and masses of willows that harbor plenty of moose and, unfortunately, hordes of vicious mosquitoes (they've been known to fly off with small dogs). Lots of small brook trout and increasing numbers

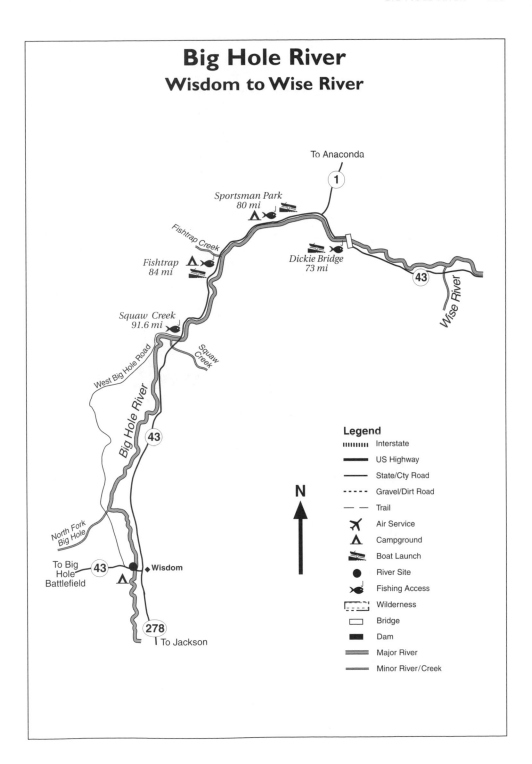

Big Hole River
Wisdom to Wise River

To Anaconda

1

Sportsman Park
80 mi

Fishtrap Creek

Fishtrap
84 mi

Dickie Bridge
73 mi

43

Wise River

Squaw Creek
91.6 mi

West Big Hole Road

Squaw Creek

Big Hole River

43

Legend

‖‖‖‖‖	Interstate
▬▬	US Highway
—	State/Cty Road
- - - -	Gravel/Dirt Road
— —	Trail
✈	Air Service
⛢	Campground
🚤	Boat Launch
●	River Site
✕	Fishing Access
⟦⟧	Wilderness
▭	Bridge
▬	Dam
▬▬▬	Major River
══	Minor River/Creek

N

North Fork
Big Hole

To Big
Hole
Battlefield

43

♦ **Wisdom**

278

To Jackson

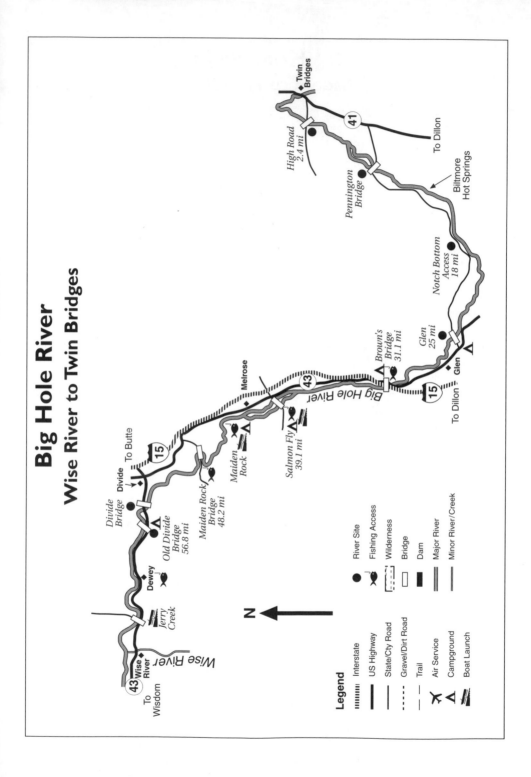

Big Hole River
Wise River to Twin Bridges

Legend

▐▌▐▌▐▌	Interstate
▬▬▬	US Highway
———	State/Cty Road
········	Gravel/Dirt Road
– – –	Trail
✈	Air Service
◬	Campground
⚓	Boat Launch

●	River Site
✈	Fishing Access
▨	Wilderness
☐	Bridge
■	Dam
▬	Major River
—	Minor River/Creek

N

To Wisdom
43 Wise River
Wise River
Jerry Creek
Dewey
Old Divide Bridge 56.8 mi
Divide Bridge
Divide
To Butte
15
Maiden Rock Bridge 48.2 mi
Maiden Rock
Melrose
Salmon Fly 39.1 mi
Big Hole River
43
Brown's Bridge 31.1 mi
Glen 25 mi
Glen
15
To Dillon
Notch Bottom Access 18 mi
Biltmore Hot Springs
Pennington Bridge
High Road 2.4 mi
41
To Dillon
Twin Bridges

An early spring float on the Big Hole brings hordes of caddisflies and lots of trout to net. Here, Jim Nave picks the killer pattern.

of grayling can be taken in the headwaters, too. A few rainbows may pick at your fly also.

For most flyfishers, the Big Hole's prime water begins at Squaw Creek. Extending from Squaw Creek downstream to the Divide Bridge, flyfishers can bring up some larger grayling—fish stretching to 15 inches—along with a smattering of healthy brook trout. Brown trout and rainbows also begin showing up in the catch. The upper river is especially appealing to flyfishers who lack a boat or raft. With its big grassy banks, it provides excellent wade fishing and plenty of room for backcasts.

According to Lyle Reynolds, a lifelong Big Hole resident who runs Sunrise Fly Shop in Melrose, the upper river fishes best early in the season, before water temperatures rise and water levels dip due to lessening runoff and irrigation demand.

"The upper section has flatter water than the other sections, and that can be really advantageous for a dry-fly fisher," Reynolds said. "It's best early in the season when the water is still cool. In March, April, May and June, that section will hold good numbers of browns and rainbows, all the way up to Squaw Creek. But they move downstream in late June and early July. They'll return to the upper section during fall when the temperature cools."

Fortunately, the best months to fish the upper section coincide with excellent water conditions.

During March, hatches are few, except for the occasional Baetis emergence. Due to a lack of bugs, flyfishers pound the banks with large, weighted streamers for tremendously hungry browns, brookies and rainbows. Grayling rarely fit a size 4 bugger in their dainty mouths.

"In that early season, you can do really well with those buggers," Reynolds said. "You can really take some nice brown trout. We've seen a number of them over 24 inches.

"If I had to choose the best float in that section, I'd pick the Sportsman's Access to Jerry Creek Bridge, which is about 12 miles. You can pitch buggers the whole way, or you might get into the caddis hatch that begins in April. It is best on the middle and lower river, but it can be excellent up top, too."

In the fall, the upper Big Hole's trout and grayling concentrate on a diminutive morsel—the Trico mayfly.

For the flyfisher, Trico hatches may provide feast or famine. They are not easy to master, but once understood, they provide excellent opportunities to take very large trout on size 20 or smaller dry flies. In the minds of many, taking large trout during a Trico hatch borders on religion.

Tricos generally emerge in the morning or evening. They molt overnight, turning into sexually mature spinners. In the morning they congregate in dense clouds above the river. After mating, the males fall to the river with spent wings. The females dunk their fannies on the surface and deposit eggs. Then they, too, die and fall to the river as spent spinners.

"The Tricos start in mid-August and run through mid-September," Reynolds said. "You'll generally find the spinnerfall starting around 9AM, and it will extend, with fish feeding heavy, until about 1 PM."

Flyfishers should expect to find pods of wary trout rising greedily to Tricos. The problem posed to an angler is this: How can you get a fish to eat your fly when so many naturals are on the water? Fortunately, it's not an impossible task, but these tiny flies, which can be difficult to see on the water, and light 6X and 7X tippets are required. If you can't master Tricos, don't fret. Good fishing can be had on the river immediately after the Trico spinnerfall.

"In the afternoon, the wind will blow spent Tricos out of the eddies and back-waters and into the main current," Reynolds said. "You'll get some really nice fish feeding out in the main current, and they seem to take a small, size 16 or 18, para-chute Adams really well. They will also take a hopper. In fact, hoppers work well on the upper stretch through August and September."

The upper river gives way to the middle section at the entrance of the Wise River. The middle section extends from that point downstream to Melrose. Through that section, the Big Hole becomes wider and faster with some deep undercut banks and sizable rapids. Willows shade the banks in many places. Huge cliffs and rock formations create some strikingly deep holes.

Browns and rainbows dominate in that water, although the rare brook trout or grayling will occasionally show up in the catch. Fighting a fish in that section's fast water, whether wade fishing or floating from a raft or boat, can be challenging, to say the least.

The upper Big Hole is prime dry fly water, offering a variety of species. On any given cast, a flyfisher may strike a rainbow, brown, whitefish, grayling or, in this case, a modest brook trout landed by Katie Hall.

"The middle section provides more pocket water, and that can provide really good fishing with woolly buggers or nymphs," Reynolds said. "During April and May, especially, I like to fish woolly buggers in that section. We nail some really big fish. It's about as good as you can ask for. You can just hit those undercut banks or the pockets behind rocks and islands, and the fish will be there."

The middle section, especially the canyon stretch, is best known for its massive, early Grannom caddis hatch, a size 14, gray wing and dark green bodied insect, which may come off anytime between a week prior and a week after Mother's Day. The *Brachycentrus* sp. hatch extends into early May, but its most productive fishing will last just a few days.

For those who are unfamiliar with the Mother's day caddis blitz, it's unforgettable. While the hatch is heavy and predictable, unfortunately, water conditions are not, which can make the hatch hit or miss on any given day. And that limits the chance of success for a visiting flyfisher. However, Montanans revel in the uncrowded conditions.

"In my opinion, it's the best hatch this river has to offer," Reynolds said. "It's way more productive than the salmonfly hatch, and there aren't very many people on the water. There are a lot of bugs, however. I've seen them so thick, the water just looks white. During the main hatch, we catch 50 or 60 fish a day, and we get some really good ones.

"If I could only choose a week to fish the river each year, I'd pick it in April or May because of the caddis hatch and because there are not very many people on the water. At that time the guides haven't started taking clients, so there is very little boat pressure.

"I think the best fishing takes place in the canyon stretch, and I think that is where the emergence is heaviest. I like to work a size 14 or 16 elk hair caddis or an X-caddis on top and drop a pheasant tail nymph off of it. The pheasant tail is good because the fish will hit it when it swings. It looks just like a real caddis swimming to the top."

While the main blitz only lasts a few days, caddis are present on the Big Hole from April though July, and the fish are normally keyed in on those bugs.

However, visiting anglers should consider the nature of Montana's weather during the spring months before planning a trip.

Heavy rains or major runoff may swell the Big Hole and other rivers overnight. Conditions are tentative at best. In fact, trying to hit the spring hatches, including the caddis emergence, is a crapshoot. If anglers arrive with the notion that they are going to catch lots of trout, no matter what the conditions offer, they are likely to go home disappointed. However, if they arrive with an open mind and figure they'll spend their down time, if the river is high, in the Blue Moon Saloon or Wise River Club shooting the bull with locals while advancing their angling knowledge, they'll be perfectly happy.

"It's really hard for somebody to come in and hit the hatch," Reynolds said. "If you happen to be on the water during the three or four days when the hatch is heaviest, consider yourself very fortunate. It all depends on the weather and the water conditions, and they are never very predictable in Montana, especially during spring."

To assure yourself the best chance to hit that Mother's Day caddis hatch, here's what you should do:

- Save money for a "Big Hole" fund that will allow you to catch a plane and fly out of town on a moment's notice. By saving money ahead of time, you won't feel the pain in your pocketbook when you have to book flight reservations on one day's notice.

- Call Lyle Reynolds at Sun Rise Fly Shop, George Goody at Montana Fly Company in Melrose or Frank Stanchfield at Troutfitters in Wise River every day to check on river conditions and the extent of the caddis hatch. These three will have all the knowledge from their guides who watch the river (by that I mean they fish the river diligently) prior to and during the hatch.

- Last, pray for a mild runoff so you can get on the river when the bugs do come off.

The scene of many wild nights—the ever-inviting Wise River Club.

Flyfishers should be aware of a river closure that is in effect between Divide Dam and Melrose Bridge from December 1 to the third Saturday in May. The catch limit, which hopefully doesn't concern you because you are going to practice catch and release, is four trout with three under 13 inches and one over 22 inches. Other river restrictions include artificial flies and lures between Dickie Bridge and Melrose Bridge. All grayling and cutthroat must be released.

The Big Hole's middle section gives way to the lower section at Melrose. From Melrose, extending to the Big Hole's confluence with the Beaverhead River, flyfishers should expect a trout population consisting of mostly browns. However, there are some good rainbows to be taken in the lower section, too.

Dry-fly fishers will particularly like the flatwater stretches. Nymphers should concentrate on the numerous broad riffles.

"The lower section offers good dry-fly fishing, and it has some excellent nymph runs," Reynolds said. "Just look for a nice riffle dropping into a deeper hole, and you'll find lots of fish.

"The lower river fishes really well late in the summer when hoppers come off," he added. "There are lots of big grassy banks at the edge of hayfields, and the hoppers fly right out of them onto the water. From late July into October, you can fish a hopper all day long, and you'll take some big browns."

While a flyfisher might catch a trophy trout anywhere on the river, most locals agree that the largest fish come from the waters between Wise River and Melrose. If Reynolds is any indication, those in pursuit of trophies should keep a weighted streamer on their line and pass up the likes of an elk hair caddis.

"I think a woolly bugger works as well as anything," Reynolds said. "It gets down in the rocks and under the banks where the biggest fish hide. You won't see the 28-inchers up top slurping dry flies. I've seen a fish that weighed 16 pounds taken on the Big Hole, and the biggest one I caught was 28 inches, but they don't come easy."

One pattern that I've had much success with on the Big Hole is the yellow yummy. Essentially, it's a large, size 2 woolly bugger tied with yellow rabbit fur strips. Rubberlegs are often attached, and an obscene amount of lead is always wrapped onto the hook.

While each section of river definitely holds a period when it provides the best fishing, the entire river is productive throughout spring, summer and fall. Because winters are severe in the Big Hole, flyfishing during cold months is not enjoyable or productive.

In general, here is a rundown of the Big Hole's top hatches:

Watch for caddis from early April through July. We know about the Mother's Day caddis hatch, but there are equally significant emergences extending from June through August. These insects, the spotted sedge and the little sister sedge, exist in phenomenal abundance, and they are the mainstay during lazy summer evenings. Golden stones are also present on the Big Hole, and they are most significant between mid-June and the end of July. The big salmonfly hatch and the big crowds usually arrive around the first week of June. The hatch will last for a couple weeks, and just getting a drift boat or raft on the water can provide a challenge. Pale morning duns emerge in mid-June, and they are present through July. Emergences and spinnerfalls are equally important. Grasshoppers start showing up in late July, and they will draw fish to the top through September. Tricos make their appearance in late August extending through September. Baetis mayflies can be encountered anytime between September 1 and late October.

With such varied hatches and good water conditions, any angler who fishes the Big Hole extensively will find themselves asking The Big Question: "Is this the best trout river in Montana?"

Reynolds, and he's not alone with his opinion, thinks so.

"I would say it's the best river in the state, because it doesn't have nearly the pressure you might see on the Madison, Bighorn, Missouri or Yellowstone," he said. "It clears quickly, too. We get about a week of clouded water, and then it turns coffee color again just the way we like it. Other rivers are blown out for a month or more each year. Above all, I think this is a good river for dry-fly fishermen—more so than any other. We have lots of hatches, and they all bring fish up. Plus, this is just beautiful country to look at and float through."

For visiting or resident anglers alike, the Big Hole should be a big draw. You can fish the stately rivers like the Yellowstone, Missouri and Bighorn, but until you've sampled the Big Hole, you certainly can't call your visit to Montana complete. The Big Hole River and its unique valley offer a glimpse of Montana the way it used to be. My suggestion: visit the valley and its river soon, before it, too, changes.

Stream Facts: Big Hole River

Seasons
- Open third Saturday in May through November 30. Extended whitefish season/ catch and release trout December 1 to third Saturday in May, except Divide Dam to Melrose Bridge is closed to all fishing December 1 to third Saturday in May.

Special Regulations
- All grayling and cutthroat must be released.
- Limit on brook trout: 20 fish.
- Tributaries upstream from Divide Dam: open entire year for brook trout.
- Dickie Bridge to Divide Dam: artificial flies and lures only.

Trout
- Rainbow, brown, brook, cutthroat. River also holds grayling.
- Rainbow, cutthroat, brook trout and grayling populations heaviest in upper river. Brown trout are dominant in the lower river. Most trout average 12 to 17 inches. Grayling run eight to 16 inches.

River Miles
- Twin Bridges—0
- Brown's Bridge—31
- Maiden Rock Bridge—48
- Old Divide Bridge—56.8
- Dickie Bridge—73
- Sportsman Park—80
- North Fork Big Hole—102
- Wisdom—116

River Flows
- Runoff begins in late April and peaks in June. By July 4, water conditions are ideal.

River Characteristics
- The upper river provides lots of classic flat-surfaced dry-fly water with lots of room for backcasts. The middle sections are fast and roily with brushy banks. The lower river slows down with some deep pools holding large browns. Undercut banks are abundant.

Fishing Access Downstream from Wisdom
- Fishtrap—84
- Sportsman Park—80
- Dickie Bridge—73
- Old Divide Bridge—56.8
- Maiden Rock Bridge—48.2
- Salmon Fly—39
- Brown's Bridge—31
- Glen Bridge—25
- Notch Bottom—18
- High Road—2.4

Area Fly Shops
- Sunrise Fly Shop, Melrose, MT, 406-835-3474
- Troutfitters, 62311 Highway 43, Wise River, MT, 406-832-3212
- The Montana Fly Company, Melrose, MT, 406-835-2621
- Harmon's Fly Shop, 310 S. Main, Sheridan, MT, 406-842-5868
- Frontier Anglers, 680 N. Montana St. Dillon, MT, 406-683-5276
- Fishing Headquarters, 610 N. Montana St. Dillon, MT, 406-683-6660; 800 753-6660
- Four River's Fishing Company, 205 S. Main, Twin Bridges, MT, 406-684-5651
- Big Hole River Outfitters, Wise River, MT, 406-832-3252
- Complete Fly Fisher, Hwy. 43 Wise River, MT, 406-832-3175
- Great Divide Outfitters, Charcoal Gulch, Divide, MT, 406-267-3346

Campgrounds
- Fishtrap
- Sportsman Park
- Old Divide Bridge
- Maiden Rock
- Salmon Fly
- Brown's Bridge
- Glen

BIG HOLE RIVER MAJOR HATCHES

Insect	J	F	M	A	M	J	J	A	S	O	N	D	Flies
Caddis		█	█	█	█	█	█	█					Black Caddis Pupa #16-18; X-Caddis #16-18; Emergent Sparkle Pupa #16-18; Hemingway Caddis #16-18; Tan Caddis #16-18; Elk Hair Caddis #16-18
Trico							█	█	█				Parachute Adams #18-20; Spent Wing Trico #18-20; Griffith's Gnat #18-20; CDC Biot Trico #18-20; Hairwing No Hackle Trico #18-24
Little Yellow Stonefly					█	█	█	█					Stimulator #16-18; Elk Hair Caddis #16-18; Golden Stonefly Nymph #16-18; CDC Little Yellow Stone #14-16; Henry's Fork Yellow Sally #14-16
Cranefly					█	█	█	█	█	█			Cranefly Larvae #10-16
Baetis			█	█	█				█	█			Olive Cripple #16-20; Parachute Adams #16-20; Sparkle Dun #16-20; Hare's Ear Nymph #16-20; Pheasant Tail Nymph #16-20; Poxyback Baetis #16-20
Salmonfly *Pteronarcys californica*					█	█							Seducer #4-8; Stimulator #4-8; Bitch Creek Nymph #4-8; Kaufmann's Stone #2-6; Brook's Stone #2-6; Bitch Creek Nymph #4-8; Black Rubberlegs #2-8
Golden Stone *Hesperoperla pacifica*						█	█						Whitlock's Golden Stone Nymph #4-8; Montana Nymph #4-8; Betts' Brown Stone #4-8; Whitlock's Revised Golden Stone #4-8; Poxyback Biot Golden Stone #6-12
Pale Morning Dun					█	█	█	█					Sparkle Dun #14-20; Parachute Adams #14-20; PMD Cripple #16-20; Poxy Biot Nymph #16-20; Lawson's Thorax Dun #16-20; Lempke's Extended Body PMD #16-18; Hare's Ear Nymph #16-18; Pheasant Tail Nymph #16-18; CDC Floating Nymph #16-18; Half Back Emerger #16-18

Big Hole Grayling

A grayling let loose in a mayfly factory just might die from overindulgence. The reason: grayling are voracious and they don't know when to quit eating.

That is why most flyfishers find them appealing. They can literally save the day when trout, like rainbows and browns, are feeling least cooperative.

Unfortunately, fluvial grayling only live in clear, cold, healthy river systems and that type of water is hard to find in the West. Therefore, most anglers only consider grayling when they head to the far north—Alaska, British Columbia and the Yukon.

However, there are grayling to be caught in the West, and Montana's Big Hole may be the best place to do it. In fact, the Big Hole is the only Western river with a viable population of fluvial grayling. With two good water years in a row, grayling numbers are rebounding after slumping to 22 a mile in 1987.

Today, it's estimated there are 70 grayling in each mile of the upper Big Hole. Biologist Pat Byorth hopes their numbers may eventually push 200 a mile. While that number seems low compared to the Bighorn's 6,000 trout per mile, that is a significant number when considering the grayling's appetite and propensity to inhale dry flies.

"Right now it looks real promising for the grayling," Byorth said. "The population has stabilized, and it resembles what it was in the early '80s before a series of drought years hit hard. With better water quality the past two years, the water temperature has stayed down and fish have had good spawning opportunities.

"We see a good representation of all age classes, but there is still a lot of room for recovery," he added. "The highest population we have ever sampled was 107 a mile in the late '70s. In a couple years, I think we will see numbers like that. If that is the case, it's feasible to see the numbers go as high as 180 to 200 a mile under the best possible circumstances. However, we just don't know for sure because we've never seen it that high."

Grayling, *Thymallus arcticus*, are best known for a sail-like dorsal fin that facilitates navigation in fast water. The rest of their body, including a small mouth and forked tail, resembles a mountain whitefish. Don't let that appearance fool you. Grayling are far more sporting and beautiful than whitefish. Their colors intensify from drab gray or silver to a purple cast when caught. It's like they are so mad that you've interrupted their feeding binge that they hold their breath and count to 10. Their dorsal fin offers rows of turquoise spots.

Big Hole River grayling feed on a variety of aquatic insects, and they are almost always caught feeding on the surface when a decent hatch or spinner fall occurs.

"Mostly, they eat small aquatic invertebrates," Byorth said. "In the Big Hole they stick to caddis and mayflies. They really gorge on the nymphs, but they eat the adults, too."

Big Hole grayling numbers are highest between Wisdom and Wise River, and that is where I have found good numbers. Most of those grayling run between eight and 12 inches, but a few prime specimens push 15 inches. That is about as large as Montana's fluvial grayling get. However, a friend, Dan Summerfield, landed a 16-incher on the Madison River, of all places. The Madison does not hold a large population of grayling.

While anglers may find Big Hole grayling munching caddis and pale morning duns along the grassy or rock-strewn banks or in the slack seams behind islands and obstructions, they seem particularly fond of the mouth of feeder creeks, backwaters, and sloughs.

"They are attracted to that placid water," said Fred Thomas (author's father), a grayling connoisseur who has chased that fish on many of Alaska's backwaters and the upper Big Hole. "They don't like to work in the main current. Instead, you will find them in the seams and slackwater pools. That slow water is also where mosquitoes, gnats, and other insects congregate."

Grayling are not fussy about patterns or tippet size. Tie on a 5X tippet followed by a size 16 PMD, dark-bodied elk hair caddis,or a parachute Adams, and you should be able to catch Big Hole grayling all summer.

When you do land a grayling, consider its plight. Its very existence in the Lower Forty Eight is precarious at best. Fight the fish quickly, keep it in the water, and use forceps to remove the hook. Then, gently point it into the current until it has regained strength and is ready to part company. And don't even think about taking one to the taxidermist—catch and release is required on grayling throughout the Big Hole.

Jim Nave holds a true Montana treasure—a Big Hole River fluvial grayling. The Big Hole offers the last substantial western grayling population, a fish that rises eagerly for dry flies.

Beaverhead River

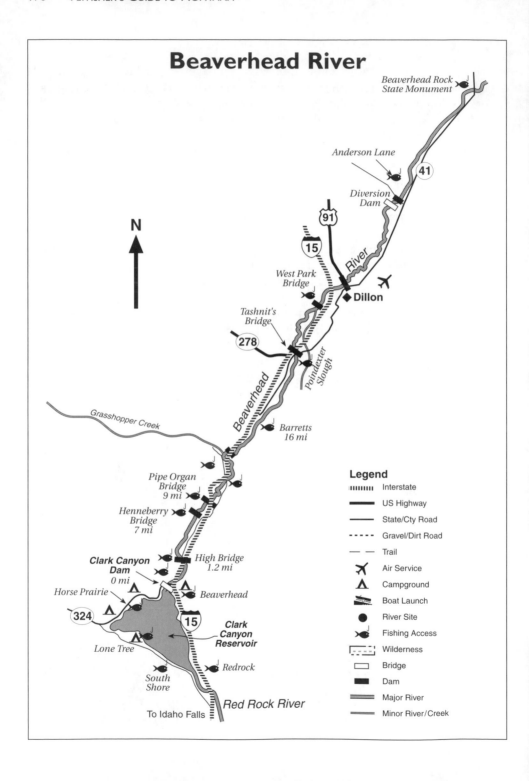

Beaverhead Rock
State Monument

Anderson Lane

41

Diversion
Dam

91

15

West Park
Bridge

◆ **Dillon**

Tashnit's
Bridge

278

Poindexter Slough

N

Grasshopper Creek

Beaverhead

Barretts
16 mi

Pipe Organ
Bridge
9 mi

Henneberry
Bridge
7 mi

**Clark Canyon
Dam**
0 mi

High Bridge
1.2 mi

Horse Prairie

Beaverhead

324

15

**Clark
Canyon
Reservoir**

Lone Tree

South
Shore

Redrock

Red Rock River

To Idaho Falls

Legend

⅏	Interstate
▬	US Highway
—	State/Cty Road
-----	Gravel/Dirt Road
– –	Trail
✕	Air Service
⛰	Campground
🛶	Boat Launch
●	River Site
🐟	Fishing Access
⬚	Wilderness
▭	Bridge
■	Dam
▬	Major River
—	Minor River/Creek

BEAVERHEAD RIVER

Compared to some of the broad, brooding waters of the West, the Beaverhead River seems a little paltry. To the untrained eye, its willow-laced banks contain a narrow, serpentine flow that looks awesome for small brookies and little else.

However, looks can be deceiving. Anglers with a trained eye who test the Beaverhead's depths will find the greatest population of large brown trout in Montana, possibly in all of the West. It has always been that way, and barring any catastrophic disasters, it should always be that way. The river's trout habitat is ideal, and it suits brown trout particularly well, although there are a number of large rainbows in the upper system, too.

Despite healthy numbers of large fish, you are not going to go out and slay one big brown or rainbow after another. The river is simply too difficult for the average flycaster. But fishing can be quite productive, and with each cast a flyfisher could hook the trout of a lifetime.

Always tempting, forever frustrating, the Beaverhead demands stealth, patience and ingenuity. Just ask Montana Fish, Wildlife and Parks' biologist Dick Oswald. He seems particularly amused at the flyfisher's plight when working the river.

"The real monsters don't come easy," Oswald said. "In fact, they are much harder to catch than the smaller browns and rainbows. And that's good in the face of increased pressure, which is what we are seeing on the river now.

"Some people who have fished the Beaverhead for 20 years remember the good old days when they caught significant numbers of large fish. They ask me to put total catch-and-release regulations on the entire river. I laugh because there are more trout in the river than there ever have been. It's just a hell of a lot tougher to catch a good fish now than it was before."

A good fish on the Beaverhead stretches 18 inches or more. Specimens to 30 inches exist. In a 1996 electrofishing survey, Oswald wrapped his mitts around a brown that weighed 11 pounds. Rumors of browns to 15 pounds have circulated. In my mind those rumors could very well be true, but we fishermen know the exaggeration power of our peers. Until some lucky angler displays a photo of an absolutely prehistoric-looking Beaverhead brown (just before releasing it back to the river, I hope), I remain a cautious, yet enthusiastic, skeptic.

"I've been here in Dillon for 16 years, and I only remember a half-dozen monsters being caught between the dam and High Bridge," Oswald said. "But we handle large fish like crazy in our surveys. There are piles of them in there. It's just real rare that anybody nails one.

"The general fisherman wants success," Oswald added. "He's doing what the average fish responds to. If I was bent on catching a huge brown, I would do something completely atypical, like working tarpon flies in the deepest holes for hours on end. However, you aren't going to have a high success rate doing that. You need serious patience and a lot of drive to get one monster fish. Your odds of taking one of those are astronomically low when you're drifting an elk hair caddis on the surface."

During winter, flyfishers can get on the Beaverhead below Pipe Organ Bridge (pictured). Above the bridge, the river is closed until opening day to protect spawning rainbows.

Actually, the odds of taking many of the Beaverhead's trout in any size lessens when a flyfisher ties on a dry. There are times when anglers find fish up top slurping duns, spinners and emergers, but the Beaverhead has always been known as, and will continue to be called, a nymph and streamer fishery.

However, things have changed on the river in the last decade. No longer can a flyfisher chuck a big yuk bug under the banks and expect a strike. The yuk bug was the ticket in the 1960s, 1970s and even the early 1980s. Today, small nymphs like a size 22 midge pupa are standard fare, and they must be fished in an effective manner, meaning they must be bounced seductively along the bottom rocks for a flyfisher to be successful.

"The Beaverhead is not really conducive to dry-fly fishing," says Dick Sharon at Fishing Headquarters in Dillon. "Nine out of 10 fish are caught subsurface, and that is particularly true of the upper river. If a person is going to the Beaverhead for dry-fly fishing, he is definitely going to the wrong river. He should be hitting the Big Hole.

"We spend most of our time nymphing with small stuff like pheasant tails, peeking caddis and midge larvae," Sharon offers. "The smaller the fly the better. We find a good spot on the river, get out of the raft and work the water thoroughly. When I'm really feeling athletic, I love to throw streamers. They have always worked well on this river, and they still do today. But you have to pop them into the cubby holes right along the banks, and most folks can't hit the spots with weighted streamers. Most of their flies end up in the trees. There are spots on this river where some trees look like they've been decorated with Christmas tree ornaments!"

The Beaverhead begins at the base of Clark Canyon Dam, about 10 miles south of Dillon. From the dam, the river charges north, 100 yards downstream before its

Author's father, Fred, and sister, Kim, pose with a Beaverhead brown. Throughout summer, nymphs, such as hare's ears, pheasant tails, caddis and midge larvae, consistently take fish.

first bend—a physical feature that marks the nature of the Beaverhead for the rest of its course.

In fact, the river continues to twist, rarely running in a straight line for more than 100 yards, which creates an abundance of deep pools, undercut banks, choice runs and shallow riffles—killer trout habitat in excess. It's estimated that 1,500 to 2,000 trout fin in the prime, most popular, and heaviest-fished water extending from the dam at Clark Canyon downstream to Barrett's Diversion Dam. There are a number of public access sites in that section, such as Clark Canyon Dam, High Bridge, Henneberry and Pipe Organ Bridge, that facilitate easy access. During high water years, wade fishers will find the river is simply too deep to wade effectively when the water is up. Floatfishers, who can row from one prime hole to another, are at a distinct advantage.

Flyfishers will want to work the river above Grasshopper Creek during the spring and early summer, when high water turns Grasshopper into a muddy, rushing torrent. It clouds the Beaverhead below its confluence and severely limits a flyfisher's options.

From Barrett's Diversion Dam downstream through Dillon, access sites thin out, but trout numbers remain relatively stable and large fish persist. If a flyfisher is looking for a more private venture than the upper river offers, try floating between Barrett's and Tashnit's Bridges just south of Dillon.

"Really, there is a tremendous trout population all the way to Dillon," Oswald said. "There are lesser numbers of large fish in the lower sections, but in relation to the entire population, you handle a high percentage of large fish extending from Barrett's all the way to Twin Bridges. It's just that total numbers taper off.

"I think people are making a big mistake if they don't fish below Barrett's and even below Dillon," Oswald said. "We do find the greatest number of large trout just below Clark Canyon, but they don't come easy. I think a guy has a real good chance of taking a very large brown on the lower sections."

While large fish persist, trout populations do drop to levels that range between 350 and 550 fish a mile below Dillon, where the river flattens and straightens out a bit and becomes a little more conducive to the dry-fly fisher.

The Beaverhead's most significant hatches begin with small stoneflies, Baetis mayflies and midges during spring. However, the upper river from Clark Canyon Dam to Pipe Organ Bridge remains closed from November 30 through the third Saturday in May to protect spawning rainbows. Below Pipe Organ the river remains open all year, but fishing is somewhat unproductive through the winter and spring months.

"It's just tough conditions during winter," Oswald said. "Anytime the water temperature is under 50 degrees, you are pushing the limit of productive fishing conditions. I've had people tell me they do well on nice winter days, but generally the fish are just resting during winter, and they are tough to catch."

When the upper river opens, flyfishers should expect to see some yellow sallies (small stoneflies), Callibaetis mayflies, extensive caddis hatches, and as always, midges.

By July, pale morning dun mayflies make their appearance, and fishing can really perk up. Most of the action can be had on PMD nymphs, but a flyfisher who encounters a rising brown or rainbow during a PMD emergence or spinnerfall has a good shot at taking that fish on a size 16 or 18 parachute PMD or a rusty spinner. Just remember, the water is crystal clear, and light tippets will be required. That combination makes it nearly impossible to catch the largest fish.

Caddisflies continue their emergence through the summer, and flyfishers can target the caddis during afternoons and evenings. An elk hair caddis is standard fare for the Beaverhead, but a Hemingway caddis, an X-caddis or a LaFontaine deep sparkle pupa or emergent sparkle pupa are excellent options, too.

Grasshoppers are present on the Beaverhead in late July through early September, but their importance is limited on the upper river where willow-lined banks form a barrier between the water and the irrigated fields where hoppers thrive. However, on the lower river, where undercut banks run adjacent to fields and willows are less prevalent, hopper patterns can draw large browns to the surface from mid-July through mid-September.

Trico mayflies can be found on the water from mid-July through August. Their presence can be detected by a morning spinnerfall that coincides with an emer-

Small dogs and young swimmers beware—the Beaverhead hosts some monster brown trout. Scott Brown drilled this "once-in-a-lifetime buck" on a pheasant tail nymph. (Scott Brown Photo)

gence. At times Tricos can literally blanket the water, and a flyfisher's challenge is not to get a fish to eat, but rather how to get a fish to eat your tiny imitation when so many other naturals are floating on the water. Then, if you do hook a fish, it's a matter of landing a monster on some thread-like leader—5X, 6X, even 7X may be required under the most challenging conditions while stalking the most wary fish.

In late August extending well into September, a seldom heralded hatch occurs, and some of the best fishing of the year occurs. *Diptera tipulidae,* commonly called craneflies, are most active after warm, late summer rainshowers or early in the season when the first high flows of the year wash them from the muddy banks en masse.

During those times, cranefly larvae imitations like a muskrat or a Western cranefly larva work well. When adult craneflies are active some big browns and rainbows will rise to the top and pound them. Flies that skate across the surface will draw strikes. The ginger spider, ginger variant or Darbee cranefly are effective patterns. However, Tim Tollett at Frontier Anglers and Sharon at Fishing Headquarters harbor local patterns that are probably most effective. Stop in at their shops before you hit the water.

In September, extending through the end of the general fishing season, flyfishers will encounter strong Baetis mayfly hatches. The Beaverhead's trout, possibly sensing their last good meal until spring, are more than eager to slurp in Baetis nymphs, emergers and even dries.

By late November there may be a few Baetis holding strong, but the midge hatch takes over in importance and these hatches can be massive. That is the way it remains through April.

During winter you can expect the river to be uncrowded. Only hard-cores are willing to brave the elements and fish in frigid weather. However, that doesn't hold true during the Beaverhead's prime months, which extend from late May through October. At times in certain sections (especially the upper river), flyfishers may literally be lined up within yards of each other, flailing away at a prime hole. For me, the sight is almost sickening. It reminds me more of the western Washington steelhead rivers of my youth than it does a secluded Montana trout river. But that is the face of flyfishing in the late stages of the 20th century, and those who can't accept it had better head for the high mountain lakes or a small stream that lacks easy access.

"Relative to everywhere else, crowding isn't much of a problem on the Beaverhead, but compared to five years ago, it's a mess," Sharon says. "Respect is very important here because the river is so small. If you piss somebody off, realize that at some point during the day, you are probably going to pass right by them again.

"A lot of people are complaining about it (pressure), but I have not seen a lot of impact on the quality of fishing," Sharon adds. "There are some spots that are attractive to everyone, but there are a million other spots that don't get much pressure at all and they hold huge fish. However, during high water years, the problem is exacerbated by limited areas to fish."

High water can limit access to the river and a flyfisher's success itself. Most anglers agree that when the Beaverhead runs 600 to 800 cfs, conditions are prime. During high water years, the river may run 1,500 cfs through mid-September, and that can make for difficult wading, although floatfishers find decent conditions. When the water sinks to 200 or 300 cfs, which it does during some winters, a raft or drift boat may scrape bottom in the shallower riffles, but fish become concentrated in the prime habitat and fishing remains excellent.

Because the Beaverhead is so notorious for its large trout, especially browns, many anglers arrive with bloated expectations. They dream of rods bent double, straightened hooks, and at least a couple times during a week-long stay, holding those notorious five-pounders.

Unfortunately, the Beaverhead's trout are tough to catch. They present a true challenge to the flyfisher. On certain days, when everything seems perfect, flyfishers can drill 15 to 20 fish, with a few stretching 20 inches or more. However, on the average day, a few fish may come to net, a few more may be missed or broken off and, always, the brush will account for a few of your flies. Those who arrive with modest expectations will always find success on the beautiful Beaverhead. Those who just have to land some monster trout to make their trip a success are simply asking for a let-down. For those who harbor such lofty aspirations, plan at least five days on the river. More days spent on the water will heighten your chances for success.

Stream Facts: Beaverhead

Seasons
- Clark Canyon Dam to Pipe Organ Bridge open third Saturday in May through November 30.
- Downstream from Pipe Organ open all year.

Special Regulations
- Limit: three trout, only one over 18 inches and only one rainbow.

Trout
- Rainbow and brown trout ranging from 12 inches to 15 pounds. Brown trout make up the greatest share of large trout. Rainbow populations are highest in the upper river.

River Miles
- Twin Bridges—2.4
- Beaverhead Rock—26
- Poindexter Slough—59
- Barretts Diversion Dam—63.5
- Grasshopper Creek—66
- Pipe Organ Bridge—70.5
- Henneberry—72.7
- High Bridge—78.7
- Clark Canyon Dam—79.5

River Flows
- Peak flows arrive in late May and June when flows run over 800 cfs.
- Prime fishing occurs with flows ranging between 200 and 800 cfs. Flows below 300 cfs provide difficult floating conditions.

River Characteristics
- The Beaverhead is a narrow, deep river that winds like crazy and harbors a ton of brush on its banks. It runs about 12 to 18 yards wide in most places. The trout hold below riffles in the runs and pools and under cutbanks.

Fishing Access
- Clark Canyon Dam
- High Bridge
- Henneberry
- Pipe Organ Bridge
- Grasshopper Creek
- Barretts Diversion Dam
- Poindexter Slough
- West Park Bridge
- Anderson Lane

Area Fly Shops
- Sunrise Fly Shop, Melrose, MT, 406-835-3474
- Troutfitters, 62311 Highway 43 Wise River, MT, 406-832-3212
- The Montana Fly Company Melrose, MT, 406-835-2621
- Harmon's Fly Shop 310 S. Main, Sheridan, MT, 406-842-5868
- Frontier Anglers 680 N. Montana St. Dillon, MT, 406-683-5276
- Fishing Headquarters 610 N. Montana St. Dillon, MT, 406-683-6660; 800-753-6660
- Four River's Fishing Company 205 S. Main, Twin Bridges, MT, 406-684-5651
- Big Hole River Outfitters Wise River, MT, 406-832-3252
- Complete Fly Fisher Hwy. 43 Wise River, MT, 406-832-3175

Camping
- Horse Prairie at Clark Canyon Reservoir
- Lone Tree at Clark Canyon Reservoir
- Clark Canyon campground, just downstream from Clark Canyon Dam

BEAVERHEAD RIVER MAJOR HATCHES

Insect	J	F	M	A	M	J	J	A	S	O	N	D	Flies
Caddis			■	■	■	■	■	■	■	■			Black Caddis Pupa #16-18; X-Caddis #16-18; Emergent Sparkle Pupa #16-18; Hemingway Caddis #16-18; Tan Caddis #16-18; Elk Hair Caddis #16-18
Trico							■	■					Parachute Adams #18-20; Spent Wing Trico #18-20; Griffith's Gnat #18-20; CDC Trico #18-20
Little Yellow Stonefly						■							Stimulator #16-18; Elk Hair Caddis #16-18; Golden Stonefly Nymph #16-18
Cranefly								■	■				Cranefly Larvae (brown, gray, orange) #10-16
Baetis				■			■	■	■				Olive Cripple # 6-20; Parachute Adams #16-20; Sparkle Dun #16-20; Hare's Ear Nymph #16-20; Pheasant Tail Nymph #16-20; Poxyback Baetis #16-20
Pale Morning Dun						■	■	■					Sparkle Dun #14-20; Parachute Adams #14-20; PMD Cripple #16-20; Poxy Biot Nymph #16-20; Lawson's Thorax Dun #16-20; Lempke's Extended Body PMD #16-18; Hare's Ear Nymph #16-18; Pheasant Tail Nymph #16-18; CDC Floating Nymph #16-18; Half Back Emerger #16-18
Midge	■	■	■	■	■	■	■	■	■	■	■	■	Griffith's Gnat #18-20; Standard Adams #16-20; Palomino Midge #16-20; Serendipity #16-20; Brassie #18-20; Disco Midge #16-20
Grasshopper								■	■				Dave's Hopper #2-8; Meadow Hopper #2-8

BEAVERHEAD RIVER TRIBUTARIES

Red Rock River

Not technically a tributary of the Beaverhead River, the Red Rock River feeds Clark Canyon Reservoir, which ultimately starts the Beaverhead at the base of its dam.

If the Red Rock was not tied up with so much private property, you would read about the stream in every major national sporting magazine. Red Rock holds really big brown and rainbow trout, and it offers excellent hatches throughout summer on its lower end while providing opportunities to catch healthy grayling in its upper reaches, which begin in the Centennial Mountains just west of Idaho's famous Henry's Lake.

The river falls under general regulations (open third Saturday in May through November 30), but its limiting factor is a matter of access rather than season. However, there are several options to consider on the lower river: you can pay a fee to cross some ranch lands or gain access to the river at several bridge crossings. If you choose that method of access, do not allow yourself above the high water mark—landowners do not appreciate trespassers. Launching a small boat or raft from one of the bridges is not easy and, truthfully, the Red Rock is best waded. If you are going to float, a floattube is more ideal for the stream because it's small, ranging between 10 and 15 yards wide in most places. Boats and rafts take up the entire stream, it seems.

Access is easy on the upper river, from upper Red Rock Lake to the headwaters. That's where you will find those grayling and some nice-sized cutthroats. During spring, some huge cutthroat/rainbow hybrids move out of upper Red Rock Lake and into the river. Unfortunately, by opening day water conditions often cancel fishing plans. Besides, fishing the river as it winds through dense willow patches is taking your life in your hands—cow moose with calves have an ugly way of wrecking a positive fishing experience.

Both upper and lower Red Rock Lakes are closed to fishing, as is the channel between the two. Productive fishing begins below Lima Reservoir and extends downstream to Clark Canyon Reservoir.

During summer, after high water subsides, flyfishers should expect heavy-duty caddis hatches in June and July. Morning and evening fishing can be awesome. PMDs will draw trout to the surface in late June, July and August. During August, grasshoppers crash on the river's surface, furnishing some of the West's best hopper action. Bulky Red Rock trout often show no mercy when a big Dave's or Joe's hopper plops down in front of them.

While access is definitely a problem on the river, Red Rock provides some of the best dry-fly fishing in the state. Its lower section runs through flat agricultural lands. Its faces range from classic flat-surfaced spring creek-like current through wide open meadows to long glides under cutbanks and overhanging willows—prime dry-fly water throughout.

To reach Red Rock, take Interstate 15 south from Dillon. The Red Rock dumps into the south end of Clark Canyon Reservoir. To gain access to the very lowest end, take Exit 37 off the Interstate and follow the side road back toward the reservoir. The river is located east of the road. To reach the upper river above upper Red Rock Lake, follow Interstate 15 through Lima. At Monida (Exit 0), follow a dirt road east toward Red Rock Pass. Access signs will lead you to the river.

Remember, the upper Red Rock is remote country. Bring all the necessities with you (groceries in Dillon for sure). You'll want extra food, water, gas, and fishing gear. There are no fly shops or sporting goods stores within 30 to 40 miles of the upper river.

Grasshopper Creek

It's a hung jury on this stream—fish Grasshopper during spring or early summer when the water is high, and you are bound to hate it. Hit the creek after runoff when it runs clear and solid insect hatches come off, and you will fall in love.

Grasshopper Creek begins in the Pioneer Mountains at Big Hole Pass, about 38 miles northwest of Dillon, just north of Bannock, where the first major gold strike was made in the state.

In its headwater reaches, Grasshopper offers small brookies, a nice hot springs (Elkhorn Hot Springs), a campground, and small ski area (Maverick Mountain).

The best fishing Grasshopper has to offer rests downstream near Bannock. Unfortunately, most of the land around Bannock is private and access is difficult. Water quality diminishes downstream, but there are still a few trout around. Look for some browns and rainbows in the 16- to 20-inch class on occasion.

Look for typical summer hatches on Grasshopper. Flyfishers should see caddis between May and September, especially in the late afternoon and early evening hours. PMDs emerge between July and August, Trico mayflies in late August and September, and Baetis when the temperature cools in September and October.

Grasshopper is not a stream to float; it is a small stream, with maybe 20 or 30 feet of water maintained between its banks on average. Wade fishing is the most productive way to attack the stream. Note: During high water or after severe thundershowers, grasshopper will run cloudy.

Grasshopper falls under general regulations: open third Saturday in May through November 30.

Clark Canyon Reservoir

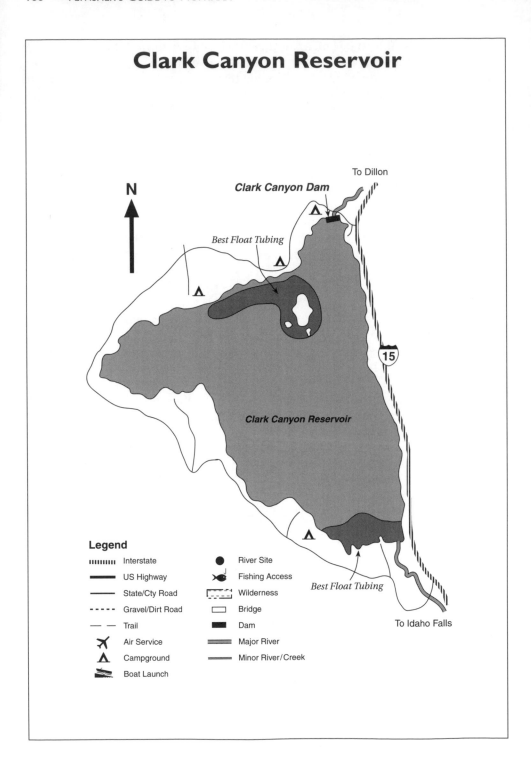

N

To Dillon

Clark Canyon Dam

Λ

Best Float Tubing

Λ

Λ

15

Clark Canyon Reservoir

Λ

Legend

� Interstate		●	River Site
▬ US Highway		⇲	Fishing Access
— State/Cty Road		▱	Wilderness
- - - - - Gravel/Dirt Road		▭	Bridge
— — Trail		▬	Dam
✈ Air Service		▬	Major River
Λ Campground		—	Minor River/Creek
⛴ Boat Launch			

Best Float Tubing

To Idaho Falls

CLARK CANYON RESERVOIR

Clark Canyon Reservoir rests in the Centennial Valley next to Interstate 15, just 20 miles south of Dillon. The interstate offers access to most of the east shore while Highway 324 provides ample access to the west side. A narrow dirt road, in a few places still concrete, which is accessible from I-15, leads anglers to the south end of the reservoir.

Many of Montana's top flyfishers consider Clark Canyon the premiere trophy stillwater fishery in the state. With its large fish, beautiful scenery and easy access, that statement is tough to argue. Most of the time, Clark's big fish are more than willing to rise to your fly.

The reservoir, which covers about 6,000 acres when it is full, is best known for its rainbow trout, fast growing fish that reach impressive length, although it has a decent population of large brown trout, too.

"The growth rate in Clark Canyon is exceptional," says Dick Oswald at Montana Department of Fish, Wildlife and Parks. "A (4.5-inch) rainbow stocked in June will measure about 14 inches the following May. Generally speaking, a three-year old spring fish will average about 21 inches. At four years old they will measure about 22.5 inches. Our Eagle Lake rainbows at full maturity range between five and seven pounds. A few whoppers reach 12 pounds."

Clark Canyon also offers enormous brown trout that will occasionally eat a fly. They are best known as lockjawed creatures that hold tight to the bottom. Normally, that is the case with browns, but on occasion, some unknown set of elements puts them on the feed, and they can be taken on a variety of subsurface patterns.

"Our brown trout are not caught as frequently as the rainbows," Oswald says. "They are always harder to catch, no matter where you are. There are some huge fish in the reservoir—some that go ten pounds or more—but you don't see them very often."

Despite the huge trout, the reservoir receives little pressure when compared to the Beaverhead River—the area's biggest draw. Flyfishers who fail to fish the reservoir and strictly focus on the river are making a big mistake, especially if they spend more than a couple days in the area.

Prime flyfishing at Clark Canyon begins sometime between late March and mid April, just as the winter ice sheet begins to break. Even small openings in the ice can provide good opportunities.

Look for leech patterns, such as Canadian red mohair leeches or olive bunny leeches, to draw the most strikes. Midge patterns may also be fished effectively.

In June, Callibaetis mayflies begin popping and surface activity can be strong, especially during the morning hours. They seem to emerge especially heavy on the south shore, mainly near the mouth of the Red Rock River. Nymphs, such as hare's ears and pheasant tails, and dry flies like Callibaetis cripples, a parachute Adams, and gray sparkle duns, work well. Midges will hatch with the Callibaetis, partially coating the water at times.

Damselflies show up in July, and they may extend into August. Rainbows, especially, key on those big damsel nymphs. Areas with lots of submerged aquatic vegetation, such as the south end of the reservoir near the inlet of the Red Rock River, will typically provide the best fishing during the damsel hatch.

Callibaetis and midge patterns become effective again in early fall, from September through October. Spring and fall also offer relatively sparse angler numbers. On weekdays you can have the reservoir to yourself. During summer, recreational boaters and anglers pulling hardware, like big strings of Pop Gear, vie for the choice areas.

Bank fishing can be decent at times, but it can be a boring affair, unless you milk a cooler full of your favorite beverage between strikes. Most shore fishers chuck large hunks of lead, trailed by a gob of nightcrawlers or, don't scream, Power Bait. They take some big trout on those setups, too.

The shore-bound flyfisher is best served by a variety of nymph and streamer patterns. Those patterns can be cast out and stripped back in, but the most effective retrieve is the wind-aided drift, which consists of letting the wind push your fly and strike indicator slowly into shore. Large strike indicators (essentially bobbers) work best, especially when visibility is limited by whitecaps. Some large trout are taken during the spring in that fashion.

Flyfishers who have a boat or floattube at their disposal should target the south end of the reservoir where the Red Rock pours in. There are plenty of submerged willows in that area that must hold a treasure trove of broken-off flies. Fortunately, the big browns and rainbows that hang out in that section are pretty aggressive, too. The willows and the accompanying submerged vegetation grow dense numbers of damselflies, scuds and leaches. Trout are drawn to that smorgasbord every day of the year.

Wherever you fish at Clark Canyon, one fly that will work when all others may fail is the Sheep Creek Special, which was created by George Biggs of Jerome, Idaho, around 1969.

The hackle of the Sheep Creek is wound sparsely. Various shades of olive are used for the body. The wing is a thin segment of mallard breast feather. Sizes 6, 8 and 10 work best.

I've found the Sheep Creek effective during all seasons and in all types of weather. So have my friends—in fact, Dan Summerfield landed two big rainbows and a modest brown on Sheep Creek Specials.

Clark Canyon is not a difficult water to fish, but it can be temperamental. Sometimes the reservoir produces and sometimes it doesn't. Patience plays a large part in an angler's success—those who have faith in the reservoir and choose to remain on the water through bouts of boredom are bound to score when the bite turns on. During spring and fall, remaining on the water means wearing layers of

A modest Clark Canyon rainbow in the net!

clothing like polar fleece garments from Patagonia, which happens to have an outlet store in Dillon. Also, try the Capilene® underwear by Patagonia.

Possessing a floating and a sinktip line encourages success, too. In fact, if the trout are up top eating midges, the floating line will serve best. However, if there is no visible hatch and the fish are holding deep, a sinktip or fullsink line is the ticket.

Changing tippets for varying situations will add to a flyfisher's success, as well. If you are fishing up top to rising trout, go with a 10-foot long, or longer, leader and taper it down to 5X. When fishing nymphs and streamers deep, try a shorter leader like a 7.5-footer and don't worry about going down to 3X—the heavier tippet will aid in landing large fish, especially those hooked near the submerged willows.

If you are going to stay at Clark Canyon overnight, there are two maintained campgrounds—one at the north end of the lake and the other on the south shore. There are also two boat ramps. One is located just south of Clark Canyon Dam, and another rests on the west side shore. Both can handle large boats.

If a motel sounds more appealing than a night next to a windy reservoir fending off packs of hungry skunks and mischievous coyotes, head for Dillon, just 20 miles north and grab a motel room for the evening.

Although a number of factors can influence the outcome of a flyfishing venture on Clark Canyon Reservoir, a heavy wind and lockjawed trout playing large roles, the reservoir remains one of Montana's top bets for large fish. With persistence, any flyfisher with average skills can land a five-pounder here. That says a lot for Clark Canyon.

CLARK CANYON RESERVOIR MAJOR HATCHES

Insect	J	F	M	A	M	J	J	A	S	O	N	D	Flies
Midges													Palomino Midge #18-20; RS-2 Emerger #16-18; Serendipity #16-20; Parachute Adams #16-22; Griffith's Gnat #16-20
Damselfly													Marabou Damsel #10-12; Six Pack #10-12; Swimming Damsel #8-12
Scud													Scud (gray, olive) #16-18
Leech													Rabbit Strip Leech (olive, black, brown) #2-6; Mohair Leech #2-8; Marabou Leech #4-8; Woolly Bugger #2-8

MADISON RIVER

The Madison River might be Montana's most revered natural feature. Flyfishers have flocked to the river for 80 years, and the action hasn't disappointed. The river and its banks are glorified in every major sporting publication in America.

The Madison River and Montana are inseparable partners. Legendary flyfishers like Joe Brooks honed their craft there. Even today, many flyfishers don't feel they've arrived until they throw a line in one of the river's brood riffles.

On a very good day, the Madison may place 15 or more good trout in your hand. On a bad day, it offers impressive Western scenery to the max. And there is always a dedicated horde of flyfishers to offer worthy conversation, whether while sharing a beer on the banks of the river or at a bar or restaurant in Ennis, West Yellowstone or Three Forks. The Madison Valley is trout country, and the towns around it thrive on that aura. At every bar, cafe or espresso stand (yes, even in Montana; "give me a double tall skinny with a dose of bourbon!") conversation swirls around the hatches, the runoff, the boat that wrapped itself around the big boulder, the big brown that was landed in the braids, the rainbow that broke off by Slide or the unexpected summer snowstorm that dumped four inches of the big white stuff on those oars and that drift boat.

For the flyfishing fanatic, this is good country to call home. It seems everyone has a vested or emotional interest in the river and its fishing—that is a quality that is hard to identify in many portions of the West.

The Madison begins in Yellowstone National Park where the Gibbon and Firehole rivers, both dandy trout streams, meet. From there it flows west out of the park and through Hebgen Reservoir and Quake Lake, which offer excellent flyfishing opportunities for big browns and rainbows. At its outlet from Quake Lake at Slide Inn, the true Madison begins (the stretch of river most people refer to when speaking about the Madison and its flyfishing). From Slide to Ennis Lake, the river is affectionately labeled, "The 50-Mile Riffle."

Through that section it provides excellent hatches and a variety of water, ranging from shallow rocky riffles to deep pools and braided channels. Big salmonflies, golden stoneflies, nemora stoneflies and blue-winged olive, pale morning dun, gray drake, green drake, callibaetis and March brown mayflies exist. Tons of caddis—a variety of species—swarm over the river during spring and summer, too.

Below Ennis Lake, the Madison splits the Bear Trap Canyon, providing roily water, dangerous rapids and some awfully large and difficult trout. Below the canyon, the river becomes shallow, slows down and broadens. Limited opportunity exists in the canyon. Below the canyon, spring, fall and winter fishing is best—the water temperature rises too high during summer.

The Madison has gained much press lately for its problems. In fact, it was the Madison that brought national attention to the effects of whirling disease, that insidious infection that knocked off about 90 percent of the Madison's rainbow population during the early and mid-nineties. It's anyone's guess whether the river will rebound from its whirling disease woes. The fact is this: the river holds a decent

Upper Madison River

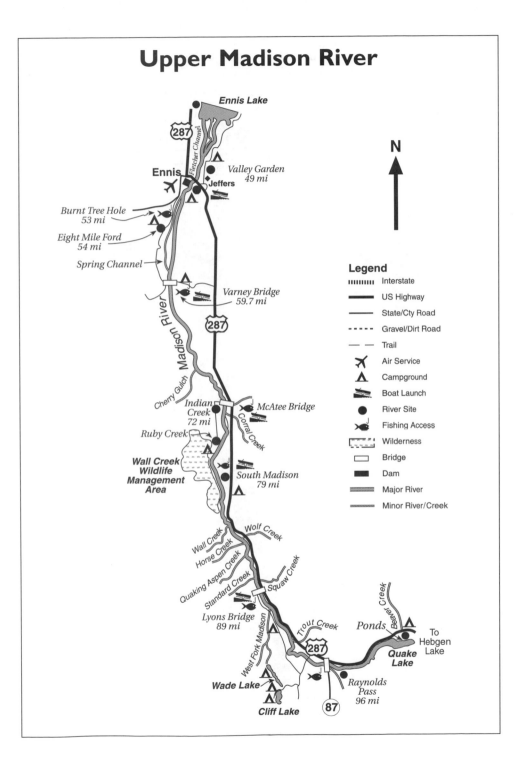

N

Ennis Lake

287

Fletcher Channel

Ennis

Valley Garden
49 mi

Jeffers

Burnt Tree Hole
53 mi

Eight Mile Ford
54 mi

Spring Channel

Madison River

287

Varney Bridge
59.7 mi

Cherry Gulch

Indian Creek
72 mi

McAtee Bridge

Ruby Creek

Corral Creek

Wall Creek Wildlife Management Area

South Madison
79 mi

Wolf Creek

Wall Creek
Horse Creek
Quaking Aspen Creek
Standard Creek
Squaw Creek

Lyons Bridge
89 mi

West Fork Madison

Trout Creek

Beaver Creek

Ponds

To Hebgen Lake

Quake Lake

Wade Lake

Raynolds Pass
96 mi

287

Cliff Lake

87

Legend

▥▥▥▥	Interstate
▬▬▬	US Highway
———	State/Cty Road
- - - - -	Gravel/Dirt Road
— —	Trail
✈	Air Service
▲	Campground
⛴	Boat Launch
●	River Site
✦	Fishing Access
▨	Wilderness
▭	Bridge
■	Dam
▰▰▰	Major River
══	Minor River/Creek

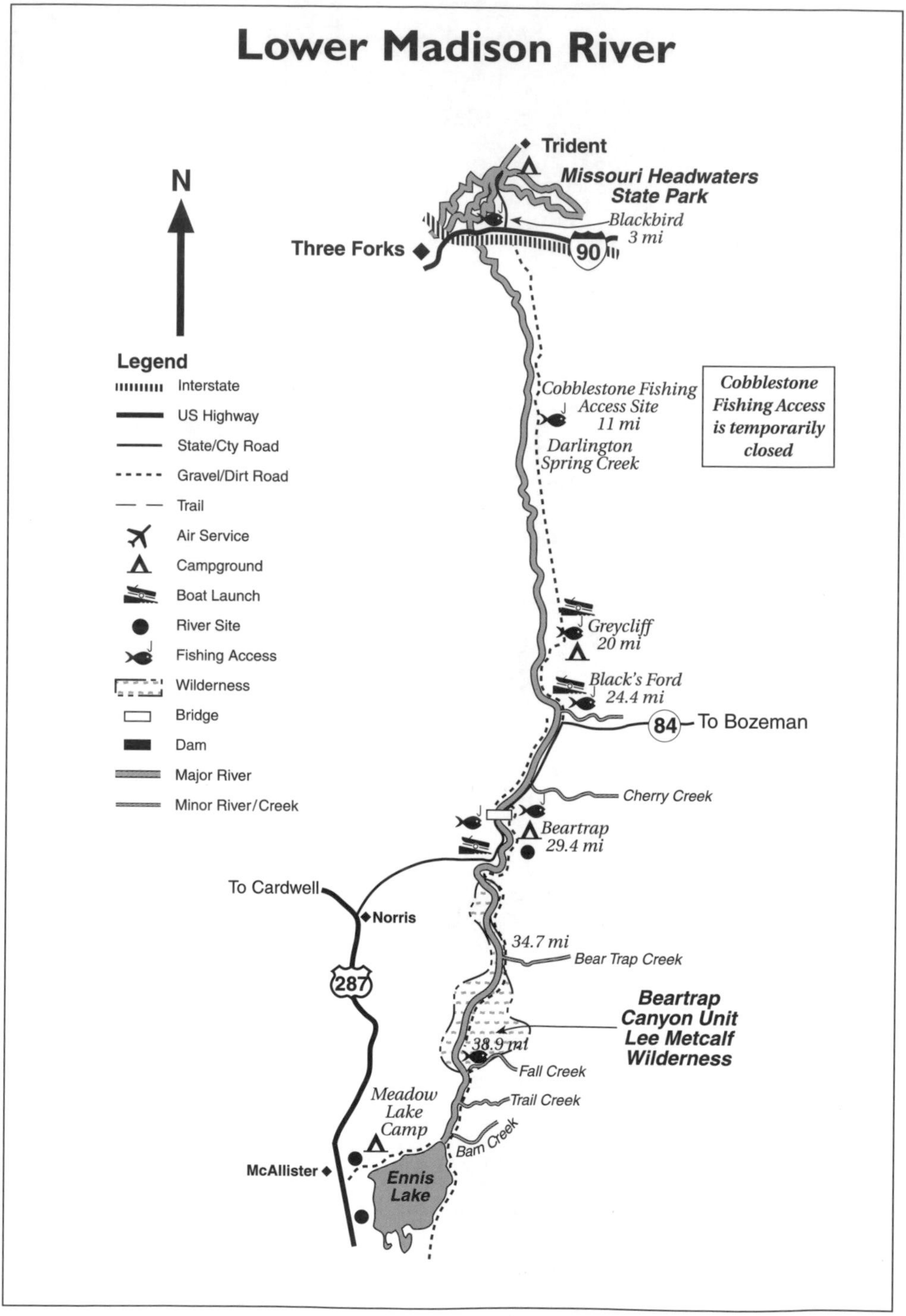
Lower Madison River
N
Legend
Interstate
US Highway
State/Cty Road
Gravel/Dirt Road
Trail
Air Service
Campground
Boat Launch
River Site
Fishing Access
Wilderness
Bridge
Dam
Major River
Minor River/Creek
Trident
Missouri Headwaters State Park
Blackbird 3 mi
Three Forks
90
Cobblestone Fishing Access Site 11 mi
Cobblestone Fishing Access is temporarily closed
Darlington Spring Creek
Greycliff 20 mi
Black's Ford 24.4 mi
84
To Bozeman
Cherry Creek
Beartrap 29.4 mi
To Cardwell
Norris
34.7 mi
Bear Trap Creek
287
Beartrap Canyon Unit Lee Metcalf Wilderness
38.9 mi
Fall Creek
Trail Creek
Meadow Lake Camp
Barn Creek
McAllister
Ennis Lake

population of large rainbows and healthy numbers of various size brown trout. Fishing can't compare to what it was in past decades, but the river is still a good one.

Following is a rundown of the hatches and flyfishing opportunities on the Madison throughout the season.

Confluence of Gibbon and Firehole Rivers in Yellowstone Park to Hebgen Lake

Seasonal opportunity is the best way to describe the Madison inside Yellowstone park extending downstream to Hebgen Lake. Flyfishers will not find many fish in that section at certain times of the year, but when they do, the fishing can be awesome—especially for large trout.

Fishing season begins in Yellowstone Park on May 25 and ends November 3. On the opener, expect to fish small midge patterns. The water will still be cold, and the river's premier hatches are a couple of weeks away. A size 18 Griffith's gnat or parachute Adams should draw strikes when risers are encountered.

Caddis hatches begin by the second week in June, and they can be prolific. Size 14 and 16 spent partridge caddis, elk hair caddis, ram caddis, Henryville caddis and Hemingway caddis, all tied with a dark body, work best.

"The caddis hatch typically lasts all day, with the peak arriving around dark," says Dick Greene at Bud Lilly's Trout Shop in West Yellowstone. "You'll see the hatch from the confluence (Gibbon, Firehole) all the way down to Hebgen Lake. Wherever you can get good access, you'll find the caddis and trout working them. I like it best near Baker's Hole, just above the bridge, in the evenings."

While the caddis provide good action, nothing gets the Madison's fish or flyfishers so jacked as the salmonflies. They are normally present on the park stretch by June 10, just when the water temperature hits 55 or 56 degrees.

"You will see more of them up in the Firehole Canyon, but you do see some all the way downstream to Barns Hole," Greene says. "One mistake people make during the salmonfly hatch, when the water is high, is wading out too deep. You don't have to get out far; the fish are on the banks, and you can dead-drift a big stonefly nymph in the seams and eddies next to shore. I like to fish a big size 2, 4 or 6 girdle bug or Bitch Creek nymph. Kaufmann's stones are good, too."

The park section can be quite crowded during the salmonfly hatch, as hordes of aluminum airstreams head through for their annual family vacation. Stay out of the traffic jams and on the river.

If you are trying to get away from people, try the Beaver Meadows and Barns Hole areas. You can park outside the park boundary off of Highway 191 or at Baker's Hole Campground.

"You can hike a mile or two upstream from the highway and find some pretty decent water with fewer people," Greene says. "Through that section, the river meanders a lot. There are boggy areas filled with holes, downed trees and beaver dams to negotiate. That keeps most people away. There are also a lot of grizzly bears in that area, and the Baker's Hole campground is restricted to hardside camping only, no tents. All of that combined keeps a lot of people off the river."

If salmonflies aren't doing it for you in mid-June, keep an eye out for green drakes —the hatch can be significant when it occurs. CDC captive duns, standard green drake Wulffs, paradrakes and cripples work well.

By the end of June, water temperatures rise drastically in the Madison due to thermal springs draining into the Firehole. Hatches shut down and the river's trout shut off. Time to focus on other waters.

However, by September, cool nights chill the water and insect hatches resume. Look for solid hatches of Trico and Baetis mayflies to carry dry-fly fishers through fall. Tricos and Baetis patterns are most productive during late morning and afternoon, when the sun reaches above the cliffs and warms the water. Try light tippets of 5X, 6X and even 7X when the fish are on the rise. Olive sparkle duns, parachute Adams and cripples will draw strikes when the Baetis are on top. Tricos can be matched with size 18, 20 and 22 parachute Tricos, Griffith's gnats and downwing Trico spinners.

While dry-fly fishing appeals to some, the Madison's big draw during fall is the opportunity to throw meaty streamers to some awfully large rainbow and brown trout that move out of Hebgen Lake.

"Prime time on the Madison is late September and October, when you really have the chance to hit some trophy fish. We have some Eagle Lake rainbows in Hebgen that run upstream the same time that the browns do," Greene says. "As soon as you get the first cold snap of fall, such as four or five days of 30 to 40 degrees, you'll see them move upstream. I look for the fish to hold in the deeper runs and the tailouts of riffles. I'll dead-drift size 2, 4 and 6 streamers like light and dark spruce flies, copper zonkers and white zonkers. Size 6 and 8 Prince nymphs and San Juan worms work, too. Egg patterns can also be effective in October.

"The biggest trout I've caught during fall was a 25-inch brown," Greene says. "Within a half-hour of taking that fish, I caught a 22-inch brown, a 20-inch brown and a 19-inch rainbow. Then I got interrupted by some buffalo. The fish will move quite a bit from day to day, so when you find them, you can usually catch more than one. If they move upstream, move with them."

To fish the park's late season, 4mm or 5mm neoprene waders are advised. Temperatures can range from 20 to 70 degrees during the day. Most days, 40 or 50 degrees will be the high. Bring neoprene gloves, extra clothes and something warm to drink. Also, be advised that an early snowfall can close the gates to Yellowstone Park until it can be removed from the highway, usually by noon. Sit back in a cafe with a mug of coffee and wait for the snow to clear; you can learn a lot about life and, of course, flyfishing in Montana when frequenting cafes.

When fishing the park stretch of the Madison, flyfishers can lodge and dine in West Yellowstone. There are lots of excellent eateries, coffee shops and plenty of hotels. Check out the fly shops while you're in town, too: Bud Lilly's, Blue Ribbon Flies and Madison River Outfitters all have top-of-the-line equipment and guides. They keep tabs on spawning movement and hatch progression, so it pays to swing in, ask a few questions and stock up on local fly patterns, which normally work better than those brought from home.

Between Varney Bridge and Ennis, side channels of the Madison hold good fish. Stalk the banks carefully.

Quake Lake to Lyons Bridge

This is an excellent stretch of water for the winter flyfisher, but it has been closed at times to protect spawning rainbows. Those regulations may change again as the effects of whirling disease are known.

If you can get at it between the end of February and the general opener on the third Saturday in May, you will catch fish on a variety of small patterns.

"They seem to like tiny flies in that roily water," says Eric Swedman at Madison River Fishing Company in Ennis. "A lot of fish will move into the side channels where they eat nymphs. Beadhead serendipities and hare's ears work really well. Anywhere the water is deep and slow you should find fish."

You can gain access to that section at Raynolds Pass Bridge. Walk up or downstream through the braids. Swedman prefers the south side of the river upstream from bridge.

If regulations keep you from this stretch during winter, don't fret. Late spring, summer and fall fishing can be productive, too.

"When the pre-runoff warm weather arrives, we get the first big hatch of black microcaddis," Swedman says. "Then, after runoff you see a variety of caddis ranging from size 12 to 18 through the summer. You can fish standard hairwing patterns (elk hair caddis, stimulators) in the fast water. In the slower flat stretches you need a LaFontaine sparkle emerger or soft hackle instead of dries because the fish can be tough."

Salmonflies and golden stones are present in this section, and they can provide decent fishing, especially the goldens, in late June. This section is the place to look when other areas are blown out by runoff. Because this section flows above the

The Madison Range offers a perfect backdrop for a day on the water. What's better than working the Madison with a bent rod held high on a beautiful day?

confluence of the West Fork Madison, it remains clearer than sections downstream. Unfortunately, regulations restrict boats.

"The golden stones run size 14 and 16, and an elk hair caddis or a stimulator matches them," Swedman says. "The golden stones are a big deal because they fish well in the fast water. You can just work them through the riffles and pick up fish."

Other insects encountered during summer include PMDs in July and August, Callibaetis in late July and August, and beetles throughout summer.

"They love beetles in that stretch," Swedman insists. "I just like to work a foam beetle when nothing else is really happening. They pound it."

Lyons Bridge to Varney Bridge

Floating is legal in this section, and that is probably the most effective way to fish the river, although wade fishers enjoy good success, too.

Hatches begin with the caddis emergences of late spring and early summer. The bugs can be so thick that they almost hamper a flyfisher's efforts at times. Imagine 30 million nachos to choose from—it wouldn't take long to fill up!

"It's almost too intense," Swedman says. "You see blankets of caddis on the water in late June and early July, and the fish are gorged on caddis pupa and salmonfly nymphs. It's tough to get them to eat a fly. It's better to wait until after the initial caddis blast to fish. In mid-July through the summer, you'll see caddis in the mornings and evenings, and it can be quite productive."

Golden stoneflies and salmonflies are present in late June and early July, sometime between June 25 and July 1. They can offer decent action, but Swedman says the hatch moves through fast, providing just a couple days of prime fishing. And it can be tough to hit ideal conditions.

"Everybody comes out and floats between McAtee Bridge and Varney Bridge when the salmonflies are out," Swedman says. "It's a zoo, but the fishing can be pretty fun when you get trout coming up to a size 4 dry fly. But I've only really hit it twice.

"Sometimes the water will be really off-color and high, but you only need 10 inches to a foot of visibility to fish the big nymphs," Swedman adds. "I like to fish a big black woolly bugger or olive and white bunny fur pattern. Really anything, if it's big and black and on the bottom, will work. Just pound the banks."

As the water clears in July, the Madison becomes a hopper and attractor dry-fly river in a big way. Dave's and Joe's hoppers, double humpies, royal Wulffs, stimulators and elk hair caddis account for most of the river's fish.

"You get PMDs, Callibaetis and caddis, but we mostly fish hoppers and dry-fly attractors," Swedman said. "Also, there is a nocturnal stonefly, such as a skwala, that comes off in mid-July. Very few people see this bug, but if you turn over a log at that time, you will see them scurrying around. I like to fish with a size 6 stimulator for those."

Varney Bridge to Ennis Lake

You can drift a boat between Varney Bridge and Ennis, but boats are restricted downstream between Ennis and Ennis Lake.

That is probably a good regulation, because there would be twisted masses of Lavros, Hydes and Yellowstone Drifters wrapped around logjams and boulders during high water—the river curls and braids continuously through that section. Round a tight bend in the river and say your prayers if a log is in the way. That goes for some of the water between Varney Bridge and Ennis, too. But the appeal of the salmonfly hatch in this section is enough for most of us to launch our boats anyway.

"I think the section from Varney Bridge to town has some of the nicest water on the entire river," says Swedman. "The fish population thins out a bit, but it's a great place to wade fish. And it's big fish habitat. You have lots of braids, classic deep runs, big pools and tailouts. Above Varney Bridge the Madison is more pocketwater."

The time to hit this section is between June 25th and July 10 — usually there will be some salmonflies hovering in the air. If not, assure yourself that nymphs will work by turning over a few boulders near shore. Twisting, snarling, three-inch long bugs should defend their nests. When the hatch really comes off, the bankside brush and grass will be alive with salmonflies crawling out of their carapaces. Hordes will migrate up boat launch ramps.

"I like to fish this section in late June when the salmonflies are coming off," Swedman says. "You can usually take fish on the big nasty nymphs and sometimes on dries. If the salmonflies don't cut it, you can fish caddis patterns in the evenings and do really well."

Below Ennis, wade fishers can work the braids with caddis patterns any night during summer and catch fish. But the real attraction to that water arrives during fall, when some large browns move out of Ennis Lake and into the lower reaches of the river to spawn.

"There are some browns that come out of the lake, but it doesn't seem like there are too many of them," Swedman says. "You sure have the chance to take a large fish on streamers during late September and October, but it's not red hot. It's a good idea for someone who wants to go in and spend a day just searching for one or two large fish."

Ennis Lake to Three Forks

The lower Madison differs from the upper river drastically; gone are the intense pocketwaters and riffles between Quake Lake and Ennis Lake. It becomes a shallow, silt-bottomed tailwater, with massive weedbeds, some decent hatches and a tendency to become too warm for trout during the summer season.

So what do you do? Write this 30-mile stretch off as nonproductive? According to Dave Kumlien at Montana Troutfitters in Bozeman, that would be a big mistake. Especially if you are an off-season flyfisher.

"The lower Madison is a fantastic off-season river," Kumlien says. "It really differs from the upper sections, but this is a good brown trout stream with a lot of nice fish. I'd rate it equal to any section of the Madison and surrounding area streams for streamer fishing." You can fish the lower Madison effectively anytime between September 15 and June 15, and it all starts during winter with solid midge hatches, followed by the Baetis mayfly.

"You don't see a lot of action in January and February, but in March things pick up," according to Kumlien. "You'll see good midge hatches and some blue-winged olives. The only thing that can set fishing back is if they increase flows by releasing more water from Ennis Lake. Usually, that won't happen until May, so you get a good month and a half of Baetis and midge action."

Rising water levels will most likely affect fishing in May, just when the Mother's Day caddis blitz begins. If the water level remains consistent, the caddis hatch can provide outstanding action. But when the water rises, dry-fly and emerger fishing is a bust. The only option is to throw big streamers, and that isn't such a bad option.

"A guy with a boat can fish big streamers when the river is as high as 5,000 or 6,000 cfs," Kumlien says. "Just throw the big junk streamers, because the trout don't give a darn about the water level—they'll still eat. Crustaceans and leeches are awfully big in terms of trout food here, so the guys who really get the big browns use crayfish patterns. Some guys like to get real detailed with those patterns, and they put pinchers on them. All I've found that to do is twist my leader. I think a brown woolly bugger works better than anything. You'll pick up a lot of fish averaging 10 to 12 inches, but there are bigger browns in here. A true 20-incher is rare, but the size of the fish seems to be increasing."

Generally, the lower Madison will run high through May and June. By late June the river drops, and caddis patterns will take fish in the evenings. A few salmonflies may be seen about, but the hatch is minimal compared to the festivities going on upstream. By July, the river warms and the fishing shuts off almost totally. There is still some action to be had during the morning and late evening hours, but midday fishing is not productive.

"There is one hatch in August that can provide some decent action, but it's not fantastic," Kumlien says. "We do see a big white mayfly that comes off in size 12, and fish do get on it and eat it, but it's not a dense hatch. We just use a royal Wulff to match it."

Wade fishing is a big attraction on the lower Madison. It has a firm bottom, not as slippery or bouldery as the upper river, and almost anyone can keep their footing during decent flows.

Prime flows for wading range from 1,200 to 1,800 cfs. Anything near 2,000 cfs or above makes for tricky footing at best. Because most of the lower Madison's prime fishing occurs during the off season, neoprene waders, polar fleece gloves, a Gore-Tex jacket and a stocking cap should be standard gear.

Those items are handy if you are floating the river, too. However, if you float the Beartrap Canyon, you might want to throw in a survival suit. And make sure your will is prepared before starting downstream—people die here.

The Beartrap Canyon, located just below Ennis Lake, harbors some nasty waves and rapids. Undoubtedly, some very large trout live there. But they are mostly out of reach for the flyfisher, which means the canyon is better avoided. Why risk your life if you're not guaranteed a 12- to 15-pounder?

"I don't recommend that people float the Beartrap Canyon," Kumlien says. "Some people can float down it and do fine, but it will kill those who don't. It's so short, just seven miles, with so much danger involved, it's not worth it. You can't fish it effectively anyway, so why try? If you just want a whitewater trip and you don't want to fish and you know what you are doing, go for it."

For those who want to fish the Beartrap, trails run down both sides of the river below the dam. Strong-legged flycasters can wade out and probe the water with big stonefly nymphs, caddis pupa and pheasant tail nymphs or streamers. Beyond a half-mile downstream, the footing becomes treacherous and forward progression ceases.

If you choose to avoid the Beartrap, launch a boat or raft at the Warm Springs/Beartrap access site and float to Black's Ford access site, which is about seven or eight miles. There are plenty of good spots to get out of the boat and wade fish, so this float can take all day if you want.

Another option is to put in at Black's Ford and drift downstream to Greycliff access site. It's a short float, best run in a half-day. A healthy full-day float would take you from Greycliff all the way downstream to the Blackbird access site at Three Forks, but the water downstream is less productive due to dropoffs in trout populations.

If you do take that float, plan a full day and try to stop at Darlington Spring Creek ("the ditch") at the Cobblestone access site (no boat access). Darlington hosts some large rainbow and brown trout, but they are as picky as you might find anywhere. Long, light leaders, delicate patterns and stealth are required.

When floating the river during spring or fall, keep one rod rigged with a woolly bugger and another with a light tippet and a Baetis imitation. You or your partner can pitch a bugger to the banks as you float. When a riser or pod of risers is sighted, grab the dry-fly rod and throw it.

In the big scheme, the Madison River is not the noted rainbow trout fishery that it used to be. Whirling disease has certainly made an impact on the number of trout

Even during winter, the Madison offers solid brown trout. Here, the author displays a 17-incher taken on a size 22 disco midge.

in the river, but perhaps more importantly, it has caused the Madison's fine reputation to falter, and that is a shame. The Madison still hosts some of the best trout water in the world, with strong populations of browns, and it offers some of the most unique flyfishing towns Montana has to offer. The Madison, even with fewer rainbows, is still worth fishing.

"The dry-fly people are really complaining about the Madison," Swedman says. "Overall, the river hasn't been as good as it used to be, but we still get some flurries of activity that are tough to beat. It's just turned into a brown trout stream, and browns are more difficult to catch.

"We hear gloom and doom every day, but we still see a lot of traffic on this river. We fish the Yellowstone, the Big Hole, the Beaverhead and the Missouri, and we have a good time. But you can go out here and wade fish for a half day and catch a half dozen nice fish, too—good ones. You are still looking at trout populations around 2,500 to 3,000 a mile, and that is impressive. I still think the Madison is one of the best rivers in the state."

Stream Facts: Madison River

Seasons
- Yellowstone National Park open third Saturday in May through November 4.
- Yellowstone National Park boundary to Hebgen Lake open third Saturday in May through November 30. All rainbow trout must be released.
- Hebgen Lake to Quake Lake open entire year.
- Quake Lake to McAtee Bridge open third Saturday in May through end of February.
- McAtee Bridge to Ennis Bridge open all year.
- Quake Lake outlet to Varney Bridge, artificial lures only/catch and release for trout.
- Varney Bridge to Ennis Lake, all rainbows must be released.
- Ennis Bridge to Ennis Lake open third Saturday in May through end of February.
- Ennis Dam to mouth of river open all year.

Trout
- Mostly browns with lesser numbers of rainbows, cutthroats and grayling. Most trout average 12 to 18 inches. A few hogs top five pounds.

River Miles
- Missouri River Headwaters State Park—0
- Blackbird access site—3
- Cobblestone access site (no boat access)—11
- Greycliff access site—20
- Beartrap access site—24.4
- Madison Dam—40.3
- Ennis Dam—50.6
- Burnt Tree access site—53
- Varney Bridge—59.7
- McAtee Bridge—72
- Lyon Bridge—89
- Slide Inn—101.4
- Hebgen Dam—109.1
- Yellowstone National Park boundary—126.2
- West Yellowstone—133.4

River Flows
- Flows increase in March and April, and they peak in late May and June. Conditions are usually prime by July 4, just as the salmonflies emerge. On the lower river, below Ennis Lake, flows drop substantially in July, August and September. Fishing is less productive at that time.

Dangers
- Only the most experienced rafters should attempt the Beartrap Canyon.

Fishing Access
- There is plenty of access in all sections of the Madison.

Area Fly Shops
- Madison River Fishing Company, 109 Main Street, Ennis, MT, 406-682-4293
- Headwaters Angling, Highway 287, Box 964, Ennis, MT, 406-682-7451
- The Tackle Shop, 127 Main, Ennis, MT, 406-682-4263
- Thompson's Angling Adventures, Box 130, Ennis, MT, 406-682-7509
- Gallatin River Guides, Highway 191, Big Sky, MT, 406-995-2290
- East Slope Anglers, Highway 191, Big Sky, MT, 406-995-4369
- The River's Edge, 2012 N. 7th Ave., Bozeman, MT, 406-586-5373
- Montana Troutfitters, 1716 W. Main, Bozeman, MT, 406-587-4707
- Bozeman Angler, 24 E. Main, Bozeman, MT, 406-587-9111
- Blue Ribbon Flies, 309 Canyon, West Yellowstone, MT, 406-646-7642
- Madison River Outfitters, 117 Canyon St., West Yellowstone, MT, 406-646-9644
- Bud Lilly's Trout Shop, 39 Madison Ave., West Yellowstone, MT, 406-646-7801
- Jacklin's Fly Shop, 105 Yellowstone Ave., West Yellowstone, MT, 406-646-7336
- Arrick's Fishing Flies, 125 Madison Ave., West Yellowstone, MT, 406-646-7290

MADISON RIVER MAJOR HATCHES

Insect	J	F	M	A	M	J	J	A	S	O	N	D	Flies
Midges	■	■	■	■	■	■	■	■	■	■	■	■	Griffith's Gnat #18-22; Palomino Midge #16-22; Parachute Adams #16-22
Caddis				■	■	■							Emergent Sparkle Pupa #14-16; Cased Caddis #14-16; Elk Hair Caddis #14-18; Hemingway Caddis #14-16
Green Drakes						■							Parachute Adams #14-16; Olive Sparkle Dun #14-16; Quigley Cripple #14-16; Hare's Ear Nymph #14-16; Pheasant Tail Nymph #14-16
Trico									■				Polywing Trico #18-22; Parachute Adams #18-22; CDC Trico #18-22
Baetis				■	■				■				Parachute Adams #16-20; Olive Sparkle Dun #16-20; CDC Baetis #16-20; Hare's Ear Nymph #16-20; Pheasant Tail Nymph #16-20
Pale Morning Dun							■	■					Parachute Adams #16-18; Yellow Sparkle Dun #16-20; PMD Cripple #16-20; Poxyback PMD #16-20
Golden Stone						■	■						Stimulator #2-6; Kaufmann's Stone #2-4; Golden Stonefly Nymph #2-4
Salmonfly							■						Bird's Stonefly #2-4; Kaufmann's Stone #2-4; Bitch Creek Nymph #2-6; Stimulator #2-6; Brown Woolly Bugger #2-6

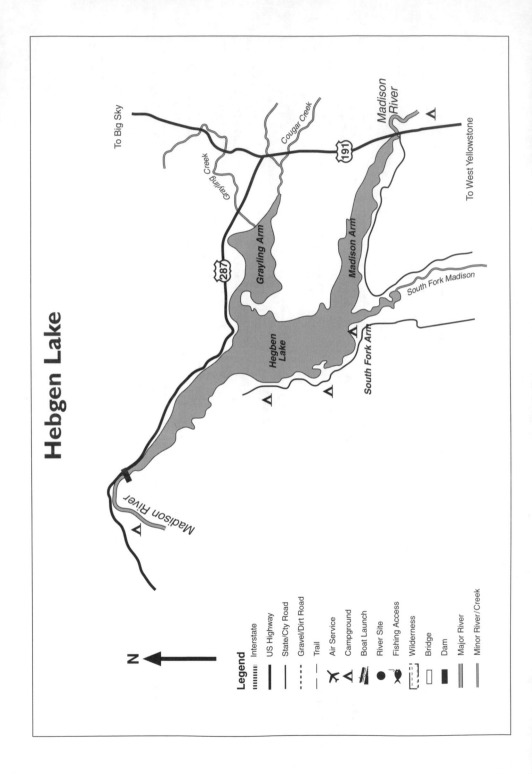

Hebgen Lake

To Big Sky

Cougar Creek

Grayling Creek

Madison River

191

To West Yellowstone

South Fork Madison

287

Grayling Arm

Madison Arm

South Fork Arm

Hebgen Lake

Madison River

N

Legend

Interstate

US Highway

State/Cty Road

Gravel/Dirt Road

Trail

Air Service

Campground

Boat Launch

River Site

Fishing Access

Wilderness

Bridge

Dam

Major River

Minor River/Creek

HEBGEN LAKE

When midsummer arrives in the Rockies and flyfishers start mumbling something about gulpers, they can only be speaking of one place—southwest Montana's Hebgen Lake.

Hebgen is synonymous with the term gulper, which was spawned on that water, and refers to the sound that the lake's trout, both rainbows and browns, make when they suck in a diminutive morsel from the surface. And we're talking about some hefty trout eating small flies, no less.

Hebgen, a 16-mile long, three-mile wide reservoir, rests in southwest Montana, just west of the Yellowstone Park boundary and just north of the Idaho state line. West Yellowstone, Montana, is a short drive from its shores.

Despite its remoteness, flyfishers from around the country make treks to the lake during spring, summer and fall to taste some of the best dry-fly lake fishing that Montana, if not the country, has to offer. Rainbows and browns to five pounds are commonly caught, and even an occasional eight-pounder. Larger fish are hooked and lost. Hatches come off like clockwork. The only thing that can ruin a trip to the lake is the wind—if you let it.

"The true gulper fishing on Hebgen that you hear so much about doesn't really get started until late July or early August when the Tricos start up," says Dick Greene of Bud Lilly's Fly Shop in West Yellowstone. "You'll see Tricos emerging around 6 or 7 AM, but the real spinnerfall, which is most important, doesn't really happen until 11 AM. Unfortunately, that is quite often when the wind chooses to kick up."

Fishing tiny Trico mayflies on an incredibly smooth lake surface may seem impossible upon first consideration, but flyfishers do take Hebgen's trout on these diminutive patterns. Successful anglers focus their attention where the bugs live, and they are not afraid to tippet down to 5X or 6X.

"During the Trico hatch, which runs from late July through the first week of September, you can just sit in a floattube or wade out into the lake and sight-fish to cruisers," Greene said. "You want to focus your effort on the Madison Arm, especially where you can find weedbeds. The fish seem to congregate in those areas.

"I like to fish dry flies to those trout, but there can be so many bugs on the water at one time, it would seem amazing if a fish actually ate your fly," Greene added. "I use CDC or twinkle spinners, but they are very difficult to see on the water, and if the wind comes up, it's a waste of time. So typically, I'll throw a size 18 pheasant tail flashback in front of cruising fish, because I think they see nymphs under the surface better. They just snatch them up and run. Normally, I'll use a 12- to 15-foot leader tapered down to 5X. To really reach the fish, you need to cast about 30 feet. If the wind comes up, it's good to have a powerful rod like a 9-foot, 6-weight."

While gulper fishing is Hebgen's big draw, Callibaetis mayflies also play a key role in a flyfisher's success. While not present in such staggering numbers as the Tricos, often Hebgen's trout seem partial to larger mayflies.

"You work with Tricos in the morning, and then around 11 AM, you start to see the Callibaetis, and you hope the wind doesn't come up," Greene said. "I like to

Hebgen Lake holds some huge rainbow and brown trout. Here, Scott Brown reaches for a big rainbow during the August gulper rise.

fish a parachute sparkle Callibaetis in a size 14. Callibaetis cripples and parachute Adams also work. Often, I'll tip one of those with a size 14 pheasant tail nymph for a two-fly rig."

While there are some monster rainbows and browns lurking in Hebgen, the average trout is 16 to 18 inches, with a fair number going 20 inches or more. Fortunately, Hebgen fishes well during the spring, too, just as the lake's rainbows gather in the bays. During spring, try the South Fork Arm, Grayling Arm, Rumbaugh Point and Denny Creek. And take your pick—throw midge patterns for surface feeders or big streamers for aggressive rainbows that are ready to dodge up the tributaries to spawn.

"In the spring, the Madison Arm isn't as important," Greene says. "You want to focus your efforts on other bays. Usually, the ice will go off the lake in late April or early May. At that time you'll see a lot of midges. I like to use a size 16 Griffith's gnat, a parachute Adams or a palomino midge. I fish all of those in dark colors like olive and brown and peacock and black.

"I use a lot of streamers at that time, too," Greene adds. "Crystal woolly buggers in light olive and chartreuse or light brown work good. You can fish those right under the surface off a floating line, or you can go with an intermediate sinktip. The fish really cruise the surface; they aren't stuck on the bottom. I like a floating line with a 12-foot leader tippeted down to 3X. An added bonus to streamer fishing is that you can do it in the wind."

Because Hebgen is such a huge lake, it is prone to serious bouts of wind, which can eliminate fishing opportunities and create dangerous situations for floattubers and boaters. One eye should always be focused on the weather and the water surface conditions.

Access to Hebgen is not difficult to find. In fact, the only time that access is a problem is during spring when the water level is low; large boats can only launch at Lonesome Hurst boat launch in the South Arm. During summer and fall, there are plenty of boat launches available, and floattubers can get on the lake anytime simply by carrying their tubes down to the water.

To reach Hebgen, travel south from Bozeman on Highway 191 toward West Yellowstone. From Ennis, follow Route 287 southeast toward West Yellowstone—it parallels the Madison River. There are numerous campsites located around the lake, and there is National Forest access available off some of the side roads. Motels, groceries, gas and excellent fly shops are available in West Yellowstone.

Gallatin River

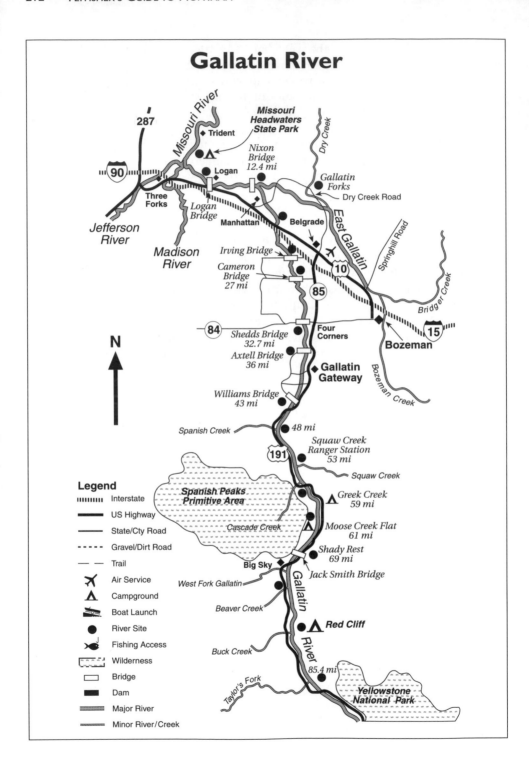

Legend

- Interstate
- US Highway
- State/Cty Road
- Gravel/Dirt Road
- Trail
- Air Service
- Campground
- Boat Launch
- River Site
- Fishing Access
- Wilderness
- Bridge
- Dam
- Major River
- Minor River/Creek

GALLATIN RIVER

Before fishing the Gallatin River, I was firmly focused on trophy trout. If a fish didn't have an adipose fin the size of a thumb and a kyped jaw straight out of a low-budget Tokyo horror flick, I really didn't want anything to do with it.

I couldn't understand why my father seemed so content with what I considered tiny trout. After fishing the Gallatin, despite its lack of arm-long trout, I have a better sense of my father's view that there is equal beauty in all trout, no matter what their size may be.

In fact, the size of a trout shouldn't diminish an observant angler's pleasure from the scent of a dense pine forest or the view of the lovely country that surrounds most trout waters, not to mention the musical sound of rapids or the gulp of a trout that is feeding from the surface. To suggest that the Gallatin River is not a worthy destination, simply because it does not hold many large trout is ludicrous; you can find many appealing aspects along its banks, including some decent size scrappy rainbows and browns. And, during fall there may not be a prettier river in the state. Riverside cottonwoods and aspens, plus a variety of bankside brush, light up in a flash of crimson, gold, tan and orange. I have not fished a prettier setting.

With its beginnings in Yellowstone Park and its termination at Three Forks, where it helps form the Missouri River, the Gallatin flows through some the most beautiful, varied country in Montana. And throughout its length, the river provides excellent trout habitat.

Population estimates place the number of rainbow trout in the upper river, from Yellowstone Park downstream to Spanish Creek, at about 3,000 a mile. From Spanish Creek downstream to its confluence with the Missouri, the Gallatin offers a mix of browns and rainbows, with total numbers approaching 3,000 a mile.

If my spiel on the merit of all trout did not change your attitude toward average sized trout, the lower river is where you should hang out; each year some dandy browns are taken there, but access to the river is mostly across private land. And that can be a difficult proposition, depending on who owns the land. The scenario upstream is different. U.S. Highway 191 parallels the river almost consistently on the upper end, where most of the river flows through Yellowstone National Park or Gallatin National Forest lands. Flyfishers can jump down the bank just about anywhere and start flogging the water immediately.

Unfortunately, those easy-access attributes and its geographic location in relation to Yellowstone Park draws hordes of anglers during summer.

You can hit the Gallatin by taking the Belgrade exit on Interstate 90 about 8 miles northwest of Bozeman, where Highway 191 south parallels the river to its headwaters.

Although activity from commercial rafters has increased, early spring, summer and fall remain prime seasons to fish the river. Winter doesn't provide many options due to frigid conditions, especially upstream from Spanish Creek through the Gallatin Canyon. And during spring, runoff is normally quite heavy, which makes dangerous conditions to any but the strongest wade fishers; fishing from a boat is not an option—it's prohibited on the Gallatin.

That restriction is due to the Gallatin's size; it is ideal for wading. In fact, in most places the stream runs just 25 to 30 yards wide. Where the river braids, 15-yard-wide sections may produce all the fish you need. There is always a variety of water to cover: shallow riffles, medium-depth runs, alluring pools and flatwater tailouts.

The Gallatin can be divided into three distinct sections: the upper river from Yellowstone Park downstream to the town of Big Sky; the middle river from Big Sky downstream to the mouth of the canyon just north of Spanish Creek; the lower river from the mouth of Gallatin Canyon downstream to its confluence with the Madison and Jefferson at Three Forks.

In Yellowstone Park, extending downstream to Taylor Fork, the Gallatin offers swift water with lots of shallow runs, complemented by some deep pools and lots of undercut banks. The terrain surrounding the stream is wide open, so backcast conditions are generous—just don't hook a wayward elk or bison, which are commonly sighted in the area.

What you want attached to the end of your line is one of the wild brown, rainbow or native cutthroat trout that frequent the area. Most of the fish will run eight to 11 inches, but there are enough 15-inchers to keep things interesting. And there is always the possibility of hooking a brown that might stretch 16 to 19 inches.

The Gallatin and its tributaries in the park stretch are ideal for a young flyfisher. Attractor dry flies and standard nymphs take fish. When specific mayflies or caddis need to be imitated, a parachute Adams or an elk hair caddis in the appropriate size and color will cover most situations. Most of the water can be waded from one bank to the other, and only short casts are required.

Just south of Big Sky, the Gallatin changes its face, and anglers who fish the river early in the season should take note: below the mouth of Taylor's Fork, the river can be snarling, ugly, muddy and unfishable from May through June. However, above Taylor's Fork, spring anglers seeking clear water can have a feast. But clear water can crowd the river with anglers.

Beginning at Big Sky, the river is characterized by its surrounding terrain: steep timbered slopes, massive, vertical granite outcroppings and red sandstone cliffs. Try to find a more beautiful setting to catch a trout—you will be hard pressed to find one.

Anglers who like fast pocket water will enjoy the canyon, but flycasters who are more in tune with flatwater spring creeks or big, wide rivers like the Missouri or Yellowstone may feel out of their element.

The canyon section requires tight (watch that backcast), precise presentations, quick mending (drag-free drifts are needed) and the ability to wade in fast water over slick rocks and boulders. Felt-soled boots are a necessity! While the upper river provides good opportunities for young flycasters, the canyon stretch can be somewhat treacherous. However, even during July and August when other area rivers warm up, the cool, shaded Gallatin Canyon section fishes well.

Through the canyon, flycasters test spunky rainbows and some larger browns. Don't expect trophies—a 14-inch rainbow through the canyon is considered a good fish. A 16- to 19-inch rainbow or brown is a monster.

The Gallatin Canyon offers a variety of options; pocketwater, broad riffles and deep runs. Rainbows and browns abound.

Those who seek larger trout should test the lower section, which runs through agricultural land in a broad valley. As mentioned, access is more difficult, but the Montana stream access law once again saves the responsible sportsman from the wrath of landowners.

Pick any bridge crossing on the lower river and walk up or downstream from there within the high water mark.

The lower river is characterized by broad runs and some deep pools. Braided channels offer some fast riffles. All types of dry flies and nymphs will take fish here. Streamers draw strikes in the spring and fall when rainbow and brown trout, respectively, spawn.

The lower river provides fairly easy wading as well as good opportunities for young flyfishers, although it does broaden out a bit. Forty-foot casts may be required in some situations. On any given cast, a 20-inch plus rainbow or brown could be hooked.

Below Four Corners, fishing declines due to massive dewatering. It's a fact of life for the Gallatin flyfisher, and it's not likely to change. During high water and during fall, that section is worth looking at, but it's not the river's premier opportunity.

While it is difficult to describe specific hatches for an entire river, the Gallatin receives hatches throughout its length that vary in timing by a week or less.

Beginning in March or April, just as the first sunny days of the year begin, the Gallatin receives a decent emergence of blue-winged olives or Baetis. Those insects hatch best at midday, extending to 4 PM. Early season caddis are also present through March, April and May. The first "major" hatch begins in late June when salmonflies

The entire Gallatin is beautiful and productive, but you can't beat the scenery near Rock Haven.

crawl out of the bottom rocks and take wing, like pterodactyls. The smaller golden stone follows the salmonfly emergence by a week. Cross your fingers and hope that the river is not blown out.

In July and August, caddis and mayflies dominate. Pale morning duns and green drakes are especially important mayfly emergences — PMDs hatch throughout the river; green drakes come off best in the upper section.

Grasshoppers, ants and beetles also take their fair share of fish during late summer and early fall. Best stretches for terrestrials are the upper section in the park and the lower section between the mouth of the canyon and Four Corners.

In September and October, caddis, Baetis and mahogany duns are the ticket. Crowds clear out by October 1 and dedicated flycasters have entire sections of the river to themselves. If the fish aren't working over caddis and mayfly patterns, tie on a big streamer and let 'em have it.

When you catch a fish, consider releasing it back to the river. Growth rates in the Gallatin are extremely slow. In fact, Mark Lere at Montana Fish, Wildlife and Parks suggests that a 13- to 15-inch trout in the river will be about five to seven years old!

"This river just doesn't produce a lot of fish over 13 inches," Lere said. "And it seems that overwinter survival is the main controller, not harvest."

In early October, there's no better looking trout stream in the state. With cotton-woods aglow, anglers can fish for spawning browns and hungry rainbows.

However, some local anglers do not buy that line. In fact, Steve French at Gallatin River Guides in Big Sky, would like to see catch and release regulations on much of the river. "It takes a long time to grow a large fish in this river," French said, "and they just don't get a chance to grow. Go ahead and let people keep an eight- or 10-inch fish, but require them to put back the larger trout. An extensive catch and release section would solve everything."

Anglers don't have an option to keep a fish if they tangle with native cutthroats or grayling. Both of those fish are less abundant than browns or rainbows and they are protected under regulations.

While you are not likely to catch a behemoth trout on the Gallatin River, trophy trout anglers should not pass by its appealing banks. Those small trout in the Gallatin are eager to rise at a dry fly and the river itself is one of the prettiest, most easily accessible stream that you will ever fish. That, in itself, merits a trip.

If you want to camp by the river, there are good sites throughout its length. As mentioned, most of the upper and canyon stretches are bordered by National Forest lands. You can camp in designated or non-designated sites through those stretches. If you prefer a hotel room for the evening, try the Best Western (Buck's T-4 Lodge) just south of Big Sky or the Gallatin Gateway Inn at Gallatin Gateway. There are also a number of private lodges that offer cabin rentals and excellent dining. The Half Moon Saloon, just south of Big Sky, offers a killer bloody Mary and the best bar view in Montana. At Four Corners, the Korner Club bar and grill serves good pizza, salads and sandwiches. The Exxon at Gallatin Gateway, just off Highway 191 serves a pretty good breakfast—try the prime rib, eggs and browns, served on Sundays.

Stream Facts: Gallatin River

Seasons
- Open all year.

Special Regulations
- Closed to fishing from boats from Yellowstone National Park to the East Gallatin River. Catch and release on grayling.

Trout
- Good numbers of rainbow and brown trout with a few cutthroats and grayling. Average trout will run six to 12 inches. Most large fish frequent the lower sections, below Spanish Creek.

River Miles
- Missouri River Headwaters State Park—0
- Gallatin Forks—12. 5
- Shedd's Bridge—32.7
- Gallatin Canyon Bridge—45
- Squaw Creek Bridge—53
- Greek Creek—59
- Moose Creek Flat—61
- Shady Rest—69
- West Fork Gallatin—70
- Taylor Creek—85.4
- Yellowstone National Park Boundary—88.8

River Flows
- Runoff peaks mid-May and may persist through mid-July. River clears quickly above Taylor's Fork.

River Characteristics
- Most sections are 20 to 30 yards wide with lots of pocket water broken by large boulders. Wade fishing is prime during winter and spring and again when high water ends. Fall brings lots of brown trout to the river's lower end.

Fishing Access
- Numerous public sites scattered along the river. Many bridge crossings offer access to the lower river.

Area Fly Shops
- Gallatin River Guides, Highway 191, Big Sky, MT, 406-995-2290
- East Slope Anglers, Highway 191, Big Sky, MT, 406-995-4369
- The River's Edge, 2012 N. 7th Ave., Bozeman, MT, 406-586-5373
- Montana Troutfitters, 1716 W. Main, Bozeman, MT, 406-587-4707
- Bozeman Angler, 24 E. Main, Bozeman, MT, 406-587-9111
- Blue Ribbon Flies, 309 Canyon, West Yellowstone, MT, 406-646-7642
- Madison River Outfitters, 117 Canyon St., West Yellowstone, MT, 406-646-9644

GALLATIN RIVER MAJOR HATCHES

Insect	J	F	M	A	M	J	J	A	S	O	N	D	Flies
Grasshopper							■	■	■				Dave's Hopper #2-8; Meadow Hopper #2-8;
Midge	■	■	■	■	■	■	■	■	■	■	■	■	Griffith's Gnat #16-20; Parachute Adams #18-22; Pheasant Tail Nymph #16-22
Salmonfly *Pteronarcys californica*					■	■							Seducer #4-8; Stimulator #4-8; Bitch Creek Nymph #4-8; Kaufmann's Stone #2-6; Brook's Stone #2-6; Bitch Creek Nymph #4-8; Black Rubberlegs #2-8
Baetis				■	■								Olive Cripple #16-20; Parachute Adams #16-20; Sparkle Dun #16-20; Hare's Ear Nymph #16-20; Pheasant Tail Nymph #16-20; Poxyback Baetis #16-20
Golden Stone *Hesperoperla pacifica*						■	■						Whitlock's Golden Stone Nymph #4-8; Montana Nymph #4-8; Betts' Brown Stone #4-8; Whitlock's Revised Golden Stone #4-8; Poxyback Biot Golden Stone #6-12
Caddis					■	■	■	■	■	■			Elk Hair Caddis #14-18; Diving Caddis #14-16; X-Caddis #14-16; Drifting Cased Caddis #14-18; Emergent Sparkle Pupa #12-18; Deep Sparkle Pupa #12-18; Electric Caddis #14-16; Caddis Variant #14-16
Pale Morning Dun						■	■	■					Sparkle Dun #14-20; Parachute Adams #14-20; PMD Cripple #16-20; Poxy Biot Nymph #16-20; Hare's Ear Nymph #16-18; Pheasant Tail Nymph #16-18; CDC Floating Nymph #16-18; Half Back Emerger #16-18
Mahogany Dun									■	■			CDC Emergent Crippled Dun #14-16; Sparkle Dun Mahogany #14-16; CDC Spinner #14-16; Comparadun #14-16; Pheasant Tail Nymph #14-16
Green Drake / Little Western Green Drake						■	■						Olive Sparkle Dun #10-16; Cripple #10-16; Green Drake Emerger #10-16; Comparadun #10-16; Hare's Ear Nymph #10-16

EAST GALLATIN

If you were floating down the stream, and you did not glance northeast to the Bridger Mountain Range, you might believe you were fishing the Beaverhead River.

But you are not fishing the Beaverhead. Instead, you are on the East Gallatin River, just 15 minutes north of Bozeman, casting dry flies on one of the least noted, yet truly excellent, streams in the state.

In size and character, the East Gallatin, which originates in the southern Bridgers, is much like the Beaverhead: its banks are brushy; its holes deep; it has a nutrient-rich silt bottom and abundant and varied aquatic insect populations; and it winds like a dazed and confused rattlesnake. It carries a very healthy population of rainbow and brown trout, somewhere near 5,000 a mile over five inches (some much larger), and it demands a measure of stealth.

Its trout are not as big on average as the Beaverhead's, and it does not provide much public access, but it definitely offers Beaverhead-like habitat just outside a metropolitan hub—that is a hard attribute to find anywhere in the West. Bozeman and its residents are fortunate to have a stream like the East so close.

"The East Gallatin is very similar to the Beaverhead, but it is not a tailwater, so it isn't quite as fertile and it doesn't grow so many large fish," says Dave Kumlien at Montana Troutfitters in Bozeman. "There are some large fish in there, but most of them will go 14 to 18 inches; a fair number will go 20 inches or more. It's not the place to go for big trout, but biologists shocked a fish from the same hole several times that weighed about 10 pounds. There aren't too many of those around."

A major reason why the East Gallatin is ignored by resident and visiting anglers alike is that you must gain access across private land to fish it. There are several bridge crossings that allow access to the water, but a wade fisher must keep below the high-water mark, and that can be difficult on a stream that twists severely—those corner holes are deep. If you are going to float, and you can't secure launch and takeout sites on private land, you will have to haul your boat, raft or canoe down and, of course, up some nasty banks. For that reason, a canoe or small raft with a light frame is the way to go. A 16-foot McKenzie would eat up half the East Gallatin, and you would drag it across the bottom rocks half the distance of your float.

For aspiring floaters, Kumlien offers this warning: "People who float the East should be aware of fences that cross the entire stream. Also, the river meanders so much, it takes forever to float from one point to another. You don't just sail right on down it. Take everything you need for a long day: water, food, sunblock, etc."

An attribute of the East Gallatin is that you can fish it almost any day of the year. And normally, you can find some fish rising.

During winter, the East rarely ices over and when it does, it is usually in localized areas. Other portions are wide open. Crazed flyfishers, who don't mind cold fingers, frozen ears and painful toes, can test the water with relatively strong chances for success from early November through March.

The East Gallatin's hatches begin with midges during winter, extending from New Year's Day through April. Look for a few fish rising to midges on the warmer days

*Greg Henry and Shadow probe a prime run for big browns and rainbows on the
East Gallatin, just 10 minutes outside of Bozeman.*

—any time the temperature rises above freezing. Standard midge imitations, like
midge larvae, suspender midges, Griffith's gnats and parachute Adams work fine.

However, because the river harbors a flat surface in many portions, especially in
the tailouts of pools and runs where fish like to congregate and feed during winter,
long, light tippets are often required. Make sure you carry 6X tippet material.

As winter and spring begin their annual tug-o-war in late March and early April,
look for Baetis (blue-winged olive) mayflies to join the hatch menu. After dining on
diminutive midges all winter, the East Gallatin's trout will have their noses pointed at
the surface, ready to inhale those olives at will.

"It's hard to beat a parachute Adams to match those Baetis," Kumlien said. "But,
a blue-winged olive sparkle dun is good, too. I like to go with size 18 or even size 16
in the spring. The spring Baetis will run larger than those you see during fall. A 9-foot,
6X leader is long enough and light enough to fish those Baetis."

As spring gives way to summer in early June, look for solid caddis hatches. As
with most silt bottomed, brushy banked streams, the East provides excellent caddis
action throughout summer. A flyfisher can just about count on evening caddis activity every day between early June and late August.

"Once they start in June, they will be around all of the time," Kumlien says. "When the hatch is coming off and fish are rising, you can use any standard adult caddis pattern and they'll take," Kumlien added. "Prior to the hatch, nymph patterns work great. I like a big serendipity or a caddis larvae best. Prince nymphs will work well, too. If they shy away from the adults, try emergers. Go with olive soft hackles or caddis emergers in sizes 14 and 16. You can fish them separately or in tandem with a dry fly like an elk hair caddis, parachute caddis or Hemingway caddis. The fish will feed right up through dark, and you will find them everywhere, not just along the banks, when they are on the caddis."

Another insect to look for during the early season is the cranefly. While the cranefly will never gain much recognition due to its sparse emergence schedule, it does bring some big fish onto the feed.

"The East Gallatin has a fair number of craneflies, and I always try to match them when I'm on the river during late spring and early summer," Kumlien says. "They seem to come out best right after a strong rain. I just throw a Bitch Creek nymph, and the fish take it."

Pale morning duns are present on the East Gallatin beginning in late June and extending through July. As with PMD emergences anywhere in the state, they get the trout frothing on the East. "The emergence is what you want to key on," Kumlien says. "I haven't heard much about or even seen a significant spinnerfall, so I don't think it's really important here. The emergence begins around 10 or 11 AM, and it can last all afternoon. Light cahills, parachute cahills, cripples and sparkle duns work good for the PMDs."

While the East does not have any large stoneflies (giant salmon and giant golden), it does offer the little yellow stonefly, and that insect can be quite significant to the trout. Imagine that you have subsisted on tiny midges, Baetis and a few middling caddisflies all winter and spring, and a larger, more vulnerable stonefly floated by—you would probably go out of your way to eat it, too. That would compare with dining on cheese and crackers all winter, to wake one morning and find the table stacked with Big Macs.

Watch for the little yellow stoneflies in all of the riffles. They will bounce along the riffles, dunking their fannies and dropping eggs. The trout will gorge as those insects hit the water. To match the stoneflies, try throwing a size 14 or 16 stimulator or elk hair caddis. In the riffles a flyfisher can get away with 5X or even 4X tippet. Don't hesitate to skip a pattern across the top.

As July gives way to August on the East Gallatin and the surrounding hayfields turn brown from the persistent sun, grasshoppers become extremely important as a food item for trout. In fact, an angler can get on the water at any of the bridge crossings and walk upstream or downstream all day with only a hopper tied to the leader —a size 8 or 10 Joe's will take trout from late morning through late afternoon.

At the same time, the river enjoys a heavy emergence of tiny Trico mayflies that offer some of the most challenging, if not best, fishing of the season.

"You actually see the oscillating clouds of Tricos," Kumlien said. "It's not quite like you might see on the Missouri, but this is a significant hatch on the East Gallatin.

You won't catch a huge East Gallatin brown on every cast, but they are there in the deep holes, sulking like ornery dogs. The auther caught this five-pounder on a tinsel bugger.

Their emergence is in the morning, but the spinnerfall is what you want to hit around 10 or 11 AM. The trout won't be podded up much, but you can walk the banks and spot isolated risers the whole way.

"During a Trico emergence, the fish can be pretty tough," Kumlien added, "so you might have to tippet all the way down to 6X or even 7X for a real picky fish."

If delicate fishing during a Trico hatch doesn't sound appealing, wait until fall. From late September through November, the river's brown trout become aggressive as they gear up to spawn. During that time frame, large, weighted streamers bounced along the bottom rocks will draw nasty strikes. Focus on the medium-depth runs, the deeper holes and the tailouts of riffles. And don't forget the mouths of feeder creeks —often they will stack up with browns as the fish bide their time to leave the main river and shoot upstream into a relatively foreign environment.

You can reach the East Gallatin by traveling north from Bozeman on Interstate 90 to the Belgrade exit, where you head north on Dry Creek Road. Or you can head out of Bozeman on Highway 10. The creek lies to the north of Interstate 90, running just past the airport, and it turns through numerous hayfields and backyards on its way to Manhattan.

While the East Gallatin may never gain the notoriety of its nearby neighbors— the Gallatin, the Madison, the Jefferson—it is a first-rate stream with some awfully nice fish. Beginning under the watchful eye of the Bridgers, extending nearly 30 miles to its confluence with the Gallatin near Manhattan, the East Gallatin is truly Bozeman's backyard stream.

EAST GALLATIN RIVER MAJOR HATCHES

Insect	J	F	M	A	M	J	J	A	S	O	N	D	Flies
Midge	■	■	■	■	■	■	■	■	■	■	■	■	Griffith's Gnat #18-20; Standard Adams #16-20; Palomino Midge #16-20; Serendipity #16-20; Brassie #18-20; Disco Midge #16-20
Pale Morning Dun						■	■						PMD Cripple #16-18; Sparkle Dun #16-18; Blond Humpy #16-18; Parachute PMD #16-18; Whitlock Red Squirrel Nymph #16-18; Rusty Spinner #16-18; Woven PMD Nymph #16-18
Caddis						■	■	■					Black Caddis Pupa #16-18; X-Caddis #16-18; Emergent Sparkle Pupa #16-18; Hemingway Caddis #16-18; Tan Caddis #16-18; Elk Hair Caddis #16-18
Trico								■	■				Parachute Adams #18-20; Spent Wing Trico #18-20; Griffith's Gnat #18-20; CDC Trico #18-20
Little Yellow Stonefly						■	■						Stimulator #16-18; Elk Hair Caddis #16-18; Golden Stonefly Nymph #16-18;
Cranefly					■	■							Cranefly AirThru #10-16; Cranefly Larvae #10-16
Baetis				■	■				■	■			Olive Cripple #16-20; Parachute Adams #16-20; Sparkle Dun #16-20; Hare's Ear Nymph #16-20; Pheasant Tail Nymph #16-20; Poxyback Baetis #16-20

JEFFERSON RIVER

It bears a president's name, but that is about the only legitimate way to compare the Jefferson River to the nearby Madison and Gallatin Rivers. The Jeff, despite its title, is not worthy of much consideration, especially for out-of-state flyfishers.

And that is unfortunate, because the Jefferson could be one of the state's top trout waters if it were not for local irrigators, whirling disease and the nuances of Mother Nature. Those forces combined keep the Jefferson's trout population highly subdued.

However, before you turn to the next section, there are a couple of tidbits to consider: the Jefferson holds some huge brown trout, up to 15 pounds, and they are suckers for sculpin patterns.

The Jefferson is a large, deep, lumbering river that flows 80 miles northeast from its origin at Twin Bridges to its confluence with the Madison, Gallatin and Missouri Rivers near Three Forks. The river can be divided into three distinct sections: the upper river from Twin Bridges to Cardwell, the canyon section, and the lower stretch from Sappington Bridge downstream to its confluence with the Madison and Gallatin at Three Forks.

Throughout its length, the Jeff is characterized by a lazy current that provides easy floating options for beginning rafters and boaters. Too bad the fishing can't be described that way!

But there are some fish to catch: the best options are in the upper river where brown trout average 14 or 15 inches. On the lower river, browns will stretch about 12 inches on average.

Historical population estimates place the number of brown trout at about 700 a mile. However, in 1990 that estimate dropped to 370 a mile, and in 1996 the number slumped to 290. Before you throw in the towel, there is hope—that population decline came on the heals of a decade of drought. Three good water years in a row, 1995–1997, may have alleviated that trend.

While brown trout may boost their numbers, rainbows likely will not. In 1996, biologists discovered whirling disease in the Jefferson, and infection rates in juvenile rainbows are comparable to those in the Madison, where 90 percent of its rainbow population perished.

Due to that decline, rainbows are catch and release only. While news on the Jefferson sounds grim at best, there will always be some large fish in the river and the flyfisher who targets them specifically should land some monsters.

"The Jefferson is a river we sort of ignore around here until fall," said Scott Waldie who runs Four Rivers Fishing Company in Twin Bridges. "It's just not as dependable as the Big Hole or Beaverhead. But it does provide a good fall fishery. That is when the big browns move, stacking up below the mouths of tributary streams like Hell's Canyon Creek, the Boulder River and Willow Creek."

While most browns stage in front of the feeder creeks, don't overlook the entire river. According to Waldie, trout can be found in some unusual places.

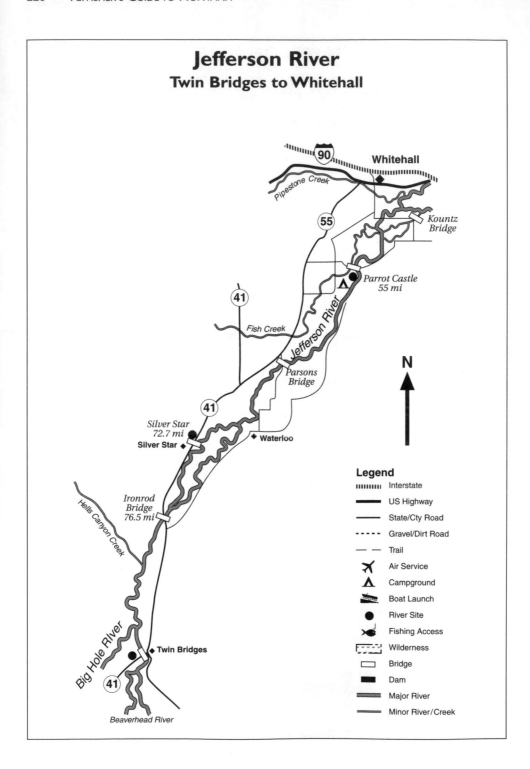

Jefferson River
Twin Bridges to Whitehall

Whitehall

Pipestone Creek

Kountz Bridge

Parrot Castle 55 mi

Fish Creek

Jefferson River

Parsons Bridge

N

Silver Star 72.7 mi
Silver Star ♦ **Waterloo**

Legend

Interstate
US Highway
State/Cty Road
Gravel/Dirt Road
Trail
Air Service
Campground
Boat Launch
River Site
Fishing Access
Wilderness
Bridge
Dam
Major River
Minor River/Creek

Ironrod Bridge 76.5 mi

Hells Canyon Creek

Big Hole River

♦ **Twin Bridges**

Beaverhead River

Jefferson River
Whitehall to Trident

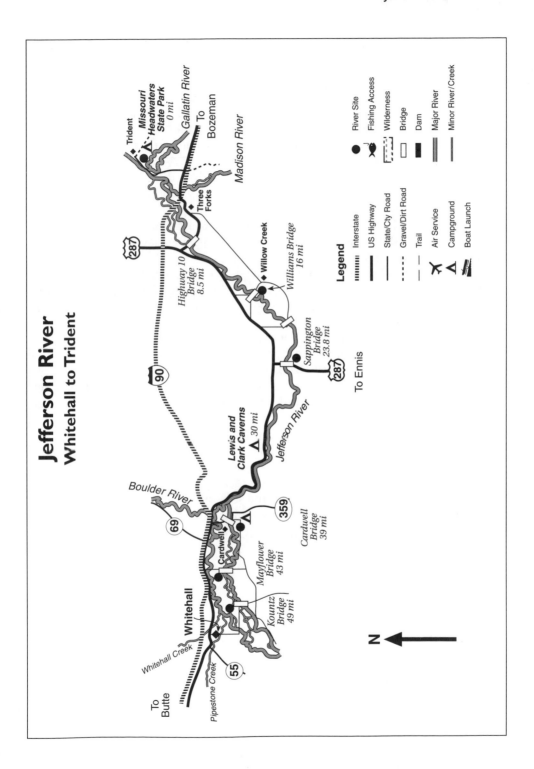

Trident

Missouri
Headwaters
State Park
0 mi

Gallatin River

To
Bozeman

Madison River

Three
Forks

Willow Creek

Williams Bridge
16 mi

Highway 10
Bridge
8.5 mi

287

Sappington
Bridge
23.8 mi

90

To Ennis

287

Lewis and
Clark Caverns
30 mi

Jefferson River

Boulder River

69

Cardwell

359

Cardwell
Bridge
39 mi

Mayflower
Bridge
43 mi

Whitehall

Kountz
Bridge
49 mi

Whitehall Creek

55

Pipestone Creek

To
Butte

N

Legend

Interstate

US Highway

State/Cty Road

Gravel/Dirt Road

Trail

Air Service

Campground

Boat Launch

River Site

Fishing Access

Wilderness

Bridge

Dam

Major River

Minor River/Creek

"I've found browns in the fall, kind of out in the middle of the river in about three feet of water," he says. "They lay out there where the water really moves and exposes the gravel they need to spawn."

Popular patterns for the Jefferson, especially during fall, include woolly buggers, gray ghosts, zonkers, bunny leeches and, of course, muddler minnows and woolhead sculpins. Big browns don't get huge by eating tiny mayflies. Overall, the Jefferson is not big-time aquatic insect water. It does harbor some decent hatches, but the minnows provide sustenance for big trout.

While fall is definitely the best time to probe the river, there are fish to be caught throughout the seasons. They are just a little tougher to find and hook than on the Big Hole or Gallatin. But the Jefferson has its moments.

"If you hit it right, you will never have a better day of fishing anywhere," Waldie says. "You'll have fishing that you can't believe—50 fish in a day with many of them running 14 to 18 inches."

During spring and summer, watch for excellent caddis hatches, especially late in the day. Caddis are supplemented by Baetis during spring and fall, pale morning duns during July and August, Tricos in August and September, and grasshoppers through late summer and fall.

The best way to get at trout is to float the river. Wading can be productive, but the Jefferson is broad and deep, and it can't be crossed in some areas. If a pod of trout is munching mayflies on the opposite bank, you're out of luck.

But with a boat or raft, flyfishers can wander from one bank to another when trout are spotted, and long, drag-free drifts can be placed in front of risers; lead-laced streamers can be pounded along the banks.

There are a number of good put-in and take-out sites; possibly the best floats wander between Twin Bridges and Cardwell.

While it's easy to overlook the Jefferson, it's not unusual for a flyfisher to want large brown trout and a piece of water to themselves. You're not going to find that combination on many of Montana's big-name streams. However, the Jefferson offers both options. If you arrive with modest expectations as far as numbers of fish, you are likely to enjoy your visit; anything else and you'll wander away frustrated.

Stream Facts: Jefferson River

Seasons
- Open all year.
- Catch and release only for rainbow trout.

Trout
- A mix of browns and rainbows. Most fish run 10 to 15 inches. During fall some big browns can be had.

River Miles
- Missouri River Headwaters State Park—0
- Williams Bridge—16
- Sappington Bridge—23.6
- Cardwell Bridge—39
- Kountz Bridge—49
- Iron Rod Bridge—76.5
- Beaverhead River—88.5

River Flows
- Flows rise in April and peak sometime in late May or early June. By early July the water is usually back in shape.

Fishing Access
- Excellent public fishing access sites located throughout the river

Area Fly Shops
- Sunrise Fly Shop, Melrose, MT, 406-835-3474
- Troutfitters, 62311 Highway 43, Wise River, MT, 406-832-3212
- The Montana Fly Company, Melrose, MT, 406-835-2621
- Harmon's Fly Shop, 310 S. Main, Sheridan, MT, 406-842-5868
- Frontier Anglers, 680 N. Montana St., Dillon, MT, 406-683-5276
- Fishing Headquarters, 610 N. Montana St., Dillon, MT, 406-683-6660; 800-753-6660
- Four River's Fishing Company, 205 S. Main, Twin Bridges, MT, 406-684-5651
- Big Hole River Outfitters, Wise River, MT, 406-832-3252
- Complete Fly Fisher, Hwy. 43, Wise River, MT, 406-832-3175

Ruby River

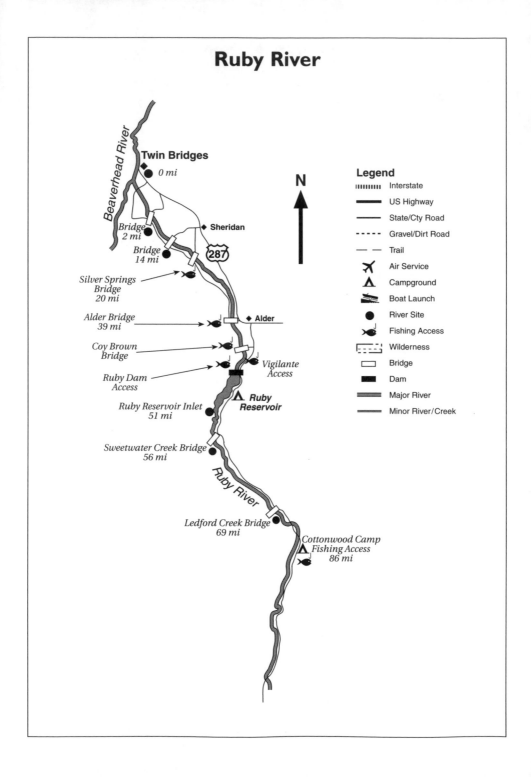

N

Twin Bridges
● *0 mi*

Beaverhead River

*Bridge
2 mi* ●

● *Sheridan*

*Bridge
14 mi* ●

287

*Silver Springs
Bridge
20 mi*

*Alder Bridge
39 mi* ● *Alder*

*Coy Brown
Bridge*

*Vigilante
Access*

*Ruby Dam
Access*

▲ **Ruby
Reservoir**

*Ruby Reservoir Inlet
51 mi* ●

*Sweetwater Creek Bridge
56 mi* ●

Ruby River

*Ledford Creek Bridge
69 mi*

Cottonwood Camp
▲ *Fishing Access
86 mi*

Legend
|||||||| Interstate
▬▬▬ US Highway
—— State/Cty Road
- - - - Gravel/Dirt Road
– – Trail
✈ Air Service
▲ Campground
🚤 Boat Launch
● River Site
🐟 Fishing Access
⌁ Wilderness
▭ Bridge
▬ Dam
▬ Major River
— Minor River/Creek

RUBY RIVER

For many seasons, the Ruby River was an afterthought in the minds of Montana's dedicated anglers. For a pocket-heavy few, the river and its posh lodges acted as a private playground. For those relying on public access, the river offered nothing.

Instead of visiting that productive stream, ordinary flyfishers passed by the Ruby, casting a glare at the beautiful valley and stream, before launching their drift-boats on southwest Montana's other delights, including the Beaverhead and Big Hole Rivers.

That all changed in 1997 when the Montana Department of Fish, Wildlife and Parks secured several public fishing access sites on the Ruby. That was no small task, considering how vehemently local landowners tried to keep the public away, occasionally threatening aggressive action, even when anglers had legally gained access to the river from bridge crossings.

Today, the new public access sites are an angler's treat. Walk up to the river, wade in deep if you like and cast a fly on the water without fear of taking a bullet in the back—the Ruby is once again public.

According to Dick Oswald, a biologist for FWP, the new access sites open the door to some great fishing opportunities—as long as anglers treat the land with respect.

"There certainly has been a faction out there who hasn't wanted us to get access to the river," Oswald says. "These leased access sites were needed badly. Now people can get to the river, but they must be respectful of the land: clean up any litter, remain within the river corridor and stay out of people's hayfields. If we mistreat these access areas, we are playing right into the hands of the people who don't want us on the river."

While the Ruby suffered from a serious fish kill in 1994 and continues to endure the effects of whirling disease, the river is on the rebound, and there are plenty of brown trout, mixed in with a few rainbow trout, to be had.

"We saw a real bad population decline downstream from Sheridan in 1994 that was timed with the outbreak of whirling disease," Oswald says. "Since that time, we've seen good recruitment of fish into that section. Anywhere upstream from Sheridan has been good all along. Right now, I'd say the entire Ruby has good numbers of large fish, and overall trout densities are high."

A large fish in the Ruby doesn't turn heads the way a big brown or rainbow from the Beaverhead or Big Hole Rivers might. Instead, a large Ruby River brown may stretch 18 inches. A few 20-inch-plus fish can be found in the Ruby, but an angler should not expect to catch one. However, an 18-inch trout is an impressive specimen when considering the size of the Ruby: it's a small, willow-choked, meandering affair, with plenty of undercut banks and medium-depth holes, but it doesn't scream of giant trout, with one noted exception.

"There is a short tailwater section below Ruby Dam that supports some large browns and a rainbow population that spills out of the reservoir," according to Oswald. "There aren't a lot of rainbows in that section, but there is some

Flyfishers can gain access to some of the upper Ruby over public land. Look for a smattering of modest rainbows and browns. (Tom Harman Photo)

opportunity." (The river is closed to angling from the Ruby Dam outlet channel upstream to the dam.)

To maintain productive angling opportunities, the limit for the Ruby has been set to three trout, with only one over 15 inches. Also, grayling, which were introduced to the upper river above Ruby Reservoir, are strictly catch and release.

The upper river offers not only grayling but lots of cutthroats and rainbows in the National Forest lands. On the lower few miles of the upper river, before it dumps into Ruby Reservoir, there are some resident brown trout available, but access is difficult if not impossible.

When fishing the Ruby this summer, expect the presence of caddisflies. Especially in the afternoon and evenings, LaFontaine sparkle emergers, X-caddis and elk hair caddis bring fish to the top. Pale morning dun mayflies also draw strikes when they emerge in July. Trico mayflies may be present on the water in August, and tiny downwing patterns are required for success.

Maybe the most effective way to catch the Ruby's trout is to drift a grasshopper along its banks. Brown trout, even the big brutes, do not like to allow passage of a hopper. Typically, they dart out from an undercut bank and tear those helpless, kicking insects under the surface. They do the same to Joe's hoppers, Madame Xs and stimulators.

As should be expected on a brown trout stream, the big, ugly stuff also draws strikes. Woolly buggers, zonkers, sculpins, leeches, and minnow patterns, such as dace and sucker renditions, are very effective, especially late in the day extending into evening when big browns go on the prowl. Even mice patterns, stripped across the surface in the moonglow, are known to fool the Ruby's brown trout.

Anglers who visit the Ruby River may want to cast a fly on Ruby Reservoir, too. According to Oswald, the reservoir has made a big recovery since it was drained in the early 1990s.

"It's been going gangbusters since it was dewatered in 1994," Oswald says. "We have strong numbers of two- and three-year-olds. The three-year-olds are near their maximum size—they'll go 17 to 19 inches. By the end of the first year, fish measure 13 inches. Those are phenomenal growth rates. Eventually, I think we'll get back to some normal growth rates, but it's been neat to see these fish prosper the way they have."

While fishing can be decent from shore, flycasters who use a floattube enjoy better success rates. Damselflies, scuds, leeches and mayfly nymphs draw strikes throughout summer.

For many years, the Ruby River and its excellent trout fishing options have been out of reach for the common angler. Today, FWP should be commended for their work securing public access sites. Don't take their effort or your opportunity to fish the Ruby lightly. Respect that opportunity: pick up after yourself and others when fishing the stream. In the end, we control our fate and the fate of the next angling generation in regard to fishing this wonderful stream.

Stream Facts: Ruby River

Seasons
- Upstream from Ruby Reservoir, third Saturday in May through November 30. Below Ruby Reservoir, open year-round.

Trout
- Rainbow, cutthroat and brown trout. Most of the rainbows and cutthroats reside above Ruby Reservoir. Brown trout, some quite large, dominate the river below the reservoir.

River Miles
- Confluence with Beaverhead River—0
- Silver Springs Bridge—20
- Alder Bridge—39
- Ruby Dam—47.9
- Ruby River inlet—51
- Sweetwater Creek Bridge—56
- Ledford Creek Bridge—69
- Cottonwood Camp—86

River Flow
- Runoff peaks in early June and tapers off by mid-July.

River Characteristics
- The Ruby River above Ruby Reservoir is a small stream bordered by private properties its lower end. The lower river, below the reservoir, is a medium size, placid, meandering stream that is bordered entirely by private property.

River Access
- Silver Springs Bridge
- Alder Bridge
- Coy Brown Bridge
- Vigilante
- Ruby Dam
- Upper river above reservoir has numerous access sites on Forest Service and BLM lands

Area Fly Shops
- Four Rivers Fishing Company, Twin Bridges, MT 59754, 406-276-8768
- Ruby Springs Lodge, Alder, MT, 800-278-RUBY—Full surface lodge including private access to the lower Ruby and numerous, challenging, yet excellent spring creeks.
- Sunrise Fly Shop, Melrose, MT, 406-835-3474
- Troutfitters, 62311 Highway 43 Wise River, MT, 406-832-3212
- The Montana Fly Company Melrose, MT, 406-835-2621
- Harmon's Fly Shop 310 S. Main, Sheridan, MT, 406-842-5868
- Frontier Anglers 680 N. Montana St. Dillon, MT, 406-683-5276
- Fishing Headquarters 610 N. Montana St. Dillon, MT, 406-683-6660; 800 753-6660
- Big Hole River Outfitters Wise River, MT, 406-832-3252
- Complete Fly Fisher Hwy. 43 Wise River, MT, 406-832-3175

SOUTHWEST HUB CITIES
Dillon
Elevation – 5,057 • Population – 3,991

Dillon is a friendly college town located in southwestern Montana, surrounded by four impressive mountain ranges—the Beaverheads, Tendoys, Centennials, and Pioneers. The famous Beaverhead River flows through Dillon along with Poindexter Slough. Flowing west to east across the northern part of the county is the Big Hole River, which joins the Beaverhead, and eventually becomes part of the Missouri River. Clark Canyon Reservoir, located about 20 miles south of town, provides excellent fishing for large rainbow and brown trout.

Beaverhead County is Montana's largest beef producer and is one of the largest counties in the nation, with an area larger than Connecticut and Rhode Island combined. Much of the surrounding terrain consists of plains and sagebrush, dotted with antelope, elk and mule deer.

ACCOMMODATIONS
Sundowner Motel, 500 North Montana / 406-683-2375 / 32 rooms, cable / Dogs allowed / $$

Super 8 Motel, 550 North Montana / 406-683-4288 / 46 rooms, cable / Refrigerators and microwave ovens in some rooms / Dogs allowed / $$

Five Rivers Lodge, 13100 Hwy 41 North / 406-683-5000 / Private access to blue-ribbon flyfishing waters (rivers and spring creeks)

CAMPGROUNDS AND RV PARKS
Beaverhead Marina and RV Park, 20 miles south on I-15, exit 44 on Clark Canyon Reservoir / 406-683-5556 / 2 tent and 31 RV spaces / Full facilities including docks, gas, and boat ramp

Skyline RV Park, 3 miles north of Dillon on Hwy 91 / 406-683-4903 / 5 tent, 38 RV spaces / Full facilities

RESTAURANTS
Anna's Oven, 120 Montana Street / 406-683-5766 / 7AM–4PM / Breakfast and baked goods

Buffalo Lodge, I-15 20 miles south of Dillon at Clark Canyon / 406-683-5088 / Open 10:30AM–9PM / Features burgers and steaks

Lion's Den, 725 North Montana / 406-683-2051 / 11AM–10PM / Steak, prime rib, cocktails

The Mine Shaft, 26 South Montana / 406-683-6611 / 11AM–11PM / Wide variety of steaks

Town Pump, 625 North Montana / 406-683-5097 / Open 24 hours for breakfast, lunch, and dinner

VETERINARIANS
Veterinary Hospital, 935 South Atlantic / 406-683-2385 / Dr. Knorr and Dr. Nelson

FLY SHOPS AND SPORTING GOODS
Hitchin Post Sporting Goods, 125 North Montana / 406-683-4881
Frontier Anglers, 680 North Montana / 406-683-5276
Fishing Headquarters, 610 N. Montana / 406-683-6660
Bear Creek Angler, Box 334, Gallatin Gateway, MT, 59730 / 406-763-4201

SHUTTLES
Lower Madison Shuttle / Kathy Fredericks / 406-763-4201 or 406-580-2772

AUTO REPAIR
B&L Auto Repair, 250 North Railroad / 406-683-6733
Dillon Auto Repair, 624 East Glendale / 406-683-5214

AIR SERVICE
Iverson Aviation / 406-683-4447 / Call for information

MEDICAL
Barrett Memorial Hospital, 1260 South Atlantic / 406-683-2323

FOR MORE INFORMATION
Dillon Chamber of Commerce
Box 425
Dillon, MT, 59725
406-683-5511

Ennis

Elevation – 4,927 • Population – 790

Ennis is located on the banks of the Madison River. It is a small ranching and tourist community situated in a broad valley between the Gravelly and Tobacco Root Mountains to the west and the Madison Range to the east. The terrain consists of montane forest and intermountain grasslands. Flyfishers will view Ennis as a major trout hub; the city breathes fishing during the summer season.

ACCOMMODATIONS
Riverside Motel, 346 Main Street / 406-682-4240, 800-535-4139 / Open
May–December / Cabins, some with kitchens / All have cable, refrigerator, picnic table, and gas grill / Located on the Madison River / Dogs are welcome, $3 per dog / Reservations are necessary / Your host is Robert Hines
The Sportsman's Lodge, P.O. Box 305 / 406-682-4242 / 18 lodgepole pine cabins, 11-unit motel / Cable, restaurant, and lounge on premises / Dogs allowed, $5 per dog / Reservations recommended

CAMPGROUNDS AND RV PARKS
Elkhorn Store and RV Park, ½ mile south on Hwy 287 / 406-682-4273 / Open year-round / 12 tent and 13 RV spaces / Full facilities except for laundry

OUTFITTERS

Diamond J Ranch, REC Orvis Outfitter, P.O. Box 816, Ennis, MT 59729 / Call M–F 8AM–5PM / 406-682-7404 or 682-4867 after 5PM / 1,200 private ranch acres
Gary Evans Madison River Guides, PO Box 1456, Ennis, MT 59047 / 406-682-4890

RESTAURANTS

Continental Divide Restaurant, Downtown Ennis / 406-682-7600 / Open for dinner summer through mid-fall / One of Montana's finest restaurants / Your hosts are Jay and Karen Bentley
Ennis Cafe / 406-682-4442 / Breakfast, lunch, and dinner
Kathy's Wild Rose Restaurant / 406-682-4717

VETERINARIANS

White and White Veterinary Hospital and Supply, 5098 Hwy 287 / 406-682-7151
Douglas B. Young, DVM / 406-682-7956

FLY SHOPS AND SPORTING GOODS

Madison River Fishing Company, 109 Main Street / 406-682-4293
Headwaters Angling, Highway 287, Box 964 / 406-682-7451
The Tackle Shop, 127 Main / 406-682-4263
Thompson's Angling Adventures, Box 130 / 406-682-7509

AUTO REPAIR

D&D Auto / 406-682-4234

AIR SERVICE

Ennis Airport, 8 miles south of town / Contact Madison Valley Aircraft / 406-682-7431

MEDICAL

Madison Valley Hospital / 406-682-4274 / Emergency 406-682-4222

FOR MORE INFORMATION

Ennis Chamber of Commerce
P.O. Box 297
Ennis, MT 59729
406-682-4388 / If no answer try Ed Williams, Chamber President, 406-682-4264

Bozeman

Elevation – 4,793 • Population – 25,000

Known for its blue-ribbon trout fishing and great skiing, Bozeman is a rapidly growing resort and college town. There has been a recent population boom, resulting in crowded conditions and high prices. However, Bozeman has a lot to offer the flyfisher. There is still a small town atmosphere with big city amenities: good air service, shopping, fine restaurants, and outdoor activities. The terrain consists of montane forests and intermountain plains. Gallatin Valley's economy is based on agriculture. Bozeman is bordered by the Bridger Mountains northeast of town, Gallatin National Forest and the Gallatin Range to the south, and the Madison Range to the southwest.

ACCOMMODATIONS

Days Inn, 1321 North 7th Avenue / 406-587-5251 / 80 rooms / Cable, continental breakfast / Dogs allowed, $25 deposit / $$

Fairfield Inn, 828 Wheat Drive / 406-587-2222 / 57 rooms, 12 suites w/kitchenettes / Continental breakfast, pool, and jacuzzi / Dogs allowed, no restrictions / $$-$$$

Gallatin River Lodge, 9105 Thorpe Road / 406-388-0148 / Beautiful lodge near the Gallatin River / Guided flyfishing trips available (make reservations early)

Super 8, 800 Wheat Drive / 406-586-1521 / 108 rooms, cable / Dogs allowed, no restrictions / $

The Bozeman Inn, 1235 North 7th Avenue / 406-587-3176 / 45 rooms / Outdoor pool, sauna, cable / Mexican restaurant and lounge / Dogs allowed for a $5 fee / $$

CAMPGROUNDS AND RV PARKS

Bozeman KOA, 8 miles west on US 91 / 406-587-3030 / Open year–round / 50 tent and 100 RV spaces / Full services including laundry and store

RESTAURANTS

Bacchus Pub and Rocky Mountain Pasta Co., 105 East Main / 406-586-1314 / Breakfast, lunch, dinner / *Bacchus* 7AM–10PM / Sandwiches, burgers, salads, soups, and daily special entrees / $$ / *Pasta Company*, 5:30PM–10PM / Fine dining, pasta and seafood / $$$

John Bozeman's Bistro, 242 East Main / 406-587-4100 / International and regional specialties / Breakfast and lunch: $$ / Dinner: $$$

Mackenzie River Pizza Company, 232 East Main / 406-587-0055 / M–F 11:30AM –10PM, Sun 5–9PM / Fancy pizzas, pasta, salad / $$

O'Brien's, 312 East Main / 406-587-3973 / M-Sun 5PM–9PM / Continental cuisine / $$$

Crystal Bar, 123 East Main / 406-587-2888 / Open every day / Beer Garden / Will pack lunches / $$

Spanish Peaks Brewery, 120 North 19th / 406-585-2296 / Lunch M–F 11:30AM– 2:30PM; Dinner daily 5:30PM–10:30PM; Brunch Sat–Sun 11AM–2PM / Italian cuisine, microbrewed ales / $$-$$$

VETERINARIANS

All West Veterinary Hospital, 81770 Gallatin Road / 406-586-4919 / Gary Cook, Honor Nesbet, David E. Catlin, DVMs / 24-hour emergency service

Animal Medical Center, 216 North 8th Avenue (behind Kentucky Fried Chicken) / 406-587-2946 / Sue Barrows, DVM / Emergency service

FLY SHOPS AND SPORTING GOODS
Bob Ward and Sons, 2320 West Main / 406-586-4381
Powder Horn Sportsman's Supply, 35 East Main / 406-587-7373
The River's Edge, 2012 North 7th Avenue / 406-586-5373
Montana Troutfitters, 1716 West Main / 406-587-4707
Bozeman Angler, 24 East Main / 406-587-9111
Bear Creek Angler, Gallatin Gateway (Guide service only) / 406-763-4201

AUTO RENTAL AND REPAIR
Budget Rent-A-Car of Bozeman, Gallatin Field / 406-388-4091
Avis Rent-A-Car, Gallatin Field / 406-388-6414
Hertz Rent-A-Car, Gallatin Field / 406-388-6939
College Exxon Service, 723 South 8th Avenue / 406-587-4453
Frank Manseau Auto Clinic, 715 East Mendenhall / 406-586-4480
E.J. Miller Service and Towing, 28373 Norris Road / 406-587-0507

AIR SERVICE
Gallatin Field Airport, 8 miles west of Bozeman / 406-388-6632 / Served by
  Delta, Horizon, Skywest, and Frontier Airlines / Charter service available

MEDICAL
Bozeman Deaconess Hospital, 915 Highland Boulevard / 406-585-5000.

FOR MORE INFORMATION
Bozeman Chamber of Commerce
1205 East Main
P.O. Box B
Bozeman, MT 59715
800-228-4224

West Yellowstone
Elevation – 6,666 • Population – 1,000

West Yellowstone rests on the western edge of Yellowstone National Park and it is
an ideal location for flyfishers to call home for as long as they want. There are endless miles of rivers and lakes to explore in the area and almost all of them are on public land. West is bordered by the Gallatin and Targhee National Forests. You should
not have any trouble finding a nice spot to stay, whether in a plush hotel or an
improved campground. West also hosts excellent eateries, lively bars and some nice
bookstores. There are many flyshops, well-stocked, waiting for your visit.

ACCOMMODATIONS: WEST YELLOWSTONE
Alpine Motel, 120 Madison Avenue / 406-646-7544 / $
Best Western, 201 Firehole Lane / 406-646-9557 Hwy 2 West / 406-293-8831 / $$
Best Western, 103 Gibbon Lane / 406-646-7373 / $$

Campfire Lodge, 8500 Hebgen Lake Road / 406-646-7258 / $$
Lakeview Cabins, Hebgen Lake Road / 406-646-7257 / $$
Campobello Lodge/Bar-N-Ranch, 3111 Targhee Pass Hwy / 406-646-7121 /
    Access to private spring creeks and ponds available

CAMPGROUNDS AND RV PARKS
KOA Campground, West of West Yellowstone / 406-646-7606 / $$
Hebgen Lake Lodge, motel and tent campground, Highway 287, West Yellowstone
    / 406-646-9250 $$
Hideaway RV Camp, Corner of Gibbon Avenue / 406-646-9049 / $

OUTFITTERS
Beartrap Outfitters, 19 Madison Avenue / 406-646-9642
Madison River Outfitters, 125 Canyon / 406-646-9644

RESTAURANTS
Alice's Restaurant, 1545 Targhee Pass Road / 406-646-7296
Cappy's Bistro, 104 Canyon Road / 406-646-9537

FLY SHOPS AND SPORTING GOODS
Bud Lilly's Trout Shop, 39 Madison Avenue / 406-646-7801
Blue Ribbon Flies, 315 Canyon Road / 406-646-7642
Arrick's Fly Shop, 37 Canyon Street / 406-646-7290
Jacklin's Fly Shop, 105 Yellowstone Avenue / 406-646-7336
Madison River Outfitters, 117 Canyon Street / 406-646-9644
Eagle's Tackle Shop and Sporting Goods, 9 Canyon Street / 406-646-7642

AUTO REPAIR
Budget Rent-A-Car, 131 Dunraven / 406-646-7882
Big Sky Car Rentals, 415 Yellowstone Avenue / 406-646-9564

AIR SERVICE
West Yellowstone Airport (SkyWest Airlines) / 406-646-7351

FOR MORE INFORMATION:
West Yellowstone Chamber of Commerce
40 Yellowstone Avenue
West Yellowstone, MT 59758
406-646-7701

Central Montana

There are more famous places to fish in Montana, but you will have trouble finding a better river than the Missouri—its spring creek-like waters hold throngs of solid, really hard-fighting rainbows along with some awfully large browns.

On a good day, the Missouri will give up between 10 and 20 trout ranging between 14 and 18 inches. If you are really lucky, you may hook into a brown better than 20 inches. Every year, a 10-pounder or two comes to net.

While many only consider the Missouri River when heading to central Montana, the region offers a lot more—its streams and lakes aren't promoted in movies, but they offer first-rate flyfishing in some beautiful and typical Montana surroundings.

Take, for example, the Smith River. If you can acquire a permit to float the river (it's limited), launch your boat or raft at Camp Baker and settle in for a long ride—the next take-out point is 61 glorious miles downstream.

Throughout the float you will pass through a canyon with massive 200-foot-tall cliffs and lush, green meadows while casting at the fine riffles, deep pools and seductive runs. Brown trout are the staple on the Smith—on a good day you might bring 30 or more to net. And what's more important, you can experience Montana the way it used to be—wild.

The Yellowstone River flows through southcentral Montana, offering a truly grand river for the taking. Once labeled "The Yankee Stadium of Flyfishing," the Yellowstone offers over 100 miles of quality water, ranging from its headwaters in Yellowstone National Park to its most beautiful stretch in the Paradise Valley near Livingston to a point where it ceases as quality trout water east of Big Timber. Throughout, you might hook a strong-willed rainbow, brown trout, or the river's original inhabitant, the native cutthroat. It's an unbeatable combination: killer scenery and awesome trout water.

If you just want to hop off the road somewhere to fish for a couple hours, you can do that in central Montana. Little Prickly Pear Creek (some big rainbows and browns), the Dearborn (an underrated, wild and scenic float), Big Spring Creek (see Spring Creek section), the Musselshell River (trophy browns in solitude), the Marias River (an undiscovered rainbow and brown trout tailwater), the Boulder River (classic mountain trout water), and the Stillwater (pocketwater to the max), among others, are easily accessible.

If you're looking for stillwater opportunities, get your fill during May at Canyon Ferry Reservoir. You can catch enough five-pound rainbows in one day to make your arm sore for a week!

Overall, central Montana is a flyfisher's paradise—it offers easy access or remote solitude with excellent flyfishing opportunities, including some meaty trout, available with whatever option you choose.

Missouri River

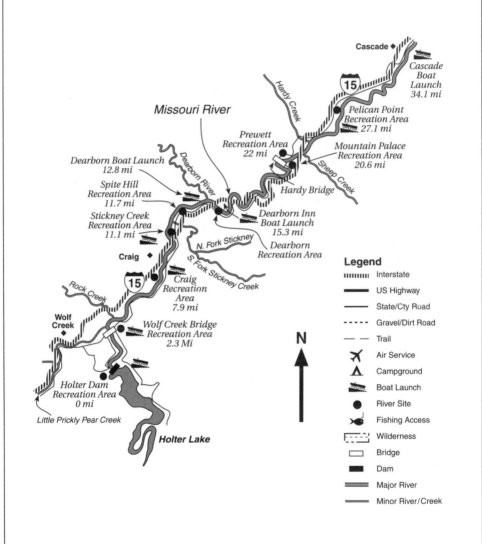

Cascade ◆

Cascade
Boat
Launch
34.1 mi

15

Hardy Creek

Pelican Point
Recreation Area
27.1 mi

Missouri River

Prewett
Recreation Area
22 mi

Mountain Palace
Recreation Area
20.6 mi

Dearborn Boat Launch
12.8 mi

Dearborn River

Sheep Creek

Spite Hill
Recreation Area
11.7 mi

Hardy Bridge

Stickney Creek
Recreation Area
11.1 mi

Dearborn Inn
Boat Launch
15.3 mi

N. Fork Stickney

Dearborn
Recreation Area

Craig ◆

S. Fork Stickney Creek

Legend

⊪⊪⊪⊪	Interstate
——	US Highway
—	State/Cty Road
- - - -	Gravel/Dirt Road
– — –	Trail
✈	Air Service
⛺	Campground
🚤	Boat Launch
●	River Site
🐟	Fishing Access
⌷⌷⌷	Wilderness
▭	Bridge
▬	Dam
━━	Major River
═══	Minor River/Creek

Rock Creek

15

Craig
Recreation
Area
7.9 mi

Wolf
Creek

Wolf Creek Bridge
Recreation Area
2.3 Mi

N
↑

Holter Dam
Recreation Area
0 mi

Little Prickly Pear Creek

Holter Lake

MISSOURI RIVER

When studying a map, the Missouri River might appear quite intimidating to a fledgling flyfisher. Its size and its length—a wide, blue twisting line on the chart that runs halfway across the state—often raises this question: "Where in the hell do you fish the river?"

Once that question is answered—by the way, you fish between Holter Dam and Pelican Point, where trout populations are most dense—the only intimidating factor is the Missouri's width and its apparent lack of good trout water.

You will not find classic riffle-run-pool habitat like you see on Rock Creek or the Gallatin River. Instead, the Missouri resembles a giant flat-surfaced spring creek with all the trimmings—massive insect hatches and abundant rainbow and brown trout that grow very large. Unfortunately, they hold a propensity to shun even the most delicately presented dry fly, especially late in the summer season. However, there are proven methods that take fish during those times, and we will cover those in a moment.

One day on the Missouri can teach a flyfisher many things about trout and trout water, not the least being that a drift boat or raft can be very advantageous, especially when the river is running high and fast (8,000 to 16,000 cfs) as it can be anytime between mid-April and August 1.

The Missouri is most easily waded when the river drops below 5,500 cfs. Prime floating conditions are between 5,500 to 8,000 cfs. Drift boats are preferred over rafts on the big river for their excellent anchor systems and their comfort during long floats. While casting from a boat or from shore, a 9-foot, 6-weight or 5-weight rod will work fine. If pitching big, weighted woolly buggers during spring or fall, a 7-weight might be best.

The Missouri begins at Three Forks where, of course, three noted trout streams, the Madison, Jefferson and Gallatin, feed it. From Three Forks, the river twists and turns north for 60 miles before it dumps into Canyon Ferry Reservoir near Helena. Then the river slices between a canyon for 25 miles where it dumps into Holter Reservoir.

From Holter Dam extending downstream across half the state, the Missouri is broad and powerful before slowing down at the manmade monstrosity called Fort Peck Reservoir, which actually provides some great flyfishing opportunities for big northern pike. However, productive trout fishing ceases just south of Great Falls. As mentioned, the best fishing on the river is restricted between Holter Dam and Pelican Point, which gives flyfishers about 25 miles of wonderful water to work.

In that stretch, rainbow trout ranging between eight and 22 inches are commonly caught. Brown trout are less abundant, but they still show up quite often, and their size normally ranges between 14 and 21 inches. Large specimens, both browns and rainbows, are a possibility on the Missouri, but it is best known for an amazing number of solid 16- to 18-inchers. It should not be expected to produce a ton of trophies.

On a good day, a dozen rainbows between 12 and 19 inches will be landed. A few browns may come to net also, and they could range to 20 inches or more. Expecting more than that from the Missouri or, for that matter, from any other trout stream is setting yourself up for disaster. It should be known, though, that several fish over 10 pounds are landed each season, with the best chances for a fish like that arriving in fall. If your luck is great, one of those fish may have your name on it.

There really isn't a bad time to fish the Missouri. It has excellent insect hatches every day of the year. In fact, winter fishing can be very productive, and you can, essentially, have the river to yourself. That is not the case during the popular summer and fall months.

During winter, expect heavy midge hatches. Millions of the small, biteless bugs will hover over the surface, gathering in clusters to mate. Trout love to eat these bugs when they are most vulnerable, which, of course, is when they cluster. Makes sense, doesn't it? Wouldn't personal preservation be a lower priority during the middle of an orgy?

Big midge hatches last from November through March, but on any given day you might be blown off the river or stymied by calm, but freezing, cold weather. When I spoke to a Trout Unlimited gathering in Great Falls one January, my ambition was to fish the river. A minus-30 temperature reading and a howling wind kept me off the water that morning. I visited the Charley Russell Museum instead, and I found it to be a very worthwhile diversion.

If you can get out on the river during winter, watch for rising trout. Tiny dry flies, such as a size 20 parachute Adams, Griffith's gnat, or a royal Wulff, will draw strikes up top, but the best offerings cruise under the surface. In fact, a San Juan worm trailed by a scud or a midge pupa is tough to beat.

One winter day I watched my friend, Kent Sullivan of Missoula, land one big scrappy rainbow after another on a San Juan worm from a run at the tailout of an island. There are few places in the world that produce trout like that. Each fish was solid, running 14 to 17 inches, and didn't seem at all disturbed by their brothers and sisters being pulled from the water next to them. Fishing like that separates the Missouri from 90 percent of Western rivers. And the fishing gets better as the year progresses!

According to Garry Stocker, who runs Montana Fly Goods in Helena and guides extensively on the river, the best fishing begins with a strong Baetis hatch in late April. And at that time of the year, after having subsisted on midges all winter, trout are keyed on the small mayflies, which make a good meal.

"You'll find the Baetis mixed in with midges during April, and then it turns to pretty much Baetis by May," Stocker says. "The fish will be holding next to the banks in pods. You'll find them anywhere that current seams come together, such as the end of islands and where braided channels meet.

"Typically, I like to throw a parachute Adams or a Baetis parachute in size 18 to 22," he adds. "An advantage to fishing the early Baetis hatch is that the fish aren't leader shy. They get that way by midsummer, but in April and May you can cast small flies on 5X tippet. I stick to a 9-foot leader at that time, because there can be some wind to deal with and a longer leader is nearly impossible to turn over in that wind."

Broad and flat, the Missouri River tailwater resembles a giant spring creek. Long casts, light tippets and tiny flies are often required. (Garry Stocker Photo)

Following the Baetis is a great caddis hatch. Typically beginning in May and early June, the caddis hatch will last all summer long and provides maybe the best overall action of the year. In fact, Stocker would choose the caddis hatch as the top emergence on the river, the one he would fish if it was his only option.

The caddis hatch begins near the Dearborn River and pushes upstream as the days lengthen and the weather warms. Heaviest emergences occur between mid-June and August.

"When it gets started, it comes off around 3 PM and runs till dark," Stocker says. "It gets extremely heavy the last hour of light, and that is typical of the hatch throughout summer. During that last hour of light, you'll be spitting them out of your mouth and pulling them off your glasses. The trout will be going crazy, slurping down emergers and adults like mad.

"A size 16 cream, light brown or rust-colored elk hair caddis works best, and I like to trail it with a spent caddis because they often eat emergers that are swinging in the surface film," Stocker added. "One key to fishing the hatch is understanding rise forms…you have to watch them."

When trout are eating emergers, not adults, the head never breaks the surface. You will only see the dorsal fin and tail come out of the water. If you only offer an elk hair caddis at that time, you won't catch many, if any, fish. You must give them the emerger when they're focused on that stage of the hatch."

The bread and butter hatch of summer arrives in mid-June when pale morning duns come off en masse. The emergence and spinnerfall are both important stages of the hatch.

"You see the emergence around 3 PM, and then the spinnerfall around 6 or 7 PM," Stocker says. "Sometimes, especially on extremely hot days, the emergence and spinnerfall happen right at dark, and that can make conditions difficult because those events coincide with the caddis emergence. It's tough to determine which insect they (the trout) are taking. And their choice can change from one pod of trout to the next."

Effective patterns for the PMD hatch include a size 16 or 18 PMD cripple or a sparkle dun. A parachute Adams will pull fish to the top in a pinch.

Following the PMDs, which peak in late June and last through mid-August, are the Tricos. Not to witness a dense Trico spinnerfall on the Missouri River at least one time would be depriving yourself of a true spectacle. The bugs can be so thick that they look like clouds hovering above the river, oscillating in the wind. An angler could find himself staring at the bugs complacently while trout froth the water just a few yards away. But to witness the event, you are going to have to get your butt out of bed early. The Tricos usually come off around 6:30 or 7 AM.

"We see the emergence in the early morning and the spinnerfall around 11 AM," Stocker says. "Spinners will pile up in the riffle corners and eddies, and there can be so many bugs on the water that fishing is tough. Instead of matching the Trico directly, I use a caddis or a small parachute Wulff. They are easier to see and the fish take it.

"If I have to match the Tricos, I go with a parachute Trike or an H&L. You should be able to get way with 5X tippet, but a wary fish will require 6X or even 7X. But it can be very difficult to hold a 17- to 22-inch trout on that tippet. That's the trade-off. The fish are in good shape, they are in the football mold, and they are hot. They can pop a light tippet as though it didn't exist! "

Trico fishing peaks in mid-July and lasts through August. By that time, if you have been lucky enough to spend a number of mornings on the river fishing Tricos, you'll be ready for a change of pace. And after tossing minuscule size 22 flies for a month, there is no greater contradiction than a grasshopper. Tossing a hopper up against the bank when you are used to throwing Tricos is like crash landing a Cessna.

"Hopper fishing is usually best in the afternoons, from 2 to 6 PM," Stocker offers. "Pay close attention to the wind in relation to a farmer's field. A bank right next to a field is going to be best. In a situation like that, you want to fish the banks but don't forget about the middle of the river, either. Guys that fish the middle of the river will take some good fish. I would almost always run a beadhead dropper off the hopper. A caddis pupa or a Prince nymph works best."

Hopper fishing dies sometime in September or October, just as the first hard frosts hit Montana. However, that does not mean a flyfisher needs to tie on a small dry fly to take fish. In fact, fall may be the best time to pitch large offerings, especially size 2 woolly buggers.

"In the fall the brown trout start their spawning runs, and fishing can be excellent, especially for large trout with woolly buggers," Stocker said. "I think the best

"That's right, I drilled this nice 'bow." Happy flyfisher hoists a typical Missouri River rainbow. (Garry Stocker Photo)

fishing happens on the lower section below the mouth of the Dearborn. It's more rocky down there, and the fish hold in the water along the banks. Really concentrate on the riprap banks. And just pound the holes along those banks. We catch a lot of fish over 20 inches. A few go 24 to 26 inches."

Because the river is deep, flyfishers may want to throw a fullsink line during fall. According to Stocker, a fullsink will get you down to the trout much faster than a floating line, even with weight added.

"A guy fishing a fast sinkline versus a guy with a floating line will catch a lot more fish during fall because it gets down so much faster and it's more maneuverable," Stocker explains. "I'd fish that sinking line off a 9-foot, 5- or 6-weight rod."

Brown trout and rainbows also spawn in the channels between Canyon Ferry, Hauser and Holter Reservoirs. The channel between Canyon Ferry and Hauser is nearly impossible to fish, due to its depth and heavy current.

The channel between Hauser and Holter is a little more manageable.

"It's best if you fish it from a motorboat, but you can hike down to it," Stocker says. "The best access is right at Hauser Dam, where you can just walk downstream Or you can drive down from Beaver Creek. It's a long, windy road, but it takes you right to the river. You don't need four-wheel drive if the road is dry, but if it gets wet you need it.

"We catch a couple of 10-pound browns out of there each fall," Stocker adds. "We see some rainbows to eight or 10 pounds, also. It's all good throughout the channel between the end of September into November."

You don't have to throw the big bugs during fall to catch fish. In fact, if a dry-fly fisher wants some action, there are plenty of Baetis to match, and a size 16 parachute Baetis or Adams would be ideal.

The Baetis hatch can be so productive that Jerry Lappier at Missouri River Trout Shop in Wolf Creek rates it over the caddis hatch as the Missouri's premier emergence —the one hatch he would fish over all others.

"If I were rating the hatches without the crowds, I'd take the caddis," Lappier says. "But during summer there can be crowds of people on the river. In the fall, you have blue-winged olives and few people, and the fish are really on them. It (the emergence) only lasts about five or six hours a day, from 11 AM to 5 PM, but in that time you can really drill them.

"The Baetis hatch really peaks about the second week of October, and it lasts through the first real cold days of November. An advantage to fishing during fall is that you can get away with a 5X tippet—something you can't always do at other times. The flies are smaller, so you will want to go with a size 18 Adams or royal Wulff to match the duns. An RS-2 emerger or a soft hackle will cover emergers. Sparkle duns and cripples work very well, too. You can use a size 16 when fishing the cripple patterns.

"Another advantage to fall fishing is that the people you do encounter are pretty hard-core flyfishers—you see very few bait fishermen," Lappier adds. "Also, you can fish the lower river successfully. In fact, people tend to migrate to the lower river where the water is slightly warmer. The fish will be podded up, and the fishing will be fabulous. I like to fish upstream, take the first trout off the bottom end of the pod, and then work my way up through them. However, a downstream presentation is probably the most effective of all."

No matter what hatch you hit on the Missouri, you're bound to have good luck. However, because the river is regulated by dams, the flow can change overnight and send fishing into a tailspin.

According to Stocker, increasing the flow will put trout off the feed for one day. When the flow is decreased, fish immediately get more aggressive. Prime flows for floating range from 5,500 cfs to 8,000 cfs. However, prime wading occurs below 6,000 cfs. That flow range usually occurs between late June and early July, although it always varies, so it pays to call Stocker or Lappier ahead of your arrival date.

It isn't difficult to gain access to the Missouri, despite lots of private property along its banks. Those with boats and rafts, of course, have total access to the river.

Boaters can put in at Holter Dam and float down to Silver Bridge, about 3 miles, or to Craig, an excellent 7.5-mile float. Craig to the mouth of the Dearborn River is another popular float, and it is about 7 miles.

No matter where you decide to float or wade in the Missouri's prime trout stretch, the river will not disappoint. It is unquestionably one of the state's best rivers —many people would argue it is the state's best stream—and its trout are as strong as you might find anywhere. It is also an easy river to reach from any direction: from the west you can follow Highway 200 from Missoula. Take Highway 287 junction south to Craig. From Bozeman to the south, take Highway 287 north near Three Forks to Townsend and then follow Highway 12 northwest to Helena. From the east at Lewistown, just follow Highway 200 west to Great Falls and cruise down to Craig.

Stream Facts: Missouri River

Seasons
- Downstream from Three Forks—open all year.

Special Regulations
- Portions of the Missouri River are closed from Toston Dam to Canyon Ferry Reservoir between March 1 and June 15.
- Toston Dam to Canyon Ferry: All brown trout between 18 and 24 inches must be released.
- Below Canyon Ferry Dam as posted — closed entire year.
- Hauser Dam downstream to Holter Dam — catch and release for brown trout.
- Holter Dam to Cascade — only one brown trout over 22 inches.

Trout
- Rainbow and brown trout. Rainbows dominate the population, but there are decent numbers of brown trout, too. Flyfishers can expect both rainbows and browns to average 15 to 17 inches. A few fish will stretch past 20 inches.

River Miles
- Missouri River Headwaters—0
- Toston Dam—21.9
- Townsend—42
- Canyon Ferry Dam—68
- Holter Dam—110
- Silver Bridge—112
- Craig—117
- Dearborn River—124
- Hardy Bridge—132
- Cascade—145

River Flows
- Between Holter Dam and Cascade, where the best fishing takes place, flows build in May and peak in June. By early July the river drops and prime water conditions occur. Floating is best between 5,500 and 8,000 cubic feet a second. Prime wading occurs below 6,000 cfs.

River Characteristics
- The Missouri between Holter Dam and Cascade displays a flat surface that resembles a giant spring creek. Floating is not difficult and novice boaters can manage fine.

Area Fly Shops
- Montana Fly Goods, 2125 Euclid Avenue, Helena, MT, 406-442-2630
- Fly Fisher's Inn, 2629 Old U. S. Highway 91, Cascade, MT, 406-468-2529
- Big Sky Expeditions, 2125 Euclid Ave. Helena, MT, 800-466-9589
- Missouri River Trout Shop & Lodge, Wolf Creek, MT, 406-235-4474
- Missouri River Expeditions, 114 Forest Park Drive, Clancy, MT, 406-933-5987
- Montana Troutfitters, 1716 Main, Bozeman, MT 59715, 406-587-4707
- The River's Edge, 2012 N. 7th, Bozeman, MT, 406-586-5373
- Wolverton's Fly Shop, 210 5th St., Great Falls, MT, 406-454-0254
- Montana River Outfitters, 1401 5th Ave. South, Great Falls, MT, 406-761-1677

MISSOURI RIVER MAJOR HATCHES

Insect	J	F	M	A	M	J	J	A	S	O	N	D	Flies
Midge	██	██	██	██	██	██	██	██	██	██	██	██	Griffith's Gnat #18-24; Standard Adams #16-24; Palomino Midge #16-24; Serendipity #16-24; Brassie #18-24; Disco Midge #16-24; Reverse Suspender Midge #18-24
Pale Morning Dun						██	██						PMD Cripple #16-22; Sparkle Dun #16-22; Parachute PMD #16-22; Rusty Spinner #16-22; CDC Transitional Dun #18-22; Woven PMD Nymph #16-20; Hare's Ear Nymph #16-20; Pheasant Tail Nymph #16-20
Caddis							██	██					Black Caddis Pupa #16-18; X-Caddis #16-18; Emergent Sparkle Pupa #16-18; Hemingway Caddis #16-18; Tan Caddis #16-18; Elk Hair Caddis #16-18; Soft Hackle #14-18
Trico								██	██				Parachute Adams #18-20; Spent Wing Trico #18-20; Griffith's Gnat #18-20; CDC Trico #18-20; Z-lon Trike #18-22
Baetis				██	██				██	██			Olive Cripple #16-24; Parachute Adams #16-24; Sparkle Dun #16-24; Olive Thorax #18-24; Hare's Ear Nymph #16-22; Pheasant Tail Nymph #16-22; Poxyback Baetis #16-22; RS-2 Emerger
Grasshoppers								██	██				Dave's Hopper #6-8; Meadow Hopper #6-8

MISSOURI RIVER TRIBUTARIES

Little Prickly Pear Creek

With the Missouri River looming in its backyard, Little Prickly Pear Creek and its generous population of sizable rainbow and brown trout will never gain the distinction they deserve—the creek is an excellent small water trout fishery that is often passed up by visiting anglers and savored silently by locals.

The creek, however, is not the place to spend an entire weeklong trip—long stints severely increase your odds of being bitten by two-fanged serpentine creatures. And there are plenty of them, some quite large and fast, residing in the rocky shoreline habitat. Rather, the Little Prickly Pear offers an interesting diversion from extended days on the Missouri, especially during late spring, just as general fishing season opens on the third Saturday in May. That is when some sizable rainbows, Missouri River spawners, can be found in the lower reaches of the creek, especially below the Interstate 15 bridge. Above the bridge, flyfishers will find smaller rainbows and browns still worthy of dry-fly and nymph imitations.

If you choose to fish upstream from the bridge, pack a variety of fly patterns in your vest: light and dark caddis, numerous mayfly species and, of course, hoppers, may be encountered during the summer season. Downstream from the bridge during spring, larger weighted patterns, such as woolly buggers, egg sucking leeches, woolhead sculpins and Troth bullheads, work wonders. Just remember to slip those trout into a net and don't remove them from the water. Their spawning efforts ensure the propagation that makes the Missouri River one of the world's best rainbow fisheries.

Also, don't mess with Little Prickly Pear's spawning brown trout—not only is it illegal (the creek is closed to fishing below the bridge between Labor Day and the general opener), it's downright ruthless. Those browns need a chance to boost their population.

The only factor that can ruin a trip to Little Prickly Pear, other than having a hissing rattlesnake hanging from your ankle by two fangs, is high, muddy water. That can occur in late April, with premature runoff, or later in May and June when the state's snowpack heads out of the high country in earnest. You will be able to tell if the creek is fishable by glancing from the interstate, which runs above the creek. If the creek looks blown out, give it a few days to settle. As soon as it starts dropping and clearing, rainbows that have not raced back into the big river will be ready to perform.

To reach Little Prickly Pear, follow I-15 north from Helena. From I-15 you can parallel the middle and upper portions of the creek by following the Sieben Canyon Road. Most of those portions run through private land and permission must be gained to fish the creek. On the lower end, access is available from the interstate via the Helena National Forest.

Dearborn River

Almost anywhere else in the West, the Dearborn River would be held in high regard by its state's flyfishers. But in Montana, with the big name rivers calling to us, the Dearborn goes virtually untouched.

Not touched that is, except by a local following. And that local following prefers to fish the river early in the season when the water level and, therefore, access, is prime. It doesn't hurt that some large stoneflies frequent the Dearborn in March, April and May.

Large stoneflies—skwalas—are often ignored on lesser Montana rivers. Most flyfishers only consider far west Montana's Bitterroot when chasing the hatch. But the Dearborn, along with many other medium size streams, offer that insect, too. According to Stocker, the Dearborn's skwala hatch is worth hitting.

"We have to make a tough decision when it comes to the skwala hatch," Stocker said. "We can either float the Smith for four days or hit the Dearborn. Almost every year, we will do at least a float or two on the Dearborn. It can be really good."

Unfortunately, access is not good on the Dearborn. The river cuts through mostly private land on its path to the Missouri. Most floaters put in where Route 287 crosses the Dearborn north of Wolf Creek. Because access is so limited, the next public take-out point is on the Missouri River downstream from Craig. From the 287 bridge to the confluence with the Missouri, the Dearborn spans 19 miles. Ideally, floaters would take two days to cover the water. However, a one-day float eliminates the need to camp; camping sites along the river are limited at best. There are several state land sections touching the river, but you have to have the directional instincts of a mallard to locate them. Floating that stretch could take much longer if you launch a boat or raft after the water recedes; you'll be dragging your craft over gravel bars much of the way.

Fishing can be excellent anytime you can get at the water with standard caddis and mayfly imitations taking rainbows and browns that average 12 to 15 inches, with a few to 20-plus. During fall, the lower section, including the mouths of Paul, Sawmill and Flat Creek, can be extremely productive for large browns that move out of the Missouri to spawn. Streamers are your best choice at that time.

Sun River

While access limits flyfishers on the Dearborn, it is water—a severe lack of it at times—that inhibits productive fishing on the Sun River.

Numerous irrigation dams pull water out of the river and its reservoirs through summer, which makes life difficult for trout and troutfishers. Fortunately, rainbows, cutthroats, browns and brookies are hearty, resilient creatures, and a few of them manage to survive under those marginal conditions. It's these trout, most in the eight- to 12-inch range with a few reaching many pounds, that offer decent opportunities for local flycasters. For out-of-state flyfishers or Montanans visiting from other areas of the state, the Sun is a day or two side-trip away from big name rivers. It is not a top-rated stream, but it flows through some interesting country, and it does hold some good fish.

The Sun River begins with the North Fork Sun, which curls around the east edge of the Bob Marshall Wilderness. It meets the South Fork Sun at Gibson Reservoir, about 20 miles northwest of Augusta. It's there, at Gibson, that the Sun's real problems begin. In fact, from Gibson Reservoir the Sun flows a couple miles through a short canyon before backing up at Diversion Dam, a small reservoir that holds some decent cutthroats, rainbows and brookies. Gibson Dam and Diversion Dam feed Pishkin and Willow Creek Reservoirs, and because of the requirements for those reservoirs, they drop severely during summer.

Below the reservoirs, the Sun also feels the effects of dewatering, but there are some large browns to be had and the scenery is excellent. In fact, from Diversion Dam downstream about 20 miles, the Sun flows through a steeply-sloped canyon with all the scenery you need. There are a variety of water types to fish—deep holes, rocky runs, shallow riffles and flat glides. It's all good water and the trout seem particularly fond of muddler minnows, woolly buggers and rabbit strip leeches, although they will rise to caddis patterns when a hatch comes off.

While larger streamers take the most fish on the lower river, attractor dry flies are the ticket along the forks of the Sun. Royal Wulffs, double humpies, a parachute Adams, renegades and elk hair caddis will draw strikes. Standard nymphs, such as hare's ears, pheasant tails, caddis larvae and beadheads, work wonders, too.

To reach the upper Sun, take Willow Creek Road west from Augusta. About six miles out of town, turn north on Sun River Road, which parallels the canyon. Sun River Road takes you to Gibson Reservoir. Trails lead the adventurous flyfisher up the forks. Gear up before you head out of a hub city—there are few amenities in Augusta, especially if you are looking for any flyfishing gear.

SMITH RIVER

If you fish Montana's big-name rivers, you will find company unless your toes and fingers can handle wintry weather, which keeps most flyfishers off the water from early November through April. However, there is one prime Big Sky water, exceedingly beautiful and trout-productive, that sees relatively light pressure during the excellent spring and early summer season.

While other streams like the Missouri, Beaverhead and Bighorn founder under nearly unbearable numbers of rod-waving lunatics, the Smith River in west central Montana receives a limited number of floaters—a maximum of nine float parties a day, controlled by a permit system. And because there is severely limited access, wade fishers are also sparse. A flyfisher's primary companions are bears, hawks, golden eagles, mule deer and elk.

This is a unique option in some of Montana's most secluded country. If you launch a boat or raft on the river at Camp Baker, the next take-out point lies 61 twisting, trout-rich, no-turning-back river miles away! That's too many isolated miles for many people, but just the perfect amount for trout addicts who enjoy a measure of solitude. The glitch is this: drawing a permit to float the river is becoming increasingly difficult.

The Smith River begins just south of the Castle Mountains southeast of White Sulphur Springs. The best water twists between sheer canyon walls, slopes of thick timber and around bends in the river formed by sheer cliffs on one side and vast meadows on the other. The most productive trout water rests in those 61 miles between Camp Baker and Eden Bridge (the standard take-out point).

While floating the river, flyfishers can hook plenty of rainbow and brown trout, with the occasional Goliath ranging to 20 inches or more. For definition purposes, the Smith is a brown trout river. Not a trophy brown trout stream, but a river that, at its best, can kick out 30 or 40 fish between 12 and 17 inches in a day. Its rainbows are less often encountered, but according to local flyfishers, their numbers are increasing, especially in the lower river.

"The Smith is a freestone stream that snakes like crazy," says Garry Stocker at Montana Fly Goods, a veteran guide on the river. "Most of the way, you have 300-foot tall rock walls on one side of the river and big beautiful green meadows on the other. As far as I'm concerned, it's the most beautiful river in the state. It's where I go when I have vacation time. You feel enclosed when you are on it. You can't see out of the canyons in most places. It gives you a sense of wilderness. It looks untouched. You feel like you are in the middle of nowhere, and that is a great thing."

Plus it has hungry trout that aren't afraid of eating the big, easy, ugly stuff.

The Smith fishes well all year, however, winter fishing is a bust due to extremely cold temperatures and ice jams along the river. Winter unleashes its grip on the water sometime in March, but floating the river at that time is sketchy at best.

"The last guy to attempt the Smith before April 1 came back with a picture of 18 inches of snow on his boat," Stocker says. "We really don't even see many people floating it in April because of the weather, but the fishing is good at that time. It's just

Smith River

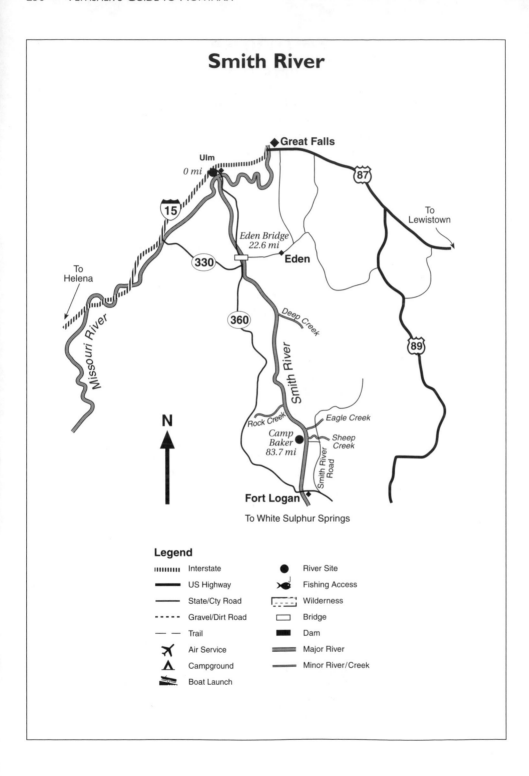

Great Falls

Ulm
0 mi

87

To
Lewistown

15

*Eden Bridge
22.6 mi*

330

Eden

To
Helena

360

Deep Creek

89

Missouri River

Smith River

N

Rock Creek

Eagle Creek

*Camp
Baker
83.7 mi*

*Sheep
Creek*

Smith River Road

Fort Logan

To White Sulphur Springs

Legend

ⅢⅢⅢ	Interstate	●	River Site
▬▬	US Highway	✺	Fishing Access
—	State/Cty Road	⌐---¬	Wilderness
- - - -	Gravel/Dirt Road	▭	Bridge
— —	Trail	▬	Dam
✈	Air Service	▬▬▬	Major River
⛺	Campground	▬▬▬	Minor River/Creek
⛴	Boat Launch		

a matter of the weather; you could sail right through with nice temperatures or it could dump a pile of snow, and you might not be able to get out of your boat."

Poor weather or not, the skwala stonefly begins its emergence on the Smith in mid-April, and it is present on the water through mid-May. The Smith's trout chow on skwala nymphs and adults during that time. Fortunately, simple patterns will draw strikes, and delicate presentations are not required.

"You don't see a lot of bugs when the skwalas are coming off," Stocker says. "If you see one or two on the water, you start fishing them; the fish will be keyed in. It can be a really productive hatch, and there just aren't very many people on the water."

Patterns like a size 12 olive bullethead skwala or elk hair caddis draw strikes up top. Prince nymphs and olive skwala nymphs with peacock dubbing will take fish underneath. Try sizes 8 through 12.

"We fish a lot of yuk bugs and woolly buggers, too," Stocker says. "There is a warm time frame from noon until 4 PM when the fish are really active. Before or after that you can't beat the woolly buggers."

Dry-fly fishers can also find action during spring when decent hatches of blue-winged olives come off. Watch for sporadic rise activity, not full-blown surface feeding. You will not encounter the olives or the rising trout throughout a float. Instead, you'll find isolated pods of trout feeding up top. Keep one rod rigged with a dry-fly tippet and a BWO pattern and another rod strung with a heavy tippet and a bugger. You can pound the banks with buggers and switch quickly to your dry-fly rig when you eye a riser.

"In the lower sections, you'll run into some fish that get on those olives pretty good, but it's not great," says Stocker. "You'll do much better at that time if you throw stone-fly patterns. The fish do key on the Baetis, but bigger patterns are more productive."

The Smith's main event arrives in mid-May when the big salmonflies come off. Catching lots of large trout during the salmonfly frenzy is as easy as flyfishing can get. Drawing a permit anytime in late May and June, however, is very difficult. If you do draw a permit, pray that water conditions will be suitable for fishing. High, muddy water with less than a foot of visibility is your nemesis. And high water will be present from early May through June. In extended high water years, the big flows may last until mid-July.

"Traditionally, the salmonflies get going about May 18 or 19," Stocker explains. "They will run through the first week of June. It can be awesome or it can be a blowout for fishing. Usually in low water years, the hatch will last just a few days. It will start near Ulm and move upstream about five miles a day. When the fishing is on, we've popped 100 a day in a boat with guys who knew what they were doing. You can catch a lot of them on size 4 and 6 Kaufmann's stones or up top on size 4 and 6 stim-ulators or Bird's stoneflies."

While salmonflies get the notoriety, the golden stoneflies, which are present on the Smith between mid-June and mid-July, are equally significant to the trout and trout fishers who mimic them. That statement is true of many Montana streams—salmonflies are the glory bugs; golden stones get no respect.

"When the golden stones come off, you can float up to a flat and see fish just going crazy everywhere," Stocker says. "We use size 10 and 12 golden stimulators to match the stoneflies—that's the best fly by far. We do get some on yellow double humpies, but you're crazy if you don't fish stimulators."

Another early summer hatch of note is the brown drake, a size 10 mayfly that is well worth a trout's attention. The drakes are present in greatest numbers on the lower river. Size 10 paradrakes or a parachute Adams work well. Cripple patterns will draw strikes, too.

"The last week of June is the best time for brown drakes," Stocker says. "It can be significant when it happens. I think the brown drake might even have more than one emergence; it comes off around 11 AM, and then it gets prolific in the afternoon around 3 PM. You won't see a ton of fish rising, but they will really react to dry flies in the flats."

By early or mid-July, depending on the amount of water being sucked out by merciless irrigators, the Smith gets extremely low, and floaters encounter this proposition: How far can you drag a raft before you are physically deflated and can go no farther?

"A minimum flow would be 90 cfs at the old gauge at Camp Baker," says Stocker. "At the new gauge you need at least 150 cfs. On the other end, I wouldn't float if it was 800 cfs and rising. But if it was 800 cfs and dropping, I'd go for it. You only need a foot of visibility to catch trout on the banks."

By mid-September, the Smith's flows rejuvenate due to lessening irrigation demand and some much-needed rain. Fortunately, the fall Baetis hatch starts up at that time, too. Hopper and angry brown trout add to the mix.

"Fall is a great time to fish the Smith," according to Stocker. "You can fish Baetis and hoppers up top, or you can strip woolly buggers underneath. The browns are really active because they are gearing up for the spawn and the temperatures are mild. It's usually around 60 or 70 degrees during the day. I've found browns stacked up below the mouth of many feeder creeks, but they really hold in front of Rock Creek. You can fish buggers and yuk bugs all day if you want. Hopper patterns and stimulators work well in the afternoons.

"If I could only fish the river one week during the year, I'd fish it sometime in September with hoppers. The fishing is as good as it gets, there are fewer people around, the weather is nice, and the water level is good."

Floating the Smith during any season is not a huge challenge. It is not a swift gradient stream. Instead, it meanders along peacefully, offering some quick riffles and rapids to wake the oarsman. The rapids are not difficult to negotiate, but an oarsman should stay alert going around any corner in the river—downed logs, boulders and unforeseen obstacles can lead to trouble.

FWP requires mandatory preregistration for private float parties and outfitters. And you must apply well in advance of your trip—before February 17 (1998 regulations). Launches are limited to nine a day, with nine launches a week set aside for outfitters during the peak season (May through June). The average float trip takes

Many consider the Smith River Montana's wildest, most scenic float. (Gary Stocker Photo)

about four days. Groups are limited to 15 people, and campsites must be restricted to preselected sites. FWP maintains 27 boat camps with 54 campsites. Eight boat camps are on FWP lands, 14 are on National Forest land, and five are leased from private landowners. To register for permits, contact the FWP regional office in Great Falls at 406-454-5840; mail to PO Box 6610, Great Falls, Montana, 59406; or e-mail fwprg4@mt.gov. To reach the Smith, drive north from Livingston on Highway 89 to White Sulphur Springs. From White Sulphur, head west for Eden. Camp Baker lies midway on the Smith River Road.

Shuttles can be arranged through any of the fly shops in Helena or Great Falls. It makes the most sense to leave your own rig at the take-out spot. That way you are not trying to meet somebody at a specific time after floating 61 miles of wild river.

If you do not draw a permit, realize there are cancellations—if you really want to get on the river, you need to hang around Camp Baker and wait for a party to cancel. Possibly the easiest way to get on the river is to hire a guide. They will float you down the river safely, which means you can fish and gawk at the scenery while they

An easy, beautiful float, the Smith requires a limited-entry permit for access. Applications are due in February. (Gary Stocker Photo)

man the oars. Also, they'll set up your tent camps, cook your meals and carry all of the gear in extra rafts. Plus, they'll provide excellent conversation and invaluable fly-fishing knowledge.

Despite the hassle of drawing a permit, the Smith rates as one of the top trout waters in the state. It flows through some of Montana's most isolated country, and it offers lots of big brown and rainbow trout. To float the Smith is to embark on an adventure; you do not simply fire up the truck, throw in a snack and rush off to the river for a few hours. Instead, planning, which is always such an integral part of a good trip, plays a huge role. If you don't plan well, you could spend four miserable days in the wilderness. That knowledge brings most of us closer to nature than many people will ever get. In itself, that should be enough to merit a trip.

Stream Facts: Smith River

Seasons
- Open all year downstream from confluence of north and south forks.

Special Regulations
- From confluence of Rock Creek to Eden Bridge—artificial flies and lures only. Three fish under 13 inches and one over 22 inches.

Trout
- Brown and rainbow trout. Brown dominate in the Smith. Rainbows are encountered more on the lower river. Average brown trout runs between 12 and 15 inches. Rainbows will stretch between 10 and 14 inches.

River Miles
- Missouri River confluence 0
- Ulm Bridge 3.6
- Eden Bridge 22.6
- Black Butte Camp 37.2
- Staigmiller Camp 37.7
- Trout Creek Camp 51.7
- Two Creek Camp 64.7
- Camp Baker 83.7
- South and North Forks 124.8

River Flows
- Flows build in late April and May and peak by June. Dewatering occurs in July, making float trips difficult through the summer. Flows stabilize in late September and October.

River Characteristics
- The Smith does not offer very much wade opportunity, so the best way to see the river is to float. However, there are a limited number of permits available for boat launches. If you do get a permit, expect a slow, placid float, accentuated by a few minor rapids and wonderful scenery throughout.

Obtaining Permits
- Drawing for launch dates is February 17. Applications must be received before that date. Remaining launches are filled on a first-come, first-served basis. Call Fish, Wildlife and Parks in Great Falls for information 406-454-5840

Area Fly Shops
- Montana Fly Goods, 2125 Euclid Avenue, Helena, MT, 406-442-2630
- Fly Fisher's Inn, 2629 Old U. S. Highway 91, Cascade, MT, 406-468-2529
- Big Sky Expeditions, 2125 Euclid Ave., Helena, MT, 800-466-9589
- Missouri River Trout Shop & Lodge, Wolf Creek MT, 406-235-4474
- Missouri River Expeditions, 114 Forest Park Drive, Clancy, MT, 406-933-5987
- Montana Troutfitters, 1716 Main, Bozeman, MT 59715, 406-587-4707
- The River's Edge, 2012 N. 7th, Bozeman, MT, 406-586-5373
- Wolverton's Fly Shop, 210 5th St., Great Falls, MT, 406-454-0254
- Montana River Outfitters, 1401 5th Ave. South, Great Falls, MT, 406-761-1677

SMITH RIVER MAJOR HATCHES

Insect	J	F	M	A	M	J	J	A	S	O	N	D	Flies
Grasshopper								▮					Dave's Hopper #2-8; Meadow Hopper #2-8
Skwala Stonefly			▮										Bullethead Skwala #6-8; Olive Stimulator #6-8; Rubberleg Brown Stone #6-8
Brown Drake						▮							Parachute Adams #14-16; Sparkle Dun #14-16; Comparadun # 14-16; Hare's Ear Nymph #14-16; Pheasant Tail Nymph #14-16
Midge	▮	▮	▮	▮	▮	▮	▮	▮	▮	▮	▮	▮	Griffith's Gnat #16-20; Parachute Adams #18-22; Pheasant Tail Nymph #16-22
Salmonfly *Pteronarcys californica*					▮								Seducer #4-8; Stimulator #4-8; Bitch Creek Nymph #4-8; Kaufmann's Stone #2-6; Brook's Stone #2-6; Bitch Creek Nymph #4-8; Black Rubberlegs #2-8
Baetis				▮									Olive Cripple #16-20; Parachute Adams #16-20; Sparkle Dun #16-20; Hare's Ear Nymph #16-20; Pheasant Tail Nymph #16-20; Poxyback Baetis #16-20
Golden Stone *Hesperoperla pacifica*						▮							Whitlock's Golden Stone Nymph #4-8; Montana Nymph #4-8; Betts' Brown Stone #4-8; Whitlock's Revised Golden Stone #4-8; Poxyback Biot Golden Stone #6-12
Caddis									▮				Elk Hair Caddis #14-18; Diving Caddis #14-16; X-Caddis #14-16; Drifting Cased Caddis #14-18; Emergent Sparkle Pupa #12-18; Deep Sparkle Pupa #12-18
Pale Morning Dun										▮			Sparkle Dun #14-20; Parachute Adams #14-20; PMD Cripple #16-20; Hare's Ear Nymph #16-18; Pheasant Tail Nymph #16-18; CDC Floating Nymph #16-18

SMITH RIVER CHECKLIST

For Two Anglers in a Boat or Raft

- sleeping bags rated
  for 0 to 10 degrees or colder
- camp shoes, like Teva sandals
- wool socks, two or three pair
- long underwear
- shorts
- two pair long pants
- two heavy shirts with long sleeves
- fleece jacket and pants
  for around camp
- stocking hat
- flashlight
- pillow
- towel

- soap
- water purification tablets
- heavy jacket
- rain jacket
- gloves
- camera/film
- sunscreen
- two-burner Coleman stove
- cookware
- food (canned and freeze-dried items)
- tent
- pop and water
- condensed juices
- matches and lighters

Tips

"One of the things we do with food on our trips is to have someone cook a roast and a ham, and we make sandwiches off of them all week. Another thing we have found is that ice in coolers makes water—if you use bagged ice, you need to put food in Zip-Loc or Tupperware containers. The best we have found to carry ice is to freeze water in milk jugs; this way we do not have melted ice water in the coolers, and when the jugs thaw, you have drinking water."

—Garry Stocker, Montana Fly Goods in Helena

According to Stocker, there are also two places to get drinking water during your Smith River float: "These springs have never been tested for quality, but nobody has ever gotten sick from them," Stocker said. "One of them is called Indian Springs and it's about 6.8 miles downriver from Camp Baker. There is also Mother Springs, just below Bear Gulch and before Trout Creek at mile 31. There is a small sign (river right) that marks the springs, but it's easy to miss.

"Really, you should take your own water unless you are familiar with the springs. Two guys should take a five-gallon container. You could also take one of the new water purifiers if you want to."

Marias River

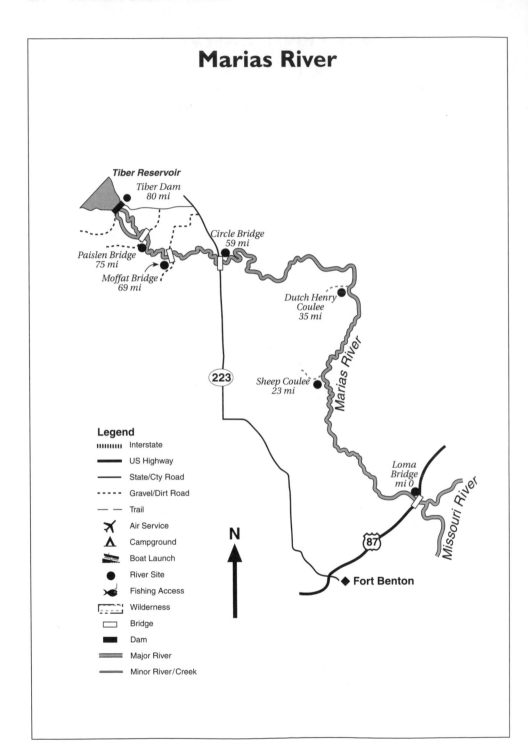

Tiber Reservoir

Tiber Dam
80 mi

Circle Bridge
59 mi

Paislen Bridge
75 mi

Moffat Bridge
69 mi

Dutch Henry
Coulee
35 mi

Marias River

223

Sheep Coulee
23 mi

Loma
Bridge
mi 0

Missouri River

87

Fort Benton

Legend

┅┅┅┅	Interstate
▬▬▬	US Highway
───	State/Cty Road
-----	Gravel/Dirt Road
— —	Trail
✈	Air Service
⛺	Campground
🛥	Boat Launch
●	River Site
🐟	Fishing Access
⌁	Wilderness
▭	Bridge
▬	Dam
═══	Major River
───	Minor River/Creek

N

MARIAS RIVER

To the common man, a trophy trout hunter's mentality may seem a little skewed. Can a flyfisher who braves the elements for hours on end, even during a blinding mid-November blizzard, really be labeled sane? If not, steer clear of Liberty County and the Marias River. There are some crazed trophy troutfishers visiting the river each fall.

The Marias twists through the lonesome prairie south of the Sweet Grass Hills, about 18 miles east of Shelby. There are few towns around, a sparse human population and very few visitors. If you want off the beaten path and a serious dose of the lonelies, you can find it on the banks of the Marias.

Historically, the Marias has not been much of a trout fishery, and it draws little attention from the visiting hordes. That disregard is understandable: the Bureau of Reclamation has sabotaged the river below Lake Elwell by maintaining high flows through summer. They drop the flow to a paltry 100 cubic feet a second or less during fall, right when brown trout require water and extra habitat to spawn.

Due to inconsistent flows, the Marias' trout population has never been called "burgeoning." Lake Elwell, also called Tiber Reservoir, is the big angling draw in the region—for all the wrong reasons. The beer-swizzling, bait-chucking, fish-bonking masses just love to troll the lake for dreaded walleyes.

However, seasonal flow changes have quietly boosted large brown trout populations in the river below Tiber Dam, and browns draw the attention of trophy seekers.

Do not expect the Marias to become the next great Montana brown trout fishery like the Bighorn; however, it is quietly becoming one of the state's best kept angling secrets. A destination for visiting anglers it is not. But for a side trip from the Missouri River, it offers solitude and the opportunity to land a hog.

The Maria River's brown trout fishery has improved steadily since Montana Department of Fish, Wildlife and Parks took strides to bolster the river's rainbow trout population beginning in 1977. While rainbows have reacted with moderate success, at best, browns are thriving—much to the surprise of biologists.

"We've seen the brown trout population quadruple since we began work on the Marias," says Bill Gardner at FWP in Lewistown. "The numbers aren't high, but there are nice individual fish. "The browns get kinda big—three or four pounds is average, and we've seen bigger fish than that. I would say this is a trophy fishery for browns, because we've seen some over 10 pounds."

Much of the work on the Marias focuses on following the natural runoff cycle—a cycle that the BOR controls. During past years, summer flows blasted downstream at 2,000 cfs. As mentioned, they dropped to just 100 cfs during fall. Fortunately, that pattern shifted in 1994, and flows are expected to resemble nature's pattern from now on.

"They release high flows during spring instead of summer," Gardner says. "That's what we want—to see big flows in June, not later than that. We want to replicate the natural hydrograph to a degree. You can't have it all like Mother Nature, but we want it to be similar."

A minimum winter flow of 500 cfs, established in 1995, should facilitate the brown trout spawn while augmenting aquatic insect and vegetation growth, and that should further improve the fishery. "Since we established constant flows, I've seen improved insect populations," Gardner says. "Especially more Baetis and *Ephemerella*. I've also seen improvement in bank cover. We hope that might provide more winter cover for the yearling trout.

"This is a big river, about two-thirds the size of the Madison, but it lacks cover. Those small fish have nowhere to go. That may be why we don't have much success with our young rainbow trout surviving their first year or two."

Fish, Wildlife and Parks stocks the Marias with 10,000 to 20,000 fingerlings and yearling rainbows each year, but records indicate few of those fish reach adult proportions—the kind you would like to find in your landing net.

"When we began this project, our goal was to get 500 trout a mile in the Marias," Gardner says. "We've experimented with different strains of rainbows, including Madison River fish. Right now we are evaluating whether stocking those fish was effective or not—whether they survive better in this environment than other strains of rainbows. As of our latest estimate in 1994, we had 392 a mile, but 90 percent of those fish were yearlings. We aren't seeing a lot of adult fish with clipped adipose fins that would indicate that Madison River rainbows are surviving any better than other types of rainbows. So there may be something else affecting the fish."—Like big hungry brown trout?

"Maybe the browns do feed on them," Gardner says. "The browns seem healthy. Whatever is happening, this fishery has not stabilized yet. But we will keep striving to get the numbers to 500 a mile, with large fish constituting a major portion."

Marias River brown trout can take up the slack when fish in other rivers around the state go off the daytime bite and turn nocturnal during midsummer, due to relatively high water temperatures.

"Even midsummer is a good time to fish because the water stays cold, about 50 to 60 degrees," Gardner says. "Hoppers will work, but the best pattern for browns is probably a muddler minnow. We have a lot of sculpins in this river."

The Marias' brown trout are not unlike any other *Salmo trutta*—they prefer to feed on minnows rather than aquatic insects. Especially during fall, muddler minnows, Kiwi muddlers, woolly buggers, zonkers and rabbit strip bunny leeches will draw strikes. And the larger the pattern the better. I like to tie those flies in a variety of colors, including yellow, green, black, brown and white, and I prefer to tie them on long-shank, size 2 hooks (purists shudder in unison).

Brown trout and the river's rainbows will also take tiny dry flies and nymphs when the situation is right. During spring and fall, expect to see some Baetis on the water. They will run about a size 18, and they can be effectively mimicked with a parachute Adams or Baetis. Some of the best fishing occurs as the bugs swim to the surface and emerge. Size 16 or 18 Quigley cripples should draw strikes during the emergences, as will a standard hare's ear nymph. Pheasant tail nymphs are also a likely choice.

When the fish are up on Baetis, work your pattern off a 5X or lighter tippet. Especially during fall, when the water is clear, browns and rainbows can be particularly leader shy.

While Marias River trout are liable to hit a big, gaudy offering or even a small dry fly or nymph if you place it in front of their snout, they are not found throughout the river. In fact, flyfishers who seek big browns and rainbows should concentrate on a 10-mile section below Tiber Dam. Below 10 miles, the river is slow and warm, which is not much of an incentive for a trophy trout. Above the reservoir, including Dry Fork, trout fishing is marginal, and the catch is made up of mostly inferior specimens when compared to those below the dam.

Fishing below Tiber Dam is most productive from a drift boat or raft, but wade anglers connect with fish, too. Expect the Marias to stretch 250 feet wide in spots as it wanders through arid prairie, grasslands and croplands for 80 miles before joining the Missouri at Fort Benton.

While you should rightfully be disappointed if you don't catch a nice brown on the river, don't arrive with inflated expectations.

"You have to expect to catch a couple big browns here a day once you're familiar with the river," Gardner says. "The pools are far apart, so you have to find where the good water lies. Skip the marginal stuff, and then it can be a productive day."

To reach the best water on the Marias, travel east out of Shelby on Highway 2. Turn south on Tiber Road, which is located about midway between Shelby and Chester. Tiber Road will lead you to Tiber Dam. Smaller roads parallel the river, and access can be found at numerous sites, although there are no official FWP access sites.

Stream Facts: Marias River

Seasons
- Open all year.

Trout
- Rainbow and some large brown trout.

River Characteristics
- The Marias runs through isolated, dry country. It is not a difficult river to float—it is mostly broad and flat. Fishing is most productive below Tiber Dam.

River Flows
- Peak flow occurs in mid-June and tapers off quickly in early to mid-July.

Fishing Access
- Public access is located at the base of Tiber Dam. Nonmaintained accesses can be found along the river.

Campgrounds
- A campground lies just below Tiber Dam. There are BLM lands along the river that offer primitive camping also.

Area Fly Shops
- Coyote's Den Sports in Chester, 406-759-5305

CANYON FERRY RESERVOIR

When late spring and the month of May arrives, you hear all kinds of derogatory remarks about Montana's rivers.

"They're too damned muddy to fish." "It's running the color of chocolate milk." "Logs, houses and bodies are the only things rising."

Many anglers wallow in their sorrow, sitting around local cafes complaining like whipped puppies. But it doesn't have to be that way. When the rivers blow out of shape, as they can between late April and mid-July each year, flyfishers should simply turn their attention toward the state's excellent reservoirs. Canyon Ferry Reservoir, a 25-mile long impoundment that lies just east of Helena, is one of the best early-season bets. For folks who want to wrap their mitts around true hogs, this is the place to be.

In fact, on any given day in May, Canyon Ferry flyfishers should do battle with numerous trout in the 18- to 20-inch range—deep-bellied rainbows that weigh between three and six pounds. Fish congregate along the reservoir's shoreline, especially where gravel beds exist in six or seven feet of water. They will remain in the shallows until spawning ceases in early June.

Granted, pitching buggers at spawning trout may not offer the demands of an early-season Baetis mayfly blitz on the Missouri River, but the opportunity to land hogs often overrides challenge as the ultimate angling reward. Believe me, fighting grandiose trout on a four-weight fly rod holds merit.

According to Rad Davis at Montana Fly Goods in Helena, mid-May to the end of the month is the prime time at Canyon Ferry.

"Once I watched my friends land 60 fish while standing in one spot in late May," Davis says. "Wherever you can find rainbows congregated, it will be like that. Usually I just walk a 20-yard stretch of the bank, and I'll catch fish all day."

Because rainbows congregate, so too do anglers. However, crowding is only a problem near campgrounds and boat ramps, where major gravel beds draw anglers in force. By walking up and down the bank, looking for trout, flyfishers can avoid competition. Of course, working the water from a boat or floattube has its advantages. However, sitting waist deep in the water, floating around in a tube, is not for the cold-blooded. Snowstorms can erupt, wind gusts can scream past, and rain squalls can douse the reservoir in May.

"There are a couple of places where it looks like Buffalo Ford (Yellowstone Park) on opening day," Davis muses. "You will see 10 or 15 guys lined up shoulder to shoulder, and they will all land fish. But that is not for me. I walk on the east side bank just up from the dam and look for fish rolling and slashing at the surface. Where there is one rainbow, I figure there will be more. Once I find some fish, I'll work a spot thoroughly."

Canyon Ferry's rainbows are not picky. They'll smack a strip-retrieved black or brown woolly bugger, and they should not shy away from egg-sucking leeches, either. Davis suggests that San Juan worms and electric buggers draw strikes, too.

It would be overstating their merit to say a Canyon Ferry rainbow fights aggressively. Due to their spawning efforts, most fish succumb after a couple strong runs. But don't take them for granted—Davis has broken a few fish off on 5X tippet before switching to 2X.

"They roll around a lot, but they are not great fighters," Davis said. "But with light tippet, they can pretty much do what they want. You can't apply enough pressure to turn them without breaking the leader. I don't think I would go lighter than 2X."

Do not expect any super-lengthy rainbows at Canyon Ferry, even though FW&P began stocking Eagle Lake and De Smet rainbows in 1990. Those strains typically live six or seven years and spawn naturally. Prior to that, FW&P stocked Arlee strain rainbows that lived just 2.5 years and rarely reproduced in the wild. Since 1990, biologists witnessed a resurgence in Canyon Ferry's rainbow population.

Eagle Lake and De Smet rainbows are stocked each year as four-inch fingerlings. They grow to 13 inches during their first year in the reservoir, and they reach 18 inches by the end of their second year. However, their growth tapers off around 20 inches during their third year in the reservoir. According to Montana Department of Fish, Wildlife and Parks, rainbows feed primarily on zooplankton, and their effectiveness at capturing that food lessons with age.

That statement reflects Davis' observations when he inspects a meaty trout before release. "They are almost all right there at 18 or 20 inches," he said. "They are solid and healthy. The largest one I've seen was caught by Gary (Stocker). It measured 23 inches."

One fish that certainly will gobble its greedy share of food from Canyon Ferry (at least for now) is the walleye, which was illegally introduced to the reservoir in the late 1980s.

Currently, yellow perch provide the food base for Canyon Ferry walleyes. But the reservoir's perch population is at historically low levels. Starving walleyes are already turning to trout to supplement their diet.

If walleye populations grow as expected, they would likely deplete their forage base, possibly including trout, in 10 or 15 years. Walleye abundance and average size would decline just like it has many times on reservoirs around the West. Currently, it is unclear whether walleye numbers can be reduced with controlled gillnetting by FWP.

A sinking line and streamers that imitate perch or small trout could be the ticket for catching Canyon Ferry's walleye on a fly. Currently, I know of nobody pursuing walleye with a fly, but there could be some decent opportunities in the spring and fall when fish move into the shallows. And you can take every one of those toothy, rotten bastards home.

While fishing the reservoir, do not be surprised if you see lots of trout giving up the ghost via a heartless whack to the head with a rock. Few of the reservoir's anglers release their catch. In fact, a recent creel survey notes that anglers execute 95 percent of all rainbow trout caught in the reservoir. Fortunately, meat-sackers must stop their slaughter after they have smacked their fifth fish. And only one trout can measure over 18 inches.

While walleyes pose a huge threat to its trout fishery, Canyon Ferry pumps out plenty of large rainbows each year in late spring. The opportunity to throw large streamers to them should be treasured during high water periods in Montana. Don't join the whining hordes who frequent Montana's cafes in late spring. Instead, let them complain about the swollen, discolored rivers while you slay huge rainbows in central Montana.

MUSSELSHELL RIVER

A mandate for central Montana irrigators to install water measuring devices on their diversion dams could change the Musselshell River from an afterthought to a destination in the minds of local and visiting flyfishers.

It's about time—the Musselshell and its wonderful brown trout have been battered for too long. In fact, on August 18, 1988, the Musselshell's best trout section, which is located about midway between Big Timber and Lewistown, ran bone dry— zero cubic feet a second. The river's brown trout, some of them very large, writhed. Talk about pathetic! Unfortunately, in Montana, ranchers get the water, and the state's outdoors people and wildlife get the shaft.

The dewatering and fish kill in 1988 should have caught nobody by surprise. Historically, the Musselshell has been drained nearly dry by each summer's end. Local populations offer little resistance to the irrigators' overindulgence. The Musselshell rests at the north end of the beautiful Crazy Mountains, which is a stronghold of the beef industry. Deer, antelope, upland game birds and, of course, brown trout offer a paltry voice when trying to shout over the constant tick, tick, tick of irrigation spigots and the decrees from Montana's deep-pocketed politicians.

Fortunately, irrigator control over the river may change, and the brown trout fishery may rebound. Not that it is too bad right now.

By April 1997, local ranchers were to have installed water-measuring devices on all diversion dams along the Musselshell's main stem and forks, which may curtail inexcusable waste of the water.

That mandate arrives on the heels of three excellent water years in central Montana, a combination that could give the Musselshell's brown trout, many running between 14 and 22 inches with a few hogs thrown in on the side, a needed boost.

"What we saw in the late 1980s was a population of older brown trout just hanging on," said Jim Darling at Montana Department of Fish, Wildlife and Parks in Billings. "Right now, because we've had a few good water years in a row, we see all age classes of trout, and they are healthy. But, the key to it all is water flow. Anything we do otherwise is worthless if we don't have adequate flows.

"We can't control the water because we are not the key players, but installing water monitors on irrigation ditches could help out."

Seth Brandenburg at the Department of Natural Resources and Conservation in Helena agreed. "Historically, a lot of the Musselshell's water was wasted early in the year," he said. "By the end of the summer, irrigators could dry the river up. We hope by monitoring the water closely, irrigators can increase their knowledge of how much water they use so there should be less waste.

"For instance, if an irrigator needs more water, he can call the dam operator at Deadman's Basin (Reservoir) and tell them to turn up the gauge to compensate for a loss of water on the main river. With better management, there should be more water left in the river, and that means more water for fisheries."

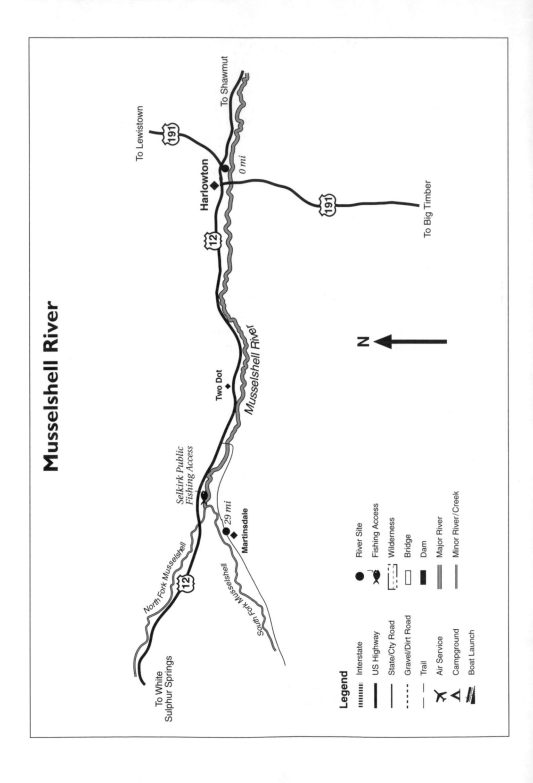

Musselshell River

To Lewistown

To Shawmut

191

0 mi

Harlowton

191

To Big Timber

12

N

Musselshell River

Two Dot

Selkirk Public
Fishing Access

North Fork Musselshell

29 mi

Martinsdale

South Fork Musselshell

12

To White
Sulphur Springs

Legend

IIIIIII	Interstate	●	River Site
▬	US Highway	🐟	Fishing Access
—	State/Cty Road	⬚	Wilderness
⋯	Gravel/Dirt Road	▢	Bridge
–	Trail	▮	Dam
✈	Air Service	▬	Major River
▲	Campground	—	Minor River/Creek
🚤	Boat Launch		

Some waters appeal to the imagination, but fishing them requires a gambler's mentality and a tolerance for disaster. That is true when speaking of the Musselshell.

It twists out of the Crazies as a small mountain stream, full of modest rainbows, browns and cutthroats, before winding through the barren, wind-blasted private rangeland where cattle, deer and antelope are left to ponder its chief purpose.

Being a long way from anywhere, few anglers mark the Musselshell on their "destination" list. Offering difficult access does little to bolster a flyfisher's determination to fish the river. However, this is known among flyfishing circles: the Musselshell holds big brown trout. In a true trophy hunter's mind, that is enough information to merit a trip.

"We found about 155 browns a mile over 12 inches," said Jim Darling at Montana Department of Fish, Wildlife and Parks. "Of course, about 21 a mile were over 20 inches. There is great fishing on the upper Musselshell for those who can get on it. It's really just a matter of getting at them."

Fortunately, flyfishers can always soak a streamer at the Selkirk public fishing access on the south side of U.S. 12 near Martinsdale. From there you can wade or float 25 miles of prime brown trout water, depending on how far downstream you prefer to wander. Actually, the intuitive flyfisher who knows how to approach ranchers in a friendly, tactful way—not by pounding on their door at 6 AM—can secure access across much of the private land that borders the river. Access is also guaranteed at the Highway 191 bridge south of Harlowton.

In the prime stretch below Selkirk, you will find small riffles, deep pools, downed logs, curious cows, lots of brush and always, undercut banks. And if you are lucky, you may find a brown trout of epic proportions.

"Most of the trout go about a pound or two," said Ron Hinand, a frequent Musselshell fisher who works at Ray's Sport in Harlowton. "But there are some big browns in there, too. It wouldn't surprise me if someone catches a fish that goes 15 pounds or more. Really, five pounders are not uncommon."

Because the river is so small, ranging between 15 and 20 yards wide in most places, there is not much room to fight a fish, and even a two- or three-pound trout can be a challenge to land.

I discovered the leader-snapping qualities of the Musselshell's trout when I visited one October afternoon, taking a break from some mind-boggling bad luck while hunting pronghorn antelope on the surrounding prairie with an apparently bent-barreled .270 rifle.

Downstream from the Selkirk access site, a good brown drilled my size 4 woolly bugger. I saw the fish only once, a brief golden slash across the surface. After the initial roll, the trout shot across stream, ducked under a bank and quickly parted my 5X tippet. It seemed like only a dream.

Most Musselshell browns are taken on large nymphs and streamers. However, there are some decent hatches on which dry-fly and small nymph fishers can focus. Remember, like browns everywhere, those Musselshell trout prefer to feed early and late in the day, which makes the afternoon hours typically unproductive.

Watch for Baetis hatches beginning in April, subsiding by late May. They will make another appearance beginning in late September, extending through October. Spring Baetis are followed by golden stoneflies, a few caddis and a healthy hatch of pale morning duns in June and July. Then, in late July, August and September, brown trout really pound grasshoppers if river conditions are decent.

"It gets a pretty good hatch of golden stones early in the summer before the water level drops," said Chris Miller at Dan Bailey's Fly Shop in Livingston. "I've also seen a decent PMD hatch that gets the fish working up top. I've caught fish on stimulators and your basic mayfly patterns. They do not seem overly picky, and there is good water above and below the public access. However, if you fish the higher sections near Martinsdale, it's a small, meandering stream with lots of undercuts and bankside brush. You can trip a lot in places, and there is not much room for backcasts. It's like fishing in a tunnel of brush."

In fact, timing is everything on the Musselshell. Flyfishers can almost always count on decent water conditions in April, May and June. But, from July 1 through mid-September, the water could be low and its temperature could be quite high. Temperatures over 65 degrees will put browns off the feed. However, the river revitalizes after irrigation ends just when the browns go on the spawn and become very aggressive.

"We get some decent hatches here, but it's pretty much a nymph and streamer show," Hinand said. "We don't get big hatches like you see on the Yellowstone or Madison. The only hatch that really brings the biggest fish to the top is hoppers.

"But Fall is the best time to fish," he added. "The water is cooling down and browns are more prone to eat streamers than at any other time of the year. They will be on their redds, or they will hold in the riffles and medium-depth runs. In some cases you can see them. All you have to do is run a woolly bugger or muddler minnow past them. They'll hit it."

Because the Musselshell is a small stream, many flyfishers approach the water with their delicate outfits. The first time a big brown peels all the line off their reel you will find them in Big Timber at Sweet Cast Angler or Boulder River Flyfishing or in Livingston shopping for a six- or seven-weight rod.

With a heavier rod, a flyfisher has the power to pull large fish away from the undercut banks and downed logs. Flyfishers may also prefer a heavier rod to throw large surface patterns at dusk, in total darkness or at dawn. Mouse patterns and large greased muddler minnows will certainly draw browns up top during low light periods, and those patterns are not ideally suited for a two- or three-weight rod.

Whatever rod you choose for the Musselshell, realize you are in for a relatively solitary experience. Few anglers choose to brave a river about which little is known. Especially when it lies an hour or more from one of the big name Montana rivers.

However, with irrigators possibly losing their stranglehold on the river, the Musselshell may soon offer trout fishing equal to better-known waters. My suggestion: get in on the action while it's still relatively unknown. A 10-pound brown may be in your immediate future.

To reach the Musselshell, turn north off of Interstate 90 onto U.S. Highway 191 at Big Timber. Follow 191 north to Harlowton (44 miles) then turn left (west) on U.S. 12. The Selkirk access is about 23 miles from Harlowton.

Food and lodging are available in Big Timber and Harlowton. However, flyfishing equipment is limited, at best, in Harlowton.

Stream Facts: Musselshell River

Seasons
- Downstream from confluence of north and south forks open all year. Forks are open from third Saturday in May through November 30.

Trout
- Brown trout and rainbows. Most trout run 10 to 15 inches but there are some enormous browns to be had, especially during the fall spawn.

River Miles
- Confluence of north and south forks—0
- Two Dot Bridge—17
- Highway 191 Bridge (Harlowton)—36
- Shawmut Bridge—63

River Flows
- The river runs low from September through mid-April. In May flows rise severely and then peak in June. By August flows are back down to low levels.

Dangers
- Numerous diversion dams.

Fishing Access
- Access is poor along the Musselshell—flyfishers must use the Selkirk public fishing access, bridge crossings, or get permission to cross private property.

Area Fly Shops
- Ray's Sports and Western Wear, Hwy 12 and Hwy 191 (sporting equipment and clothing), 406-632-4320
- Sweet Cast Angler, 151 1st Ave., Big Timber, MT, 406-932-4469
- Boulder River Flyfishing, McCloud Street, Big Timber, MT, 406-932-4063

YELLOWSTONE RIVER

Being single, often reckless and fairly thirsty, I've always judged the attributes of a town by its nightlife and local trout stream.

There are a number of good places in Montana that combine those traits— Missoula with the Clark Fork and Bitterroot, and Dillon with the Beaverhead and Poindexter Slough come to mind—but maybe no town in the Big Sky state harbors more worthy trout right out its back door and equally enticing specimens indoors as Livingston.

For those who breathe our sport, those who must surround themselves with the ultimate flyfishing atmosphere, Livingston and its backdoor fishery, the Yellowstone River, will always call to the young single man in pursuit of wild trout. Whether they ever move to Livingston or not, the town represents a tangible place where life is good, trout fishing reigns king and heaven is just a step out the back door.

Where else can you find excellent fishing for three trout species, all running to substantial size, right behind town? Where else can you head so many directions to find equally enticing trout on smaller streams? And where else can you find so many entertaining bars, eateries, coffee shops and hotels in a quaint Western town? If you are familiar with a better place, call me! I'm there!

From Livingston, anglers can head directly south or east to fish the Yellowstone. To the north twists the Shields River, the Musselshell and Big Spring Creek; to the east are the Boulder and Stillwater rivers; to the west are the Madison, Gallatin, East Gallatin and the Jefferson. Even with those enticing smaller streams so close, the Yellowstone is Livingston's definitive water, due to the number of famous personalities and flyfishing gurus who visit its banks every year, if not by its size alone.

There is so much water to fish on the Yellowstone, so many localized hatches and so many various conditions, the river can actually be broken down into distinct sections, each offering something different for the flyfisher. An angler could spend his or her entire life on the Yellowstone and not come to grips with all of its complexities. Entire books have been written on the subject, and still there is much to know.

The Yellowstone begins in the high Absaroka Mountains in Yellowstone National Park, where tumbling tributaries rush into the main river. Those tributaries and the mainstem above Yellowstone Lake offer a bastion for Yellowstone cutthroat trout. Many of these fish never see a fly cast over their snouts during the entire year. Access to the upper river and its tributaries is by foot or horse only. You can't drive to the edge of the river, hop out of a truck and pitch a line. To fish the headwaters, a flyfisher must first don boots and spend a day hiking. Due to that requirement, the fish are not fussy; they'll fight each other for a properly presented dry fly or nymph. For those of us who spend much of our time on challenging waters like the Bighorn, Missouri and Beaverhead, the option to catch eager cutthroats, many to 18 inches, is a treasured opportunity. Just watch out for Mr. Griz.

The headwaters of the Yellowstone join at Yellowstone Lake, where excellent fishing for cutthroats, most of them over 13 inches, can be found from shore. The fish are not picky here, either: present a woolly bugger, scud, leech or even a dry-fly attractor

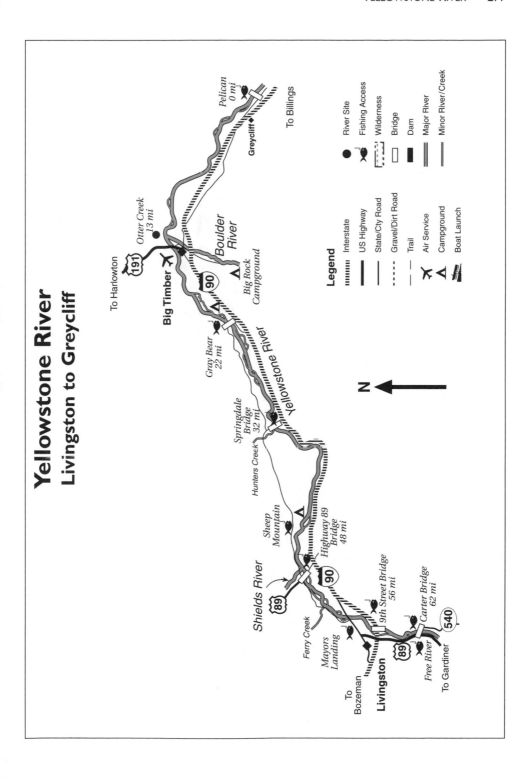

Yellowstone River
Livingston to Greycliff

Pelican
0 mi

To Billings

Greycliff

Otter Creek
13 mi

To Harlowton

191

Big Timber

Boulder
River

90

Big Rock
Campground

Gray Bear
22 mi

Yellowstone River

Springdale
Bridge
32 mi

Hunters Creek

Sheep
Mountain

Highway 89
Bridge
48 mi

Shields River

90

89

Ferry Creek

9th Street Bridge
56 mi

Carter Bridge
62 mi

540

Mayors
Landing

89

Free River

To
Bozeman

Livingston

To Gardiner

N

Legend

▓ Interstate	● River Site	
━ US Highway	✦ Fishing Access	
│ State/Cty Road	▭ Wilderness	
┊ Gravel/Dirt Road	▭ Bridge	
┈ Trail	▮ Dam	
✈ Air Service	│ Major River	
⛺ Campground	│ Minor River/Creek	
◢ Boat Launch		

Yellowstone RiverYellowstone River
Emigrant to Livingston

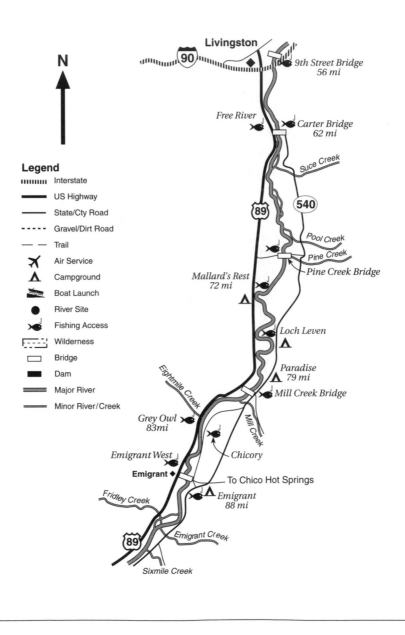

Legend

ⅡⅡⅡⅡⅡ	Interstate
▬▬	US Highway
──	State/Cty Road
- - - -	Gravel/Dirt Road
— —	Trail
✈	Air Service
⛰	Campground
🚤	Boat Launch
●	River Site
🐟	Fishing Access
⬚	Wilderness
▭	Bridge
▬	Dam
▬▬	Major River
──	Minor River/Creek

N

Livingston

90

9th Street Bridge
56 mi

Free River

Carter Bridge
62 mi

Suce Creek

89   540

Pool Creek
Pine Creek

Pine Creek Bridge

Mallard's Rest
72 mi

Loch Leven

Paradise
79 mi

Mill Creek Bridge

Eightmile Creek

Mill Creek

Grey Owl
83mi

Emigrant West

Chicory

Emigrant

To Chico Hot Springs

Fridley Creek

Emigrant
88 mi

89

Emigrant Creek

Sixmile Creek

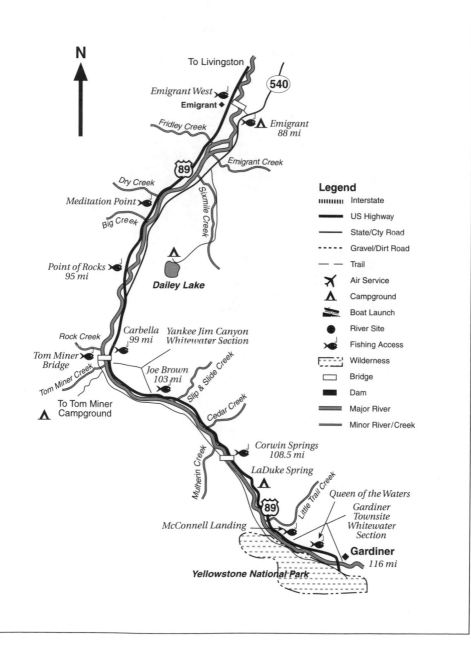

Yellowstone River
Gardiner to Emigrant

N

To Livingston

540

Emigrant West
Emigrant ◆

Fridley Creek

Emigrant
88 mi

89

Emigrant Creek

Dry Creek

Sixmile Creek

Meditation Point

Big Creek

Point of Rocks
95 mi

Dailey Lake

Legend

ıımıını	Interstate
▬	US Highway
—	State/Cty Road
- - - -	Gravel/Dirt Road
– –	Trail
✈	Air Service
⛢	Campground
🛥	Boat Launch
●	River Site
🐟	Fishing Access
⌐ ¬	Wilderness
▭	Bridge
▬	Dam
▬	Major River
—	Minor River/Creek

Rock Creek

Carbella
99 mi

Yankee Jim Canyon
Whitewater Section

Tom Miner
Bridge

Joe Brown
103 mi

Slip & Slide Creek

Tom Miner Creek

To Tom Miner
Campground

Cedar Creek

Mulherin Creek

Corwin Springs
108.5 mi

LaDuke Spring

Little Trail Creek

Queen of the Waters

Gardiner
Townsite
Whitewater
Section

89

McConnell Landing

Gardiner
116 mi

Yellowstone National Park

The standard scene at Buffalo Ford in Yellowstone Park—shoulder to shoulder with anglers, everyone catching native cutthroats.

in the shallows, almost anywhere on the lake, and you're bound to take fish. Large streamers, worked during the spring and fall, may also draw strikes from large lake trout, which are an unwelcome guest—they are, potentially, a thorn in the side of the native cutts and the entire Yellowstone ecosystem. Time will tell if the illegally introduced and highly predacious lake trout will have a major impact on the cutthroats.

The river changes as it exits the massive lake, essentially becoming a giant spring creek. It's been mentioned that the section of the Yellowstone, extending from Yellowstone Lake downstream to Yellowstone Falls, is the most fertile stretch of trout water on Earth. After fishing the river several times, you'll likely agree.

That section of the river opens July 15, and in sync with its opening, sees a massive migration of people to the river. Opening Day resembles a zoo, with anglers lined up within yards of each other, artificial flies whipping past ears. But everyone, it seems, catches fish, and the entire spectacle is what you make of it: if you despise other people's presence, you're set for a downfall; welcome their company, and you'll witness some interesting antics, not the least being a parade of anglers wading deeper and deeper into the river only to find the cutthroats rising for PMDs five feet off shore.

The Yellowstone meets its most significant obstacle at Yellowstone Falls, a plunge of over 300 feet that is both visually exquisite and terrifying at the same time: any fly-fisher who sees the falls must wonder what it would be like to go over them in waders, playing that once-in-a-lifetime cutthroat trout.

Below the falls, the river cuts through an impossibly steep canyon. Access to this section is nonexistent. The only possible way to fish it would be by helicopter, dropping monster streamers 30 feet down off sinktip lines, one arm wrapped in a death grip around the safety bar, the other extended out to the side, whipping a fly wand. There must be some true hogs in that water, but fishing from a helicopter would be all too much like the bass pro circuit for my liking.

Fortunately, downstream in the Black Canyon of the Yellowstone, there are opportunities to fish from the ground. However, you better be ready to test your lungs—fishing the Black Canyon is an up and down affair over rocky, rattlesnake-infested terrain.

The Black Canyon begins at Roosevelt, where a trail leads down to the river. That trail extends to Gardiner, which is about 20 miles and a three-day hike away. Most anglers tromp down the trail, fish within a mile or two of their first glimpse of the river, then head back uphill. Throughout the canyon, there are sections of water that offer easy access and others that would require a swim to reach. Cutthroats dominate in the canyon, but introduced rainbows and brown trout navigate that water, too.

The Black Canyon opens on Memorial Day weekend, and depending on runoff, especially out of the often muddy Lamar River, fishing can be hit or miss. If runoff is delayed or mild, the first two weeks of the season can be killer. If runoff arrives on schedule, the river will run high and fast anywhere between Memorial Day and late July. During a normal year, if there is such a thing, the canyon's stonefly hatch runs from late June through July. Big fish migrate to the banks and pound stonefly nymphs and adults with abandon. Almost every year, there is a window of opportunity for fly-fishers who want to hit the hatch. But it's much easier for a resident flyfisher to take a day off work to fish the water than it is for a visiting angler to arrange a plane flight on a moment's notice.

The Black Canyon does not provide your typical salmonfly hatch for a couple reasons: there are no boats floating downstream (it's not allowed) and you usually have the river to yourself, which is in sharp contrast to accessible rivers where the salmonflies come off. Thirty-fish days are not unheard of in the Black Canyon during the salmonfly hatch; 10 fish should be expected every time.

Upstream casts and tight, drag-free bank drifts are the ticket during the hatch. Don't bother with the middle of the river—the fish are in the shallows sucking in nymphs or monster adults writhing on the surface.

Fortunately for the Yellowstone, its quality trout water extends outside the park, over 100 miles downstream past Big Timber. Through that stretch you will find native

During fall, you can catch some nice browns in the Yellowstone's side channels below Livingston. Here, Dan Summerfield displays a dandy.

cutthroats in good numbers and size, along with rainbows and increasing numbers of browns.

What you likely will not find, especially if you are a small stream fisher, is familiar water. The Yellowstone is not a dainty trout stream—it is broad and brooding during runoff and its size is intimidating.

The best way to cover the water is with a drift boat or quality raft like an Achilles or Avon. By floating the river, you will not run into the access problems you can find when wade fishing the river. Also, by float-fishing, you will be able to pound both banks, which is not an option to the wade fisher during anything but the lowest of flows—the river is simply too deep and powerful to cross in most places.

During an average year, the Yellowstone will run up to its banks or a little more, tearing down unsuspecting cottonwoods, through July 4. In extreme high water seasons like 1996, the river will not pull into shape until sometime in August. Ideally, you'll find the river running 6,000 cubic feet a second or lower from July 4 on through the season. Prior to that, during high water, the Yellowstone might scream past its banks at 20,000 cfs. Each year, the river creates new channels and abandons others, which makes each season's first venture astream a refreshing learning experience.

Within Montana, the Yellowstone can be divided into many major sections, but we will break it down into three here: Gardiner to Emigrant, Emigrant to Big Timber, and Big Timber to Billings. For our purposes, the true quality trout water ceases about 40 miles below Big Timber, although trout do show up below that point.

The stretch between Gardiner and Emigrant is best known for its salmonfly hatch. For some reason, these big insects come off best higher on the river, and if you hit the hatch right, the valley that it flows through lives up to its billing—Paradise.

The Paradise Valley extends from Gardiner, almost 60 miles downstream, to Livingston. The Absaroka and Beartooth Mountains rise above the river to the east, and the valley bottom is broad and flat. The Yellowstone winds endlessly as it pushes through the valley, and there might not be a prettier float in the world. Cutthroats, browns and rainbows are equally mixed here, and some of them are large—it's not uncommon to catch a cutthroat, brown or rainbow over 20 inches.

Most of the water provides easy floating, but in Yankee Jim Canyon, between Gardiner and Emigrant, it's no cakewalk, especially when flows are up, which can be anytime between April 20 and the end of July. Unless you can handle Class III rapids, don't try the canyon with a raft or boat.

Tthere are some large fish holding behind the big rocks right in the middle of the rapids, but it's just hard to get a fly at them when you're hanging on for your life. If you do fish that water, try high density sinking lines and extremely large streamers.

If you're bent on fishing the upper section but you don't want to attempt the Canyon, you can put in at McDonnell Landing, LaDuke Spring or Corwin Springs access sites. Just make sure that you don't float past the Joe Brown access site—it's the last take-out before the canyon. Below Yankee Jim, the river settles down, and you can cast at leisure again.

You can also float or wade the section from Yankee Jim to Emigrant when the water is down. The river here is slower than it is in the canyon, the riffles are broad and defined, and the banks also hold a lot of fish.

If you decide to float, you can put in at the Carbella access site and float to Point of Rocks, which is about 4.5 miles. You could also float from Point of Rocks to Emigrant, which is a nice 8-mile drift. If you want to fish mostly from a boat, try Carbella to Emigrant, which is about 12.5 miles and a full day.

Hatches vary from section to section on the Yellowstone, and the upper river is no different. From December through February, you'll see a smattering of midges, and fishing can be decent because the water temperature is boosted by hot springs entering the river. The midge hatch really comes into its own in late March.

However, at that time, an angler may choose to focus on Baetis mayflies—the trout do, so why shouldn't you? Baetis will extend through April and into May.

While the Yellowstone isn't noted as a major mayfly fishery, it hosts a pretty decent March brown drake hatch in late April, extending into May. It's a hit and miss affair, depending on the nuances of runoff. If the river stays in shape, there can be some quite good fishing during the afternoon hours. Parachute Adams, gray sparkle duns, hare's ear nymphs and pheasant tail nymphs will draw strikes.

Generally, the upper river blows out by May 10 and fishing is unproductive. However, in mid-June the salmonfly nymphs make their migration to shore, and any visibility along the banks can mean productive fishing. Bitch Creek nymphs, woolly buggers and Kaufmann's stones pounded along the banks draw strikes.

When the river shapes up, flyfishers will find the salmonfly hatch going full bore. Usually, by July 1 there will be big *Pteronarcys* flying about, which brings large fish to the surface in droves. At the same time, golden stones, yellow sallys and green drakes may bring trout up top, too. If you can't get any takes by throwing the big stonefly patterns, take a crack at the river with yellow sallies or green drakes—sometimes the trout will key on a lesser insect.

Caddis dominate a trout's diet as the river drops in mid- to late July, but there will be a smattering of mayflies tempting trout to the surface, too. After that, hoppers take over, and the Yellowstone, throughout, is an excellent hopper river.

By late September, the weather cools, the elk start bugling and the Baetis mayfly makes its second appearance of the year. Size 16, 18 and 20 comparaduns, sparkle duns, and parachute Baetis patterns will draw strikes.

The next distinct section of river to explore runs from Emigrant to Livingston, and it's probably the most popular reach on the entire river for good reason: it's close to town, offers lengthy floats and excellent hatches, and it has a nice population of trout, including a solid portion of fish, especially browns, over 18 inches.

There are two particularly intriguing overnight options through this stretch. At the upper end of the section is Chico, home of Chico Hot Springs and Resort. Chico's rooms, lounge, and hot springs are always inviting, and the food is gourmet. You'll find all sorts of characters running around the place, and the word on trout fishing always flows freely through its halls.

If you are not going to stay at Chico and you are not going to camp, try the Murray Hotel in Livingston. It's an interesting place, with a lounge, rustic yet attractive rooms, a hot tub on the roof, and Parks Reece's art gallery located on the second level. On the lower level is the Winchester Cafe, and it may be tough to find a better steak anywhere in the state.

The Yellowstone between Emigrant and Livingston is not difficult to float, and the water is fairly easy to read. You do not find the pocketwater that you might in Yankee Jim Canyon, and you won't find much braiding until you near Livingston. Most of the fish lie in riffled corners that are spread out between long, glassy glides. Throughout the section, fish hold to the banks, and that is where successful flyfishers target their casts.

As the river exits Paradise Valley and takes its sharp turn east at Livingston, it becomes broad, yet diverse, with numerous braided channels, steep bluffs and rock formations, and broad riffles offering all types of holding stations for trout. As the river continues downstream past Sheep Mountain and on to Big Timber, it becomes powerful and wide with lots of good banks and some monster riffles. It's all good water, though not very different from the upper reaches. This is also water where you won't find many anglers. Paradise Valley is the river's glory, but it is also the apex of angling activity. If you truly can't live with another angler anywhere about, the river between Sheep Mountain and Big Timber, or even below that point, is the place to fish. There are plenty of side channels in this section, and they harbor trout all year. During spring the side channels will remain fishable longer than the main river. They also become fishable quicker than the main river when the water drops after runoff.

While this entire section receives a healthy salmonfly hatch, its most noted emergence is the early season caddis, which begins in mid-April and peaks the first week of May. As always on the Yellowstone, water conditions play a major role in the success of anglers during the hatch.

If conditions are prime, you may not find a better hatch anywhere in the West. Billions of caddis swarm through the air. Billions more coat the surface of the river, congregating in writhing balls of insects in the slack waters near shore. Yet more cling to the willows and other bankside vegetation. And it's not like the fish don't notice the event. They plow through the water, their noses just above the surface, inhaling every caddis they can find. It's a major event as flyfishing hatches go, and every fly-fisher should visit the Yellowstone during this time, even if there is a flock of anglers for company.

Despite the emergence of bugs and the recklessness that trout display in devouring the winged hordes, the caddis hatch is no cakewalk: Trout may key in on one specific stage of the hatch, and if your flies don't match the actual insect in question, you're SOL—screwed, I tell you.

You'll need patterns that mimic cased caddis nymphs, also patterns that mimic swimming and emerging pupa and, of course, adults.

Here is a list of patterns that will work for each stage:
- Cased Caddis: Prince nymph, rock-rollers, beadhead caddis, free-living caddis
- Caddis pupa: LaFontaine deep sparkle pupa, beadhead caddis pupa, olive soft hackle, Lafontaine emergent sparkle pupa, X-caddis
- Caddis adult: Elk hair caddis, Goddard caddis, Hemingway caddis, caddis variant

Even with those patterns in hand, the hatch can prove frustrating to a novice fly-fisher. If it's your first time dealing with this hatch, book a guide who can limit your frustration and put you into plenty of fish. Be sure to call ahead, because dates in April and May are booked solid often a year in advance.

Caddis are not the only option in this section. Look for solid midge hatches during winter on the warmest days. In March and April, expect some decent Baetis action. Also, during that time frame, the river's rainbows will seek out the mouths of spring creeks and tributary streams to spawn. Any exposed gravel in the mainstem could be used, too. Egg patterns, if you want to fish those, are very productive during the spawn.

By the first week of May, the river could be blown out, and it may not be fishable until mid-June or, during the very worst years, late July. If you can get at the water by mid-June, there will be lots of big stoneflies, both goldens and salmonflies, to work.

When you fish the Yellowstone River, expect to catch whitefish. Here, John Huber displays the merit of a whitey taken on a dry fly.

In July, flyfishers will find a variety of caddis to match, especially during the evening hours. During the day, look for yellow sallies, green drakes and maybe even some PMDs, which extend into August. By the end of the month, hoppers will come out, and by the middle of August they will be the ticket.

The stretch between Emigrant and Livingston offers prime hopper banks, and you can spend the entire day floating the river, popping hoppers off the banks. The trout will find them.

During September, you'll see the return of Baetis along with midges. Hopper fishing will taper off, but the big brown trout get active toward streamers as they gear up for the fall spawn, which is not to be missed. Quite possibly, this section of the river offers the best opportunity in the state for a monster fall run of brown trout. Because the river braids extensively in the lower reaches of this section near Livingston, prime spawning habitat exists in side channels. It pays to work away from the main river and into the side channels occasionally.

There are plenty of public access sites throughout this section—the only determining factor when choosing a place to launch is this: how far do you want to go?

From Big Timber downstream to Reedpoint and beyond, the Yellowstone is a forgotten river, even though it contains healthy trout populations—mostly browns but good numbers of rainbows and cutthroats, too—and good scenery. The Beartooths mark the southern sky, and the Crazy Mountains, one of the most beautiful mountain ranges I've ever seen, race off to the north.

In this section, you will find long, deep holes just below the riffles. Due to this habitat and the fact that few people fish the river here, you just know that that one brown trout, a fish to turn your back to the river and call it a day, if not a week or year, lurks somewhere. Streamers thrown off sinking lines are about the only way to reach those leviathans. But throwing streamers isn't the only way to take fish in this section.

Watch for hatches of Baetis and March browns in March and April, until the river blows out in early May. Don't expect to get back on the water until sometime in July.

When the water slows down, expect golden stoneflies, yellow sallies and a variety of caddis to carry you through the day. In August, concentrate on the PMDs and the hopper fishing. Later in the month, work the Trico spinnerfall in the mornings and early afternoons.

By early September, nights are cool and fall fishing begins in earnest. Baetis, Tricos and hoppers will draw fish up top, but streamers are the ticket for large brown trout.

From Reedpoint downstream to Billings, anglers can still pick up a few trout, but warmwater species like walleyes take over the show. However, access is difficult in that stretch.

If you are going to fish the lower sections and you don't want to camp out, try The Grand Hotel in Big Timber. It's rustic, yet fancy, and provides nice rooms, a gourmet dining room and a comfortable lounge where you can kick back in boots, jeans and a flannel shirt if you want.

Really, when you get right down to it, there is likely not another trout stream in Montana, maybe not in the entire West, that offers such a variety of options for the flyfisher. And if history is the mark of a trout stream, the Yellowstone has it all. There are so many big names in flyfishing who have cut their teeth and spent large portions of their lives on the river that you can almost feel their presence, urging you to explore the next bend, riffle, boulder, or pool, every nuance the river has to offer.

From its sparkling headwaters on the lip of the Continental Divide to its wonderful native cutthroats in Yellowstone Lake, from its educated trout at Buffalo Ford to its lung-burning challenges in the Black Canyon, from its wild ride through Yankee Jim Canyon to its backdoor opportunity at Livingston, and from the underrated challenges of large trout between Big Timber and Reedpoint, the Yellowstone is the most classic of rivers. Every visiting flyfisher and every resident fisher should take a trek to this big river at least once in their life. Plan plenty of days on the water and don't show up during runoff. The river, its scenery, its bankside towns and its trout will not disappoint.

Stream Facts: Yellowstone River

Seasons
- Yellowstone National Park boundary to Emigrant Bridge open all year.
- Pine Creek Bridge to I-90 Bridge at Billings open all year.
- Emigrant Bridge to Pine Creek Bridge open third Saturday in May through November 30. Extended whitefish season and catch and release on trout open December 1 through third Saturday in May.
- Inside Yellowstone National Park open July 15 through November 4.

Trout
- Rainbows, browns and cutthroats all present in good numbers. Most fish average 14 to 16 inches, but there are decent opportunities for fish in the four- to six-pound range. Cutthroats must be released in Yellowstone Park and from Gardiner downstream to the I-90 bridge at Billings.

River Miles
- Greycliff—0
- Big Timber—13
- Gray Bear—22
- Springdale Bridge—32
- Shields River—48
- Mayor's Landing—54
- Livingston—56
- Carter Bridge—62
- Mallard's Rest—72
- Mill Creek Bridge—79
- Grey Owl—83
- Emigrant—88
- Point of Rocks—95
- Tom Miner Bridge—99
- Joe Brown—102.5
- Corwin Springs—108.5
- Gardiner—116

River Flows
- Flows peak in late June and July. During high water years, the river may run muddy and high from mid-May through early August. Spring and fall offer the most predictable water conditions.

River Characteristics
- The Yellowstone is a big river that runs through some of the prettiest country in Montana. Aside from periods of high water, the river offers easy floats.

Access
- Although the Yellowstone runs through private property for most of its length, there are numerous public fishing access sites that offer unlimited opportunities.

Area Fly Shops

Livingston
- Dan Bailey's Fly Shop, 209 West Park Street, 406-222-1673 or 800-356-4052: Flies, fishing equipment, clothing, and accessories
- George Anderson's Yellowstone Angler, Rt 89 South, P.O. Box 660, 406-222-7130: Flyfishing specialties, outdoor clothing
- Wilderness Outfitters, 1 mile south of town on Rt 89, 406-222-6933: Guns, shells, clothing, and accessories
- Hatch Finders Fly Shop, 113 West Park Street, 406-222-0989

Gardiner
- Parks' Fly Shop, PO Box 196, Gardiner, MT, 406-848-7314

Other Areas
- Big Sky Flies and Guides, Hwy 89, Emigrant, MT 59027, 406-333-4401
- Gallatin River Guides, Highway 191, Big Sky, MT, 406-995-2290
- East Slope Anglers, Highway 191, Big Sky, MT, 406-995-4369
- The River's Edge, 2012 N. 7th Ave., Bozeman, MT, 406-586-5373
- Montana Troutfitters, 1716 W. Main, Bozeman, MT, 406-587-4707
- Bozeman Angler, 24 E. Main, Bozeman, MT, 406-587-9111
- Blue Ribbon Flies, 309 Canyon, West Yellowstone, MT, 406-646-7642
- Madison River Outfitters, 117 Canyon St., West Yellowstone, MT, 406-646-9644
- Sweet Cast Angler, 151 1st Ave., Big Timber, MT, 406-932-4469

YELLOWSTONE TRIBUTARIES

To cover the major Yellowstone River tributaries in one section is almost not giving them their due. These streams, the Stillwater, Boulder, Shields, Rock Creek, and the Clark's Fork, are first-rate fisheries in themselves. Place one of these waters near, God forbid, Seattle, Atlanta, Los Angeles or New York, and their banks would be trammeled to death by eager flycasters.

In Montana, we are fortunate to have an abundance of excellent waters that are adequately chronicled in the pages of national sporting magazines. However, therein lies the problem: many resident and visiting flycasters focus only on the big name waters that receive coverage, and they miss out on some of the best fishing the state has to offer. Any of the following streams could merit a week-long visit. Fish the Yellowstone for a few days, but do try to sneak away to one of the smaller streams, where undiscovered treasures lurk.

Stillwater River

Talk about misnaming a river—the Stillwater is anything but calm. Instead, it offers a steep gradient and fast flows that prove ideal to anglers who excel in pocket-water conditions.

The Stillwater begins in the Absaroka Mountain high country, just north of the Yellowstone National Park boundary, under the watchful eye of Wolverine Peak, which sits at 10,440 feet. This is wild, rugged country, complete with grizzly bears, mountain goats and probably a few wolverines. To fish the headwaters, where good numbers of small brook trout, cutthroats and rainbows dine, you'll need a heavy-duty set of lungs and a large backpack—the only way in is by trail, and it's about 24 miles from the trailhead off of Nye Road to the headwaters. Because of its isolation, fish are eager to eat anything that floats. Throw them royal Wulffs, stimulators or a parachute Adams—they'll gobble them down. Small nymphs and larger streamers are good choices if, for some reason, the fish won't take dries.

Below the trailhead, the river is closely paralleled by Nye Road, and access is relatively easy at bridge crossings, where Gallatin National Forest touches its banks, and at established access sites, including Woodbine and Buffalo Jump. Camping is available at the Old Nye Picnic Site between the two access sites. Numerous Forest Service campgrounds exist upstream.

Below Buffalo Jump, the river runs through mostly private land, although access can often be gained by knocking on a door. Brown trout are regularly hooked in that stretch, along with rainbows and brook trout. If you can't gain access across a rancher's land, put in at one of the public access sites and float downriver. Moraine, Castle Rock, Cliffswallow, Absaroka, Whitebird, Swinging Bridge and Fireman's Point offer access any time you want it. Note: the river can become a torrent during runoff, and it can drop drastically low during late summer—two situations that do not facilitate floating.

With concern about overharvest and the need to protect spawning trout, the limit on browns, rainbows and cutthroats was reduced to two fish, with only one over

Stillwater River

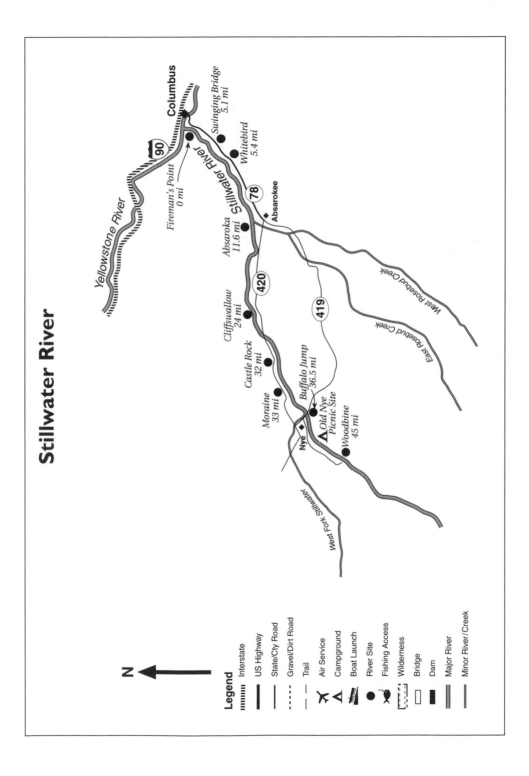

Legend

Interstate
US Highway
State/Cty Road
Gravel/Dirt Road
Trail
Air Service
Campground
Boat Launch
River Site
Fishing Access
Wilderness
Bridge
Dam
Major River
Minor River/Creek

N

Columbus

Swinging Bridge 5.1 mi
Whitebird 5.4 mi
Fireman's Point 0 mi
90
Stillwater River
78
Absarokee
Absaroka 11.6 mi
420
Cliffswallow 24 mi
419
Castle Rock 32 mi
Buffalo Jump 36.5 mi
Moraine 33 mi
Nye
Old Nye Picnic Site
Woodbine 45 mi
West Fork Stillwater
West Rosebud Creek
East Rosebud Creek
Yellowstone River

13 inches in 1989. Fortunately, that is where the regulations stand today. The Stillwater is open to fishing all year.

It's estimated that there are nearly 3,000 trout per mile in the lower river, while numbers are lower in the upper reaches. Fish grub on a variety of hatches that follow each other in two-week increments. Watch for excellent pre-runoff fishing in March and April, when Baetis mayflies, the Mother's Day caddis, midges, and small brown and tan stoneflies draw strikes. One advantage to fishing the river during spring is the opportunity to hit rainbows running up the river out of the Yellowstone. Some of those fish top 20 inches.

After runoff, which can be severe (don't even try wading the river during high water), look for pale morning duns and caddis. Hoppers are standard fare from late summer through early fall. In late September and October, big browns can be taken on streamers as they move upriver from the Yellowstone.

If you have questions about water conditions or hatch timing, call Rainbow Run Fly Shop in Billings, 406-656-3455.

Boulder River

For most flyfishers, there comes a time to get off the main rivers and up into the mountains. You can do just that on the Boulder River south of Big Timber—its headwaters lie in the Absaroka-Beartooth Wilderness, just below 11,300-foot Mount Douglas, and much of its upper section is contained between steep, densely timbered slopes.

It's not as though you are giving up much in the fishing department, either. There are good populations of rainbows in the upper river and a solid mix of browns and rainbows on the lower end. Hatches are quite heavy, and the fish really key in on them. The only problem you'll find on the Boulder is access.

The river can be divided into two sections at Natural Bridge and its 70-foot falls. Natural Bridge, which collapsed in 1988, is about 33 miles from the Boulder's confluence with the Yellowstone. For migratory browns and rainbows, the falls mark the end of their upstream movement.

Above the falls, access is better in the river's 25-mile jaunt to its origin. Anglers bump into pockets of private land, but most of the upper river is bordered by Gallatin National Forest and there is easy access—park your truck off the road, don waders and hit the river.

The upper river is characterized as a medium-sized stream that cuts through a glacial valley. It has a steep gradient that is laced with lots of boulders providing classic pocketwater action. It has wide, rocky riffles that fish move into when the weather warms, and it provides a few glassy slicks where delicate dry flies are a must. The section between Natural Bridge and Two Mile Bridge (six miles) is catch and release only for rainbows, artificial flies and lures only. The entire river is open all year, with two-trout limit and only one over 13 inches.

The lower river is virtually surrounded by private land, and access is tenuous at best. The Boulder is not an ideal stream to float, so anglers are limited to their own

Boulder River

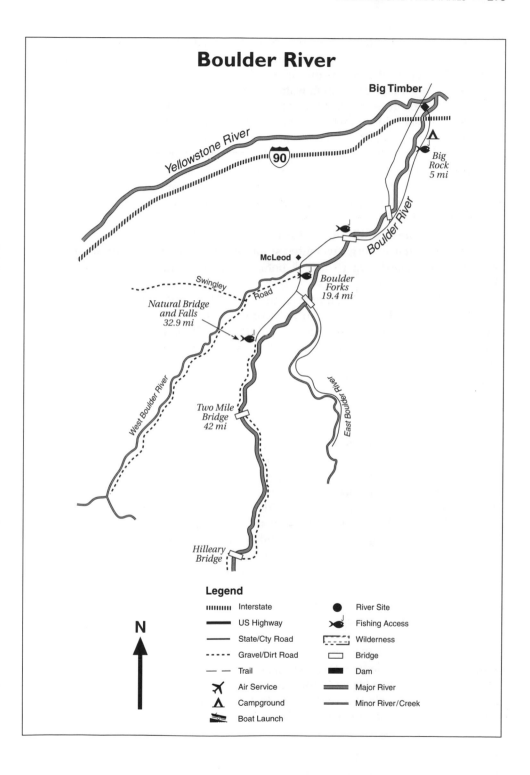

Big Timber

Yellowstone River

90

Big Rock 5 mi

Boulder River

McLeod ◆

Swingley Road

Boulder Forks 19.4 mi

Natural Bridge and Falls 32.9 mi

West Boulder River

East Boulder River

Two Mile Bridge 42 mi

Hilleary Bridge

Legend

‖‖‖‖	Interstate	●	River Site
▬▬	US Highway	🐟	Fishing Access
—	State/Cty Road	⬚	Wilderness
----	Gravel/Dirt Road	▭	Bridge
— —	Trail	◼	Dam
✈	Air Service	▬▬▬	Major River
⛺	Campground	▬▬	Minor River/Creek
🚤	Boat Launch		

N

desire and endurance when fishing the river on foot. The West Fork Boulder also provides that option, and fishing can be quite good. Just watch out for unruly landowners. If you stay below the high water mark, you can tell them where to go! If you hop out of the stream and over the high water mark, they have reason to chastise.

Overall, there are eight public access sites on the river: three state fishing access sites from Natural Bridge downstream, and five upstream U.S. Forest Service campgrounds. The Forest Service also maintains campgrounds on the upper east and west forks. The two access sites on the lower river are called Boulder Forks and Big Rock.

Throughout the river, watch for small stoneflies, Baetis mayflies and caddis in late March, April and May. Salmonflies and green drakes come off as the water begins to build in May. Watch for PMDs in July and August, along with the terrestrials like hoppers and ants.

In the fall, some awfully large browns move out of the Yellowstone and into the Boulder for the spawn. Large, weighted streamers can pull browns out of the deeper runs and holes. Don't forget to work behind boulders and bankside obstructions where the current settles.

To reach the Boulder River, head south from Big Timber on Main Street (Route 298). The road parallels the river for its entire length. If you can't gain access across private land on the lower river and you want to avoid Boulder Forks, head upstream and tempt the upper river's rainbows and cutthroats. The scenery is awesome and, again, the fishing is quite good.

For water conditions and hatch updates, call Sweet Cast Angler or check with the Livingston fly shops.

Shields River

This is an easy stream to overlook, except by flyfishers who realize the merit of the Shields' spring rainbow and fall brown trout runs that provide an excellent opportunity to hook a big fish on a small stream.

Unfortunately, the Shields twists through mostly private land, and access can be a hassle. However, there are enough bridge crossings off of Highway 89 south of Wilsall and off the side roads that cross the stream north of Wilsall to allow the adventuresome angler enough opportunities to get on the river. Just remember to stay below the high water mark that the stream access law requires.

The Shields runs almost 82 miles from its origin in the Crazy Mountains to its confluence with the Yellowstone a few miles northeast of Livingston. The lower 40 miles parallel Highway 89. The upper river heads northeast at Wilsall into the Crazies. A few tributary streams run into the river out of the Bridger Mountains to the west.

The Shields is a small river by anyone's standard. In most places it's a short cast wide. In other spots you may have to apply a modest single haul to reach the opposite bank. Only in a few places is the stream deep enough that you can't see bottom during clear water periods. In other words, this is a good river for beginners. However, its rewards often come in a size that some flyfishers wait a lifetime to catch.

Shields River

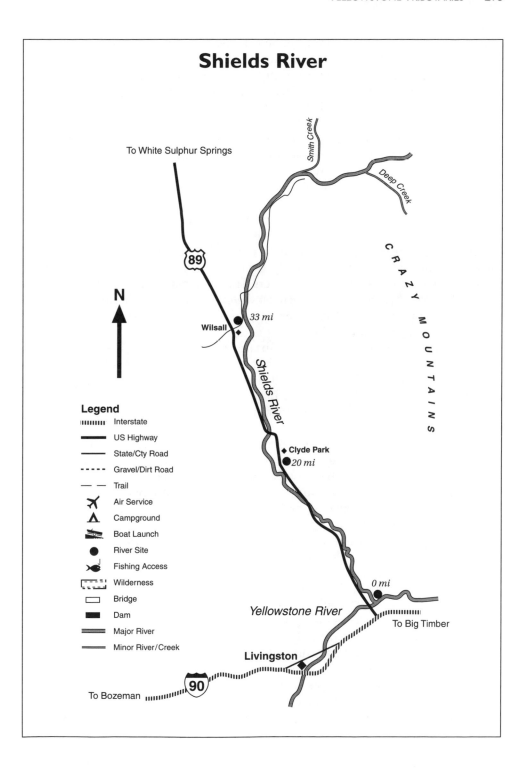

To White Sulphur Springs

Smith Creek

Deep Creek

89

N

Wilsall ● 33 mi

Shields River

C R A Z Y   M O U N T A I N S

Legend

⦚⦚⦚⦚⦚⦚	Interstate
▬▬▬	US Highway
——	State/Cty Road
- - - - -	Gravel/Dirt Road
— —	Trail
✈	Air Service
⛰	Campground
🚤	Boat Launch
●	River Site
🐟	Fishing Access
⌁	Wilderness
▭	Bridge
▬	Dam
▬▬▬	Major River
——	Minor River/Creek

● Clyde Park
● 20 mi

● 0 mi

Yellowstone River

To Big Timber

Livingston

90

To Bozeman

Insect hatches on the Shields can be diverse. You may bump into some Baetis and small stoneflies during pre-runoff in April and early May. After runoff, look for caddis, PMDs, hoppers and ants. Baetis may appear again during fall.

To reach the Shields, take the White Sulphur Springs exit from Interstate 90 east of Livingston or take the Old Clyde Park road east out of Livingston.

The Shields is open from the third Saturday in May through November 30. An extended whitefish season and catch and release for trout on artificial flies and lures only runs from November 30 through the third Saturday in May. The entire river is catch and release for cutthroat trout year-round.

Rock Creek

When flyfishers speak about Montana's Rock Creek, invariably they are referring to that mountain gem in the far west region of the state.

However, there is another Rock Creek, this one a Yellowstone River tributary via the Clark's Fork of the Yellowstone that provides excellent fishing throughout. And it twists through a bastion of neon-clad skiers. That information obviously will strike a chord with some flyfishers: yes, you can leave your spouse at the ski area and hit the river even during winter—Rock Creek is open for fishing all year; however, it will freeze over during extended cold spells.

Rock Creek begins high up in the Absaroka-Beartooth Wilderness area off the Beartooth Plateau, just east of Mount Rearguard, which soars 12,204 feet.

Obviously, winter fishing near the headwaters is an afterthought. However, the Beartooth Highway parallels the river for its entire upstream length, offering easy summer and fall access through National Forest lands. There are six public campgrounds upstream from Red Lodge.

Downstream at Red Lodge, extending to its confluence with the Clark's Fork, the creek flows through private lands, although there are a couple of public access sites. Permission to fish may often be gained by knocking on a door.

Often, Rock Creek will not come into its prime until mid-July, after runoff. At that time, expect solid caddis hatches, some small stoneflies (yellow sallies) and a variety of mayflies, including PMDs.

Don't expect large fish in Rock Creek. Instead, be happy with an eight- to 12-incher in the upper river. Below Red Lodge you could bump into a 15- or 16-incher, with an absolutely rare fish close to 20 inches. Expect browns and rainbows.

To reach Rock Creek, follow I-90 west from Billings or east from Livingston. From Billings, take U.S. Route 212 south at Laurel. From Livingston, take State Route 78 south at Columbus. Red Lodge has great accommodations, excellent eateries, many interesting shops and lively nightlife. For water conditions and hatch updates, call Yellowstone Troutfitters in Red Lodge, 406-446-3819.

Clark's Fork of the Yellowstone

Due to irrigation demand and soupy, chocolate milk-colored irrigation returns, the Clark's Fork is not what it could be. Instead, it is a stream to shake your head at when passing by its lower reaches.

But, by the time you reach the upper eight miles of the river, just before it dumps south into Wyoming, it's time to stop your truck and rig a flyrod.

In those upper reaches between the state line and Bridger Bend, expect a smattering of cutthroats, browns and rainbows, some of them to 15 inches or more. Also expect some challenging pocket water conditions.

The section in Wyoming is said to fish better than Montana's portion. A Wyoming license is all you need to find out for yourself.

Keep an eye out for typical hatches on the Clark's Fork. Small stoneflies, plenty of caddis, a few PMDs and terrestrials, like hoppers and ants, should keep fish rising. If you go underneath, try a beadhead hare's ear or pheasant tail, or tie on a big sculpin or woolly bugger (size 4)—the big browns and rainbows hammer them.

To reach the upper Clark's Fork follow U.S. Route 310 south from Laurel. Turn left off of 310 onto State Route 72 just south of Bridger.

CENTRAL HUB CITIES
Great Falls
Elevation–3,333 • Population–55,000

Great Falls is located in northcentral Montana at the confluence of the Missouri and Sun Rivers. It is Montana's second largest town and home to the famous Charlie Russell Museum, which is well worth a side trip when fishing the nearby Missouri, Sun, Dearborn or Smith rivers. The Lewis and Clark National Forest lies south of Great Falls and the rest of the county consists of intermountain and plains grasslands. Agriculture is one of the main industries of the county.

ACCOMMODATIONS
Budget Inn, 2 Treasure State Drive / 406-453-1602 / 60 rooms. Dogs allowed, grassy area / $$

Comfort Inn, 1120 9th Street South / 406-454-2727 / 64 rooms / Dogs allowed in smoking rooms only, $5 charge, grassy area / Spa / $$

Edelweiss Motor Inn, 626 Central Avenue West / 406-452-9503 / 20 rooms / Dogs welcome, grassy area / $$

Super 8 Lodge, 1214 13th Street South / 406-727-7600 / 117 rooms / Dogs allowed, grassy area / $$

TownHouse Inn, 1411 10th Ave South / 406-761-4600 / 108 rooms / Dogs allowed, $5 charge per dog / Grassy area, pool, restaurant / $$

CAMPGROUNDS AND RV PARKS
Dick's RV Park, ½ mile east off exit 278 on 10th Avenue South / 406-452-0333 / Open all year / 10 tent and 140 RV spaces / Showers, laundry, and store

Great Falls KOA Campground, SE edge of town at 10th Avenue South and 51st / 406-727-3191 / Open all year / 22 tent, 116 RV spaces / Showers, laundry, store, and cabins

RESTAURANTS
4B's, 4610 10th Ave South / 406-727-3366 / Open 24 hours

Elmers Pancake and Steak House, 1600 Fox Farm Rd, next to Budget Inn / 406-761-2400 / Open 6AM–10PM for breakfast, lunch, and dinner

El Comedor Mexican Restaurant, 1120 25th Street South / 406-761-5500 / Open 7 days, 11AM–11PM for lunch and dinner / Imported beers

Jaker's Steak, Ribs, and Fish House, 1500 10th Ave South / 406-727-1033 / Open for lunch and dinner

FLY SHOPS AND SPORTING GOODS
Big Bear Sports Center, 4800 10th Avenue / 406-761-6300

Prairie Sporting Goods, 802 2nd Avenue North / 406-452-7319

AUTO RENTAL AND REPAIR
Budget, Great Falls International Airport / 406-454-1001

Hertz Rent-A-Car, Great Falls International Airport / 406-761-6641

Carl's Exxon, 2300 10th Ave South / 406-761-1342 / Open 7 days / Towing
Westgate Exxon, 416 Smelter Ave NE / 406-452-1271 / Open 7 days / Towing

AIR SERVICE
Great Falls International Airport, 15 South / 406-727-3404 / Serviced by
  Northwest, Delta, and Horizon airlines.

MEDICAL
Columbus Hospital, 500 15th Avenue South / 406-727-3333
Montana Deaconess Medical Center, 1101 26th Street South / 406-761-1200

FOR MORE INFORMATION
Great Falls Chamber of Commerce
P.O. Box 2127-A
Great Falls, MT 59403
406-761-4436

Montana Department of Fish, Wildlife, and Parks, Region 4
4600 Springs Road
Great Falls, MT 59406
406-454-3441

Bureau of Land Management
812 14 North
Great Falls, MT 59406
406-727-0503

Benton Lake National Wildlife Refuge
922 Bootlegger Trail
Great Falls, MT 59406
406-727-7400

Lewistown

Elevation – 3,960 • Population – 6,051

Lewistown is a long way from anywhere, nestled at the foot of the Judith, Moccasin and Big Snowy mountains, about 128 miles northwest of Billings and 105 miles west of Great Falls. This hub of central Montana is in the exact center of the state. It is a trading center for the ranchers and farmers in the area.

Lewistown is the seat of Fergus County. Fergus County, like most of central Montana, produces beef cattle and grain products in the form of wheat and barley. The county is large and has a wide variety of terrain and vegetation types including mountains with montane forest and intermountain grassland, and rolling hill country with shrub and plains grasslands. Both are interspersed with ranch and farmland. The northern boundary of Fergus County is the Missouri River. The Judith River and its tributaries flow north into the Missouri River system. The county has numerous other creeks and small streams with mixed types of habitat along their water courses. Big Spring Creek and the Musselshell River are the two main attractions for flyfishers.

Upland bird hunts can be combined with fall fishing trips; sharptail and sage grouse, Hungarian partridge, pheasant and forest grouse abound.

ACCOMMODATIONS

Mountainview Motel, 1422 West Main Street / 406-538-3457 or 800-862-5786 / Reservations suggested / 31 rooms, 3 kitchenettes, 1 house (day or week) / Dogs allowed / Your hosts are Jim and Virginia Woodburn / $$

Yogo Park Inn, 211 East Main / 406-538-8721 or 800-437-PARK / Reservations suggested / 124 rooms, dogs allowed / Golden Spike Lounge and Yogo Steak House / $$

B&B Motel, 420 East Main / 406-538-5496 / 36 rooms, kitchenettes / Dogs allowed / $$

OUTFITTERS

Pigeye Basin Outfitters, Peter B. Rogers, HCR 81, Box 25, Utica, MT 59452 / 406-423-5223 / Accommodations and meals / Call for reservations

RESTAURANTS

Snow White Cafe, 122 West Main Street / 406-538-3666 / Daily specials / 5:30AM–10PM / Closed Mondays

Sportsman Restaurant and Casino, top of the hill / 406-538-9053 / Dining, 6PM –10PM / Lounge, 8AM–2AM

Pete's Fireside Dining Room and Drive-In, 1308 West Main / 406-430-9400 / Open 7 days a week

VETERINARIANS

Lewistown Veterinary Service, Fairgrounds Road / 406-538-3663 / Dr. Vischer

FLY SHOPS AND SPORTING GOODS

The Sports Center, 320 West Main Street / 406-538-9308 / Hunting and fishing headquarters / 8:30AM–6PM

Don's sports Center, 120 2nd Avenue South / 406-538-9408

Pamida, 825 Northeast Main / 406-538-3423

AUTO REPAIR AND RENTAL

Dean Newton Olds, 519 West Broadway / 406-538-3455

AIR SERVICE

Lewistown Airport, Big Sky Airlines / 406-38-3264 / Daily service

MEDICAL

Central Montana Medical Center, 408 Wendall Avenue / 406-538-7711

FOR MORE INFORMATION

Chamber of Commerce
P.O. Box 818
Lewistown, MT 59457

White Sulphur Springs

Population– 1,002 • Elevation– 5,200

White Sulphur Springs is a full-service community located halfway between Yellowstone and Glacier National Parks on US 89 and US 12. The town, which rests in Meagher County, is surrounded by the Big Belt, Little Belt and Castle mountains. It gains its name for the mineralized, thermal waters, which are located in the city park. That water is used in the Spa Hot Springs Motel's pool.

There are a wealth of recreational opportunities in the area, with the Lewis and Clark and Helena National Forests surrounding town. The Smith River's headwaters are located in the Castles and Little Belts, and the river flows through the county to meet the Missouri at Ulm. The Smith is a famous floating river that passes through 61 miles of beautiful natural canyons cut in limestone formations. Although Meagher County is surrounded by mountains, the valley is vast and flat with shrub grasslands and croplands.

ACCOMMODATIONS

The Tenderfoot Motel, 301 West Main Street / 406-547-3303 / 20 units, kitchenettes / Dogs allowed / $

Spa Hot Springs Motel, 202 West Main Street / 406-547-3366 / 21 rooms / Dogs allowed / $

CAMPGROUNDS AND RV PARKS

The Spring Campground, on Hwy 89 / 406-547-3921 / Open 5/1-12/1 / 8 RV spaces / Water, electric, and sewer

RESTAURANTS

The Truck Stop Cafe, 511 East Main Street / 406-547-3825 / Full menu, 5:30AM–10PM

Dori's Cafe, 112 East Main Street / 406-547-2280

Cow Palace, 406-547-9994 / Steaks, seafood, and cocktails

Mint Bar, 27 East Main Street / 406-547-3857

VETERINARIANS

William H. Schender, DVM, 404 East Hampton / 406-547-3857

FLY SHOPS AND SPORTING GOODS

Lone Wolf Sporting Goods Stores, 105 West Main Street / 406-547-2176

AUTO REPAIR

Berg Chevrolet Garage, 11 West Main Street / 406-547-3514

AIR SERVICE

Airport, south of White Sulphur Springs / 406-547-3511 / Prop aircrafts and small jets

MEDICAL
Mountain View Memorial Hospital,16 West Main Street / 406-547-3384

FOR MORE INFORMATION
Chamber of Commerce
P.O. Box 356
White Sulphur Springs, MT 59645
406-547-3932

Harlowton

Elevation – 4,167 • Population – 1,049

Harlowton is located at the intersection of US Hwy 12 and Hwy 191, 93 miles northwest of Billings. It is nestled among three mountain ranges near the geographic center of the state. The Graves Hotel and other buildings on Main Street still have the native sandstone of a frontier town. The Upper Musselshell Historical Society Museum on Central Avenue contains interesting memories of the local past.

Harlowton is the county seat of Wheatland County. Hwy 12 follows the Musselshell River, and its many sandstone buttes and cottonwood bottomlands, across the county. North of the river is intermountain grassland. Plains grassland flanks the south side. The agricultural land along the Musselshell is mainly irrigated crops. The rest of the agriculture in the county is dryland farming.

ACCOMMODATIONS

Graves Hotel, 106 South Central Avenue / 406-632-5855 / Built in 1908 / 45 rooms / Bar 11AM–2AM, Restaurant 6AM–10PM / No dogs allowed / $

Corral Motel, Junction US 12 and 191 east of Harlowton, P.O. Box 721 / 20 rooms, 3 kitchenettes / Dogs allowed / $

County Side Inn, 309 3rd Street NE, P.O. Box 72 / 11 rooms / Dogs allowed / $

Troy Motel, 106 2nd Avenue NE, P.O. Box 779 / 406-632-4428 / 7 rooms / Dogs allowed / $

RESTAURANTS

Graves Hotel Dining Room, 106 South Central Avenue / 406-632-5855 / Dining room open 5–10PM / Coffee shop open all day

Cornerstone Inn, 11 North Central Avenue / 406-632-4600 / Breakfast and lunch

Wade's Cafe, 406-632-4533 / Open 7 days

VETERINARIANS

Holloway Veterinary Hospital, P.O. Box 274 / 406-632-4371

FLY SHOPS AND SPORTING GOODS

Ray's Sports and Western Wear, Hwy 12 and Hwy 191 / 406-632-4320 / Guns, sporting equipment, clothing, and source for hunting guides and outfitters

AUTO REPAIR
Leary's Exxon Service, 406-632-5814 / Open 7AM–5PM

AIR SERVICE
County Airstrip, Will Morris / 406-632-4545

MEDICAL
Wheatland Memorial Hospital, 530 3rd Street NW / 406-632-4351

FOR MORE INFORMATION
Harlowton Chamber of Commerce
P.O. Box 694
Harlowton, MT 59036
406-632-5523

Livingston
Elevation – 4,503 • Population – 6,700

Livingston is located in southcentral Montana, on a big bend of the Yellowstone River, 53 miles north of Yellowstone National Park and 25 miles east of Bozeman. It sits in the lovely Paradise Valley, surrounded by the Absaroka-Beartooth Wilderness, and the Gallatin, Bridger, and Crazy mountain ranges. Livingston is a hospitable Western town, with over 600 rooms in its hotels, motels, and bed and breakfasts. It offers excellent eateries and it is considered by many seasoned flyfishers as the the king of western trout fishing towns. Campgrounds, scenic areas and fishing access sites are readily available.

ACCOMMODATIONS
The Murray Hotel, 201 West Park / 406-222-1350 / Located downtown, next to Dan Bailey's Fly Shop / Newly renovated, deluxe, turn-of-the century hotel / 40 charming guest rooms with or without adjoining baths / The Winchester Cafe, The Murray Bar, and a large lounge are adjoining / Dogs allowed / $$

Paradise Inn, P.O. Box 684 / 800-437-6291 / Off Interstate 90, Exit 333 / 42 rooms, all ground floor / Lounge, indoor pool, jacuzzi, and restaurant / Dogs allowed, some restrictions / $$

Parkway Motel-Budget Host, 1124 West Park Street / 406-222-3840 / Reservations: 800-727-7217 / Interstate 90, Exit 333 / 28 rooms, 8 kitchenettes, 3 two-bedroom rooms / Dogs allowed, $3 charge / $$

Livingston Inn and Campground, Box 3053-A, Rogers Lane / Motel: 406-222-3600 / Interstate 90, Exit 333, ½ block north / 16 rooms / Campground: 406-222-1122 / 26 hook-ups / Pull-through spaces, showers, and laundry / $

Chico Hot Springs Lodge, Pray, Montana / 406-333-4933 / Located 23 miles south of Livingston on route 89 / Inn has 50 Rooms / Motel has 24 rooms, 4 cabins, 3 cottages with kitchens, log house with kitchen, 2 condos with kitchens / Mineral hot springs pool / Chico Inn gourmet dining room / Poolside Grill, Saloon / Dogs allowed, $2 charge / $$

RESTAURANTS

Winchester Cafe and Murray Bar, 201 West Park / 406-222-1350 / Downtown Livingston / Full-service—breakfast, lunch, dinner, Sunday brunch / Homemade desserts, espresso, fine wine selection

Chico Inn, Pray / 406-333-4933 / 23 miles south of Livingston on Route 89 / Fine dining, reservations recommended / Great wine list / Poolside Grill has great homemade food, bar

Stockman, 118 North Main Street / 406-222-8455 / Bar and restaurant / Lunch and dinner—steaks, prime rib, seafood, and burgers

Livingston Bar and Grill, 130 North Main Street / 406-222-7909 / Antique bar / Steak, seafood, and buffalo burgers

The Sport, 114 South Main Street / 406-222-3533 / barbecue ribs, chicken, burgers, cocktails, and wine

Martin's Cafe, 108 West Park Street / 406-222-2110 / Open 24 hours, 7 days / Carry-out, breakfast specials, smorgasbord on Sundays

VETERINARIANS

Colmey Veterinary Hospital, P.O. Box 521 / 406-222-1700 / Duane Colmey, DVM, ½ mile south of Livingston on Rt 89 / Pet food, supplies, grooming, kennel

Shields Valley Veterinary Service, Rt 85, Box 4321 / 406-222-6171 / Donald Smith, DVM

FLY SHOPS AND SPORTING GOODS

Dan Bailey's Fly Shop, 209 West Park Street / 406-222-1673 or 800-356-4052 / Flies, fishing equipment, clothing, and accessories

George Anderson's Yellowstone Angler, Rt 89 South, P.O. Box 660 / 406-222-7130. / Flyfishing specialties, outdoor clothing

Wilderness Outfitters, 1 mile south of town on Rt 89 / 406-222-6933 / Guns, shells, clothing, and accessories

Big Sky Flies and Guides, Highway 89, Emigrant, MT 59027 / 406-333-4401

Hatch Finders Fly Shop, 113 West Park Street / 406-222-0989

AIR SERVICE

Mission Field, east of Livingston / 406-222-6504

AUTO RENTAL AND REPAIR

Livingston Ford-Lincoln-Mercury, 1415 West Park Street / 406-222-7200 / All models, 4wd and vans

MEDICAL

Livingston Memorial Hospital, 504 South 13th Street / 406-222-3541

FOR MORE INFORMATION

Livingston Area Chamber of Commerce
212 West Park Street (Depot Center Baggage Room)
Livingston, MT 59047
406-222-0850

Big Timber

Elevation – 4,100 • Population – 1,557

Big Timber is tucked between the Yellowstone and Boulder Rivers in the shadow of the Crazy Mountains. The town is located halfway between Bozeman and Billings off I-90.

Big Timber is the county seat of Sweet Grass County. The Boulder River, which flows through town, leads south into the spectacular Absaroka-Beartooth Wilderness. To the north are the Crazy Mountains and the Musselshell River. Many Forest Service campgrounds are located in the area. In addition to the fishing, excellent wingshooting and big game hunting opportunities can be found here—but be prepared for private property. Sweet Grass County must lead the state in numbers of no trespassing signs.

ACCOMMODATIONS

Big Timber Super 8 Motel, Interstate 90 and Hwy 1 / 406-932-8888 / 39 rooms / Dogs allowed with a $15 deposit / $

The Grand Hotel, Box 1242, McLeod Street / 406-932-4459 / Recently restored with high ceilings and Victorian atmosphere, 10 rooms / No dogs / Moderate rates / A hearty breakfast is included with your room

Lazy J Motel, P.O. Box 1096, on old Hwy 10 / 406-932-5533 / 15 comfortable rooms / Dogs allowed for a small fee / $

CAMPGROUNDS AND RV PARKS

Spring Creek Camp & Trout Ranch, 2 miles south on Rt. 298 / 406-932-4387 / Open 4/1–11/30 / 50 RV and 50 tent spaces / Full services

RESTAURANTS

Frye's Cafe and Lounge, Hwy 10 West / 406-932-5242 / Breakfast, lunch, and dinner

The Grand Hotel, 139 McLeod Street / Breakfast, lunch, and dinner / Fine dining and full beverage service / Elegant / $$$

Country Pride Restaurant, Old Hwy 10 West / 406-932-4419 / Breakfast, lunch, and dinner

Timber Bar, 116 McLeod Street / 406-932-9211 / Breakfast, lunch, and dinner / 10AM–midnight

VETERINARIANS

All Creatures Veterinarian Service, 21 North Bramble / 406932-4324

FLY SHOPS AND SPORTING GOODS

The Fort, Hwy 10 East / 406-932-5992

Bob's Sport Shop, 230 McLeod Street / 406-932-5464

Sweet Cast Angler, 151 1st Ave / 406-932-4469

AUTO REPAIR
Stetson Ford, 403 McLeod Street / 406-932-5732

AIR SERVICE
County Airstrip, Justin Ferguson / 406-932-4389

MEDICAL
Sweet Grass Family Medicine, 5th Avenue and Hooper / 406-932-5920

FOR MORE INFORMATION
Sweet Grass Chamber of Commerce
Box 1012
Big Timber, MT 59011
932-5131

Eastern Montana

Eastern Montana is not about to become the next great destination area for the flyfishing masses, but it does contain the most popular river in the state—the Bighorn—along with some surprising options.

The Bighorn is to Montana flyfishing what the Statue of Liberty is to New York, what Mount Rushmore and pheasant hunting is to South Dakota, what the Space Needle is to Seattle, what the Iditerod is to Alaska—the Bighorn is Montana's signature river, a place that provides some of the best, if not *the* best, trout fishing in the world.

It is not uncommon for beginners to catch large brown trout on the Bighorn— its trout average 15 to 17 inches with many exceeding 20 inches. The river's rainbow trout run larger on average. And both species feed heavily on the river's massive aquatic insect hatches, making them prime targets of both dry-fly and nymph fishers. Pale morning duns, Baetis and Trico mayflies, a variety of caddisflies and small golden stoneflies emerge seasonally. Scuds, sow bugs, aquatic worms and minnows fill out the menu at any time.

Although the Bighorn draws most of the attention, there are other possibilities in eastern Montana, and one of the wildest exists farther north, below Fort Peck Reservoir in the lower Missouri River, where some huge rainbow trout reside.

However, a trip to that part of the Missouri is not for the faint of heart. Serpentine creatures are just waiting to sink their teeth into your ankle. Scorpions always hold their stinger at high mast. Amenities are few. Air temperature rates above 90 degrees most summer days. And those rainbows are just downright hard to catch.

In many flyfisher's minds, eastern Montana is a desolate wasteland offering little to the angler. However, everyone should try the Bighorn at least once. If you get tired of crowded conditions, venture to the lower Missouri. You'll get all the solitude you need, and possibly the largest rainbow of your life.

Bighorn River

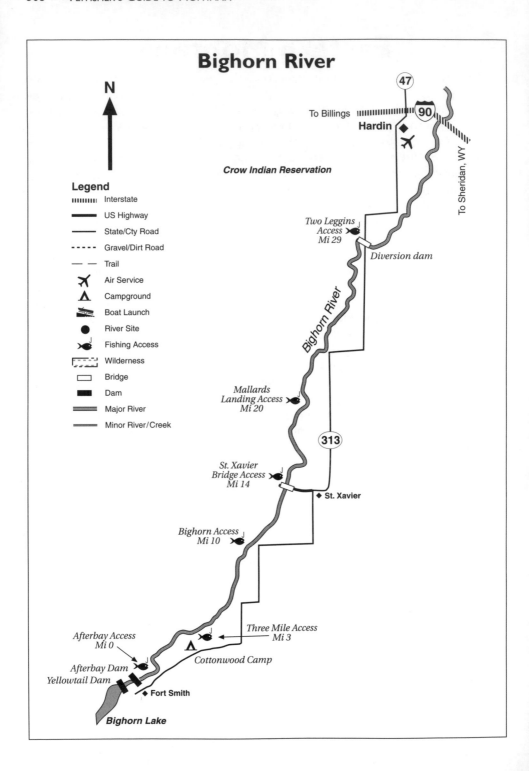

Bighorn River

After a serious stint on southcentral Montana's Bighorn River, few anglers would argue that it is not the state's most complete trout water. It offers big browns and monster rainbows throughout the year, and it produces awesome aquatic insect hatches to match. For anglers who fish the Bighorn, the river becomes a measure against which the merit of all other waters are judged.

Situated just north of the Wyoming state line, pouring out of massive Bighorn Lake, the Bighorn River cuts through some of the most desolate, historically painful, yet beautiful country in the Big Sky. Custer and his men died in the fields above the river, and if you listen diligently, their voices are present in the wind.

The Bighorn's crystalline tailwaters divide the Pryor Mountains to the west and the Bighorn Mountain foothills to the east. Along its banks, fields of wheat and alfalfa thrive. Upland birds and waterfowl visit in great numbers. Rooster pheasants are heard cackling crisply at dawn. Mallard and goldeneye ducks and big Canada geese whistle by on locked wings in the morning mist, settling by the thousands in prime feeding grounds.

But in the minds of many, the Bighorn's greatest appeal rests with its fish: hordes of brown and rainbow trout that average 15 inches and commonly reach 20 inches. For many of us, the Bighorn River and its trout reside as much in our subconscious as they do in reality.

Once you've fished the Bighorn, most waters pale in comparison, especially when they fish poorly. In other words, the Bighorn spoils a lot of anglers, making relatively productive waters appear sterile.

One of the Bighorn's appealing aspects is its year-round consistency. You can catch trout there in January, June and November and all months in between. And because it is a tailwater fishery (meaning it flows out of a reservoir), its waters, especially the upper 13 miles, are almost always clear, cold and very appealing.

The river's trout population doesn't hurt, either: in the upper 13 miles from Afterbay Dam downstream to Bighorn Access Site, biologists estimate nearly 6,000 trout per mile.

Rainbows have been in general decline in the 1990s, but they constitute the greatest portion of large fish in the river, and according to those who fish the river daily, they may be making a slight comeback. You should know that if a trout takes your fly in a shallow, rapid riffle and charges 70 yards downstream, threatening to burn the gears right out of your reel, assume that you've hooked a rainbow and you had better get moving down the riverbank quickly, unless you prefer to lose bragging rights for the day. The river's brown trout are more likely to dig hard for the bottom, as they do wherever they are found.

For most anglers planning a trip to the river, the questions are these: When is the best time to fish the river? What is the most prolific hatch? When is crowding most severe (you may literally see hundreds of boats on the river during a summer day)? And what is the river's best stretch?

Fortunately, two of those questions are easily answered: the best time to fish the river is when you can get there—hatches are normally always occurring, and when they are not, nymphing works really well. Crowding is most severe from early July through September, although a choice secret is that holidays are typically bearable (everybody thinks it will be a nightmare of mobile homes, angry wives, screaming kids, beer guzzling fools and inconsiderate anglers).

The last two questions are highly disputable. The river's upper 13 miles, where every sane angler agrees the best water lies, can be split into two sections: Afterbay Dam access to Three Mile access and Three Mile access to Bighorn access.

The upper three miles sees the most pressure; the middle and lower sections slightly less. To me, the debate is ridiculous. Fishing is excellent throughout. The only question should be logistics and how soon you want off the water. If you want a short float, go from Afterbay at Fort Smith to Three Mile, which is only, of course, three miles, but offers plenty of area to get out of a boat or raft and wade through the riffles and side channels.

If you want to spend more time in the boat floating and casting, try putting in at Three Mile and float to Bighorn. You won't have much time to wade when you float that far, especially during spring, fall or winter when the days are short, but you will see a lot of choice water. The other option is to float one stretch, take out and complete your shuttle, and then float it again!

Okay, on to hatches. There are a number of dandies on the Bighorn, but they should not intimidate anglers. Probably the most important hatch, because it occurs during summer when the greatest number of flyfishers visit the water, is the pale morning dun emergence and spinnerfall. However, as you will discover, the Baetis, midge, Trico and caddis occurrences can be equally enticing, especially during the off-season when the river is less overrun.

According to Gordon Rose at Quill Gordon Flyfishers in Fort Smith, the best hatch—the one he would hit if he could only spend a month on the river each year—is actually two hatches that often overlap; pale morning duns and caddis.

"I think the neatest time to fish here is during late summer when you have the opportunity to catch the tail end of the PMDs and the beginning of the caddis," Rose says. "I'd always aim for the late stage of the PMDs, and if you miss it, so what, you still have excellent caddis action that can last all day. In a typical year you will get PMDs from July 20 to August 20 and caddis from August 20 to September 20. If you are really lucky, you will also hit the Trico hatch that starts in September. The safest time frame for a dry-fly fisher is right around the 20th of August—you can't go wrong."

If you're going to match a PMD or caddis hatch, use precise flies and focus on specific times of day when the bugs, and likewise the trout, are most active.

The Bighorn's pale morning duns generally begin their emergence by the third week of July in the upper 13 miles. They may appear earlier, but only in that water 13 miles below the dam on the lower river. But water conditions in that section are tentative at best and trout populations take a marked dip.

The Bighorn offers some of the best brown trout fishing in the West. This fish, taken during January on a lead-eyed bugger, is a typical size.

On a typical summer day, PMDs emerge between 11 AM and 6 PM, although some days you may find two emergences—the normal afternoon occurrence and a killer, bonus hatch between 7 and 11 PM.

"You should really concentrate on the heavy riffles when the PMDs are coming off," Rose says. "PMD nymphs need lots of oxygen, and they seek that faster water."

Trout will focus on precise artificial fly patterns that best mimic each stage of the hatch and spinnerfall.

"I've got my own favorite patterns that I sell here in the shop," Rose adds. "I like a Whitlock red fox squirrel nymph or a light-colored hare's ear, both in size 16. But I sell a woven PMD nymph that accentuates the light and dark shades of the nymph best. They really take that pattern."

While fishing PMD nymphs, Rose and squadrons of other anglers find a dead-drift most effective. If the trout do not take the nymph during the drift, they often will suck it in when it swings at the tail end of the drift.

For dry flies, Rose prefers basic patterns and one monstrosity that may surprise you—the blond humpy. "At different times the fish really seem to prefer one type of dry fly over another," he says. "A size 16 parachute PMD or a size 16 or 18 sparkle dun works well, but I've found that a blond humpy can really get them, too. That pattern floats really well in a heavy riffle, and I think the humped-back profile of the fly mimics a cripple or stillborn dun."

You can fish the Bighorn during winter, but you better be ready for the weather. Here, a geared-up gal hoists a Bighorn rainbow.

As mentioned, spinnerfalls are equally important to emergences on Montana's rivers, and the Bighorn is certainly no exception.

Watch for the densest PMD spinnerfalls to occur during the evening from 7 PM extending until dark. Standard dun and emerger patterns may be shunned by the river's trout during a spinnerfall, so it pays to carry a few spinners in your fly box.

"Sometimes the spinnerfall can be really, really heavy, and it brings a lot of fish up," Rose says. "I have two patterns that work best for me—one is an amber and yellow dun, and the other is a rusty spinner. They seem to have the most preference for the rusty spinner with its Z-lon wing. They'll take that repeatedly."

As PMDs emerge, caddis may come off just as strong. Anglers should pay close attention to the fish, and if they are not receiving strikes on a PMD during a heavy emergence and trout rise, a switch to caddis is in order.

Typically, the caddis hatch peaks between 1 and 5 PM. However, quite often, that time frame is not particularly significant to a flyfisher.

"What happens with the black caddis is this," Rose says. "It hatches sporadically all day long. You can see some as early as 10 AM, but most come off in midafternoon. They immediately go to the bushes, and they really aren't a big factor for trout unless it's an overcast day. On overcast days, trout seem less wary and will feed during midday on caddis."

If you notice caddis on the water, try a scud or sow bug in the morning, trailed by a black caddis pupae. In the afternoon, try emerger patterns like an X-caddis or a size 16 or 18 black caddis with a bright green abdomen. Then prepare for the evening onslaught.

"The best action comes during evening as the caddis return to the river, just before dark," Rose adds. "Caddis won't just hop up and down on the surface, they actually go underneath the water to lay eggs. When they do that, we like to fish a version of the Hemingway caddis—it's basically tied all black and it's fairly dainty and slim. We also use a subsurface egglayer that is tied with a little green egg sack. The rest of it is tied with black (antron) that carries little air bubbles. We tie all of those in a size 18."

Bighorn anglers should also watch for a tan caddis hatch that occurs during late August and early September. A size 14 or 16 elk hair caddis will match those. It's a lesser hatch that comes off between 2 PM and dark, but it can be awfully productive.

While the late summer PMD and caddis emergences provide the most predictable dry-fly action, there are other hatches during the year that provide good opportunities, also. And one of those hatches, the midge emergence, surprisingly, offers dry-fly fishing through the winter months, extending into May. However, during the coldest months, matching those midges can prove maddeningly difficult.

"I divide the Bighorn's midge hatch into two parts," Rose offers. "The true winter midge fishing goes from December through February, and it's fairly difficult because there are single midges on the surface and they must be matched by a single dry fly that runs size 20 to 24. Later, you will get into mating midge clusters, which can be matched with a larger fly, and the fishing can be super-productive."

If you arrive on the Bighorn during the winter, make sure you bring some very tiny dry flies, sow bugs, and scuds, and plenty of warm clothes—the temperature may range from 50 above to 30 degrees below zero.

When fish are working midges up top, try a Griffith's gnat or a standard Adams. The white wing post on a parachute Adams provides a mayfly wing silhouette that the trout definitely do not key in on. If you can't catch fish on those dry flies, don't fret —most of your takes will arrive subsurface anyway.

"During winter I mainly go underneath with crustaceans like scuds and sow bugs and midge larvae," Rose says. "Actually, it's tough to beat a scud or sow bug trailed by a red or white palomino midge. A San Juan worm works alright, too, but they dig into the river bottom during winter, and the fish aren't as keyed in on them."

No matter what color midge larvae you decide to try, be prepared to change. And that goes for any midge hatch any time of the year on the Bighorn.

"Color can make a big difference with the pupa," Rose says. "They can vary from brown to red to black to olive, and the trout most certainly key in on various colors. In the winter and early spring, black and red work best. In April and May, we use a brown or olive."

During the cold season, midge pupa should be dead-drifted in slow, deep water. Trout will be less aggressive when the water is cold, and they likely will not seek fast moving larvae. One thing to keep in mind is the location that trout feed on larvae. According to Rose, it's either a foot off the bottom or within a foot of the surface, and rarely, if ever, between.

By March, anglers should see clusters of mating midges (Rose says it's one of the best dry-fly sessions of the year) riding the surface currents. Size 18 and 20 dry flies will suffice at that time—and, believe me, they are a lot easier to spot on the water than a size 24 demonic gnat.

As winter gives way to spring, sometime in April, blue-winged olives, also called Baetis, make their appearance. The Baetis hatch peaks in mid-May and tapers off in early June. Hatches typically last from 11 AM until 5 PM, with the peak emergence occurring during the warmest part of the day.

Baetis dry-fly and nymph imitations take fish consistently. Size 18 or 20 parachute olives or an RS-2 emerger are good choices up top. Underneath, hare's ear nymphs, pheasant tail nymphs and black Baetis nymphs (Rose's favorite) draw strikes off 5X tippets.

After the midge clusters and the Baetis and before the onset of PMDs, the Bighorn falls into a rut when dry flies are unproductive—nymphs, streamers and worm imitations, however, are the ticket to prime fishing.

For those who live for the dry-fly take, stay home or visit another stream. For those who enjoy the challenge of a nymph, this is the time to fish the Bighorn in relative solitude. And you will catch a lot of fish.

"Peak hatch activity and fishing pressure runs from April through September here, but there is a pretty lengthy gap in hatches that extends from the first week in June through mid-July," Rose says. "You have to look real hard at those days in June and July when it's just real nice—70 or 80 degrees in the afternoons. The crowds are way down, and the nymph fishing is great. You will not catch fish up top, but you can catch as many fish as you would on dries in August. It's just one big trade-off. You will see lots of people when the flies are on top."

If you are not into nymphing and the crowds don't bother you, avoid that time and hit the PMD or caddis hatches, or try some truly mind-boggling fishing when the Tricos make their late summer/early fall appearance.

Tricos are tiny mayflies that persist in massive numbers on the Bighorn. Typically, they will emerge in the evenings, mature overnight, and return to the river in the morning to mate (in massive swarms above the river) and lay their eggs.

Despite their size, most are size 18 to 24, Tricos definitely catch the eye of trout. Fortunately, on the Bighorn, Tricos run quite large (as Tricos go)—you can generally get away with a size 18. Spent-wing Tricos, parachute Adams and parachute Tricos all

What's better than a big, golden-hued brown? The author took this fish on a size 4 woolly bugger.

take fish. Generally, 5X or 6X leaders are required—7X when you get some dirty dog of a trout that is extremely leader shy and paranoid.

"Usually, spinners land on the water around 10 AM," Rose says. "The cooler the night is the later the spinnerfall. I've seen it come off as late as 1 PM after a cold night."

Tricos are especially important on the Bighorn due to their ability to bring the river's largest rainbows up top. The Bighorn's rainbows are late spring spawners, typically demonstrating their spawning urge in late May and June. Most anglers leave the trout alone at that time. Guides and local fishers will snub their noses at you if they catch your streamer running in front of a trout's snout during the spawn.

After the spawn, rainbows move to deep water where they recover lost energy. And they will remain in those deep holes, noses glued to the bottom, throughout the summer. However, the big rainbows come out of hiding when the Tricos start up.

"Every year someone catches an eight- or nine-pound rainbow at that time," Rose says. "The ironic thing is that a big fish like that will come up for a tiny Trico. You actually see quite a few fish in the four- to five-pound class."

One other hatch of note is the little yellow stonefly emergence, which takes place through July. That emergence may offer the best chance for success if a young fly-fisher or a clumsy caster is in your presence.

Floating is the most effective way to fish the Bighorn.
Bank fishers are limited by private land.

Typically, yellow stoneflies hold to the fast riffles. A large attractor plopped on the water in a good chop will take fish.

"For anyone who is getting frustrated by matching the hatch and making delicate presentations on the rest of the river, little yellow stoneflies are a good thing to throw," Rose says. "You can bounce a size 16 or 18 stimulator right through the choppy riffles. It's not a heavy hatch, but there don't have to be too many bugs around for the trout to start looking for them. If you see a fish rise in a the middle of a fast riffle every five minutes or so, it's probably eating stoneflies."

For flyfishers who visit the river after October, there are several factors that influence fishing to keep in mind: the brown trout spawn and turnover of Bighorn Lake (when the water columns rotate).

"The browns start thinking about spawning when November arrives, and they won't take anything on the surface," says Rose, who doesn't endorse fishing for trout on their redds—browns during fall and rainbows during spring and early summer. "Also, the lake turns over about that time. When that happens, it puts the fishing off for a little while. It can be over and done in a week or it can last a month or more. It varies from year to year.

"What happens when the lake turns over is we get a lot of moss and algae floating down the river," Rose added. "And that makes fishing difficult because you are always taking that moss off your line, leader and flies." Another factor that can turn the fishing off is fluctuating releases from Bighorn Lake.

"They (trout) shuffle around and reorient themselves when there is a change in flow," Rose said. "Minor adjustments affect the fishing, but it doesn't shut it off. When a major change occurs, a change in flow that rates 10 percent or more of what it was, the fishing shuts down for at least a day."

The Bighorn is primarily a float-fishing river. Anglers who have access to a drift boat or raft have a much better chance of success than those who are confined to shore. And actually, gaining access to the river without a boat is a problem—the Bighorn runs through the Crow Indian Reservation, and gaining permission to fish the water is not always easy. Fortunately, the Bighorn is an easy river to float—there are quality public boat ramps, no major diversion dams, and the one set of rapids in the upper 13 miles is anything but intimidating.

Prime flows on the Bighorn run 2,000 to 5,000 cfs. Flows between 5,000 and 7,000 cfs are fishable. Anything above 7,000 or 8,000 cfs makes the river very large, spreads the trout out, and hampers a flyfisher's best efforts.

One thing that can turn a successful trip on the Bighorn into something less than desired is overzealous expectations. Yes, the Bighorn is one of the best, if not *the* best trout stream in the world, but it has temperamental days. And it is not known for producing lots of fish over 20 inches, although they are there.

Rose says, "Everyone hears tales about the Bighorn, and generally the river lives up to them. There are not many places where you can catch brown trout that consistently measure 17 inches. When you catch this river at its best, there is no better fishery in the world. It's the people who have fished this river a lot and have experienced the river in its prime who get a bad attitude. Even when the Bighorn is slow, it's better than almost anywhere. Catching 10 or 12 17-inchers, which is a slow day here, is not something to hold your head down about. Some people tend to lose sight of that.

"If people would come to this river with the expectation to just have a good time and work with what the river offers and not expect to take something from it, they will never be disappointed."

Stream Facts: Bighorn River

Seasons
- Open all year.

Special Regulations
- Catch and release only on rainbow trout between Afterbay Dam and Bighorn Access site.

Trout
- Brown and rainbow trout. The browns, which average about 15 inches, dominate. The rainbows are fewer in number, but their size is typically larger. There are plenty of both species in the Bighorn that rate over 18 inches.

River Miles
- Afterbay Dam—0
- Three Mile Access site—3
- Bighorn Access site—13

River Characteristics
- The Bighorn is an easy float, no matter how much water is being pumped out of Yellowtail Reservoir. Beginners should be able to handle the Bighorn with a boat or raft. The only large rapid is Bighorn Rapid, and it isn't much trouble.

Area Fly Shops
- Bighorn Fly and Tackle Shop, Fort Smith, MT, 406-666-2253
- Big Horn River Lodge, P.O. Box 756, Fort Smith, MT, 406-666-2368 or 800-235-5450
- Bighorn Fly and Tackle Shop, 1426 N. Crawford, Hardin, MT, 406-6650-1321
- Royal Big Horn Lodge, PO Box 236, St. Xavier, MT, 406-666-2231
- Bighorn Anglers, Route 313, Fort Smith, MT, 406-666-2233: Guided fishing and birdhunting trips
- Cottonwood Camp, One mile east of Three Mile access, 406-666-2391
- Rainbow Run Fly Shop, 2244 Grand Ave., Billings, MT, 406-656-3455
- Bighorn Fly and Tackle Shop, 485 S. 24th St. W., Billings, MT, 406-656-8257

SHUTTLE SERVICE
- Cottonwood Camp, One mile east of Three Mile access / 406-666-2391
- South Valley Shuttle, Fort Smith / 406-666-2461
- Bighorn Fly and Tackle, Fort Smith / 406-666-2253
- Bighorn Angler, Fort Smith / 406-666-2233

BIGHORN RIVER MAJOR HATCHES

Insect	J	F	M	A	M	J	J	A	S	O	N	D	Flies
Midge	■	■	■	■	■	■	■	■	■	■	■	■	Griffith's Gnat #18-20; Standard Adams #16-20; Palomino Midge #16-20; Serendipity #16-20; Brassie #18-20; Disco Midge #16-20
Pale Morning Dun						■							PMD Cripple #16-18; Sparkle Dun #16-18; Blond Humpy #16-18; Parachute PMD #16-18; Whitlock Red Squirrel Nymph #16-18; Rusty Spinner #16-18; Woven PMD Nymph #16-18
Caddis								■	■				Black Caddis Pupa #16-18; X-Caddis #16-18; Emergent Sparkle Pupa #16-18; Prince Nymph #10-18; Hemingway Caddis #16-18; Tan Caddis #16-18; Elk Hair Caddis #16-18
Trico								■	■				Parachute Adams #18-20; Spent Wing Trico #18-20; Griffith's Gnat #18-20; CDC Trico #18-20
Little Yellow Stonefly							■	■					Stimulator #16-18; Elk Hair Caddis #16-18; Golden Stonefly Nymph #16-18
Scud/Sow Bug													Bighorn Scud #16-18; Epoxy Scud #16-18; Gray Sowbug #16-18
Baetis				■	■					■	■		Olive Cripple #16-20; Parachute Adams #16-20; Sparkle Dun #16-20; Hare's Ear Nymph #16-20; Pheasant Tail Nymph #16-20; Poxyback Baetis #16-20; Halfback Emerger #18-20
Tube Worms	■	■	■	■	■	■	■	■	■	■	■	■	San Juan Worm #6-10

MISSOURI RIVER BELOW FORT PECK

To find chaos in far eastern Montana, you don't have to visit a freaked-out farmer who's finally given in to that maddening wind.

Instead, trek to the Missouri River downstream from Fort Peck Dam. Big, secretive rainbows knife through those boiling currents, inflicting their own crimson twist on some forlorn real estate —washed out territory best known for its abundance of dust, two-fanged serpentine critters and heavy doses of featureless solitude.

However, do not expect your average trout trip on this section of the lower Missouri. Success is not measured in numbers of fish. Size of trout and a unique experience are the criteria here, where you can leave your delicate presentations at home. This is not size 22 Trico water. Instead, you'll be pitching huge buggers, just hoping that one doesn't smack you on the back of the head — a severely painful proposition that occurs all too often in my life.

That trout exist in the lower Missouri is somewhat of a surprise. In fact, between Great Falls and the western edge of Fort Peck Reservoir, the Missouri runs the color of mud and it is almost devoid of trout. However, the river rejuvenates below Fort Peck Dam. Cool releases dump out of the dam and create a fertile tailwater fishery. Pike and walleyes are present below the dam, too.

If the Fort Peck rainbow trout fishery was located anywhere else in the state, it might draw fair numbers of trophy trout seekers. Meaty specimens approaching 11 pounds are reported. Two- to six-pounders are the norm.

Unfortunately, the lower Missouri is located in the heart of walleye and pike country and Montana Fish, Wildlife and Parks has no intention of changing its management policy on the lower Missouri.

"We have no plans to bolster the rainbow population anytime soon," says Bill Wiedenheft, regional fisheries manager for FWP in Glasgow. "Around here, people are pretty much interested in pike and walleyes, and that's about it. Only a few people fish for rainbows, and they fish for them with bait.

"Really, we have very little information on the fishery," he adds. "We don't have an accurate count of the trout population, and we don't even have a biologist working that stretch of river. We get information from word of mouth, and what we get isn't very detailed.

"I know that there are some big rainbows available — most will go between two and four pounds—and they feed mostly on aquatic insects. Guys catch fish during spring, and I don't know why you couldn't get them in the summer or fall."

If you are accustomed to fishing small flies for rising trout, you are in for a shock on this stretch of water. Dainty dries have no place here. Woolly buggers and muddler minnows, fished off sinking lines, are the ticket.

The Missouri below Fort Peck is a wide, powerful river that is best fished from a boat or raft. Wade fishers are severely limited. And discharges from the dam influence fishing, both wading and floating, tremendously.

"Eight thousand cubic feet a second is a lot of water coming out of the dam," Wiedenheft said, "but you can launch a boat and float the river at that level, for sure. There are several boat ramps and access sites on the west side of the river about one mile below the dam. I'd put in there and float down to a decent take-out point."

Finding a take-out spot can be difficult. Private land surrounds the river, and permission to cross that land is needed. And you better secure access before you put on the water, which means you should complete your shuttle before throwing a line. Planning to spend more than one day on the water increases an angler's chance for success in securing access and catching fish.

When floating down the river, pound the banks and strip streamers from the shallow bankside habitat over deep water. Rainbows hold near the shore to avoid heavy current, but they will dart out and nail a streamer when it passes by. Make sure to hit the seams between currents and at the tailouts of islands.

If you are in eastern Montana for some reason, whether bird hunting or traveling between fishing destinations, give the lower Missouri a try. It's definitely a challenge to fish and not for anyone but the most die-hard trophy trout hunters. But a big rainbow in the net is worth a lot of trouble.

EASTERN HUB CITIES
Fort Smith
Elevation– 5,500 • Population– 400

Fort Smith is a small town nestled at the base of the Bighorn Mountains on the Crow Indian Reservation south of Billings. If the Bighorn River was not located in its backyard, Fort Smith might die an obscure death. However, the town takes on a monumental importance when considering flyfishing gear, gasoline, snacks and shuttle service. You won't find much in the way of amenities in Fort Smith (outside of quality flyfishing gear), but you can grab essentials that will save you a trip to Hardin or Billings—a dangerous drive after dark due to windy roads and other obstacles.

ACCOMMODATIONS: FORT SMITH
Cottonwood Camp, one mile east of Three Mile access / cabin rentals / 406-666- 2391 / $$
Kingfisher Motel, North of Fort Smith / 406-666-2326 / $$

CAMPGROUNDS AND RV PARKS
Cottonwood Camp, Highway 90 north of Fort Smith / tent sites / 406-666-2391

OUTFITTERS
Bighorn River Lodge, Highway 90 North of Fort Smith / plush accomodations and guided flyfishing trips / contact Phil Gonzalez / 406-666-2368
Great Waters Outfitters, Fort Smith / 406-666-2205

RESTAURANTS
Yellowtail Market, Fort Smith / 406-666-2333

FLY SHOPS AND SPORTING GOODS
Cottonwood Camp, one mile east of Three Mile access / 406-666-2391
Bighorn Angler, guided flyfishing and bird hunting trips Fort Smith / 406-666-2233
Bighorn Trout Shop, Fort Smith / 406-666-2375
Bighorn Fly and Tackle, Fort Smith / 406-666-2253
Bighorn Troutfitters, St. Xavier / 406-6662224
Bighorn River Lodge, Fort Smith / 406-666-2368

SHUTTLE SERVICE
South Valley Shuttle, Fort Smith / 406-666-2461

Glasgow
Elevation–2,612 • Population–3,600

Glasgow is a ranching community located in the lovely Milk River Valley on the Hi-Line of Montana in the northeast section of the state. It lies 12 miles west of the Fort Peck Indian Reservation and 15 miles north of the Fort Peck Recreation Area.

The Fort Peck Recreation Area is located in the C.M. Russell National Wildlife Refuge. Fort Peck Reservoir is 245,000 acres, making it the second largest reservoir in the U.S. The C.M. Russell Wildlife Refuge extends 125 miles up the Missouri River and contains native prairies, forested coulees, river bottoms, and badlands within its million acres.

ACCOMMODATIONS

Cottonwood Motor Inn, Rt 2, ½ mile east of town / 406-228-8213

Best Western / 71 units, coin laundry, restaurant / Dogs allowed / 28 units with refrigerators / Indoor pool, sauna, cable / Very nice accommodations at reasonable rates

LaCasa Motel, 2381 Avenue North / 406-228-9311 / 13 units / Two rooms have 4 double beds each / Refrigerators in some rooms / Cable / Hunters welcome and dogs allowed / Rates very reasonable / Your hosts are Doug and Sharon Adophson

Star Lodge, Hwy West Rt 2 / 406-228-2494 / 30 units, cable, refrigerators in some rooms / Hunters and dogs welcome / Rates very reasonable / Your hosts are Bill and Shirley Fewer

CAMPGROUNDS AND RV PARKS

Shady Rest RV Park, Rt 2 East / 406-228-2769 / 4 tent sites, 40 RV sites / Water, laundry, electric, sewer, shower, store

Trails West Campground, 1½ miles west of Glasgow on Rt 2 / 406-228-2778 / 15 tent sites, 35 RV sites / Water, electric, sewer, dump, shower, store

RESTAURANTS

Cottonwood Inn Dining Room, located on Hwy 2 in the Cottonwood Motel / 406-228-8213 / Open for breakfast, lunch and dinner / Prime rib served every evening / Cocktails available, rates reasonable

Sam's Supper Club, 307 1st Avenue North / 406-228-4614 / Sam's is a popular spot for the local ranchers and town people specializing in Montana beef / Cocktails / Very good food at reasonable rates

Johnnie's Cafe, 433 1st Avenue South / 406-228-4222 / Open 24 hours / This diner is a favorite of Glasgow residents

FLY SHOPS AND SPORTING GOODS

D&G Sports and Western, 215 4th Avenue South / 406-228-9363 / Hunting, fishing
Pamida, 804 Hwy 2 West / 406-228-9845

AUTO REPAIR

Dan's Auto Clinic, 802 Second Avenue South / 406-228-2604

AIR SERVICE

Glasgow International Airport, east of town / 406-228-4023

MEDICAL

Community Memorial Hospital, 216 14th Avenue South / 406-482-2120

FOR MORE INFORMATION

Glasgow Chamber of Commerce
110 5th Street South
Glasgow, MT 59230
406-228-2222

Department of Fish, Wildlife, and Parks
Hwy 2 West
Glasgow, MT 59230
406-228-9347

BLM Office
Hwy 2 West
Glasgow, MT 59230
406-228-4316

Red Lodge

Elevation – 5,555 • Population – 1,875

The majestic Beartooth Mountains form the backdrop for Red Lodge, the former summer camp of the Crow Indians. The town is located on Rock Creek in the middle of a triangle formed by Billings, Montana Cody, Wyoming, and Yellowstone National Park, each approximately 65 miles away. Red Lodge offers a variety of lodging including motels, condominiums, a historic hotel, and bed and breakfasts. There are two private campgrounds and numerous public campsites in the surrounding national forest areas.

The county seat for Carbon County, Red Lodge is the starting point for what is arguably the most beautiful drive in America, the 69-mile Beartooth Highway that reaches a height of almost 11,000 feet as it climbs through the Beartooth Mountains to Yellowstone National Park. This highway is usually open from Memorial Day to at least Labor Day, depending on snow depth. Good fishing can be found in nearby streams, like Rock Creek and the Clark's Fork, and in the mountain lakes. Red Lodge Mountain is high-class ski area.

ACCOMMODATIONS

Red Lodge Super 8, 1223 Broadway / 406-446-2288 / 50 units, kitchenettes, indoor pool / Dogs allowed / $

Eagles Nest Motel, 702 South Broadway / 406-446-2312 / 16 units, 2 with kitchens / Dogs allowed / $

Yodeler Motel, 601 South Broadway / 406-446-1435 / 22 rooms, in-room steam bath / Dogs allowed / $

Red Lodge Inn, 1223 South Broadway / 406-446-2030 / 12 units / Dogs allowed / $

RESTAURANTS

Bogart's Restaurant, 11 South Broadway / 406-222-1784 / Great atmosphere, bar / Mexican food, pizza, sandwiches, Italian dishes

Old Pitney Dell, south of Red Lodge / 406-446-1196 / Gourmet dining / Mon–Sat, 5–10PM

Red Lodge Cafe, 16 South Broadway / 406-446-1619 / Breakfast, buffalo burgers, homemade pie, soup / Full-service bar and lounge

The Pollard, 2 North Broadway / Newly renovated, full-service restaurant and bar

VETERINARIAN

Red Lodge Veterinary Clinic, Rt 1, Box 4025 / 406-446-2815 / John Beud, DVM

FLY SHOPS AND SPORTING GOODS

Yellowstone Troutfitters, Broadway / 406-446-3819

Outdoor Adventure, 110½ South Broadway / 406-446-3818

True Value Hardware and Variety, 101 North Broadway / 406-446-1847

AUTO REPAIR

Buffalo Bob's, north of Red Lodge / 406-446-3000

AIR SERVICE

County Airstrip, Amos C. Clark / 406-466-2537

MEDICAL

Billings Clinic, 10 South Oaks / 406-446-2412 / 8AM–5PM / Walk-in care available

Carbon County Memorial Hospital, 600 West 20th Street / 406-446-2345

FOR MORE INFORMATION

Red Lodge Chamber of Commerce
P. O. Box 988
Red Lodge, MT 59068
406-446-1718

Spring Creeks

In the natural progression of flycasters, Western spring creeks, those tremendously challenging, crystal clear, winding streams, represent the Final Frontier. After a few trial runs they may represent Shangri-La.

Flyfishers like to catch trout, so they begin on Montana's hatchery-stocked ponds or mountain streams, where small rainbows and cutthroats impale themselves on any number of bushy dry flies. Next in line are the big rivers where specialized tactics like fishing under the surface with nymphs may be applied. This I do know: a serious flyfisher can only catch so many small to middling size trout on bushy dry flies and the likes of San Juan worms before the appeal wears off.

Eventually, as a flyfisher's knowledge of insect hatches, aquatic habitats and trout mentality grow, the Final Frontier alone stands in the way—much like Mongols encountering the Great Wall of China. When challenge overrides number as the gauge of a successful day on the water, you are truly ready to test your ability against a spring creek. Here's where you can find some dandies—a few well known and others obscure—in Big Sky Country.

Poindexter Slough (Beaverhead River Tributary)

Poindexter is one of Montana's more recognized and, fortunately, accessible spring creeks. It is visible from Interstate 15 south of Dillon, has plenty of public access and produces solid numbers of 1-2 to 18-inch browns, with fewer rainbows. A few hogs of each variety also reside in the Slough, but fishing for them with 6X or 7X tippet, which is often required, is not stacking the cards in your favor.

Poindexter, like most spring creeks, is tremendously fertile. Its insect hatches don't just emerge—they arrive! And when they do, expect some large fish looking to the surface, sucking in small mayflies, caddisflies and midges.

Poindexter's hatches begin with midges during late winter (the creek remains open year-round, catch and release between December 1 and the general opener in May). Those tiny insects can get the slough's trout feeding in a big way on the warmer days of late February and March, when the air temperature ranges between the high 30s and mid-40s. Patterns like a parachute Adams, Griffith's gnat, palomino, serendipity, suspender midge or brassie will take fish during the emergence.

Baetis mayflies set the table next, and they are present beginning in mid- to late March, extending through early May. Delicate patterns, such as olive sparkle duns, parachute Baetis, an olive thorax, RS-2 emergers, pheasant tails and hare's ear nymphs, will work during the emergence.

About the time Baetis taper off, expect significant caddis activity. Caddis can be tricky to match on spring creeks: be prepared with patterns that vary in size and color and match all stages of the hatch. Effective caddis patterns for Poindexter include the Hemingway caddis, partridge and peacock, LaFontaine sparkle pupa and the standard elk hair caddis, tied sparse.

Poindexter holds a nice population of rainbows and browns. Here, Scott Brown at the moment of truth with a 15-inch rainbow.

The dream mayfly of the summer season is the pale morning dun, and it gets Poindexter's trout riled up, as it does on most Western streams. Watch for PMDs to emerge between 10 AM and 3 PM. A second emergence may occur in the evening, beginning a couple hours before dark. Match the PMDs with sparkle duns, cripples, PMD no-hackles, PMD downwing spinners and standard pheasant tail nymphs.

Watch for Tricos on Poindexter in mid-July through early September. Tricos will demand the most of a flyfisher's patience, especially on spring creeks. Try matching them with downwing Tricos or a tiny parachute Adams. Remember, you may have to tippet down to 6X or 7X. Undoubtedly, that is when you will hook the largest fish— don't ask why. Just accept the odds and do your best to land a big trout—that is what advanced flyfishing is all about.

After the Tricos, watch for a resurgence in Baetis. Except during fall, expect them to run two or three sizes smaller than they did during spring. We're talking pseudocleons, and we're talking size 22 or 24 patterns to match them. Again, good luck.

Teller Spring Creek offers big rainbow and brown trout under difficult conditions. Stealth, delicate presentations and a measure of patience are key.

If all this small fly and light, long tippet talk has you ready to throw in the towel before you even wet a line, remember, when dark sets in on spring creeks, the biggest trout get active. Large streamers and mice patterns can take some huge fish under the moonglow. Just watch out for rogue skunks and rabies-crazed coyotes.

Overall, Poindexter is one of Montana's premier spring creeks, and much of its appeal rests in the fact that you do not have to cross private property or pay a fee to fish it. That can't be said for most of the state's springfed waters. When you are in the Dillon area, take a day away from the Beaverhead and gauge your progression as a flyfisher. If you walk away from the Slough with a wet net, you're doing pretty well.

Teller Spring Creek

This wonderful little spring creek winds its way through the heart of the Bitterroot Valley, passing through vast hayfields before cutting through dense cottonwood stands full of white-tailed deer and a few moose, on its way back to the Bitterroot River.

When the Bitterroot blows out, hit Teller Spring Creek. This big brown pounded an X-caddis when the big river ran the color of chocolate milk.

Unfortunately, Teller Spring Creek rests on private land. However, it is a section of private land called the Teller Wildlife Refuge that has progressive stewards who are willing to work with the environment and anglers instead of against them like so many new, wealthy Montanans do. In fact, access to Teller can be gained several ways. First, you can simply ask permission to fish—your odds of getting on have a lot to do with the last guests' behavior, which says a lot about respecting property and obeying rules. It's catch and release only on the Teller, no driving through the fields and don't venture onto neighboring properties.

The other way to fish Teller, this one guaranteed, is to book a few days at the refuge—lodging in a cool, old house is available. You will need to inquire about packages for lodging and fishing ahead of time. Teller Wildlife Refuge does not cater specifically to flyfishers—it is a wildlife refuge first, and the opportunity to fish exists to spur interest in that unique property.

The creek is a wonderful, twisting, mostly shallow, 10-yard-wide stream, sprinkled with some deep holes, undercut banks, downed logs and a couple small diversion dams. It is not an easy creek to fish, and its trout populations are not dense. Instead, this is a place where a good day consists of one or two fish—to expect more is setting yourself up for disaster. However, those two fish could measure a combined 48 inches. My best day at Teller resulted in two fish measuring (combined) 40 inches. Sorry to disappoint—they were not taken on dry flies.

However, Teller's rainbows and browns will take dry flies when the situation presents itself. Pale morning duns, caddis, Baetis and a few Tricos are present during the summer, and you'll bump into rising fish occasionally. If dries don't produce, do some searching with small nymphs or even a leech pattern—a size 6 brown mohair is a good choice.

The Mission Mountains offer an impressive backdrop while fishing the private waters of Mission Springs. Here, Scott Brown uses stealth on a big rainbow.

Stealth is paramount here: Keep a low profile and use the brush and high grass to block yourself from a trout's vision. Bring polarized glasses—sighting a fish before it detects you is crucial. Don't be afraid to use long leaders tapered down to 6X.

If you want to fish Teller, which is located a few hundred yards off the Eastside Highway just a mile north of Corvallis, call the refuge manager, Chris Miller at 406-961-3507. Reservation inquiries should be directed to 800-343-3707.

Mission Springs

Located at the base of the Mission Mountains near St. Ignatius in western Montana, Mission Springs consists of a series of springfed, fertile ponds that offer scenery galore, along with some oversized rainbow trout.

Mission Springs offers rainbows in the two- to four-pound class, and its owners are trying to establish large brook trout in the ponds, as well. Don't count on rainbows and brookies to be pushovers, even though you can see them cruising by several yards away. At times they can be very hard to catch, and that attitude can make anglers rifle through their fly boxes in search of a perfect pattern.

Mission Springs has a variety of good hatches, beginning with Callibaetis mayflies in May. Big rainbows will cruise the ponds, always visible to the angler, searching for swimming or emerging nymphs. Hare's ear and pheasant tail nymphs work wonders during the Callibaetis hatch.

Midges are always available to trout, and they may key on those tiny flies, especially early in the morning. Micropatterns are required in combination with 6X and 7X leaders. Good luck landing a fish after you hook one on that fine tippet!

Damselflies get active by June 1, and fishing can be fantastic. Big rainbows will charge many different patterns, including marabou damsels, six packs and Henry's Lake damsels.

After the damsel hatch, caddis are a staple. A popular, effective way to fish those caddis requires an angler to place the pattern in front of a cruising fish. A weighted fly will sink to the bottom, Just as a trout reaches the fly, give a twitch. The fly will kick up silt off the bottom, and a rainbow likely will pounce on it. Soft-hackled emerger patterns work wonders.

While scenery and an opportunity to catch large fish may be the spring's main draw, maybe most interesting is the opportunity to observe trout in a fertile habitat. Anglers can absorb a lot by sitting for an hour on a bluff above the ponds, watching trout suck nymphs off the bottom or rise deliberately to dry flies on the top. You will have to pay to play at Mission. To check out the action and the rates, call Mission Springs at 406-728-6840.

Paradise Valley Spring Creeks

If you love challenging trout, fish that require tiny flies, perfect presentations and a healthy dose of patience, the Paradise Valley's trio of small, private but superb spring creeks are worth a try.

Located just south of Livingston off of Route 89 on the west side of the Yellowstone River, Armstrong and DePuy Spring Creeks offer mostly 12- to 17-inch rainbows and browns, with the occasional monster reaching five pounds or more. Nelson's, located on the east side of the Yellowstone via Route 540, offers similar specimens. But you will have to pay to fish the creeks, and you don't want to wait around to make reservations. Slots are booked solid between April and October each year.

Nelson's, about three-quarters of a mile long, best survived the heavy floods of 1996. Fishing remains steady there. However, Armstrong suffered major flooding that wiped out a diversion dam and changed the structure of the creek indefinitely. If Armstrong is rehabilitated, it will again produce excellent spring creek conditions.

All three creeks receive a prime hatch of Baetis mayflies during spring. As the Baetis taper off in May, look for solid caddis emergences. In July and August, pale morning duns take over, and flyfishers can match that hatch with sparkle duns, cripples, no-hackles and nymphs like a pheasant tail or hare's ear.

Hoppers are present during late summer, and like trout everywhere, the spring creek's residents will pay attention to those terrestrials.

Fall brings back the Baetis hatches, although mayflies generally run smaller as the weather cools. Size 20 to 24 imitations are often required.

During winter, try various midge patterns: serendipities, palominos, a parachute Adams, and Griffith's gnats draw strikes. All three creeks offer the year-round option that is so hard to find during tough Montana winters. Because they are springfed, they remain warmer than the air temperature and do not freeze over. However, to fish these creeks on a winter day when temperatures can go below 30 degrees requires warm clothing, a high tolerance for pain and a sense of adventure.

Seasonal rates vary and prices may change each year, but you can always inquire about availability and rates by calling the creeks direct. For Armstrong call 406-222-2979; for Nelson's call 406-222-2159; and for DePuy call 406-222-0221. Livingston fly shops will also book and guide trips: Dan Bailey's Fly Shop and George Anderson's Yellowstone Angler are good choices.

MZ Ranch Spring Creeks

Located a few miles north of Belgrade on Dry Creek Road, access to these spring creeks used to be one of the most closely guarded secrets in the Gallatin Valley. But in 1999, the Milesnick family started making the waters of Benhart Spring Creek and Thompson Spring Creek, along with a portion of the East Gallatin River, available to flyfishermen for a daily rod fee. Both spring creeks flow into the East Gallatin River on the MZ Ranch, offering several miles of superb and often technical fishing. The prolific hatches here are similar to the Paradise Valley spring creeks, with the addition of excellent trico action in midsummer. There is currently a six-angler-per-day limit with a daily rod fee of $50. Call 406-388-6110 for more information or to make a reservation.

A Final Word on Spring Creeks

Spring creeks offer superb, yet delicate, habitat. Whenever you fish a spring creek, tread lightly. And because most of them have silt bottoms, limit your wading, especially when flyfishers are working the water below you. It's no fun to have a pile of moss come floating by you, and it's difficult to fish a spring creek full of mud.

I've mentioned a few springfed waters worthy of your attention—do not think that I've covered all of the options. There are small spring creeks sprinkled around the state, most of them private and too delicate for me to mention here, that offer excellent options. Talk to local guides and frequent flyshops if you're looking for a secret spring creek. If you come across as a nice person, respectful of Montana's habitat and wild trout, you might gain an invitation to visit one of the lesser-known waters. Good luck!

Big Spring Creek

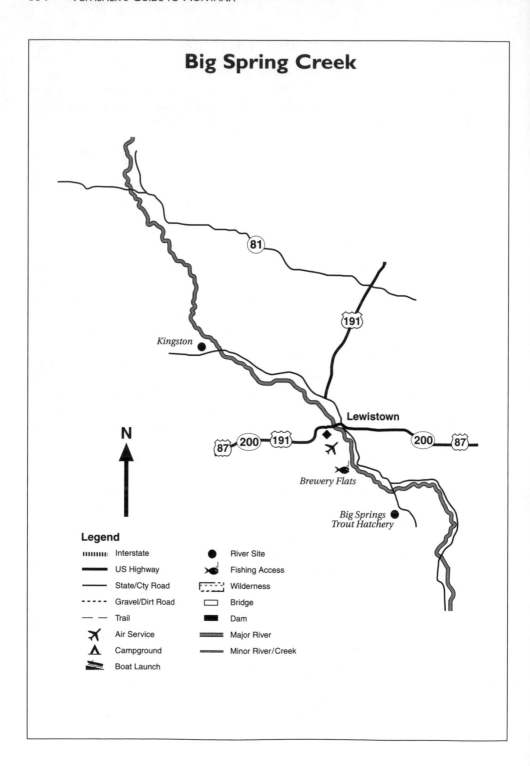

Big Spring Creek

Somewhere along Highway 191, about midway between Big Timber and Harlowton, Montana, you can search the roadside burrow pit for my coffee mug and a six pack of caddis emergers—prime flies tied during the summer season when any time spent behind the vice seams like too much time altogether.

If you find those flies, please enjoy them, but do consider the merit of a pre-1997 Ford pickup truck and the relative worthlessness of a new, stylish, ridiculously expensive and altogether hunk of junk Nissan truck.

If I had been driving my old Ford, with its triangle side window, that coffee mug and those flies would not have slid across the dashboard and flown right out the window. That's exactly what they did in the Nissan when I swerved around a big buck mule deer, narrowly avoiding an early freezer-clearing expedition.

I did turn around and search for my precious flies, but they were hopelessly lost in a 200-yard stretch of highway that I still cast weary glances at today. If I had retained those flies, I could have stayed on Big Spring Creek, but instead, my marginal patterns brought just a few takes.

Next time, soon I might add, I am buying American. And I'm going to sample the tasty attributes of Big Spring Creek the way they should be—with precise patterns and lots of takes from scrappy rainbows and browns that run 12 to 15 inches on average.

Big Spring Creek flows through the heart of Lewistown, Montana, offering an easy after work option for local flycasters. Big Spring would be a destination trout stream for visiting anglers, too, if it were not so far away from other prime waters. To reach Big Spring Creek from Livingston, an angler must drive at least 2.5 hours north. It's nearly the same distance from Great Falls or Billings. Add a half-hour to your trip if traveling from Helena. From Missoula, Butte and Kalispell, it's a three-day weekend at a minimum. And to reach Big Spring from almost anywhere, you'll have to pass a lot of prime water in the process. Due to those factors, the creek receives less pressure than other waters of similar or less productivity.

Big Spring is, essentially, a spring creek—it wells out of the ground at an amazing 64,000 gallons a minute. However, it differs from other spring creeks in that it can turn muddy any day of the summer after a heavy rain. It may turn color during spring due to accelerated flows out of its tributary streams. Despite its nuances, its size, about 10 to 14 yards wide in most places, and its fish, some up to 20 inches, make it an awesome little creek to fish. Just make sure to bring some light tippet material and a level of stealth.

"I think it's a very tough creek to fish," says Dale Pfau at Don's Sports in Lewistown, where they keep plenty of flyfishing equipment on hand, including about 2,000 to 3,000 flies at any given time. "Gosh, we have a lot of guys who come in and who think they know spring creeks and don't do well because they don't fish light enough or long enough leaders. This creek is nothing like the Bighorn or Madison, and it doesn't produce the huge hatches that those rivers do. You can take fish on dry flies here, but you have to be good. You will catch a lot more fish on nymphs."

Big Spring Creek twists along Route 426 west of Lewistown and Route 466 east of town. To the east, rainbow trout dominate; below town there are more browns. In both sections, which total about 30 miles, Big Spring meanders seemingly aimlessly until you step into the water and feel the determination of its flow. It is not a classic spring creek in that glassy surface mold. Instead, on the upper stretch Big Spring hides its trout beneath undercut banks, in deep pools formed in the curves and in the riffles that quickly drop off into deep holes. In most places, when the water is clear, you can see to the bottom—and you will see fish. Presenting a fly to them in a manner that seems appropriate is another matter. In its lower reach, which ultimately dumps into the Judith River, Big Spring Creek weaves through sagebrush and grass rangeland, and its trout-holding water is less defined.

"If the fish are active and you are a good nymph fisherman, you'll do well here," says Jim Drissell, fish culturist at Big Springs Trout Hatchery on the upper end of the creek. "But it can be especially hard to get a good drift. Most of the time you want to put a nymph near the bottom, but in the summer you can often find the fish up top during the prehatch stage. Other times you just can't buy a fish. For whatever reason, you may fish through a half-dozen nice holes in a row—places you've caught fish in the past—and not touch a fish. You know there are fish in those holes, but they won't take. Then you'll hit the next hole, and the fish will be all over what you're offering. It can be interesting."

Big Spring fishes well during spring, summer and fall, and you can even take a few fish during winter. But you'll have to throw diminutive midge patterns off of light tippets. According to Drissell, the creek does offer opportunities during the cold season, but not good enough to travel very far. For a change of pace from watching playoff football games on a Sunday, the river is ideal. To travel more than 40 miles to reach its banks between December 1 and March 15 means you live an entirely boring life.

"The best months are March through October," Drissell says. "The little blue-winged olives start things off in March and April, and they can provide some pretty good dry-fly fishing. Sometimes it's a pretty dense hatch, but overall it's not one of those super-duper emergences. It's a little sporadic—hit and miss. If I see the fish working during the olive hatch, I like to use small imitations, size 16 and 18 sparkle duns or a pheasant tail nymph."

In April and May, it's time to keep your eyes peeled for Big Spring Creek's most important food item—the caddis. Once they begin emerging, you should find them present each day through summer.

"At any given time of the year, caddis are the major food source," Pfau says. "It starts up in late spring, and fishing can be decent with caddis imitations. But in summer, caddis are the ticket. I think an elk hair caddis works best consistently. I like them in size 14 or 16 during the spring and size 10 or 12 in the summer. I drop back down to size 16 and 18 during fall. I'd fish one with a peacock body."

Drissell knows the importance of caddis on this stream, too. He will fish an elk hair caddis, also, but he swears by the sparkle pupa and soft hackles—emergent caddis patterns. It pays to carry a few in your fly box; try them just before dark.

Big Spring Creek won't produce many trophy trout, but it holds an excellent population of rainbow and brown trout. Here, Dawn Bostrom hoists a typical rainbow.

By early July, flyfishers should encounter pale morning duns on the water. Big Spring's trout will turn onto those duns during all stages of the hatch. A flyfisher should carry a few hare's ear and pheasant tail nymphs to try underneath the surface. Several parachute PMDs and cripple patterns will pay dividends, too.

According to Drissell, July is the month when visiting anglers should steer their rigs toward Big Spring Creek.

"It's really tough to pick one time to fish this creek, because it is almost always good," he says. "If there wasn't the runoff to deal with, I would say spring would be best. But rains and runoff can muddy up the creek for a month or more. By late June and July, the creek is reliable and the hatches are pretty good. There will be caddis and mayflies every day. The fish are on them and the weather is nice."

While Montana's large rivers garner all the hype, it's the small streams like Big Spring that very well might be the most fun to fish. Big Spring is a classic wade fishing water—impossible to float—and it's not a bad place to start a youngster out.

Armed with an 8-foot, 4-weight rod and a floating line, a beginner can pound away on the water and learn much in a day. They'll read water, realize that splashy presentations and clumsy wading will spook trout. And they'll discover the merit of stealth and delicate presentations. If your fishing buddy blows a hole, so what. In a few yards, the table is freshly set; you can't walk 30 yards on the upper river without encountering a prime riffle, followed by a deep hole. Just make sure to stock up on flies before you hit the water. The bankside brush gobbles up flies like candy.

Fall is not a bad time to fish the creek, either, with brown trout on the spawn, grasshoppers crashing off the banks and blue-winged olives hatching on warm days.

"Fall is an excellent season," Pfau says. "There aren't too many people fishing the creek, and all you have to do is walk the banks and look for spawning browns. You can see them in the river on the gravel beds. I like to fish with nymphs and that gets them. Sometimes I'll fish streamers. It can be really good fishing, but you do have to be careful when wading—you don't want to step on the brown trout redds."

Big Spring Creek may never achieve the legendary status that many of Montana's more accessible rivers can claim, but it is truly a great fishery. Residents of Lewistown cross their fingers, keep their mouths closed, and hope their little haven remains undiscovered. In truth, Big Spring is a long drive from anywhere to catch an average size trout. But, out in the middle of Montana, wading down the creek on a summer evening, with trout rising eagerly to adult caddis and coyotes singing from the side hills, there is not a better place to be.

To reach Big Spring Creek, travel north on Highway 191 from Big Timber. Turn east on U.S. 87 at Moore. When you reach Lewistown, grab a bite to eat at Poor Man's or Whole Famdamily on Main Street. Then pick a section of stream to fish. If you want the upper river, head east out of town. To test the lower river, head west.

Stream Facts: Big Spring Creek

Seasons
• Open all year.

Trout
• Rainbow, and brown trout. Most rainbows run 10 to 14 inches with a few to 20 inches or more. They are predominant in the upper section. Most browns will go 12 to 15 inches and they are predominant in the lower creek.

River Miles
• Upper Creek: About seven miles from Big Springs Hatchery to Lewistown.
• Lower Creek: About 24 miles from Lewistown to its confluence with the Judith River.

River Flows
• Big Spring Creek can run high and cloudy from mid May through late June. In July the river calms down and excellent conditions persist through October.

River Characteristics
• Upper River: Relatively fast water with typical riffle, run, pool, glide habitat. Brushy banks.
• Lower River: Flows through flatlands with low gradient. Lots of undercut banks.

Fishing Access
• There are several public access points located along the river. Follow high way signs.

Area Fly Shops
• The Sports Center, 320 W. Main Street, Lewistown, MT, 406-538-9308
• Don's Sports at Janeaux and 2nd Ave. S., Lewistown, 406-538-9408

BIG SPRING CREEK MAJOR HATCHES

Insect	J	F	M	A	M	J	J	A	S	O	N	D	Flies
Baetis					■					■			Olive Cripple # 16-20; Parachute Adams #16-20; Sparkle Dun #16-20; Hares Ear Nymph #16-20; Pheasant Tail Nymph #16-20; Poxyback Baetis #16-20
Caddis						■			■				Elk Hair Caddis #14-18; Diving Caddis #14-16; X-Caddis # 14-16; Drifting Cased Caddis #14-18; Emergent Sparkle Pupa #12-18; Deep Sparkle Pupa #12-18; Electric Caddis #14-16; Caddis Variant #14-16; Orange Serendipity #6-12
Pale Morning Dun						■							Sparkle Dun #14-20; PMD Cripple #16-20; Poxy Biot Nymph #16-20; Hare's Ear Nymph #16-18; Pheasant Tail Nymph #16-18; CDC Floating Nymph #16-18

Planning a Trip

So many rivers, so little time. There are so many choice trout waters in Montana, even hard-core resident flyfishers can not hit all of them in a year, let alone a lifetime. That is an almost unbearable reality for some of us.

Throw in all the prime pike and bass options and depression really sets in; work is overrated, jobs should be shunned, spouses postponed, a line thrown on the water each day of the year. Time is short. Fishing so sweet.

The situation is worse for visiting anglers—how in the heck do you quench a thirst for so many unfamiliar waters in a week? The answer is, you simply can not do it.

Many resident and nonresident flyfishers attempt to remedy their time-frame predicament by squeezing a number of well-known waters into a week long itinerary. In my opinion, that approach is set-up for disaster. You can not effectively fish more than one or two rivers or lakes in a week. River hopping—bouncing from one water to the next for a day or two at a time is normally unproductive; better to pick one or two waters and stick with them.

You will learn much about a river or lake in a week, not the least important being the nuances of local characters who frequent its banks. Tips can be shared on hatches, fly patterns exchanged and serious knowledge gained. Those who choose to river-hop will see a lot of country, meet fewer flyfishers and, likely, catch far fewer fish. Less time will be had on the water. Instead, those precious hours will be spent on the blacktop and dusty roads of Montana, gazing at the aluminum airstreams.

The Merits of Hiring a Guide

If you must fish many waters in a short time, or if you plan to fish just one stream, a guide can help you gain knowledge, and fish on the end of your, line quickly.

Realize this: most guides are hard-core flyfishers. When they usher you off the water at the end of a day, they very well might go back to the river at dark, if they don't join you for dinner or a drink, and pitch big woolly buggers for god-awfully big brown trout. They are possessed. Fish or Die is their motto. They cling fiercely to Tom McGuane's famous words, "If trout are lost, smash the state."

These men and women are good people, dedicated to their quarry and they know their local waters intimately. They know the hatches, the killer fly patterns, the prime holes and the nuances of trout. When a client really needs a fish, those guides can usually find one.

If you can afford one, book a guide for at least one day during your stay. You will learn so much about the area you are fishing, maybe even some secret, tucked-away spots, that the trip pays for itself many times over. Your money is well invested with a guide; the return is immense.

Standard guide rates in Montana fluctuate from $240 to $300. That price will provide one guide for two people, a drift boat or raft if you need one, a very hearty lunch (a guide should provide more food and drink than required), shuttle service, and plenty of great conversation. That fee does not guarantee that you will catch a fish. Rods, reels and flies are not included as rental in that price.

If the fishing is slow, don't' blame your guide; conditions vary from day to day and even the best flyfishers sometimes find themselves scratching their heads, fishless for the day. When the catching is slow, tap your guide for information, learn from them. That is what you are really paying for. Remember this: always have fun no matter what he circumstances bring. Flyfishing is an adventure. If you judge the merit of a day simply by the number of trout brought to net, you are setting yourself up for failure.

Remember too, guides should be tipped for their efforts; outfitters (guides must be licensed through outfitters) eat up between 40 and 60 percent of that guide fee you pay.

Rods and Reels: Do Not Skimp

Rods: Resident and visiting flyfishers should not jeopardize a day on the water by using flimsy equipment.

It is true, you can get by with a relatively inexpensive outfit, one that you might find for, say, $49.95 at K-Mart. However, you certainly can not count on an outfit like that to perform admirably in varied conditions, if any conditions at all.

Those cheap noodle sticks are death when the wind comes up—and the big blow can terrorize Montana's waters on any given day of the year. When you only have a day or a week to fish, losing time on the water due to insufficient equipment is a shame.

If I had to pick an all-purpose rod for Montana, I would choose a 9-foot 6-weight; it is heavy enough to punch through the wind, it has enough backbone to allow landing a large fish quickly, and yet it is light enough that you will still garner a fight from a 12-inch trout. There may be more ideal rods for certain situations, but you can get away with a 9-foot, 6-weight in any situation, aside from foul-hooking a 100-pound paddlefish on the lower Missouri!

With that said, a 9-foot 5-weight is not a bad rod choice either, in fact it covers almost every situation. And, a 9-foot 4-weight is killer for smaller streams and spring creeks, which may require long, light tippets and heavy-duty stealth.

Personally, I like Sage, Thomas & Thomas and Orvis rods; they are durable, reliable, handsome and backed by good people. I use a 9-foot 6-weight Sage, a high school graduation present from my family, on many waters in the West and it's never failed me; it's accounted for rainbows up to 8 pounds (released) on the Blackfoot Reservation lakes, and a 42-inch buck steelhead (released) in Alaska. And, after an hour-long marathon, I actually landed a 46-pound king salmon (released) on it, again in Alaska.

The Orvis I fish is a 9-foot 5-weight Trident. It has a fast action and plenty of power for a five-weight. It is an ideal rod for the larger rivers, like the Bighorn, Madison, Clark Fork and Bitterroot—all can have some serious bouts with the wind and the Trident cuts right through it. However, the rod is maneuverable enough that it sees its fair share of use on the smaller streams like the Clearwater, Musselshell and Rock Creek. When a large fish is hooked in a fast section of a small stream, like Rock Creek, that added power of a 5-weight Trident is a bonus.

Not only can guides put you on fish, they provide hearty lunches, excellent conversation and an endless source of information.

The Thomas & Thomas I use is a 9-foot 4-weight that is a dream on spring creeks and small tributary cutthroat waters. When the longest casts and major mends are not required, this is the rod to have.

Both Orvis and Sage back their rods with guarantees; snap it in a truck door or while fending off a rattlesnake and they'll replace it or fix free of charge. That is an enormous bonus when using a rod that may cost a few hundred dollars. I fish very hard with my rods, have broken them many times, and these companies back up their promise.

Reels: Your rod must harbor a reel; disk-drag, single-actions are the best. Leave that old automatic-retrieve on the shelf in the garage.

Many people consider a reel the least important element of their flyfishing equipment. I disagree. A reel with a smooth drag makes the difference between landing large fish on light leaders and breaking them off on the take.

For example, say you are fishing the Missouri River in August when the Tricos arrive in mass. A large trout, a four-pounder, is up top in a foam eddy slurping size 22 spent wing Trikes.

You tippet down to 6X, just to get the tippet through the eye of your tiny size 22 fly. Then you cast, mend the line so that you get a perfect dead-drift right over the trout's snout. First a nose appears above the river's surface and suddenly your fly is gone. The fish turns downstream, heads for the bottom, and finally feels that prick of the hook tip. He throws his head from side to side, then takes off downstream in a sizzling run.

If you have a reel with a good, light drag, you'll hold that fish when he turns and runs. A cheap reel with an unreliable drag that releases line and then locks up will bust that fish right off—the four- or five-pounder of your dreams long gone. Smooth drags are equally important when fishing for large trout in stillwaters.

Reels that I've enjoyed success with under various conditions include Abel, Marryat and STH. They all have excellent disk drags, they are beautiful and they are durable. The Marryat is particularly attractive due to its light weight and ultra-smooth drag. I've held large trout, rainbows to four pounds, on 6X tippet with the Marryat.

Leaders: For a week-long stint on Montana's rivers, you will want to carry plenty of packaged, knotless leaders. And you will want to have a varied supply. Do not head out on the river for a day without at least two 6X, two 5X and two 4X leaders. The 6X is ideal when fishing small dry flies on flat-surfaced water to selective trout. In some situations, you can't get a trout to rise on anything heavier than 6X.

A 5X tippet is the most versatile leader for Montana. It is light enough to fish dry flies, yet heavy enough to throw a weighted nymph. Plus, if you encounter some selective fish, you can tie a section of 6X tippet (from a spool) onto it.

A 4X or 3X leader is ideal for throwing the big junk, like woolly buggers, zonkers, stonefly nymphs and six-inch sculpins. A heavier tippet allows a flyfisher to pry flies out of the brush or off submerged rocks and limbs.

It is advisable to carry spools of tippet material in 5X and 6X. Sometimes 7X comes in handy, too. When your 5X or 6X leader is cut back, you can tie on a new section of tippet from a spool. Using tippet from a spool extends the life of your leader indefinitely—and it saves you money in the long run.

Flies: I try to carry as many fly patterns as possible. Every year I read articles by various outdoor writers who claim the entire spectrum of aquatic insects can be covered with, say, 10 or 12 patterns. You've seen those articles—"The Dirty Dozen" or "The Top Ten."

Those who write such articles must not fish very much, because each season, many times over, I rummage through my fly boxes, loaded with dozens of patterns, and can't come up with the proper imitation.

The stocked fly box will contain patterns to match various mayfly, caddis, stonefly, midge, moth, terrestrial, and minnow species. And it will cover all hatch stages. For instance, nymph, emerger, dun, crippled and spinner patterns should be included for each mayfly species present on Montana's waters.

Larvae, emerger, adult and spent patterns should be carried for caddis. Stone-flies should be matched by large nymphs and dries. Fishing midge hatches success-fully requires a box full of larvae, emerger, and adult patterns in various colors.

General patterns will cover moths, hoppers and other terrestrials like ants and beetles. Baitfish can be covered with various colored streamers, such as woolly buggers, sculpins and awkwardly named dandies like the yellow yummie—a Big Hole River standby.

If matching the hatch sounds like too much work and too much money, you do have another option: you can walk into a good fly shop, ask the owner to help you, and walk out with exactly the patterns required to fish a particular stream or lake suc-cessfully that day. If it seems as though the owner is trying to sell you too many flies, consider this: that man or woman probably wants you to have a great time, and they are just covering all the bases.

Weather (waders and a good rain jacket are required): Hey, you know the weather: no matter where in the world you are at any given moment, anything can happen.

In Montana, we've seen six inches of snow on the ground in July. However, on a normal July day, the temperature will peak somewhere between 80 and 90 degrees.

During spring, the temperature can range between 10 and 80 degrees. During winter—well, it's pretty darn cold on almost any given day.

What those temperature ranges suggest is the need for plenty of clothes for var-ious conditions. If you are going to be in the water wading during spring, winter or fall, use neoprene chest waders and put some layers on underneath them. During summer, a pair of lightweight waders serve best.

I use various brands of neoprene waders, and I find that Orvis and Simms are extremely durable and reliable. BARE and Hodgeman perform well for my fishing partners. A 4mm or 5mm rating will keep you warm when the water is cold. I wore my pair of Orvis Battenkill Guide waders into the Gallatin River one December morn-ing with the air temperature hovering at 5 degrees and ice building in the river from the bottom up! I had two pair of wool socks on, a pair of Lightweight Synchilla Pants and a Synchilla Snap T with a collar on up top. I remained warm for the three hours I spent in the river, and I caught a couple of browns over 17 inches!

During summer, if I am not wet wading, I'll wear a pair of Orvis breathable waders. With those on, I will not swelter under the sometimes incessant sunshine. The waders keep leeches off my legs, and they keep me warm and on the water after the sun goes down, when so many caddis swarms and mayfly spinnerfalls occur.

Rain can also be a factor for a Montana fishing trip any day of the year. A Gore-Tex coat, such as an Orvis, Patagonia or Streamline, will shed water like a sealskin. And all three will last seasons. Combined with neoprene waders, a Gore-Tex coat provides an invincible shield against the wind and rain. If you can afford one, buy a Gore-Tex jacket and bring it with you on the water every time you go out. Even on a sunny, warm day, afternoon thundershowers can drench anglers. Combine that dampness with a strong wind, and the potential to become very cold exists.

Lines: A general rule about lines is this: the more lines you carry the better. However, most situations call for a floating line.

A floating line is essential for dry-fly fishing—without it an angler is doomed. And in most instances, it is also the ideal nymph line. But a fullsink or sinktip line is handy when you really need to get deep.

On most Montana rivers, a floating line can be weighted with split shot to achieve depth when needed. However, on a lake, a fullsink, 10-foot sinktip or 20-foot sinktip is awfully handy. In fact, having a sinking line can make or break your day—when the fish hug the bottom, you have to get down to them no matter how far they go.

When choosing a floating line, flyfishers must decide between a double taper or a weight forward.

Double tapers are more delicate, and you can reverse the line on the spool once one end is worn out, which doubles the life of the line. However, a weight-forward line offers more distance when casting, and it turns over large nymphs and streamers better. But when one end is in tatters, the life of the line is over — time to head for the fly shop. I've had the best luck with Scientific Anglers' lines; they carry a variety of choices, including different colors, that are suited to all types of flyfishing situations.

Sunglasses

Behind your rod, reel, line, leader and flies, possibly the most important piece of fishing equipment you can own is a quality pair of polarized sunglasses. There are a number of companies that manufacture cheap sunglasses, and you will become acquainted with that fact if you skimp and buy a marginal pair. They will only deflect glare from your eyes and will not allow you to see into the water. And seeing into the water is key.

Let's say you are working a small spring creek with wary trout. Without polarized sunglasses, you might waltz right up to the bank without ever seeing a trout and begin casting. Every trout in the neighborhood will streak for cover at Mach 1. Instead, you need to spot fish from a distance, then stalk them like you would an unsuspecting, yet wary herd of deer or elk. Polarized glasses will allow you to do that.

Good glasses also come into play when you are floating a broad river. With polarized sunglasses, you can detect submerged gravel bars, shoals and dangerous sweepers, which will prevent the bottom of your boat from being torn off on a rock or log. You will also sight from a distance, prime holes and runs, which should buy you enough time to position the boat ideally for your company—and that means more trout brought to the net.

I fish with Action Optics and SMITH sunglasses that are built in Ketchum, Idaho, right next to the ultimate testing ground, Silver Creek. Silver Creek's trout are the trickiest you'll find anywhere, and you need an excellent pair of sunglasses to fish that fertile spring creek successfully. Fortunately, Peter Crow and many of his fellow staffers at Action Optics and SMITH are avid flyfishers. They understand the problems that difficult waters present, and their glasses show that research; I have not used more effective lenses. I've tried the Tailwater and Otis models from Action Optics, and they both perform wonderfully. I can usually see to the bottom of a river in all but the deepest places. All of their models are available in a variety of lenses that are suited to specific fishing conditions—morning, afternoon and early evening light. You can get the lenses in prescription or nonprescription. And, unlike many brands on the market, their frames are good looking; you can wear them to the river or to the bar and you don't have to feel like a poser.

Storing Your Gear on the Stream

Wherever you choose to fish in Montana, you must pack gear along with you. You'll need a vest, backpack or smaller storage compartment. Fortunately, there are excellent options for whatever method you choose.

Vests are self-explanatory; you can find a number of good ones from manufacturers like Patagonia, Columbia and Orvis. They have lots of zipper pockets in varying sizes that accommodate fly boxes, reels, extra spools, cameras, sunglasses, etc. You will not be able to spend a day astream with all the gear you need stuffed into the chest pocket of your flannel shirt.

If you opt against the vest, try a smaller storage system that attaches to your belt or one that can be strapped over your neck to ride against your chest. Wood River is carrying a large line of these smaller storage systems, and they work quite well with adjustable compartments that hold various size fly boxes. They also can be strapped to your floattube.

Another option, especially if you are hiking into a destination like Fish Creek, the upper Boulder River, the South Fork Flathead or any of the mountain lakes in the state, is the Pack Vest from Patagonia. The Pack-Vest can be used to haul in waders, rain jackets and other gear to your destination. Once there, you can detach the vest from the backpack and fish without the bulk of a pack. I have not been able to use one of the packs personally, but I hear they work great.

Another idea is the traditional fly box that hangs from your neck and straddles the chest. Most come with multiple compartments and three or four layers for storing different fly patterns. One level might be for caddis, another for mayflies, and another for nymphs, streamers and large dries. Flies on Water in Ketchum, Idaho, is offering the traditional three tier box and a similar box that is less bulky with one layer. It also includes a 4-spool tippet dispenser and magnifier light. It has enough room to harbor a few fresh tippets and forceps.

Winter Flyfishing Checklist

If you are going to fish Montana during the early spring, late fall or winter, you must wear proper clothing—warmth is everything. If you wear inadequate clothing and wade too deep, you'll be singing the high-pitched coyote blues. Here is a list of winter gear that is essential:

- Neoprene chest waders of at least 4mm thickness—a 5mm thickness is better
- Polar fleece pants and pullover shirts worn over Capilene® underwear

- Stocking cap that can be pulled down to cover ears and neck
- Wool socks with liners
- Polar fleece gloves
- A thermos with warm liquid
- A Gore-Tex raincoat
- High-energy food, like a Power Bar, Nutri Grain or, the standby, a Snickers bar

Warm Weather Flyfishing Checklist

- Rods in 4-,5- or 6-weight class
- Lines to match
- Reels with a disc drag that fit the accompanying rod
- Fishing vest or chest pack
- Forceps for removing hook from a fish's mouth
- Tapered leaders in 4X, 5X and 6X
- Spools of tippet in 5X and 6X
- Fly patterns to match caddis, mayfly, stonefly, midge, moth, grasshopper, beetle, ant and baitfish
- Dry-fly floatant (Gink or Aquel)
- Dry-fly shake (powder)
- Fishing net
- Twist-Ons or split shot
- Lightweight chest waders or hip boots
- Polarized sunglasses (next in importance behind rod, reel, line and flies)
- Long-billed ball cap
- Gore-Tex raincoat
- Lots of sunscreen
- A gallon of water
- Insect repellent
- Camera with film and wet bag (a gallon size Zip-Lock works well)
- Small flashlight

Flying In and Getting Around

You can fly into major airports in Montana, but your arrival is always weather dependent. Billings, Bozeman, Great Falls, Helena, Missoula and Kalispell all have jet service.

When you travel to Montana, try to keep all your essential gear in a carry-on bag —rods, reels, a vest, camera and flies should be packed with you. No need to tempt disaster by checking that baggage.

If you are not on a fully-guided trip or haven't driven to your destination, you will need to rent a vehicle to get around.

Remember this: a solid dirt road in Montana can turn to gumbo overnight. Rent a four-wheel drive whenever possible.

Catch and Release

Much has been written about catch-and-release angling and most of those words vehemently oppose the taking of any gamefish.

Articles on the subject read like this: Those who bonk a trout on the noggin will be dipped in whale oil and tossed to a pool of emaciated piranhas.

But how about a conscientious angler who likes to eat trout or salmon? Are there any situations where taking a fish actually benefits a population? Or, at least, doesn't damage fishing opportunity?

My answer, although I can't remember the last fish I killed, is yes. There are certain places, under a set of conditions, that allow the taking of a fish or two. However, if I see you bonking a trout on, say, Rock Creek, I just might stone your riffle and throw beaded porcupine quills at your back!

A general rule to remember is this: take a fish or two — not your limit — from a reservoir or lake. If you are fishing a river, stream or spring creek, let those trout go.

Here's why: trout grow large rapidly in lakes and reservoirs, dining on a smorgasbord of easily caught aquatic insects, crustaceans and fish. They have no current to battle, so very little of their energy is used maintaining a position in the water. Instead, they put that energy into quick strikes against aquatic insects or small baitfish. Extra energy is put into growth. In most cases, when a stillwater trout is harvested by an angler, it is quickly replaced by another solid specimen.

So visit Canyon Ferry Reservoir, the Browning Reservation lakes or Clark Canyon Reservoir, and take a fish home for dinner. Or hike into a mountain lake and satisfy your hunger with a few small trout. Mountain lakes are typically overpopulated. Taking a few fish from a lake that teems with six-inchers can only help a population.

But remember: If you switch from a lake or reservoir to a river like the Missouri, Beaverhead or Flathead, among others, the whole ballgame changes.

River and stream trout grow slowly. Most of their energy is spent maintaining a hold against powerful currents and dodging logs. What is left over is divided between foraging and growth. Because survival is so trying, stream trout rarely exceed 12 inches. Those that grow bigger have survived the odds for three or four years.

To illustrate the difference between stillwater and stream trout, check this out: in north Idaho's Lake Pend Oreille, some rainbow trout grew from fingerlings to 25-pounders in just four years. At least one reached 37 pounds by its fifth year!

In comparison, during a four-year time span, a rainbow trout in the Clark Fork, Blackfoot, Big Hole or Missouri Rivers will normally not exceed 20 inches by its fourth year. Stream trout require lots of time to grow, and unless river anglers return their catch, all of us will sing the blues when dreaming of large river trout.

While catch and release is good practice, especially in rivers, it can be taken to the extreme in some cases. And my mother, Rita, holds the title.

She caught and tried to release a 125-pound halibut in southeast Alaska. My father and his friend quickly dispatched the fish and any hope my mother had of

Forceps greatly aid a flyfisher when releasing fish. No flyfisher should leave home without a pair pinched to his vest.

being the first on record to ever willingly release a legal-size halibut. In my eyes, it was an admirable attempt. She could have started a revolution.

While the situation may change from one place to another, keep in mind that catch and release is needed on most waters. When in doubt, release a fish. If you are going to keep a fish, do so on a stillwater.

Montana Game Fish

CUTTHROAT TROUT: NATIVE SONS OF THE WEST

The favorite trout of dry fly purists, the cutthroat's lusty rises to fur-and-feather imitations gladden the hearts of novice and expert fly fishers alike.

Cutthroat usually fight stubbornly underwater and use stream flows to their advantage, sometimes even rolling with the current and twisting the line around themselves. But it is often a short-lived fight if your terminal tackle is not too delicate and you are not forced to prolong it.

Until other species were introduced in the late 1800s, the cutthroat was the only trout in much of the vast interior of the West, from the western slopes of the Sierras in California, north through Utah, Idaho, and Montana, and south to northern Mexico. The rainbow, another native trout of the West, was historically a Pacific slope fish.

Originally, the cutthroat and rainbow were considered to be descendants of the Atlantic salmon, Salmo salar. Taxonomy specialists agreed in 1990 that western trout are more closely related to the Pacific salmon. Descendants of this genus are listed as *Oncorhynchus*, which means "hooked snout."

Ironically, the taxonomists only recently caught up with the 1804-1806 Corps of Discovery. Meriwether Lewis first recorded the cutthroat for science in 1805 in western Montana. The men of the Lewis and Clark Expedition and later mountain men referred to the fish as the "trout salmon" because of its rich, orange flesh. The Yellowstone or interior cutthroat is now known by biologists as *Oncorhyncus clarki bouvieri*. The westslope cutthroat's scientific name, *Oncorhyncus clarki lewisi*, honors both captains sent west by President Jefferson to discover a route to the Pacific Ocean.

The Yellowstone cutthroat is a beautiful fish, with rouge-colored gill plates, a rose wash running across its golden flanks, and fins tinted with a translucent salmon-orange. Hundreds of round, black spots are sprinkled across its back, with somewhat larger and more heavily concentrated spots on its tail. Its name, and fame, comes from the bright orange-red slashes under its jaws. It is the ancestral parent stock of all the many interior subspecies that evolved in the Intermountain West.

It is evident the Yellowstone cutthroat once had a much broader historical range. Its taxonomic placement is based on the scientific species description made by a U.S. Army officer in 1882 from fish taken from Waha Lake, a now isolated basin north of Lewiston, Idaho.

The westslope cutthroat is native to a huge historical range that once included the entire upper Missouri River drainage in Montana and extended into Alberta and British Columbia, and a few rivers or lakes in Oregon and Washington.

As an environmental barometer of the mountains, the cutthroat is like the canary in the mine—it is the first species to be eliminated. Most of the 15 subspecies of this vulnerable, colorful fish are now largely restricted to the uppermost, coldest, headwater tributaries. A few that adapted to lower, warmer water conditions of Utah and Nevada's Basin and Range alkaline lakes and streams are largely gone or only shadows of their former glory.

Stronghold of the cutthroat is Yellowstone National Park, where the Yellowstone or interior cutthroat reigns supreme. The Yellowstone River and all of its drainages form the finest collection of cutthroat waters in the world.

Studies show the cutthroat can be easily overexploited by anglers. Even with light fishing pressure, up to half the legal-sized cutthroat in a stream are often caught. But, studies in Yellowstone show the fish are amazingly hearty. Cutthroat on the upper Yellowstone, in the park at Buffalo Ford, are caught and released an average of nine times during the river's short fishing season from mid-July to mid-October. For this reason, the fish responds well to special regulations, such as size or bag limits, or catch-and-release restrictions. They do not respond as well to hybridization with introduced species, like the rainbow.

The threat of hybridization and competition from other species is unfortunate. As the native trout that evolved in these waters, cutthroat grow at a better rate in a shorter period of time than their introduced brethren, including rainbow, brown, brook, and lake trout. Under wild trout management, cutthroat provide fish of remarkable size for the angler in all but the smallest streams. They have been known to live to 11 years of age, although six or seven is more common.

Cutthroat evolved to spawn on the spring floods common to the Northern Rockies. For this reason, a number of key tributaries with major spawning runs are off-limits to anglers during the earlier part of the fishing season, extending to late-summer on some creeks.

Spawning normally occurs in April or May; the same period rainbow spawn, which accounts for the threat of hybridization. The Yellowstone race of cutthroat spawn at three or four years of age. The westslope cutthroat is usually five when it first spawns.

The westslope cutthroat also differs from the Yellowstone race in its food choice. It primarily consumes insects and rarely feeds on other fish. This was probably an evolutionary adaptation to allow it to coexist with the predatory bull trout that shared the same waters. Fish form a sizable portion of the diet of larger Yellowstone cutthroat, which also rely heavily on aquatic and terrestrial insects.

The effects of these feeding preferences are reflected in the size differences between westslope and Yellowstone cutthroat.

Twelve to 15 inches is considered a good-size westslope, although occasional larger fish occur. Maximum growth is about three pounds, but it rarely exceeds two pounds because of its nonpiscivorous nature.

Twelve to 17 inches is the average size of Yellowstone cutthroat, with some growing more than 20 inches. It often grows to five or six pounds.

Cutthroat are most active in water temperatures between 50 and 65 degrees Fahrenheit. They can be found in both fast and slack water, although they are less fond of exceptionally fast waters than rainbows. Like all trout, they take advantage of whatever structural protection a stream provides, from over-hanging, willow-lined banks to midstream boulders, logjams, streambed depressions and deep pools at the base of riffles.

Never pass a logjam or a bank side feeding lane protected by an overhanging tree without working it closely. Riffles also are prime feeding grounds of cutthroat and provide prodigious action, especially at the lip of a deep pool.

The cutthroat's reputation for eagerly rising to a dry fly remains paramount in most fly fishers' minds. Larger cutthroat will hit a stonefly or hopper pattern with slashing strikes rivaling the ferocity of rainbows or browns. Casting to the feeding frenzy on the lip of a riffle during a heavy caddis or mayfly hatch can bring a host of fish between eight and 20 inches to the net. At the same time, a hit during selective, sipping rises to tiny mayflies will startle the angler who hooks a lunker lurking beneath the still waters.

A standard set of dry flies to attract cutthroat should include elk hair caddis, stimulators, yellow sallies, humpies, Adams, pale morning dun, blue-winged olive, light Cahill, and parachute hare's ear. Nymph and emerger patterns for each of these can be equally effective, especially on riffles. Effective sizes for both dry and wet caddis and mayfly patterns can range from No. 10 to 16 in spring and early summer. By late fall, you may have to go as small as No. 18 and 22.

When all else fails, or on big or heavy waters, you can always fall back on standard attractor flies like the renegade, royal Wulff, royal coachman, royal Trude, Goddard caddis, or irresistible.

Cutthroat also succumb to the usual assortment of small streamers, muddlers, weighted nymphs, woolly buggers, super renegades and rubber-legged patterns. Sizes No. 8 to 14 generally work best.

Cutthroat can be the least shy of the trout family. Occasionally, you can get amazingly close to feeding fish. On some streams, they may even be right underfoot, feeding on nymphs your boots stir up from the gravel. One time, I witnessed huge Yellowstone River cutthroats allowing numerous size 14 March brown drakes to drift over their heads. They wouldn't touch them. Then, unbelievably, a shy kid dropped a Cheeto off a bridge and a big fish pounded it. I talked him into dropping a few more and each time the offer was accepted.

But never underestimate the cutthroat. It is not a brown trout with a lobotomy, as some would disparage this remarkable fish. It can be easy to catch and it can be exactingly selective as it keys in on a specific mayfly or caddis hatch with the resolute intensity of one of its so-called educated brethren.

Either way, cutthroat are a joy to catch and behold.

Cutthroat Trout Identification

Yellowstone Cutthroat Trout (*Oncorhyncus clarki bouvieri*)

The body coloration on the back ranges from silver-gray to olive-green, with yellow-brown flanks, orange-tinted fins, and reddish gill-plates. The large round spots on the body are more closely grouped toward the tail, which is slightly forked. The

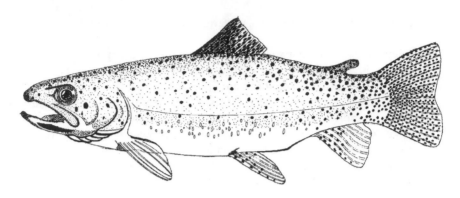

Westslope Cutthroat Trout (Oncorhyncus clarki lewisi)

spotting is less dense than on a rainbow, particularly at the tail. The pale-crimson wash along the flanks is often bright-red during spawning. Cutthroat-rainbow hybrids display most of the rainbow's coloration and spotting, and the throat slashes are light-orange to almost indistinct.

Westslope Cutthroat Trout (*Oncorhyncus clarki lewisi*)

The coloration of a westslope cutthroat is richer than a Yellowstone cutthroat's, with many small, irregularly shaped black spots across the back, concentrating on the tail and rarely extending below the midline. The Westslope variety is generally steel-gray on the flanks with an olive back and a white belly. Gill-plates are dusky-red and a pale-crimson swath extends along the flanks. The belly may be bright red during spring spawning season. An oval parr mark is also seen along midline.

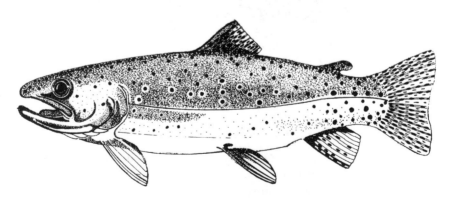

Yellowstone Cutthroat Trout (Oncorhyncus clarki bouvieri)

RAINBOW TROUT: MIGHTY LEAPER

Far and away the most exciting fighter of the trout family, the rainbow always pulls something from its bag of tricks, from cartwheeling leaps to reel-sizzling runs to repeated dashes away from the net.

In waters containing other trout species, there's no doubt in an angler's mind when a rainbow is on the end of the line. A rainbow never hesitates in its frenzied quest for freedom. It often leaps more than once in its desperate panic to throw the hook. Even small fish offer a strong and agile fight. Large fish hooked on light tackle or a delicate leader tippet leave the angler only one option—give the fish its head and hope the line is long enough for the first run. Your prayers won't always be answered, even on the second or third run. A rainbow rarely comes to the net willingly.

Anglers should use the heaviest terminal tackle conditions permit to make the fight as short as possible and not unduly tire out the fish. Always use a good-sized, soft-meshed net so you aren't inclined to manhandle the fish as you attempt to land it.

The feisty rainbow's acrobatic leaps and speckled, multi-hued beauty—described by a whimsical writer of the past as "sheened like a Kang Shi porcelain vase"—make it one of the most popular game fishes in the world. A native of coastal drainages of the northern Pacific, it has been transplanted throughout North America, Europe, and South America.

It gets its name from the crimson to pinkish-red band along the midline of its flanks. This reddish band may be absent in lake dwellers, which are generally more silver in total appearance. It is marked across its head, back, and upper flanks with many small, irregular black spots that are concentrated the heaviest on its squarish tail.

The rainbow trout, *Oncorhyncus mykiss*, was reclassified as part of the western salmon genus, *Oncorhyncus*, in 1990. Its former classification was with the Atlantic salmon genus, *Salmo*. Its former species name, *gairdneri irideus*, was replaced with *mykiss* because the Japanese description of the rainbow preceded descriptions made in the western United States in early 1800s.

Generally, the average rainbow is 12 to 16 inches, with the potential in nutrient-rich waters for fish over 24 inches. In trophy lakes, a rare rainbow can reach 20 pounds. Land-locked monsters approaching this size take on the appearance of a pot-bellied pig.

The rainbow is a spring spawner, like the cutthroat, which leads to hybridization when the species coexist. The rainbow also reaches sexual maturity earlier, at ages two or three years. In hatcheries, they often spawn at one year of age. The life span of the rainbow is fairly short. Few live beyond five or six years of age.

Rainbow waters can be fast or slow, but chances are they will be found in faster moving and more turbulent waters than cutthroat or browns. Larger fish are found in the prime holding areas favored by all trout, like overhanging banks, obvious feeding lanes or sheer lines, in front of or behind mid-stream structures, or at the head of deep pools. While more active in morning or evening, they will move far up into a riffle even at high noon during a prime hatch, using the moving water as cover. Dark, cloudy days will set the fish on the prowl at any hour. The heaviest mayfly hatches regularly occur on these types of days, too.

The rainbow is most active in waters 45 to 75°F. Peak activity is in waters around 60 degrees.

They are highly aggressive fish and will vigorously defend a feeding territory, especially against other salmonids of the same size.

Rainbows' eat anything they can catch and swallow. All sizes of rainbows depend heavily on aquatic and terrestrial insects. Larger fish prey on smaller fish, too, and are known to take small mammals like mice or meadow voles. While opportunistic, larger rainbows tend to be very selective and key in on a particular food source, especially during a multi-hatch of mayflies or caddisflies. They also may concentrate on a particular stage of a hatch, keying on the nymph, emerger, or adult flying form, or, later, the dead, spinner form. Lake dwellers tend to be more piscivorous.

The selective-feeding nature of large rainbows requires more patience and skill of a fly fisher. For those willing to be patient, it boils down to approach and presentation. Approach a feeding fish slowly and quietly to present a fly into its feeding lane. The key is a short-as-possible cast and a drag-free float through that lane. Most rainbows will not move to intercept a fly outside their feeding paths, so keep trying to put your fly right on the mark. Often, presentation is more critical than a perfect hatch match. If a fish shows an interest, present the fly again immediately. If your first choice doesn't work, rest the fish and try a different pattern. Above all, don't let your expectations cloud your appreciation of the challenge. A day on the stream is valuable, no matter how many fish you net.

Of course, all bets are off during major fly hatches, like the salmon fly or western green drake. These "Big Macs" of the aquatic insect world bring up trout of all sizes. Wariness is abandoned. This also applies during prime grasshopper activity.

The standard set of dry flies to attract rainbows is much the same as for cutthroat but, again, presentation is more of a factor. It should include elk hair caddis, stimulators, yellow Sallies, humpies, Adams, pale morning dun, blue-winged olive, light Cahill, and parachute hare's ear. Nymph and emerger patterns for each of these can be equally effective, especially on riffles. Effective sizes for both dry and wet caddis and mayfly patterns can range from No. 10 to 16 in spring and early summer. By late fall, you may have to go as small as No. 18 and 22. Micro patterns of midges, Callibaetis, and tricos also produce amazing results when that's the action on a particular stream. Sometimes small terrestrial patterns, like ants and beetles, work best, even during an aquatic insect hatch.

Standard attractor flies like the renegade, royal Wulff, royal coachman, royal Trude, Goddard caddis, or irresistible work as well, particularly in faster waters.

Larger streamers, muddlers, weighted nymphs, woolly buggers, super renegades, and rubber-legged patterns can be very effective for rainbows. Waders fish them deep, dredging the bottom; float-boaters pound the banks. Leech, dragon fly nymphs, woolly bugger, and freshwater shrimp patterns are effective in lakes. Sizes can range from No. 2 to 14.

Most often a rainbow will hook itself. Just hang on when your fly scores.

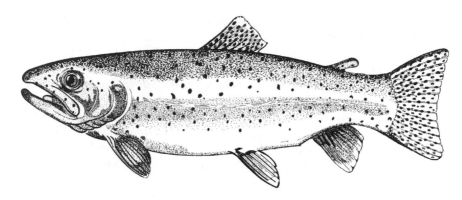

Rainbow Trout (Oncorhyncus mykiss)

Rainbow Trout Identification

Rainbow Trout, Nonmigratory (*Oncorhyncus mykiss*)

The rainbow's common name comes from a broad swath of crimson to pinkish-red usually seen along the midline of its flanks. The reddish band may be absent in lake dwellers, which are generally more silver in appearance. River rainbow coloration ranges from olive to greenish-blue on back, with white to silvery belly. They are marked with many irregularly shaped black spots on the head, back, and tail that extend below the midline.

BROWN TROUT: CRAFTY BRUTES

The brown trout's well-deserved reputation for wariness demands a dedicated effort on the part of anglers seeking one of these crafty brutes.

Most fly fishers pursue browns with large, heavy nymphs or streamers, but they rise well to a dry fly when big flies like stone flies or hoppers are present or a mayfly or caddis hatch is heavy enough to be profitable.

When hooked, browns run long and deep, although they will jump, especially in shallow-water runs or on riffles. They fight the hook with a bullheaded tenacity that can strip line from a singing reel more than once.

The brown's scientific name, *Salmo trutta*, declares it as the "true trout." It was introduced into the West in the late 1880s from stocks originating in Scotland and Germany. Many anglers commonly refer to it as a German brown.

Its basic coloration is an overall golden-brown, with the back ranging from dark-brown to greenish-brown, and its sides and belly ranging from light tan to lemon-yellow or white. The back and flanks are marked with many large black or brown spots. The few red spots on the lower flanks are surrounded by light blue-gray halos. There are very few or no spots on its squarish tail.

Longer-lived than North American species, browns have been known to grow to sizes exceeding 30 pounds in the United States and up to 40 pounds in Europe. The U.S. record, 33 pounds, came from the Flaming Gorge Reservoir on the Green River on the southwestern Wyoming-northeastern Utah border.

The older the fish, the bigger, and more wary the brown trout. They normally grow about four to six inches a year the first three years. Growth slows to about two inches a year after this, but browns have been know to live up to 15 years. Still, depending on environmental variables such as water temperature and available food, size can range widely. Average fish on some streams may range from 10 to 12 inches and up to two pounds, which is still a respectable fish. On others, lunkers over 25 inches and five to 10 pounds may be common.

The preferred habitat of the brown is large rivers and lakes at lower elevations, although it can grow to remarkable size in small streams with adequate cover or deep pools. It is generally thought the brown is able to adapt to warmer waters than North American species, but the brown's most active periods mirror those of the rainbow. It is active in waters ranging from 45 to 70°F, with activity peaking at 60 degrees.

Cold water, in fact, spurs the brown's autumn spawning runs. Late-October through December are the times trophy hunters most heavily flog the waters.

Browns first spawn at three or four years of age. They can spawn in lakes in shallow waters, but most move up into tributary streams. In rivers, browns are known to make long upstream runs to tributaries, but also spawn in shallow waters of their resident streams. In rivers with dams halting their upstream runs, they will go to extraordinary lengths to spawn, even to the extent of turning over cobble-sized rocks to create their redds.

A large spawning male can be distinguished from a female by its hooked lower jaw. This morphological adaptation is called a kype.

Browns rarely hybridize with brook trout, which also spawn in fall. One case was reported in California on a tributary to Lake Tahoe. The hybrids are called "tiger fish" and are sterile. Some Western states now stock a few streams with hatchery-bred hybrids.

Anglers pursuing browns in Montana will be going after wild fish. The typical realm of larger, wild browns can be summed up in a single phrase: "Under the cover of darkness."

Small browns can be found in most waters common to other trout species. Larger fish prefer quieter waters than cutthroat or rainbows, and more than other species they hold up in areas where they feel safest and don't have to expend undo energy to feed.

By day, browns hide out in the darker cover provided by deep pools, overhanging banks, and bankside or midstream structures like log jams and large boulders. The other essential element to good brown hiding places is a steady supply of food streaming into or close by their hangouts.

A big brown will lay claim to the same prime spot for years. When it succumbs to old age or an angler, another large brown fills the vacancy.

Older browns are nocturnal feeders as well as being very active during early-morning or evening hours and on heavily overcast days. At these times, they'll move out of the deeper waters of lakes to cruise the shallows, or come out of their stream-side haunts on feeding excursions.

An angler planning to linger into the night should scout out the area first, or only attempt it on well-known home waters. He needs to know the obstacles to avoid when casting to things that go plunk in the night and, for his own safety, to prevent getting into a precarious situation.

Browns are known for their piscivorous nature, which contributes to their ability to obtain massive body weight. They even eat their own kind, but they also feed on a large variety of other organisms, including aquatic and terrestrial insects, mollusks, and crayfish.

To entice them from their deeper hiding places, a lot of anglers resort to the chuck-and-duck technique of casting large nymphs to large trout. These heavy patterns in sizes No. 6 to 2 include large stone fly nymphs, woolly buggers, zug bugs, and super renegades. They are bounced off the bottom or drifted just above it. Also effective in similar sizes are streamers, like marabou or bullet-head muddlers. Zonkers and spruce flies that imitate sculpin or other bait fish also are effective.

Both styles of wet flies can be used to pound the banks, too, by both drift boat and wading anglers. The same goes for large, buggy styles of dry fly patterns. In either case, hit the places with the thickest cover the hardest.

Stonefly hatches bring large browns up in spring just like other trout. In mid-summer, a hopper bounced off a grassy bank or tossed up under an overhanging tree can be deadly. Smaller dry flies, including large drakes, caddis patterns, and stimulators in No. 10 to No. 14, occasionally bring up a good-sized fish if they float directly through a feeding lane. Browns will move the least of all the trout to intercept a fly. Still, under the right conditions, they will move up into a riffle to grub for nymphs or take emergers. And when there's a carpet hatch, they will slurp down huge quantities of micro-flies, like midges, Tricos, and Callibaetis. Western anglers pursuing these cruisers call them gulpers and revel in the experience of taking a 20- to 25-inch fish on a No. 20 or 22 hook.

Whether you use wet or dry patterns, you can expect to lose more than a few if you are getting them into the haunts where large browns reside. That is one of the costs of going after one. Also expect to spend more time on the water. Studies show that for every five rainbow or brook trout taken, one brown is caught.

It is sometimes easier to tie into one during the fall spawning season, but some anglers frown on this practice because the fish are more vulnerable at this time and their redds can be damaged by waders. Other trophy hunters attempt to intercept large browns in long, deep runs on their upstream migrations and in the tail waters of dams blocking spawning runs. Autumn weather plays a major role in this pursuit. You can encounter conditions commonly associated with steelhead fishing, when days of spitting rain, or snow, prove to be the most rewarding.

Any time of the year, a brown in the net is a flyfisher's reward earned the hard way.

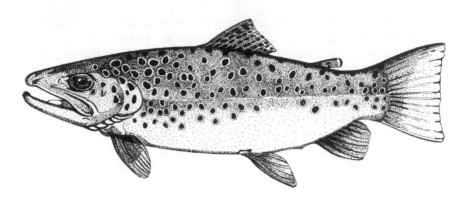

Brown Trout (Salmo trutta)

Brown Trout Identification

Brown Trout (*Salmo trutta*)

The coloration of a brown trout is generally golden-brown with a dark-brown to greenish-brown back. The sides and belly range from light brown to lemon-yellow. There are well-spaced large black or brown spots mixed with a few red spots on the sides with light blue-gray halos. The adipose fin usually has an orange border. There are very few or no spots on the squarish tail.

The brown was introduced to the United States from Europe in the 1800s.

BROOK TROUT: HIGH COUNTRY BRAWLERS

The flamboyant brook trout is the painted porcelain doll of the trout world. A beautiful fish, it is almost bird-like in the brilliance of its colors.

Brookies offer stubborn, scrappy fights with leaps rivaling the rainbow's and frantic, line-tugging runs.

Native to East Coast and Canadian waters, the brook trout, Salvelinus fortinalis, is actually a char like lake trout, bull trout, Dolly Varden, and Arctic char. Both trout and char belong to the same family, Salmonidae. The main difference between the two is that char have light spots on dark backgrounds. Trout have dark spots on light backgrounds. Both prefer cold water environments, but char seek out the coldest water.

Introduced into the West in the 1880s, the brook trout is a resident of pure cold waters of headwater mountain streams and alpine lakes.

Unfortunately, its eastern reputation as a scrappy fighter is lost to most western anglers because it tends to overpopulate the waters in which it occurs, thereby stunting its growth. The short growing seasons of alpine lakes also contribute to its diminutive size. But many high country hikers don't mind. They love to catch "plate-size" brookies because they are excellent table fare, often rated as the best among the trout species.

Average size in most western waters is eight to 12 inches, although its potential is much greater. Brook trout sometimes take up residence in lower lakes, reservoirs, and beaver ponds, where they may grow to a substantial size and provide a tussle worthy of their renown as excellent game fish. A two- or three-pounder taken from one of these waters is considered a good-sized fish.

The brook trout's most distinctive markings are white and black edges on the fronts of its lower fins. It is dark green or blue-black on its back, fading to white on the belly. Numerous wavy worm-like lines, or vermiculations, cover its back and dorsal fin. Scattered red spots surrounded by blue halos are seen on its flanks. The belly and lower fins of a spawning male are brilliant red in autumn.

Montana's flyfishers should be aware of two other chars that harbor a similar appearance to brook trout.

The bull trout, *Salvelinus confluentus*, was previously considered an inland version of the coastal Dolly Varden, *Salvelinus malma*. Bull trout caught in all Montana waters must be released. It has no worm-like markings like the brook trout, and white edges on lower fins are less distinct.

The lake trout, *Salvelinus namaychush*, was introduced into the West in the late-1880s. Also called Mackinaw, it inhabits large, deep lakes, but it is occasionally washed through dams into the rivers below. Its overall coloration is gray. It has no colored spots like the brook trout or the bull trout. The lake trout's tail is deeply forked. The tail of both brook trout and bull trout is square.

Brook trout reach sexual maturity in two or three years. Its life span ranges from six to 10 years, although a fish over five is rare. It is a fall spawner and breeds in both streams and lakes. It hybridizes with other trout species. Introduction of the brook trout into the West, habitat loss, and pollution are the main contributors to the demise of the native bull trout throughout much of its former range.

There is at least one record in California of brook trout naturally cross-breeding with the fall-spawning brown trout, an introduced European species. The two are crossbred in hatcheries. The hybrids are called "tiger trout" due to their yellowish coloration marked with dark, wavy stripes. Some states also cross brook trout with lake trout in hatcheries for introduction into a few lakes. These hybrids are called "splake."

The brook trout is the classic coldwater fish. Anglers who like to fish small waters can do well seeking it out in the churning pocket waters and small pools of cascading mountain streams. In quieter waters, it can be found lurking under overhanging stream banks and under log jams. Beaver pond and lake haunts include the edges of weed beds near deep pools and along bushy banks. As the summer heats up, they often hang out in the cooler water at the mouths of tributary streams or spring inflows.

Rarely found in waters with prolonged temperatures above 65°F, it is most active in waters ranging from 45 to 65 degrees. Activity peaks at 58 degrees.

Its primary food base is aquatic insects and other small aquatic invertebrates, but brookies will also attack terrestrial insects with abandon. Larger brook trout eat small fish, including their own kind.

In fast waters, high-floating buggy patterns, like the Goddard caddis or humpy, and easily seen attractor patterns like the Royal Wulff or Royal Trude work best. Standard nymphs can include the gold-ribbed hare's ear and caddis emergers. The new beadhead patterns eliminate the bother of dealing with split shot. Streamers also can be effective in streams and lakes. Leech and freshwater shrimp patterns, dragonfly nymphs, and woolly buggers are good producers in lakes and ponds.

Some consider the brook trout only slightly less gullible than the cutthroat. On small streams or alpine lakes where populations are profuse, brookies offer a good chance for young anglers to practice their fly fishing skills.

Brook trout can be overexploited like the cutthroat, particularly by hotspotting anglers going after big fish in a lake or pond. Most often, though, larger fish are more cautious, usually active only in the early morning or evening hours or on heavily overcast days. On quiet waters, such as smooth flowing streams and beaver ponds, they should be approached slowly and quietly, taking advantage of available cover.

Many fly fishers like to pursue brook trout with light tackle, like a 2-weight rod or one of the smaller backpacking models. A substantial brookie taken on one of these is a true challenge.

Large or small, a brook trout in the hand is a portrait of beauty taken in a picture-postcard setting.

Brook Trout Identification

Brook Trout (*Salvelinus fontinalis*)
The most distinctive markings on a brook trout are the white and black edges on the front of the lower fins, the wavy or worm-like markings on the back, and scattered red spots surrounded by a blue halo on the flanks. Brook trout are dark green or blue-black on the back to white on the belly. The belly and lower fins turn brilliant red on spawning males in the fall. The tail is square.

Brook trout were introduced in the West in the 1880s.

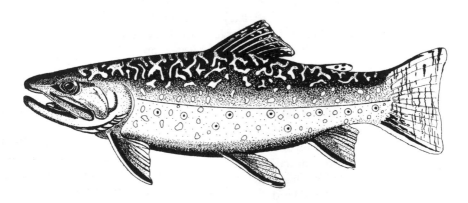

Brook Trout (Salvelinus fontinalis)

BULL TROUT: PERSECUTED PREDATORS

Once pursued like the coyote with a bounty on its head, even poisoned in attempts to eradicate it, the bull trout has gained new-found respect as a gauge of the health of the Pacific Northwest's wild forests and mountain streams. But the bull trout hangs on the brink of extinction.

It is found in only 42 percent of its native streams in Idaho, Montana, Oregon, and Washington. In 1994, the U.S. Fish and Wildlife Service found that bull trout warranted protection under the Endangered Species Act, but declined to list it. The decision was repeated in 1995.

There were two reasons given: there are too many other species in danger of extinction; and the states' political and wildlife officials prefer to attempt to save the species without federal intervention. Programs to protect bull trout and encourage their comeback are under way in all four states. The efforts will be a long uphill battle if they are to avoid their greatest fear—another northern spotted owl fiasco. But aside from curbing harvest of the fish, Montana and the others have only limited control over habitat protection on the broad expanses of federal forest lands within their borders.

The Rodney Dangerfield of coldwater fish, it got no respect from old time fishermen and biologists. Because of its predatory nature, it was persecuted as a cannibal and slaughtered for preying on so-called good trout.

But even with modern reconsideration by anglers of bull trout as a trophy fish and by biologists ranking it as an indicator species, respect may have come too late.

In their petition for endangered species listing, environmentalists said bull trout populations and habitat were seriously degraded by logging, forest road building, cattle grazing, mining, dam construction, irrigation, pesticides and home construction in flood plains. Other threats to the fish have included overfishing—particularly during spawning runs—poaching, and introduction of non-native char species that out-compete and hybridize with bull trout.

Their key importance to the Northwest is their dependence on pristine waters, clean and silt-free, cold and oxygen-rich. This makes bull trout a prime indicator species to monitor the health of forest ecosystems and watersheds. Sharing the same wilderness waters are native salmon, steelhead, and cutthroat trout.

Native to inland waters of northwestern North America, the bull trout, *Salvelinus confluentus*, is a char, not a trout. It is long-lived and grows to trophy proportions. An average adult from a large river or lake weighs three to eight pounds. Fish as large as 20 pounds are common. The U.S. record, 32 pounds, came from Northern Idaho's Lake Pend Oreille in 1949.

Formerly lumped with the Dolly Varden, *S. malma*, the bull trout was reclassified as a separate species in the early 1970s. The Dolly Varden is more common to the coastal waters of Canada and Alaska. Arctic char, found in the Northwest Territories and Alaska, and brook trout and lake trout, native to eastern North American waters, are in the same genus.

364 — Flyfisher's Guide to Montana

Fall spawners, bull trout are known for migrating 50 to 150 miles to their spawning beds. Sexual maturity occurs at four to five years of age and individual fish spawn every two or three years. Siltation covering the redds or water temperatures rising above 41 degrees can be lethal to the eggs.

The species was once common from the headwaters of the Yukon River in Canada to as far south as northern California. Today it is essentially extinct in California and occurs in only the Jarbridge drainage in Nevada. The largest remaining population outside Idaho's Lake Pend Oreille region is in Montana's Flathead Basin. Washington and Oregon also have significant populations. Some bull trout along the West Coast are anadromous and go to sea like salmon and steelhead.

Chars are distinguished from trout by their light spots on a dark background. Trout have dark spots on a light background.The spots on a bull trout's olive-green to bronze back and flanks are pale-yellow, orange, or red. There are no spots on the dorsal fin and no black line on the ventral fin.

A key feature in identifying brook trout is the white line followed by a black band on the leading edge of its orange-colored ventral fin. It has markings or spots on its dorsal fin. The spotting pattern along its flank includes pale red spots surrounded by blue halos.

The lake trout differs from both with its overall grayish coloration, dull markings, and deeply forked tail.

While it's not a spectacular fighter, bull trout resist the hook with dogged tenacity. Downstream flights can be long and strenuous. Terminal tackle, which consists mostly of large streamers that include saltwater patterns, is tied onto 10-pound leader tippets because of the fish's great strength and toothy mouth.

Bull trout are most active at dawn and dusk. During the day, they hide out in the deep pools of streams, among the roots of undercut banks, or in large logjams. They are vulnerable to bank casters on lakes because they prowl shallow waters and the mouths of tributaries looking for prey fish.

Bull Trout Identification

Bull Trout (*Salvelinus confluentus*)

Bull trout are olive green to brown above and on the sides with shading to white on the belly. They lack the worm-like marking seen on brook trout, and the white border on the fins is less distinct. There are no spots on the dorsal fin. There are yellow spots on the upper body and red or orange spots on the flanks, but no blue halos around spots like in brook trout. The tail is square.

Lake Trout Identification

Lake Trout (*Salvelinus namaychush*)

Lake trout are dark gray or gray-green on the head and upper flanks. The belly is slightly gray to white. They have irregularly shaped gray spots on the back, sides, dor-

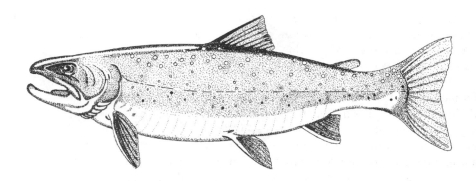

Bull Trout (Salvelinus confluentus)

sal fin, and tail. No pink or blue spots. The white border on the fins is less distinct than in brook trout. The tail is deeply forked.

Lake trout are an introduced species.

MOUNTAIN WHITEFISH: UNHERALDED GAMEFISH

One of the most abundant game fish in Montana, the whitefish gets little respect from fly fishers on trout-rich waters.

There is almost a social stigma against taking whitefish wherever found. Fishing for whitefish is most popular in winter when they are more active than trout. There are winter whitefish seasons on many drainages, which often become de facto catch-and-release seasons for trout.

Some anglers scorn the whitefish because they presume it competes with trout, however, the two species evolved to occupy separate niches in a shared habitat. There is no biological evidence that high whitefish numbers harm trout populations.

While it is in the same family as trout, salmon, and char (*Salmonidae*), the whitefish's silvery body is slender and almost round in cross-section. It has a small head and tiny mouth, with a slightly overhanging snout. Its scales are large and coarse. Like its cousins it has an adipose fin.

The most common species in the Northern Rockies, the mountain whitefish, *Prosopium williamsoni*, prefers clear, cool streams. It is also found in some lakes. The species was first recorded for science by the Lewis and Clark Expedition.

Mountain whitefish average 10 to 12 inches, but on nutrient-rich streams 18- to 20-inch fish are relatively common

Whitefish hang out in deep pools and shallow, slow-water runs. They feed actively in riffles on mayfly nymphs and caddis larvae. Surface feeding on adult insects occurs most often toward evening.

Among the best wet flies for whitefish are small green-colored nymphs, caddis larvae, and emergers. Beadhead patterns are very effective. Perhaps because of their

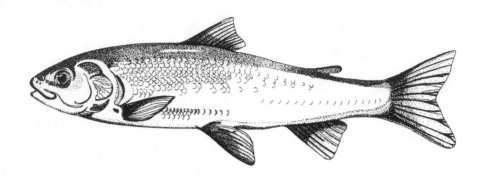

Mountain Whitefish (Prosopium williamsoni)

small mouths, many whitefish fail to take a dry fly when they strike. These misses can be frustrating, but they are also a sign that actively rising fish aren't trout.

Whitefish spawn in late-fall and remain active through the winter. Midge patterns can be productive at this time.

Whitefish Identification

Mountain Whitefish (*Prosopium williamsoni*)
Light grayish blue on back, silvery on sides, dull white belly. Scales large. Small mouth without teeth. Body almost round in cross-section.

Native to Western U.S.

BASS: PUGNACIOUS ACROBATS

Acrobatic leaps and a line-sizzling skirmish are guaranteed when tying into a smallmouth bass, considered by many to be the most dynamic fighter among freshwater game fish. Largemouth bass are husky brawlers that also rocket into the air before ripping off line in a run for cover.

Unlike trout, bass have no adipose fin. The dorsal fin is long with two distinct parts, stiff spines in front and softer rays in back; scales are large and obvious. The key difference between the two black bass species is the size of the mouth. The jaw of the largemouth extends behind the eye; the jaw of a smallmouth ends in front of the eye.

Largemouth bass, *Micropterus salmodies*, and smallmouth bass, *M. dolomieui*, are members of the sunfish family, *Centrachidae*. It includes the sunfishes, crappies, and other basses. Native to North America, only one member of the family, the Sacramento perch, was originally found west of the Rocky Mountains. Many species have been introduced successfully all over the world.

The native range of largemouth and smallmouth bass overlapped from southeastern Canada south to Georgia and throughout the Great Lakes and Mississippi drainages.

The Florida strain of largemouth grow much larger than their northern cousins, and even in some Western waters may exceed 20 pounds. Most transplants to the West belong to the northern strain. Size can range from one to 12 pounds, although a five-pounder is considered a good largemouth anywhere.

Largemouths live in warmwater lakes and ponds, and quiet backwaters and sloughs of streams. They prefer clear water with good cover like weed beds, reeds, lily pads, or flooded snags, but also do well in somewhat barren irrigation reservoirs with radically fluctuating water levels.

Smallmouth bass inhabit cool, clear lakes and streams with rocky and gravel bottoms and shoals. Size averages one to three pounds. A five-pounder is considered a trophy; an eight-pounder, a monster.

Both species are photosensitive and retreat to shadowy lays or deeper waters on bright days. They are more active at dawn and dusk, and in water temperatures above 50 degrees. Optimum water temperatures are 60 to 70 degrees.

The males of both species jealously guard egg nests and newly hatched young in spring. The determined defense of their progeny against predators makes them very vulnerable to anglers at this time.

Lakes and reservoirs that hold both bass and trout are called two-story fisheries. In summer, bass typically stick to the warmer waters closer to shore and trout retreat to the cooler depths. In streams, smallmouths orient toward the banks or along cliff walls, and prefer slower and warmer holding areas than trout.

Black bass are voracious fish eaters, and can be instrumental in curbing population explosions of panfish and nongame species. They take both aquatic and terrestrial insects and other invertebrates. Smallmouths display a strong preference for crayfish. Largemouths are known to take frogs and mice—and other "things that go bump in the night."

Intrepid bass hunters pound reed lines and shoreline shallows after dark or before dawn with noisy popping bugs, hair-mice, diving bugs like the Dahlberg Diver, and large streamers, muddler minnows, and woolly buggers, No. 3/0 to 6. The same techniques are employed throughout the day, usually with slightly smaller flies.

Most fly fishers favor spun-hair or cork-bodied popping bugs with bushy tails and rubber legs. The theory is that the bass will hang on to soft-bodied patterns longer that plastic lures. Be wary of patterns with extra-stiff weed guards. They may push the fly away from the fish's mouth.

Because of the size and wind-resistance of the fly patterns, a rod in the 8-weight 9-foot range is more effective for largemouth bass fishing. Lightweight rods and smaller flies and streamers offer lots of fun on panfish, especially for children.

Generally, dry fly action on lakes is better with largemouths and panfish than smallmouths. Bronzebacks tend to hold deeper in lakes, around bottom structure and boulders.

Effective smallmouth flies in streams are weighted nymphs, woolly worms, crayfish imitations, white marabou muddlers, and black marabou streamers for pools and riffles. Cork or elk hair popping bugs and hair-wing dry flies produce when surface action occurs.

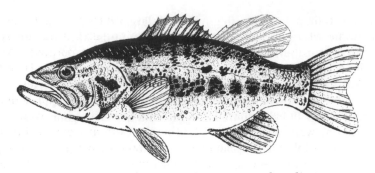

Largemouth Bass (Micropterus salmodies)

A 5- to 7-weight rod works for bronzebacks. Presentation can be less delicate than for trout and leaders can be stouter, 4-pound or heavier.

Bass Identification

Largemouth Bass (*Micropterus salmoides*)
Dark green on back and flanks, belly white. Dark, irregular horizontal band along flanks. Upper jaw extends behind eye. Deep notch in dorsal fin.

Smallmouth Bass (*Micropterus dolomieui*)
Dark olive to brown on back, flanks bronze, belly white. Dark ventricle bands on flanks. Eyes reddish. Upper jaw ends in front of eye. Shallow notch in dorsal fin.

GRAYLING: THE RELIC

The arctic grayling (*Thymallus arcticus*) is a strange creature, positively defined by its sail-like dorsal fin—an attribute that makes it not only interesting, but extremely beautiful, although some anglers still refer to the grayling as nothing more than a dressed-up whitefish.

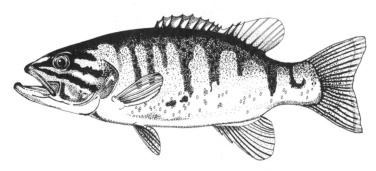

Smallmouth Bass (Micropterus dolomieui)

In Montana, grayling exist only in the coldest, clearest, purest waters. The Madison and Gallatin rivers harbor token populations and there are scattered grayling strongholds in a few high mountain lakes, mostly in northwest Montana, but the only truly viable population of fluvial grayling exist in the Big Hole River in southwest Montana. It's in a river that grayling best represent themselves.

In fact, the grayling is often regarded as the most willing to rise at a dry fly — a fact that flyfishers who know them cherish. On the upper Big Hole, where grayling populations are highest, flyfishers can take them on top any day of the summer. Grayling, which exist almost solely on aquatic invertebrates, will pound most general attractor flies; flyfishers who want to match the hatch catch an equal number, if not more, fish. Although most flyfishers prefer to catch those fish on dry flies, grayling will take nymphs like each one offered was their last meal. Standard nymphs, like a hare's ear, pheasant tail or caddis larvae will draw plenty of strikes. And, although their mouths are small, grayling will also inhale large stonefly nymphs.

The Big Hole grayling has been identified as genetically different from specimens found in the northern locals — Canada and Alaska. Due to that genetic isolation, they are listed as a fish of "Special Concern" to Montana Fish, Wildlife and Parks.

Grayling do not grow to huge size; a six-pound grayling has not been caught anywhere. In the Big Hole and the state's mountain lakes, grayling average six to 10 inches with a true monster approaching 16 inches. All fluvial grayling are protected by catch and release regulations. However, some mountain lakes offer catch and keep grayling fisheries. Wherever found, they should be cherished.

Grayling Identification

The grayling is a member of the *salmonidae* family, the smallest fish belonging to that family. Grayling are identified by their small mouths, elongated body, large scales, silver or blueish coloration, black spots along their sides and, of course, that dorsal fin. The dorsal is often punctuated by ribbing, which contains small spots that range from black to red in coloration. The top of the dorsal often harbors a pink stripe.

Grayling (Thymallus arcticus)

MONTANA FWP STATE/REGIONAL OFFICES

State Headquarters
1420 East 6th Avenue
Helena, MT 59620
444-2535

Region 1
490 North Meridien
Kalispell, MT 59901
752-5501

Region 2
3201 Spurgin Road
Missoula, MT 59801
542-3500

Region 3
1400 South 19th
Bozeman, MT 59715
994-4042

Region 4
4600 Giant Springs Road
Great Falls, MT 59406
454-3441

Region 5
2300 Lake Elmo Drive
Billings, MT 59105
252-4654

Region 6
Route 1-4210
Glasgow, MT 59230
228-9347

Region 7
P.O. Box 1630-1
Miles City, MT 59301
232-4365

Region 8
1404 8th Avenue
Helena, MT 59620
444-4720

Index

NOTES

NOTES

WILDERNESS ADVENTURES GUIDE SERIES

If you would like to order additional copies of this book or our other Wilderness Adventures Press guidebooks, please fill out the order form below or call **1-800-925-3339** or **fax 800-390-7558.**

Mail to:
Wilderness Adventures Press, 45 Buckskin Road, Belgrade, MT 59714

Ship to:

Name _____

Address _____

City _____ State_____ Zip_____

Home Phone_____ Work Phone_____

Payment: ☐ Check ☐ Visa ☐ Mastercard ☐ Discover ☐ American Express

Card Number _____ Expiration Date_____

Signature_____

Quantity	Title of Book and Author	Price	Total
	Flyfisher's Guide to Montana	$26.95	
	Flyfisher's Guide to Northern California	$26.95	
	Flyfisher's Guide to Idaho	$26.95	
	Flyfisher's Guide to Wyoming	$26.95	
	Flyfisher's Guide to Washington	$26.95	
	Flyfisher's Guide to Oregon	$26.95	
	Flyfisher's Guide to Northern New England	$26.95	
	Flyfisher's Guide to Pennsylvania	$26.95	
	Flyfisher's Guide to Michigan	$26.95	
	Total Order + shipping & handling		

Shipping and handling: $4.00 for first book, $2.50 per additional book, up to $14.00 maximum